# A Timeless Reality

### Ancient Wisdoms of the Soul & Meditation

## Shaykh Nurjan Mirahmadi

Shokran for your purchasing the book. May Allah ﷻ shower His
Divine Blessings upon you and all your loved ones.
May He keep us all with the Love of Sayyidina Muhammad ﷺ

PUBLISHED BY THE
SUFI MEDITATION CENTERS SOCIETY

A Timeless Reality
Ancient Wisdoms of the Soul & Meditation

Published and Distributed by:

Sufi Meditation Centers Society
3660 East Hastings St.
Vancouver, BC  V5K 2A9  Canada
Tel: (604) 558-4455

NurMuhammad.com

First Edition: June 2021

# TABLE OF CONTENTS

About the Author ................................................................. i

Universally Recognized Symbols................................................ vii

Realities of Tafakkur (Contemplation) ........................................ viii

What is Meditation in Sufism? ................................................. ix

Chapter 1 – Meditation..........................................................1

**Understanding Meditation** ...................................................3

What is Meditation and How is it Done? ........................................ 3

How Does Meditation Help in Our Spiritual Development?............. 9

What is the Connection Between Islam and Meditation?................... 12

How Can We Get Our Loved Ones to Pray? ................................. 14

How Can We Teach Our Children Meditation? ................................. 15

How Does Meditation Benefit Us in This Life and the Next?.......... 17

**Preparing for Meditation** ................................................. 21

What is the Recommended Dress Code for Meditation?................... 21

What is the Etiquette Before Zikr or Meditation? ............................. 22

What Should Our Diet Be Since We Started Meditation?................. 24

How Can We Keep Awake and Vigilant? ............................................. 25

How Do We Fight the Comfort of Our Ego? ..................................... 27

What Are the Benefits of Lighting Candles During Meditation?...... 30

Is it Important to Use Fragrances and Which Ones Are
Recommended? ....................................................................... 31

What is the Benefit of Holding a Rock During Meditation? ............. 32

Can We Change the Location of Where We Meditate?..................... 34

When is the Best Time for Meditation?............................................ 34

After Which Prayer is it Best to Meditate?............................................ 35

Can We Remain in a State of Meditation Throughout the Day? ...... 39

**Practicing Meditation** ................................................................ **41**

If You Are a Beginner in Meditation, Where Do You Start? ........... 41

What Should We Be Aware of During Meditation? .......................... 42

Should We Meditate in Silence or With Sound? ............................... 43

What Should We Envision During Meditation? ................................ 45

What is Grounding and How Do You Do It? .................................... 46

How Do We Place Our Hands When Grounding? ............................ 48

What Are Different Types of Meditations We Can Practice? ........... 48

What is the Best Zikr to Do During Meditation? ............................. 50

How Do We Practice the Zikr of "Hu"? ........................................... 54

What is the Importance of the Breath in Meditation? ...................... 55

What is the Purpose of Holding the Fingers During Meditation? .... 57

How Does the Nazar (Gaze) of the Shaykh Affect the Student? ..... 59

What is Hosh Dar Dam and How Do We Practice It Consistently? 67

What Happens When You Forget to Breathe During Meditation? .. 69

What if Nasal Problems Affect Your Breathing Practices? ............... 70

How Do We Know We're Progressing in Our Meditation? ............. 71

How Do We Feel the Realization that the Quality of
Our Meditation is Getting Better? ..................................................... 71

How Can We Learn and Progress in Body, Mind, and Soul
Meditation? ......................................................................................... 74

How Can We Speed Up Our Spiritual Progress? .............................. 77

Should We Continue After Becoming Consistent in Our Practices? 78

How Do We Make Our Spiritual Connection (Muraqabah)
Stronger? ............................................................................................. 79

How Can We Accelerate Our Spiritual Growth? .............................. 85

# Chapter 2 - Connecting the Heart and Accompanying a Guide

## Chapter 2 - Connecting the Heart and Accompanying a Guide..................91

**Connecting the Heart to a Guide and Importance of the Bayah**................... 93

What is the Best Way to Be Introduced to the Spiritual Teachings? 93

How Can We Be Sure This is the Right Path? .................... 94

How Do We Know Which Shaykh and Spiritual Guide to Follow? 95

Can We Follow Any Guide in the Naqshbandi Tariqah?................... 96

How Will I Know Who My Shaykh Is?.................... 97

Can We Join the Subhah (Discourse) if We're Following Another Way? ...................... 105

What Are the Best Manners in Asking For a Prayer? ...................... 106

What Are the Manners to Ask the Shaykh a Question? .................. 108

What is the Importance of the Bayah and Can We Take It From Any Shaykh?.................... 109

Can We Do the Awrad Without Having Bayah? ................. 112

Do We Need Permission for Bayah From Our Family? ................. 113

Can Unintentional Actions Cause Disconnection Between Student and Shaykh?.................... 114

**Accompanying a Guide and Importance of the Madad**............119

Can We Be in the Company of the Shaykh All the Time? .............. 119

What is the Power of the Shaykh's Nazar (Gaze)? ............................ 122

How Can We Keep a Constant Connection to the Shaykh? ........... 129

Is It Too Late to Build a Strong Connection?.................... 131

How Can We Achieve Presence of the Shaykh All the Time? ........ 136

Can the Student Become Annihilated in the Presence of the Shaykh?.................... 139

Can We Receive Guidance From the Shaykh
Through Meditation? ................................................................ 140

Should We Follow the Guidance Given to Us in Our Dreams?..... 141

Can You Tell Us About the Muhammadan Government and
Shaykh Abdul Qadir Jilani ق?................................................. 143

What is the Naqshbandi Tariqah's Relation
to Sayyidina Khidr ؏? ........................................................... 146

What is Sayyidina Ali's ؏ Importance in Sufism? ........................... 148

How Should We Ask For Madad and Make Rabita (Connection)
With the Shaykh?..................................................................... 152

Why is the Concept of Madad Important? ........................................ 158

Do Our Senses in the Heavenly Realm Show We Have
Little Control Over Ourselves?................................................. 162

What Can We Recite if Under Demonic Attack? ............................ 166

How Does the Madad Protect Us From Attacks at Night? ............. 169

What Can Be Recited for Protection Against Evil and to
Remove Fear? .......................................................................... 171

How Can We Control Our Fear? ........................................................ 173

How Do We Overcome Childhood Fears? ........................................ 174

Can We Take Advice From Anyone? ................................................. 180

How to Live Amongst Family Who Don't Have an
Understanding of Spiritual Practices? ..................................... 184

**Importance of Being of Service and Attaining Sincerity .......... 189**

How Can We Be of Service? ............................................................. 189

What Can We Do if We Feel Our Service Isn't Enough?............... 190

What Other Ways Can We Support if We Have No Income?........ 193

How Can We Be of Service if We Have No Means? ........................ 194

How Do We Reach the Station of Sincerity? ................................... 194

How Can We Honour the Shaykhs of The Golden Chain?.............198

How Can We Increase Our Love for the Shaykh? ...........................199

How Do We Know Our Connection to the Shaykh, Prophet ﷺ,
and Then to Allah ﷻ Exists?.................................................203

Can We Build Our Love For Prophet ﷺ By Praying?.......................205

How Do We Lower Our Ego and Remain Humble? .......................206

**Chapter 3 – The Daily Awrad and General Recitations...209**

**The Daily Awrad (Practice)...................................................211**

How Should We Begin the Daily Awrad and What More
Can We Recite?...................................................................211

Can We Do the Daily Awrad With Video if Needed? ......................214

What's the Minimum Awrad We Can Do When Busy? ...................216

How Can We Manage Our Time?...............................................221

On the Spiritual Path How Many Hours Should We Sleep?............222

How Do We Become Regular in Waking Up For Fajr? ..................223

If Chanting Inwards "Allah" is Difficult, What Should We Do?....223

How Do We Deal With Anxiety Attacks Even When
Doing Our Awrad? ...............................................................224

Should Zikr Be Done Loudly or Silently? .....................................225

Should We Reduce Our Zikr if We Start Seeing Things?................226

Can We Recite Different Salawats Than the Ones Recited
During Zikr? ........................................................................227

**General Prayers, Recitations, and Praisings ..........................229**

Can We Do the Fajr Awrad and What Can We
Recite for Barakah (Blessings)?............................................229

Can the Fajr Awrad Be Performed Throughout the Day? ..............231

What Can We Recite While Travelling? .......................................231

If You've Done Nothing Wrong That Day,
What Should You Recite? ..................................................................232

What Zikr Can We Recite Throughout the Day? ...........................233

Are There Salawats For Uplifting Ailments? ................................235

Are There Specific Recitations For Healing Body Pains? ...........236

What Zikr Can We Do to Overcome Constant Fear? .....................240

Can You Explain More About Durood Sharif and Salawats? .........243

Are Big Sins Forgiven With Durood Sharif? .................................244

Do We Have Permission to Recite the Naqshbandi Zikr? .............249

How Do We Maintain the Spiritual Momentum From Ramadan?. 251

What Do We Recite for Laylatul Qadr? .........................................252

Can Angels Listen to Our Recitations if We Recite Quietly? .........253

**Chapter 4 – Energy**.................................................................................**257**

**Understanding Energy and Practices for Protection**.................**259**

How Do We Identify Positive and Negative Energy? .....................259

What's the Importance and Reality of the Ta'weez? ........................265

Why Do We Lose Energy or Get Sharp Headaches
Around Certain People? ..................................................................269

Can People's Energy Reach Us Through Eye Contact? ..................272

What Are the Leaks in Energy That One Might Overlook? ............273

How Do We Protect Our Energy During Sleep? .............................276

Is There Any Remedy For Insomnia? ..............................................279

Should We Avoid Touching People When Trying to Build
Our Energy? ....................................................................................280

When Someone Else Has a Temperature
Why Can I Also Feel It? ..................................................................281

How Do We Control Body Vibrations and the Feeling of Electric Current? ...................................................................284

Are Negative Energies Attracted to Some More Than Others?......286

What is the Best Approach When We See Shaitans in Public? .......288

What is Nazma and How Do We Protect Our Energy? .................290

Can We Be of Service Spreading Light While Meditating? .............293

Should We Carry Others' Negativity if We Are Excess in Positive Energy? .......................................................................295

Is There Advice for Women Relating to Meditation or Energy?....296

Are There Special Practices for Women During Their Cycle? ........298

Are There Any Specific Practices for Women During Pregnancy? 301

Are Children Protected by Beings and How Do We Protect Their Energies? .....................................................................302

What Are the Angelic Realities of Food? ...........................................303

How Do Devils Still Influence Us if They're Imprisoned in Ramadan? .......................................................................309

Do Solar and Lunar Eclipses Affect Us Spiritually? .........................312

**Understanding Energy and Experiences During Meditation....313**

What Realities Does Practicing Meditation Open? ...........................313

Are There Physical Effects on the Body When Meditating? ...........316

Why Do Our Ears Heat Up During Meditation? ..............................317

What is the Significance of Hearing Sounds During Meditation?...318

What Does Hearing a Whistle Sound Mean When Meditating? .....320

What is the Significance of Hearing a Calibration Tone During Meditation?....................................................................322

Is It Our Voice or the Shaykh's Voice We Hear? ..............................327

How Can We Differentiate Inspirations From Whispers? ...............328

How Do We Protect Ourselves From Whispers of Satan?..............329

During Meditation is it Our Consciousness or
Our Ego Speaking?............................................................................330

How Do We Know We're Hearing the Heart and Not the Ego?...332

Why is There So Much Disturbance When Trying to Meditate?....333

What Are the Signs That Spiritual Hearing and
Sight are Opening?............................................................................334

What Does it Mean if We Start Seeing Insects and Creatures?.......335

What is Khashf and How Does it Affect Our Body and Mind?.....336

Should We Keep Notes of What We See During Meditation?........338

Is it Normal to Feel Our Body Moving During Meditation?...........339

What Does Thumping Between the Eyebrows Signify
During Meditation?............................................................................341

Why Do We Feel a Breeze During Meditation?...............................344

What Does it Mean to Have Pain in the Heart
During Meditation?............................................................................349

If the Heart Heats Up, How Do We Nourish It?.............................349

What Can We Do if We Smell Bad Fragrances
During Meditation?............................................................................351

Is Smoking Bad Spiritually and How Do We Quit Addictions?......356

What is the Significance of Happiness and Sadness
During Meditation?............................................................................359

Should We Have Spiritual Openings in Every
Meditation Session?..........................................................................360

If We've Never Had Spiritual Experiences Are We Doing
Something Wrong?............................................................................362

## Chapter 5 – Tafakkur (Contemplation) and Muhasabah (Self-examination) ........................................................... 365

**Understanding Tafakkur and Muhasabah ............................... 367**

What is the Recommended Amount of Time to
Contemplate For? .................................................................. 367

How Can We Improve Our Contemplation? .................................. 372

What is the Difference Between Zikr and Fikr? ................................ 374

Will We Know and Understand Our Seven Names During
Contemplation? .................................................................. 379

Is the Soul the Oppressor Within Us or is it the Ego? ..................... 380

How Can We Make Ourselves Believe That We Are Nothing? ...... 382

How Can We Understand the Concept of Nothingness in
Our Daily Activities? ........................................................... 384

How Can We Stop Obsessing About Certain Issues in Our Life? . 385

How Should We Deal With People Who Always Test Us? ............. 386

How Do We Know We Achieved a Level of Being Nothing? ........ 390

How Do We View Ourselves as Nothing in the Presence of
Prophet Muhammad ﷺ? ...................................................... 391

**Building Good Character Through Tafakkur and Muhasabah 393**

How Do We Stop Bad Habits? ............................................... 393

What Can We Do When We Have Flashbacks of Our Sinful Past
During Contemplation? ......................................................... 394

How Do We Counter Whispers, Negative Thoughts, and Fears
During Contemplation? ......................................................... 396

What is the Best Way to Do Muhasabah? ................................... 398

How Can We Remove Bad Character Identified
During Muhasabah? ............................................................ 400

Is There a Recitation to Jumpstart Our Humility? ...................... 402

How Do You Fix Jealousy? ............................................................... 403

Who is Iblis? ..................................................................................... 405

What is the Story of the Fallen Angels, Harut and Marut? ............. 408

Are There Any Practices to Control Sudden Feelings of Anger? .... 410

How Can We Control Our Anger? ................................................... 412

How Can We Control Our Bad Desires
With All the Media Around? ........................................................... 414

How Do We Stay Positive in Times of Uncertainty? ...................... 416

What is the Best Way to Deal With Difficulties Knowing
They Are Pre-ordained? .................................................................. 418

How Do We Keep Our Faith Strong in the Last Days? ................... 424

How Can We Keep Balance in Life? ................................................ 427

How Do We Balance Our Worldly and Spiritual Life? .................... 428

What is the Realm of Barzakh and the Realm of Malakut? ............. 431

Can We Speak on Political Matters Through Social Media? ........... 432

Should We Stop Working During Covid-19? ................................... 438

Do the Events of Covid-19 Relate to Any of the Realities
of Lataif al Qalb? ............................................................................ 438

How Can We Prepare for the Coming of Sayyidina Mahdi ﷺ? ..... 441

How Do We Know Our State of Account With Allah ﷻ? .............. 442

**Resources** ....................................................................................... 445

Daily Awrad (Practice) of Naqshbandi Tariqah ............................. 447

Al Bay'atu Fit Tariqatun Naqshbandiya
(Pledge of Allegiance to The Naqshbandi Way) ............................ 457

# ABOUT THE AUTHOR

## PROFILE

For over 25 years, Shaykh Nurjan Mirahmadi has worked hard to spread the true Sufi teachings of love, acceptance, respect and peace throughout the world and opposes extremism in all its forms. An expert on Sufi spirituality, he has studied with some of the world's leading Sufi scholars of our time.

Shaykh Mirahmadi has also founded numerous educational and charitable organizations. He has travelled extensively throughout the world learning and teaching Sufi meditation and healing, understanding the channelling of Divine energy, discipline of the self, and the process of self-realization. He teaches these spiritual arts to groups around the world, regardless of religious denomination.

## BACKGROUND

Shaykh Nurjan Mirahmadi studied Business Management at the University of Southern California. He then established and managed a successful healthcare company and imaging centers throughout Southern California. Having achieved business success at a remarkably young age, Shaykh Nurjan Mirahmadi shifted his focus from the private sector to the world of spirituality. In 1994 he pursued his religious studies and devoted himself to be of service to those in need. He combined his personal drive and financial talents to work for the less fortunate and founded an international relief organization, a spiritual healing center, and a religious social group for at risk youth.

In 1995, he became a protégé of Mawlana Shaykh Hisham Kabbani for in-depth studies in Islamic spirituality known as Sufism. He studied and accompanied Shaykh Kabbani on many tours and learned about Sufi practices around the world. Together with Shaykh Kabbani, he has established a number of other Islamic educational organizations and relief programs throughout the world.

Shaykh Nurjan Mirahmadi has received written authorization to be a Spiritual Guide from the World Leader of the Naqshbandi Islamic Sufi Order, Shaykh Muhammad Nazim al-Haqqani, as per the permission of the 41st Shaykh of the Golden Chain, Shaykh Muhammad Adil ar-Rabbani and Shaykh Hisham Kabbani. He is authorized to teach, guide, and counsel religious students around the world to Islamic Spirituality.

## IJAZAS (AUTHORIZATION)

Shaykh Nurjan Mirahmadi has taught and travelled extensively throughout the world from Uzbekistan to Singapore, Thailand, Indonesia, Cyprus, Argentina, Peru, and North America. He teaches the spiritual sciences of Classical Islam, including meditation *(tafakkur)*, subtle energy points *(lataif)*, Islamic healing, the secrets of letters and numbers *(ilm huroof)*, disciplining the self *(tarbiyah)*, and the process of self-realization *(ma'rifah)*. He teaches the Muslim communities the prophetic ways of being kind, respectful and to live in harmony with people. He emphasizes on good manners and respect, and often reminds his students that the spiritual journey begins from within and "You can't give what you don't have."

## ACCOMPLISHMENTS

One of Shaykh Nurjan's greatest accomplishments has been the worldwide dissemination of the spiritual teachings of Classical Islam through his books and online presence. The Prophet Muhammad ﷺ has told us, "Speak to people according to their levels." In an era of social media, Shaykh Nurjan's ability to reach a new generation of spiritual seekers through the Internet has been remarkable. His NurMuhammad.com website alone has over 1,500 unique visitors each day, and since its inception has seen more than 200,000 downloads of the book *"Dailal Khairat"*, 1.5 Million free downloads of *Naqshbandi Muraqabah*, and another 700,000 downloads of the *Naqshbandi Book of Devotions (Awrad)*, as well as many more articles. His Facebook pages "Shaykh Nurjan Mirahmadi" and "Nur Muhammad" combined have over 1.1 million likes and followers. Furthermore, his YouTube Channel "The Muhammadan Way" has over 9 million views, and his Google page, "Shaykh Sayed Nurjan Mirahmadi" has over 2.7 million views.

Shaykh Nurjan Mirahmadi focuses on the worldwide social media presence working on ways to bring knowledge to all seekers around the world. In 2015 he launched an Online University, called *SimplyIman.org*, to spread these traditional Spiritual Islamic teachings even further and make it accessible to all seekers around the world.

For over 25 years Shaykh Nurjan has dedicated his life to spreading the true Islamic teachings of love, acceptance, respect, and peace. He has established several non-profit organizations and has founded numerous educational and charitable organizations.

**Youtube Channels – Subscribe Today!**
- **The Muhammadan Way** – a world leading Islamic media platform with over 9 million views, featuring a library of over 1,000 videos on various topics. Join the live broadcast of Mawlid and Zikr every Thursday, Friday, & Saturday, including interactive Question & Answer sessions.
- **Divine Love: Hub-E-Rasul** – based on the acclaimed TV series with over 27,000 views and 200 episodes.
- **Shaykh Talks** – video series of short, powerful talks focusing on Spiritual Reminders and Motivational Topics.

**Muhammadan Way App (over 20,000 Users Worldwide)** – a free comprehensive resource of Islamic information for all mobile devices. Created for both Muslims and non-Muslims, it provides users with a wealth of knowledge including access to books, supplications, prayer times, month-specific practices, a media library of audio and video files, an events calendar, and much more.

**Social Media / Online Presence**
- **Facebook (Shaykh Nurjan Mirahmadi)** with over 1.1 million followers.
- **NurMuhammad.com** – a comprehensive website containing many resources covering the deep realities of classical Islam.
- **SMC (sufimeditationcenter.com)** – an outreach organization that spreads teachings to the Western audience including concepts such as meditation and charity. It reaches out to other faiths to increase peace, love, and acceptance in the interfaith environment.

**Fatima Zahra Helping Hand (fzhh.org)** – a non-profit, volunteer-based organization that supports those less fortunate. Projects are thoughtfully designed to help those in hardship to gain support and better their lives. Through a blended approach of building strong partnerships and working with local volunteers, all initiatives are easily accessible by those who are in need.

**Divine Love: Hub-E-Rasul TV Series** – launched in May 2017, this weekly half-hour Islamic television show covers a wide range of topics, focusing on spreading Prophet Muhammad's ﷺ message that Islam is a religion based on peace, love, and acceptance.

The show airs every Saturday at 1:30 pm (PST) on Joytv, reaching 7 million viewers Canada-wide. It reaches the online community through social media and through its website **huberasul.net.** For a full channel listing please visit www.huberasul.net/schedule.

**Naqshbandi Islamic Center of Vancouver** – this Center is a place for people of all faiths and beliefs to attend weekly *zikr* programs (circles of remembrance) three times a week (Thursdays, Fridays, and Saturdays). Shaykh Nurjan teaches above and beyond the principles of Islam including the deep realities of *maqam al-iman* (belief) and *maqam al-ihsan* (excellence of character).

**Hub-E-Rasul ﷺ Conference** – monthly Mawlid & Mehfil-e-Dhikr events are organized and held throughout the Lower Mainland. The aim is to revive the teachings of the Qur'an and *Sunnah* by celebrating holy events in true Islamic spirit (*Isra wal Mi'raj, Lailatul Bara'h, Lailatul Qadr, Mawlid an-Nabi* etc.)

**Simply Iman Cloud University** – an international online platform allowing people from around the world to pursue studies in various aspects of faith and spirituality from a classical Islamic perspective. Students have the opportunity to learn at their own pace and engage in an open dialogue with a teacher in real-time.

**Ahle Sunnah wal Jama of BC** – this organization is a resource for authentic content, books, and articles from the Qur'an & Sunnah from around the world. It works in collaboration with the well-known international organizations, Al Azhar University of Cairo, Dar al Ifta of Egypt and Islamic Supreme Council of North America.

**Shaykh Nurjan's Published Books** – titles are available at all major retailers and online at Amazon.

- Insan al Kamil – The Universal Perfect Being
- Rising Sun of the West
- YASEEN – Prophet ﷺ is the Walking Qur'an
- Divinely Praising Upon the Pearl of Creation
- In Pursuit of Angelic Power
- Levels of the Heart – Lataif al Qalb
- Secret Realities of Hajj
- The Healing Power of Sufi Meditation

Shaykh Nurjan's sincere mission is to globally spread the love of Sayyidina Muhammad ﷺ for our families and children. If you would like to be a shareholder in all these blessings, we invite you to support by any means possible. We hope to strengthen our efforts by joining our hands in raising the Honourable Flag of Sayyidina Muhammad ﷺ.

*Special thanks to the Team for book design and layout and to all the Transcribers.*

# UNIVERSALLY RECOGNIZED SYMBOLS

The following Arabic and English symbols connote sacredness and are universally recognized by Muslims:

The symbol عز وجل represents *Azza wa Jal*, a high form of praise reserved for God alone, which is customarily recited after reading or pronouncing the common name Allah, and any of the ninety-nine Islamic Holy Names of God.

The symbol ﷺ represents *sall Allahu 'alayhi wa salaam* (God's blessings and greetings of peace be upon the Prophet), which is customarily recited after reading or pronouncing the holy name of the Prophet Muhammad ﷺ. It commonly appears as *pbuh* (Peace and Blessings be Upon Him) in English translations.

The symbol عليه السلام represents *'alayhi 's-salam* (peace be upon him/her), which is customarily recited after reading or pronouncing the sanctified names of prophets, Prophet Muhammad's ﷺ family members, and the angels.

The symbol رضي الله عنه represents *radi-allahu 'anh/'anha* (may God be pleased with him/her), which is customarily recited after reading or pronouncing the holy names of Prophet Muhammad's ﷺ Companions.

The symbol ق represents *qaddas-allahu sirrah* (may God sanctify his or her secret), which is customarily recited after reading or pronouncing the name of a saint.

# Realities of Tafakkur (Contemplation)

إِنَّ فِي خَلْقِ السَّمَاوَاتِ وَالْأَرْضِ وَاخْتِلَافِ اللَّيْلِ وَالنَّهَارِ لَآيَاتٍ لِأُولِي الْأَلْبَابِ ﴿١٩٠﴾ الَّذِينَ يَذْكُرُونَ اللَّـهَ قِيَامًا وَقُعُودًا وَعَلَىٰ جُنُوبِهِمْ وَيَتَفَكَّرُونَ فِي خَلْقِ السَّمَاوَاتِ وَالْأَرْضِ رَبَّنَا مَا خَلَقْتَ هَـٰذَا بَاطِلًا سُبْحَانَكَ فَقِنَا عَذَابَ النَّارِ ﴿١٩١﴾

*3:190-191 – "Inna fee khalqis Samawati wal ardi wakhtilafil layli wan nahari, la ayatin li Olel albab. (190) Alladheena yadhkurona Allaha qiyaman wa qu'odan wa 'ala junobihim, wa yatafakkarona fee khalqis Samawati wal ardi, Rabbana ma khalaqta hadha batilan subhanaka faqina 'adhaban nar. (191)"*
*(Surat Ali-Imran)*

*"Indeed, in the creation of the heavens and the earth and the alternation of the night and the day are signs for those People of understanding (People of the Door of Knowledge). (190)*
*Who remember Allah while standing or sitting or [lying] on their sides and Contemplate the creation in the heavens and the earth, [saying], Our Lord, You did not create this aimlessly/ in vain; exalted are You [above such a thing]; then protect us from the punishment of the Fire. (191)" (Family of Imran, 3:190-191)*

تَفَكُّرُ سَاعَةٍ خَيْرٌ مِنْ عِبَادَةِ سَبْعِينْ سَنَةً

*"Tafakkur sa'atin khairun min 'Ibadati sab'een sanatan."*

*"One hour of contemplation is more valuable than seventy years of worship."*

Prophet Muhammad (pbuh)

# What is Meditation in Sufism?

In the words of our scholars, *tafakkur* literally means
to think on a subject deeply, systematically,
and in great detail.

In Sufism, it signifies reflection, which is the human
heart's light, the spirit's nourishment, the essence of
knowledge, and the heart and light of the
Sufi way of life.

# Chapter 1
# Meditation

# Understanding Meditation

## What is Meditation and How is it Done?

Meditation in Islamic understanding is *tafakkur* (contemplation). It's to slow our lives down in which Allah ﷻ throughout Holy Qur'an – there

are categories of *rijal* of these people, of people of realities. The people of the door. *Ulul al Baab* (Gatekeepers of the Reality), they are the people of the gate, the door, "*Ulul 'ilmi Qaaiman bil qist.*" They are the people of *tafakkur*.

شَهِدَ اللَّـهُ أَنَّهُ لَا إِلَـهَ إِلَّا هُوَ وَالْمَلَائِكَةُ وَأُولُو الْعِلْمِ قَائِمًا بِالْقِسْطِ ۚ ﴿١٨﴾

3:18 – "*Shahidallahu annahu la ilaha illa Hu wal mala'ikatu wa ulul 'ilmi qaaiman bil qist...*" (Surat Ali-Imran)

"*Allah bears witness that there is no god but He, and the angels and men of knowledge, upholding justice...*" (Family of Imran, 3:18)

Allah's ﷻ continuously making reminders within Holy Qur'an, 'None of you know but the people of *tafakkur*.'

إِنَّ فِي خَلْقِ السَّمَاوَاتِ وَالْأَرْضِ وَاخْتِلَافِ اللَّيْلِ وَالنَّهَارِ لَآيَاتٍ لِّأُولِي الْأَلْبَابِ ﴿١٩٠﴾
الَّذِينَ يَذْكُرُونَ اللَّـهَ قِيَامًا وَقُعُودًا وَعَلَىٰ جُنُوبِهِمْ وَيَتَفَكَّرُونَ فِي خَلْقِ السَّمَاوَاتِ وَالْأَرْضِ
رَبَّنَا مَا خَلَقْتَ هَـٰذَا بَاطِلًا سُبْحَانَكَ فَقِنَا عَذَابَ النَّارِ ﴿١٩١﴾

3

*3:190-191 – "Inna fee khalqis Samawati wal ardi wakhtilafil layli wan nahari, la ayatin li Olel albab. (190) Alladheena yadhkurona Allaha qiyaman wa qu'odan wa 'ala junobihim, wa yatafakkarona fee khalqis Samawati wal ardi, Rabbana ma khalaqta hadha batilan subhanaka faqina 'adhaban nar. (191)" (Surat Ali-Imran)*

*"Indeed, in the creation of the heavens and the earth and the alternation of the night and the day are signs for those People of understanding (People of the Door of Knowledge). (190) Who remember Allah while standing or sitting or [lying] on their sides and Contemplate the creation in the heavens and the earth, [saying], Our Lord, You did not create this aimlessly/in vain; exalted are You [above such a thing]; then protect us from the punishment of the Fire." (Family of Imran, 3:190-191)*

And He says that, 'Everything is praising Me and none can hear it but the people of *tafakkur.*' Throughout the Qur'an, Allah ﷻ is making

reference to a category of people whom they understood *tafakkur.* And then *awliyaullah* (saints) come into our lives and *tafakkur* is to slow down and to begin to contemplate. So, this is not about making people to be Arabs, but to teach the similarity and the Arabic words to our English understanding. So, in English, they call it meditating, to contemplate, to slow down, to get an understanding. And then Prophet ﷺ described in his *hadith* that, 'Who knows himself will know his Lord.'

4

مَنْ عَرَفَ نَفْسَهُ فَقَدْ عَرَفَ رَبَّهُ

*"Man 'arafa nafsahu faqad 'arafa Rabbahu."*

*"Who knows himself, knows his Lord."* (Prophet Muhammad (pbuh))

Again, the concept of *tafakkur*. And Prophet ﷺ describes, 'There are people whom their *tafakkur* of one hour is like 70 years of worship for someone else.'

تَفَكُّرْ سَاعَةٍ خَيْرٌ مِنْ عِبَادَةِ سَبْعِينْ سَنَة

*"Tafakkur sa'atin khairun min 'Ibadati sab'een sanatan."*

*"One hour of contemplation is more valuable than seventy years of worship"* (Prophet Muhammad (pbuh))

So, now it begins to describe the secret of *tafakkur* is so powerful that what they achieve through their soul – one hour sitting with them is like 70 years of another person's worshipness, which means it is a lifespan. So, one hour you sit with them, you may be dressed by a lifetime of somebody else's actions. It means you go about your life is not even comparable to one hour of sitting and learning *tafakkur* (contemplation) with them.

This means these are all these gifts that Allah ﷻ want to bestow. And *tafakkur* is a huge subject that we have on the website. Then go on the NurMuhammad website and begin to study that understanding. And how to slow down life, how to begin to meditate, how to understand to open the hearing and what my ears are going to hear, open my seeing, close what my eyes see from the outside and begin to see inside, what my nose is going to breathe of energy and *qudra* (power) of what it's going to bring in of the holiness of this Divine breath.

And if all of those functionalities are trying their best to submit for Allah ﷻ, then the power of the Holy Tongue. That through this tongue, Allah ﷻ will guide all of humanity. It means this is an inheritance from all of the prophets of Allah ﷻ. What made them to be prophets? It's that their hearing was for Allah ﷻ, their seeing was for Allah ﷻ, their breath was for Allah ﷻ and then Allah ﷻ bestowed a grace and a mercy upon their tongue; some of which were just prophets and others which were messengers. That they delivered the message of Allah ﷻ through the purity of their faculties. So, meditation is to stop, contemplate, open that reality – that's *tafakkur*.

*Tazakkur* is at a whole different level. It's now Allah ﷻ even asking the people of *tafakkur* and contemplation and meditation, 'Remember.'

*Tazakkur* is to remember, remember what? Remember that, 'I didn't just create you out of a vacuum and throw you onto the Earth and your whole enjoyment was supposed to be the Earth, no. You didn't even come from there. You come from paradise and I created your soul ancient.' When was your soul made? Ancient reality for your soul. *"Allamal Qur'an"* *ba'dan "khalaqal insan."*

عَلَّمَ الْقُرْآنَ ﴿٢﴾ خَلَقَ الْإِنسَانَ ﴿٣﴾

*55:2-3 – "Allamal Qur'an (2). Khalaqal Insaan (3)."*
*(Surat Ar-Rahman)*

*"It is He Who has taught the Qur'an. (2) He has created Mankind. (3)"*
*(The Beneficent, 55:2-3)*

6

'I taught your soul all of its realities and you promised Me on the day of promises.' *"Wa qalo bala."* I said, 'Am I not your Lord?' And your soul said, 'Yes, you are my Lord.' Do you remember that? No.

وَإِذْ أَخَذَ رَبُّكَ مِن بَنِي آدَمَ مِن ظُهُورِهِمْ ذُرِّيَّتَهُمْ وَأَشْهَدَهُمْ عَلَىٰ أَنفُسِهِمْ أَلَسْتُ بِرَبِّكُمْ قَالُوا بَلَىٰ شَهِدْنَا أَن تَقُولُوا يَوْمَ الْقِيَامَةِ إِنَّا كُنَّا عَنْ هَٰذَا غَافِلِينَ ﴿١٧٢﴾

*7:172 – "Wa idh akhadha rabbuka min banee adama min Zhuhorihim dhurriyyatahum wa ashhadahum 'ala anfusihim alastu biRabbikum qalo bala shahidna an taqolo yawmal qiyamati inna kunna 'an hadha ghafileen." (Surat Al-A'raf)*

*"And [mention] when your Lord took from the children of Adam from their atoms/loins – their descendants and made them testify concerning themselves, [saying to them], "Am I not your Lord?" They said, "Yes, we do testify!" [This] - lest you should say on the day of Resurrection, 'Indeed, we were of this unaware.'" (The Heights, 7:172)*

That's our goal. To go back to what you promised Allah ﷻ when He created your soul and what He bestowed of His mercy, bestowed of His gifts, bestowed of all His realities and He put upon the soul. Stop your busy-ness of your life. It's not going to be of any benefit in the grave. Use your body now to communicate with your soul's reality. Find out what is it that you promised Allah ﷻ. That's called your promise, your *ahd*, your covenant with Allah ﷻ. What was your covenant?

7

The duty of the guides is to take you back to your covenant with Allah ﷻ, not to take you to themselves, but to take you to your covenant.

إِنَّ الَّذِينَ يُبَايِعُونَكَ إِنَّمَا يُبَايِعُونَ اللَّـهَ يَدُ اللَّـهِ فَوْقَ أَيْدِيهِمْ ۚ فَمَن نَّكَثَ فَإِنَّمَا يَنكُثُ عَلَىٰ نَفْسِهِ ۖ
وَمَنْ أَوْفَىٰ بِمَا عَاهَدَ عَلَيْهُ اللَّـهَ فَسَيُؤْتِيهِ أَجْرًا عَظِيمًا ﴿١٠﴾

*48:10 – "Innal ladheena yubayi'oonaka innama yubayi'on Allaha
yadullahi fawqa aydeehim, faman nakatha fa innama yankuthu 'ala
nafsihi, wa man awfa bima 'ahada 'alayhu Allaha fasayu teehi ajran
'azheema." (Surat Al-Fath)*

*"Indeed, those who give Bayah (pledge allegiance) to you, [O Muhammad]
– they are actually giving Bayah (pledge allegiance) to Allah. The hand of
Allah is over their hands. So, he whoever breaks his pledge/ oath, only
breaks it to the detriment/ Harm/ loss of himself. And whoever fulfills
their covenant (Bayah) that which he has promised Allah - He will grant
him a great reward." (The Victory, 48:10)*

How? By bringing the love of Sayyidina Muhammad ﷺ, teaching you how to meditate, contemplate, stop, slow down, smell the fragrance, smell the roses. As soon as you begin to slow down, then 'Who knows himself will begin to know the Lord.'

مَنْ عَرَفَ نَفْسَهُ فَقَدْ عَرَفَ رَبَّهُ

*"Man 'arafa nafsahu faqad 'arafa Rabbahu."*

*"Who knows himself, knows his Lord." (Prophet Muhammad (pbuh))*

8

What governs you? What is your *rab* (lord)? Don't say your *rab* is Allah ﷻ yet because if Allah ﷻ was truly your Lord, you could walk on water. What is really your lord is all the things of your life that govern you and push you and pull you in all your desires. So, then this is the whole ocean of *tafakkur*, *inshaAllah*.

## How Does Meditation Help in Our Spiritual Development?

Meditation is not something easy that they show in our western culture that it's such an easy practice and take your clothes off and sit by the tree. Meditation is actually the last stage of a spiritual development. It's a full-fledged attack against *shaitan* (satan). And as soon as you intend to meditate, there will be a hyper-awareness of how much you're under attack from *shaitan*.

So, somebody who has never gone to a doctor – what's the word for cancer? Oncologist. They think they're very healthy. They never go to a doctor. 'Shaykh, I never go  to a doctor I'm very healthy, very healthy.' Until one day some sicknesses come to them and they go to a doctor. And the doctor says, 'Wait, you got a whole lot of problems going on. You didn't recognize anything but there are tremendous amounts of sicknesses coming out.' And all of a sudden then the person realizes how sick they are and say, 'Oh, I didn't know I was so sick!' There is no difference in the spiritual realm.

9

As soon as you intend to make meditation and sit and try to make your *zikr* (Divine remembrance) and praisings upon Sayyidina Muhammad ﷺ, do it in our system where you are playing *salawats* (praises upon Prophet Muhammad ﷺ), defending your ears from any *waswas* (whispering), you'll begin to see how difficult the process is. 'I can't sit for two seconds without something agitating me.' Now you're in the doctor's exam room. There is something wrong and Allah ﷻ wanted you to see it. You don't have the ability to sit for two minutes, five minutes, six minutes with yourself to know yourself. 'Who knows himself will know his Lord.'

مَنْ عَرَفَ نَفْسَهُ فَقَدْ عَرَفَ رَبَّهُ

*"Man 'arafa nafsahu faqad 'arafa Rabbahu."*

*"Who knows himself, knows his Lord." (Prophet Muhammad (pbuh))*

You can't play the *salawats*; you can't do all of these things, you can't put the fragrances because you're under satanic attack and *shaitan* doesn't allow you to sit, doesn't allow you to play it. That's what Allah ﷻ wanted you to know that, 'O people of *tafakkur,* stop and realize how much you are under attack!' Only at the time that you recognize your sickness is there ever a path of healing that opens. Otherwise if you're ignorant of your sickness you say, 'I don't need these people!' You don't need us, wait until you're full-fledged in difficulty, it's too late at that time.

But when they identify their problem, that's the first step in spiritual healing and spiritual development. 'I know I can't sit. I get angry, something's happening. I can't put the water on myself; I can't make *wudu* (ablution).' Those are all the first steps of awareness, that how much the person is under attack. So then they say, 'You got to be making your *zikr*, you have to make the *salawats* on Sayyidina Muhammad ﷺ. You have to keep making *"A'uzu Billahi Minash Shaitanir Rajeem Bismillahir Rahmanir Raheem,"* at least 100 times a day.

اَعُوْذُ بِاللهِ مِنَ الشَّيْطَانِ الرَّجِيْم بِسْمِ اللهِ الرَّحْمَنِ الرَّحِيْم

*"A'uzu Billahi Minash Shaitanir Rajeem Bismillahir Rahmanir Raheem."*

*"I seek refuge in Allah from Satan, the rejected one. In the Name of Allah, the Most Beneficent, the Most Merciful."*

Sitting, *"Bismillahir Rahmanir Raheem."* With every *"Bismillahir Rahmanir Raheem,"* Allah ﷻ opened a *faraj* (salvation), for a difficulty to be taken away. *Salawats* on Sayyidina Muhammad ﷺ and then sit after you make your *namaz* (prayer). If you come back and say, 'I can't even make my *namaz*,' then again that's a sign of how difficult that person is under attack. Then you email the shaykh and they try to give you

the *awrads* (daily practices), the *zikrs*, and the process that's necessary to combat that difficulty. As soon as you acknowledge it and understand it, *"Idha jaa a Nasrullah."*

11

إِذَا جَاءَ نَصْرُ اللَّهِ وَالْفَتْحُ ﴿١﴾

*110:1 – "Idha jaa a Nasrullahi wal Fath." (Surat An-Nasr)*

*"When there comes the Divine Support of Allah and the Victory." (The Divine Support, 110:1)*

Allah ﷻ never leaves the servant to be in the hands of *shayateen* (devils). That as soon as you identify it, the shaykhs pray for you. You pray for yourself that, 'I need, *ya Rabbi*, support; I understand I'm under difficulty. I'm under the oppression of *shaitan*. Grant me a *najat* (salvation); grant me a power to release myself from that difficulty, *inshaAllah*.'

## What is the Connection Between Islam and Meditation?

You have you go back into about 1917. *Shaitan* (satan) decided that his only way he is going to conquer this Earth, truly conquer this Earth, was to take away any type of *ruhani* teaching, any type of spiritual teaching, through all dimensions. So, the Islamic world from 1917, all the wars and all the governments that were put into place took away all spirituality. Even within martial arts, all spirituality, everything was taken of real spirituality, was hidden. *Shaitan* wanted to hide everything of any type of spiritual practice. So, then you look from 1917 – pretty much everything. By the time Lawrence arrived in Arabia, they completely hid all of the Sufi teachings all of which is the spiritual teachings.

12

So, very simple at that time on Earth, that's what *shaitan's* plan was. He hid all spiritual teachings so that you take the soul out of it and leave a

shell. So, they just became empty practices. As a result of empty practices, there is no spirit in anything people do now. So, when they talk, there is no spirit in them. There is no love. There is no enjoyment in it. They talk about Islam in a very dry, sort of manipulated or understood practice, as if it's something empty. And all that is remaining of Islam right now is *Jum'ah* (Friday prayer). We ask Muslims, 'What do you do for Islam?' Says, 'We go for *Jum'ah*,' and what else? 'What do you mean what else?' Everything is *bid'ah* (innovation). What are you talking about?

Our life was supposed to be Islam. The beauty of Islam is like a garden. There should be continuous *zikr* (Divine remembrance), continuous praisings, continuous *halaqas* and circles and teachings of reality but if there is nobody practicing these practices, there is definitely no reality.

That's why they just keep talking about *fiqh* (Islamic jurisprudence). How many times you can make *wudu* (ablution), how is *wudu* going to be good, how *wudu* is going to be bad, how much water you are to have for the *wudu*, what negates the water of…it goes on and on and on. Even now there's some channels in Pakistan. They talk all day long, 24 hours a day but no *haqqaiq* (realities). So, now what do they talk about? How to peel a banana according to the *sunnah* (traditions of Prophet Muhammad ﷺ), which I don't think there were any bananas at that time.

13

So, it means they're making it up. So, if you can't talk reality and there is no *haqqaiq* and there is no abundant fountain like a flowing fountain of the *Kawthar* (The Fountain of Abundance) that used to dress all of the *masjids* because they were all Sufi. Those were fountains in which Allah ﷻ was flowing of  knowledges. They would do their *zikrs*, their *halaqas*, their teachings and all of their practices. If you take the fountain away, it's just an empty shell.

## How Can We Get Our Loved Ones to Pray?

 *InshaAllah*, better to conserve or to focus on ourselves. That when I focus on myself, make sure that I'm praying, make sure that Allah's ﷻ happy with me. My actions are good, my actions are solid. My character's good. I'm an example of that reality and then, *alhamdulillah*, we leave the rest in Allah's ﷻ hands.

If the person is looking at your good character and still chooses not to pray, it means that everybody based on their coordinance. We cannot force anyone to do anything. If they look and see that you have bad character and say, 'Why should I do anything if you're bad like that?' then it's going to be difficult. If they see that we have good character and they chose still not to do and worship their Lord, then that's between them and their Lord. But again, most important is everyone is responsible for their own grave.

14

When you build yourself, pray, do all your practices, then you begin to ask, 'Ya Rabbi, that forgive me and forgive my children, forgive all my loved ones. Dress them from your blessings. Dress them from your *ni'mat* (blessing). So, then we have credibility and credit with Allah ﷻ because of our good actions and our good  character, *inshaAllah*. But as soon as we start to focus on someone else, it becomes a deficit within our own account. Because we've started to focus so much on someone else, that our actions become weak and we enter into arguments, we enter into fights, and then our own position with Allah ﷻ will become jeopardized.

### How Can We Teach Our Children Meditation?

First make sure that you are an expert in meditation. Don't think this is a children's course; this is for you a course. This is above and the most advanced courses of Islam. This is not what you see from yoga centres. This is the most advanced understandings of Islam, is *tafakkur* (contemplation). After they studied all their *shari'ah* (Divine Law), studied all their *fiqh* (Islamic jurisprudence) – at the end, the shaykhs would assign them to reach to the shaykhs of *zawq* and taste.

And the shaykhs of taste would then take you to perfect you. The moon raises you and the sun sweetens you. So, this is the last phase where the sun sweetens you because they have a very strong Muhammadan light to perfect people. It's not so much a course for children. It's more important that the adult becomes the master of *tafakkur*. The light that they bring in, the guidance and understanding that they bring in within their heart will illuminate the entire house of lights, will  bring in protection, will bring in knowledges, realities, and will bring all of the characteristics that are important for Sayyidina Muhammad ﷺ within the home.

 That's natural. Once the person is an expert in their *tafakkur*, that they continuously practice it, just by means of them sitting with their children, the children will observe how they sit and how they close their eyes, how they listen to the *salawats* (praises upon Prophet Muhammad ﷺ). And they will do as you do, not do as you say. So, our way is based on doing, not saying, *inshaAllah*.

16

## How Does Meditation Benefit Us in This Life and the Next?

If you can stop and slow down, you get to understand who you are and the reality of who our reality is. What Allah ﷻ created us for? What's the

blessings that Allah ﷻ wants to bestow upon us? Anyone whom seeking the reality of knowing themselves, no doubt, Allah ﷻ bestow His Mercy and *Rahmah* upon them. This means these are souls that become immensely blessed because as they begin to know themselves, they know all their bad characteristics and they try to stop.

As a result of getting to know themselves, they begin to witness what Allah ﷻ wants them to witness. It means they're now headed in the direction that God wants them to head into. As they are heading into that direction, taking away all of their bad characteristics, Allah's ﷻ *Rahmah* and Mercy dressing upon their souls and they become very blessed souls in *dunya* (material world) and especially in *akhirah* (hereafter). Because we just described the *akhirah*, one hour of them is 70 years of somebody else's worship. One hour.

تَفَكُّرْ سَاعَةٍ خَيْرٌ مِنْ عِبَادَةِ سَبْعِينْ سَنَةٍ

*"Tafakkur sa'atin khairun min 'Ibadati sab'een sanatan."*

*"One hour of contemplation is more valuable than seventy years of worship" (Prophet Muhammad (pbuh))*

17

So, imagine somebody who's trained in *tafakkur* (contemplation) and meditation. Real meditation, not like the western understanding of

people who sit next to a tree. This is about the people who get deep into their reality and what they promised God, what their soul was promised, and they reached to reality to be of service to humanity. If they're meditating their whole life, 24 hours of their existence is as if the 70. So, you multiply 70 years times their one day is approximately 1,700 years of your years in comparison to one of these *awliya* (saints) who are specialized in *tafakkur*. One day is 1,700 years you have to live to equal their one day of who they are. That's why Allah ﷻ then describes these are people, they are like *awtad* (pegs). They are like mountains.

$$\text{﴿٧﴾ وَالْجِبَالَ أَوْتَادًا}$$

*78:7 – "Wal jibala awtadan." (Surat An-Naba)*

*"And Mountains like Pegs." (The Tidings, 78:7)*

Why Allah ﷻ describes and why *awliya* come and say, 'Oh, the *awtad* they are like pegs, they are like mountains.' Not only because they are firm into the ground and they stop the Earth from shaking, but because the

mass that Allah ﷻ bestow upon them; they are like mountains compared to other creation. Mountains in the *barakah* and the blessing that Allah ﷻ bestow upon their souls, just from the simple mathematics of what Prophet ﷺ brought for us. One hour, 70 years.

18

Somebody trained in *tafakkur* all their life is in *tafakkur*. They don't shut their system off. Their system is continuously online and dedicated. Before, we said there's login; when you had the first Apple, you had to login 92 baud. 'Eehhh…chk,chk,chk,' and wait for the computer to connect and then get very aggravated in the house because it took forever to connect. Now what? You're live, wi-fi full speed continuously going, it never shuts off. There is no internet shutting. There is not even logging on. You just hit your wi-fi, you're on.

So, Allah ﷻ showing why. There are people whom their souls, when Allah ﷻ bestowed upon them, they are like a wi-fi. They are always on. Now they internally know how to shut their system off, then how to turn it back on but their wi-fi is broadcasting. As a result, one day with them is 1,700 years for somebody else. So, imagine you spend one day, two days, three days, five days, seven days, ten days or years with them – what their soul is bestowing of realities upon that soul, on those souls.

# Preparing for Meditation

### What is the Recommended Dress Code for Meditation?

Anytime we're taking a spiritual path and we're deep within this *dunya* (material world), we should separate our clothing. Those whom are working out and struggling and doing all their work, *alhamdulillah*. They should have a set of clothes that are specifically for spiritual program. That they take off their *dunya*, they wash, they shower, and they sit with some nice meditation clothes that completely reminds them of meditation.

And it's funny that all eastern cultures do that. So, when the kids signed up for karate, they immediately make them put on this karate suit that it look like a *sunnah* suit because it's a loose shirt, loose pants tied with a rope and immediately they feel like in the karate mode and they're going to chop and jump on everything. Same thing – that you have to get in the *sunnah* mode and meditation mode. That you take off your *dunya* clothes. You worked hard, *alhamdulillah*. Wash, shower, and now put on your *ruhani* (spiritual) clothes. That you sit and you meditate, and you cry unto Allah ﷻ in something that's nice and clean and perfumed for worshipness. And same for the *zikr* (Divine remembrance), that don't come with your work clothes to the *zikr*.

Mawlana Shah Naqshband ق used to mandate. Now a lot of these things no longer are done because the people are weak and they'll run away. So, the shaykh is trying to be as polite as possible. But in reality, Mawlana Shah Naqshband ق made a shower outside and mandated that anybody who came had to shower and then put on a nice white outfit and then sit in his presence for the *tafakkur* and the meditation, in which they meditated twice or three times a week, Mawlana Shaykh ق would say. And that was the *adab* (manners) of coming into the presence of the shaykh and the *adab* of going somewhere *ruhani* (spiritual) and special.

**What is the Etiquette Before Zikr or Meditation?**

The meditation, you can do it anytime. But for both meditation and *zikr* (Divine remembrance) is to keep your stomach empty. Try not to have big meals and then sit and think you want to meditate; you're just going to – you're not going to even levitate; you're just going to sleep. Because the body, all its energy is just to consume the food.

And the servant has to dis-attach the soul from the body. If there is no food in the stomach, then the tank is empty. When the tank is empty the soul is free to move. And the body is not needing that energy to survive and to digest. So always in the *salah* (prayer), in the *zikr*, in the practices, keep your stomach empty. That is why many people would come and be very upset – why do we eat so late? Well, because they didn't understand anything from the *zikr*. They want to go and eat big meals and go and have *zikr;* you lost the whole purpose of that *zikr*. You just sat there

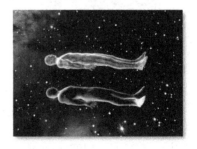

and ate a meal and just, I don't know what you did in that *zikr*. But those who want to experience the reality of the *zikr*, they keep their tank empty. As soon as they keep empty, their soul is able to feel and become subtle with the energies of the *zikr*.

They also kept a system of not wearing your work clothes with your spiritual time. Don't go from work and sit into the *zikr* with your work clothes. Keep a set of clothes that are completely separate, not from the energy of work, and that they're meant for being in Allah's 🕮 presence, not in your boss's presence. So, separate your *dunya* (material word) and your *akhirah* (hereafter) attire so that you are wearing something that's dedicated to Allah's 🕮 service.

And if you can, to shower before the association. Wash off all of *dunya* and ask to see yourself in the shower that, 'I'm washing away all of my *dunya*, and that Allah 🕮 accept my *wudu* (ablution) and my *ghusul* (shower) to be like a body that's been washed for the grave, and to be pure and purified. That, '*Ya Rabbi*, I'm coming for your *zikr*, I'm coming for your Divinely Presence.' And if we keep the *adab* (manners) of I'm coming into the presence of Sayyidina Muhammad 🕮, coming to the presence of Allah 🕮, then Allah 🕮 to reward us with that intention. Not just coming from work, sit with them for two minutes in my Adidas outfit and I'm full, I eat, and that's something else. Those are not the people who are trying to strive towards high degrees of reality, *inshaAllah*.

## What Should Our Diet Be Since We Started Meditation?

That's a very personal nature of what type of food do you like. Try to eat less before the meditation. Try to meditate on an empty stomach and know that everything has an energy. As your practices become stronger, you'll become more sensitive to the different energies. So, Mawlana Shaykh's ق teaching is that the meat has an energy.

If you eat a lot of chicken, you find yourself to be very picky, picky, picky, picky, picky. You basically take on the characteristic of that which you eat. So, it's better to be like a broccoli than a chicken. Broccoli doesn't seem like it's harming too many people but this chicken character, you know, the picky, picky, picky, picky, picky. Mawlana Shaykh ق said that, 'The chicken is always looking for a worm.' So, basically you take on the energy of all these creatures that you're eating, things you're eating.

In the Muslim world, I think they eat the lamb because it's a very passive animal. The cow is a very grazing animal and just likes to eat all day long. Before you know it, you eat too much beef and you're grazing like a cow all day long. So, you take all the characteristic and the attribute of the animal that you eat. So, then the vegetables, the food, the animals, everything in moderation. But try our best not to eat before we meditate, *inshaAllah.*

## How Can We Keep Awake and Vigilant?

The energy becomes so heavy it actually knocks you out. So, that's why in the training then the meditation was always in an uncomfortable position. As we got older, we got a little bit of arthritis in our knees, we can't do. But in our training years, we were meditating with a bench. So, we're always on the knee. And they have a little squatting bench where you can sit on your knees and it just supports yourself to be on that position of your knees. That Prophet's ﷺ teaching was to be uncomfortable, that the *hawa* and the desires, how to bring the *hawa* down.

So, our master Sayyidina Muhammad ﷺ set the example by sleeping on bamboo. He would sleep on a very uncomfortable material so that when the *Sahabi* (Holy Companions of Prophet ﷺ) awoke, they were very upset to see Prophet ﷺ having the marks of these things. They said, 'We can get you something very luxurious to sleep on.' He says, 'No, it makes it easier for me to wake up for my *Fajr*.' So, it means that was the teaching for *hawa* and the desire to go down. Make things uncomfortable.

So, if you sit in an uncomfortable position then have coffee and tea or black tea. Grandshaykh, Shaykh Abdullah Faiz ad-Daghestani ق would have eleven cups of black tea before *Fajr*. So, it means he liked it strong. So, because of the amount of energy that comes and the amount of awareness that they want to keep. And *kehwa* and coffee was actually developed by the Sufis as a means to pray their *Tahajjud* and their *Fajr* prayers. So, don't meditate on a full stomach. You'll definitely knock out and you'll take away all the *barakah* (blessing) of the energy. The energy that's coming to you has to move freely through your system. So, you can always eat nicely after your meditation, after the *zikr* nights.

Never eat before the *zikr* (Divine remembrance) if you want to feel the energy. Otherwise, the *zikr* just becomes like a place where you're going to sleep because the body is too involved into digesting the food than for you to feel the process and the movement of the energy. When you enter into a state of hunger into your practices, you feel the energy. That gives its own *himmah* and excitement that these energies are coming. And I'm feeling these

energies and to benefit from it versus making yourself to be dull or not to feel it. So, they don't eat before.

## How Do We Fight the Comfort of Our Ego?

No, you don't meditate in comfort. It means that when we were younger and didn't have arthritis – now my knees have arthritis – when we were younger, we were always meditating on our knees. There was never time when we were not sitting on our knees. And that state of discomfort was Prophet ﷺ teaching to cut your *hawa*. Cut your comfort and it will lead to cutting your desires.

And Sayyidina Muhammad ﷺ would sleep on bamboo until he had marks. And *Sahabi* (Holy Companions of Prophet ﷺ) were crying out of sadness that, 'We want to give every comfort of our wealth to you.' Said, 'No, no, I sleep in this situation so I can pray my Fajr. If I go too deep, I don't want to.'

عَنْ اَلإِمَامْ الْبَاقِرْ عَلَيْهِ السّلَامْ، قَالَ:ـ سُئِلَتْ حَفْصَةُ (عَلَيْهِ السّلَامْ)، مَا كَانَ فِرَاشُ
رَسُولِ اللهِ ﷺ فِي بَيْتِكِ؟
قَالَتْ: مِسْحًا نَثْنِيهِ ثَنِيَتَيْنِ فَيَنَامُ عَلَيْهِ، فَلَمَّا كَانَ ذَاتَ لَيْلَةٍ، قُلْتُ: لَوْ ثَنَيْتَهُ أَرْبَعَ ثَنْيَاتٍ،
لَكَانَ أَوْطَأَ لَهُ، فَثَنَيْنَاهُ لَهُ بِأَرْبَعِ ثَنْيَاتٍ .
فَلَمَّا أَصْبَحَ، قَالَ ﷺ : مَا فَرَشْتُمْ لِيَ اللَّيْلَةَ؟ قَالَتْ. قُلْنَا: هُوَ فِرَاشُكَ، إِلَا أَنَّا ثَنَيْنَاهُ
بِأَرْبَعِ ثَنْيَاتٍ، قُلْنَا: هُوَ أَوْطَأُ لَكَ .
قَالَ ﷺ : رُدُّوهُ لِحَالَتِهِ اَلْأُولَى، فَإِنَّهُ مَنَعَتْنِي وَطَاعَتُهُ صَلَاتِيَ اللَّيْلَةَ .
[ المَصْدَرْ: الشَّمَائِلَ الْمُحَمَّدِيَّةُ ٣٢٨ ، كِتَابْ: ٤٦ حَدِيثْ:٢ ]

*'An al Imam al Baqir (as) qala: suyelat Hafsa (as), maa kana ferashu
Rasulillahi* ﷺ *fi bayteka?*
*Qalat: "Meshan nathnihi thaniyatayni fayanamu 'alayhi, falamma kana
zata laylatin. Qultu: law thanaytahu arba'a thanyaatin, lakana awta a
lahu, fathanaynahu lahu bi arba'yi thanyatin.*
*Falamma asbaha, qala* ﷺ*: "Maa farashtum leyal laylata? Qalat."*

27

*Qulna: Huwa firashuka, ila anna thanaynahu be arba'yi thanyatin, qulna: huwa aw taa a laka.*
*Qala ﷺ: "Rudduhu lehalatihi alula, fayennahu mana'atni wa taa atuhu salathiyal laylata."*
*[Al Masdar: Ash Shamayel AlMuhammadiya, 328, Kitab 46, Hadith 2]*

*Our Master Imam Muhammad Al-Baqir (as) said that someone asked Ummul Mu'mineen (Mother of the Believers) Hafsa (as), "How was the bed of Prophet Muhammad (pbuh) in your house?"*
*She replied, 'It was a canvas folded into two, which was spread for the Messenger of Allah (pbuh) to sleep on.*
*On one night I thought if I folded it into four and spread it, it would become softer. I folded it and spread it that way.*
*In the morning Rasulullah (pbuh) asked, "What did you spread for me last night?"*
*I replied, 'It was the same bed, I only folded it into four so that it may become softer.'*
*Rasulullah (pbuh) said, "Leave it in its original form. Its softness deprived me of my nightly devotion and prayers."*
*[Source: Ash Shamayel AlMuhammadiya 328, Book 46, Hadith 2]*

Because teaching for us that anytime you put yourself in a discomfort, in a 'dis-ease,' you're going to bring out the power of your soul. If you sit in a very comfortable position and meditate, of course, it's going to be a sleeping competition. You snore very loud. But you go onto your knees until it hurts. You take your tea  or coffee and make sure that you're alert and then pain becomes a friend of yours. As soon as you have pain, it begins to wake, wake, wake you until you would have so much pain and your mouth is going numb and your knees and your feet going numb and that kept you awake.

And before you sleep, drink a lot of water so that your sleep and train yourself that your sleep is never deep. Don't listen to people of television. Your sleep has to be very subtle because between your sleep

and your wake is your most powerful state. So, when their sleep is light, any sound – they're alert, especially in times like now. So, when you drink a lot of water, the whole night you're waking up and washing. You become shining. Why? Because you're continuously making *wudu*. Not that, 'Oh, I have to make *wudu*.' No, this was a blessing. Every time you make *wudu*, it's a light upon light. Then you train yourself how as soon as you wash, you quickly wash. You go to the facility, wash. Sit down, pray two *rakahs Salatul Wudu* (Prayer of Ablution) and go to bed. It's all night long. You're praying and washing, praying and washing.

So, you put a difficulty upon your *hawa*. So, your four enemies have to be attacked: your *nafs* (ego), your *dunya* (material world), your *hawa* (desires), and *shaitan* (satan). If you attack these four enemies, you can unify your soul. Your soul has been quartered by them. That every desire comes to make your *hawa* to go. Every allurement, *shaitan* is sending to distract us with our *dunya*. Then

the *nafs*, everything that the *nafs* is whispering to you, to split you in a different direction and then *shaitan*. So, if we're not fighting these four enemies to bring the soul to be whole again, *inshaAllah*.

## What Are the Benefits of Lighting Candles During Meditation?

Mawlana Shaykh Adnan ق described in a talk about the beatific reality of lighting a candle. As soon as you light a candle in worshipness, Allah ﷻ creates an angel. And that angel will say *"Ameen"* during your entire  worshipness for you. At the level of angelic reality, that every imperfection the servant is doing, but because they lit this light for the love of Allah ﷻ to read.

That's why they said they would read Qur'an with a candlelight. Because as they are reciting every incorrect pronunciation and recitation, the  angel is perfecting it and saying *"Ameen, ameen, ameen, ameen."* Until the servant is finished their recitation, that angel exists for all of eternity. You turn off the fire, but the angel exists continuously saying *"Ameen"* to the servant. And that's why very spiritual people light lots of candles because there are angels coming into existence by that reality and they're continuously saying *"Ameen"* for the servant. Don't burn your house, please. They don't know how to use candles and they put it near a curtain and say, 'Shaykh I burned my apartment down.' *Astaghfirullah!* So be very careful, especially if you have little kids. They come and hit the glass and jars. Be very careful when you're using candles, *inshaAllah*.

30

### Is it Important to Use Fragrances and Which Ones Are Recommended?

It's open to choose fragrances maybe that are special for you, amber, sandalwood and rose, soft rose like *ghulab*, like a rose water. They are very special fragrances and these fragrances that have to be used, they have to be for heavenly beings because the

*mu'min jinn* (believing unseen beings) and the *malaika* (angels) they take pleasure in those fragrances. When we fragrant an area it makes them happy because they're living in that environment, praying in that environment and the reality of aromatherapy is angelic therapy.

That when you smell these fragrant fragrances an angelic energy begins to dress the servant until Allah ﷻ open the power of their breath and their smell that when they're breathing they feel an energy and the power of their smelling is of an angelic reality. That they begin to smell the angelic fragrances, the beatific fragrances that energize and dress their soul.

At the same time, it begins to open the angelic smell in which they can smell the badness of character. That when people have a bad heart and bad character and too many sins, they are of a very bad smell. That the smell of the *nafs* (ego) and smell of the sins that the *nafs* put upon *insan* (human being) is of a horrific nature and it's important to fragrance an area for these energies and for these realities.

31

At the same time because most people don't understand the unseen realm, we don't use these wild herbs. Don't use the fragrances from the jungle because you attract all the jungle creatures. And some of these areas where the natives practice, they didn't practice pure spirituality, but they practiced calling upon spirits. The *jinn* world is ten times more than our world. For every snake we have they have ten times more. For  every bear we have they have ten times more; for every wolf we have they have ten times more. So, if you release these fragrances in the home of pines and woods and make your house smell like a wild jungle then you're going to have jungle creatures attracted to that fragrance. And you're going to have very bizarre energies within the house of the believing person.

So, it means there are very specific Islamic fragrances. The *bakhoors* (incense), the ambers, the sandalwood, those are fragrances that the angels and the *mu'min* beings and spirits appreciate. As a result, they come and they begin to clean out everything negative. So, our cleansing and our cleaning of a space is by the fragrances in which Prophet ﷺ preferred. And these are our *bakhoors* and our fragrances, *inshaAllah*.

### What is the Benefit of Holding a Rock During Meditation?

For now you can hold the hand to feel the energy and the pulse so that you are in tune with your energy that's coming into your heart. For those who want to hold a rock, and the significance of a rock – there are certain stones that can heat up and they produce a tremendous amount of energy. And Allah ﷻ describe throughout Qur'an that the rock, your heart is like a rock. He says, 'No, not a rock because rocks even can gush water from.'

ثُمَّ قَسَتْ قُلُوبُكُم مِّن بَعْدِ ذَٰلِكَ فَهِيَ كَالْحِجَارَةِ أَوْ أَشَدُّ قَسْوَةً ۚ وَإِنَّ مِنَ الْحِجَارَةِ لَمَا يَتَفَجَّرُ مِنْهُ الْأَنْهَارُ ۚ وَإِنَّ مِنْهَا لَمَا يَشَّقَّقُ فَيَخْرُجُ مِنْهُ الْمَاءُ ۚ وَإِنَّ مِنْهَا لَمَا يَهْبِطُ مِنْ خَشْيَةِ اللَّهِ ۗ وَمَا اللَّهُ بِغَافِلٍ عَمَّا تَعْمَلُونَ ﴿٧٤﴾

*2:74 – "Summa qasat quloobukum mim ba'di zaalika fahiya kalhijaarati aw-ashaadu qaswah; wa inna minal hijaarati lamaa yatafajjaru minhul anhaar; wa inna minhaa lamaa yash shaqqaqu fayakhruju minhul maaa'; wa inna minhaa lamaa yahbitu min khashyatil laa; wa mal laahu bighaafilin 'ammaa ta'maloon." (Surat Al-Baqarah)*

*"Thenceforth were your hearts hardened: They became like a rock and even worse in hardness. For among rocks there are some from which rivers gush forth; others there are which when split asunder send forth water; and others which sink for fear of Allah. And Allah is not unmindful of what ye do." (The Cow, 2:74)*

It means they have a reality and they have a *zikr* (Divine remembrance) and its Allah's ﷻ creation and the *zikr* of different stones are important. The different crystals like rose crystal, they have a tremendous heat. For someone who wants to meditate and spark their energy and it's not sparking, like a science class you can use a catalyst. That something that will speed the process of feeling the heat and that would be a rose quartz. Himalayan salt – same thing. This is a cleansing nature. The *zikr* of salt is a cleansing reality. So, when you hold the Himalayan salt and you make your *tafakkur* (contemplation), you begin to feel a heat coming and begin to feel yourself lighting up and heating up. That salt also has a cleansing, so it takes away a lot of negative energy from *insan* (human being), *inshaAllah*.

## Can We Change the Location of Where We Meditate?

Sure, you can change it to where you think it's more energy there or more convenient there. It's just important to have a place – a place in which you make like a *maqam,* that you make it something you know sanctified, something holy. And many holy beings will come to pray there to make it a holy location. As long as you set it up, they will come. What's the expression? 'Build it and they will come.' Exactly. So, if you do good things for good beings, Allah ﷻ will inspire these good beings, 'Go pray there.' So that that servant can be protected and helped.

## When is the Best Time for Meditation?

*InshaAllah,* after *Asr.* Because it's the moment in which the Earth – everything is shutting down. And from *Salatul Tahajjud,* or *Asr* to *Maghrib.* Or from *Salatul Tahajjud* to *Fajr, inshaAllah,* when everything is slow and shut down, and people are not busy on the network. This *dunya* (material world) is like a big internet. If people are busy in the middle of the day, the connection is not going to be good and it's based on a *dunya* understanding energy. When everybody's sleeping, Allah ﷻ

describes the signal is very strong. That's why He recommends to come and pray *Salatul Tahajjud* where the Divinely Presence is very close to *insan* (mankind), because the energy is very strong, *inshaAllah.*

## After Which Prayer is it Best to Meditate?

All the *salahs* (prayers) are blessed. The meditation will be most powerful at *Fajr* time and *Maghrib* time. This means that this moment of *faraj* and *Tahajjud* and *Fajr* is a birth, is a birth of a day in which three veils of darkness are being lifted and there is a *najat* and a salvation forf creation. When the servant is in *tafakkur* (contemplation) from *Tahajjud* to *Fajr,* all the way to the rising of the sun, there is a tremendous energy that's being released, *"Salaamun hiya hattaa mat la'il Fajr."*

سَلَامٌ هِيَ حَتَّىٰ مَطْلَعِ الْفَجْرِ ﴿٥﴾

*97:5 – "Salamun, hiya hatta matla'il Fajr." (Surat Al-Qadr)*

*"Peace it is until the emergence of dawn." (The Power, 97:5)*

It means that there's a *salaam* (peace) from Allah 'ﷻ that's dressing the souls. And that's why Allah 'ﷻ – we said in the talk before – be like a bird. Have love in your heart like a bird, the *hadith* of Prophet ﷺ.

عَنْ أَبِي هُرَيْرَةَ عَنِ النَّبِيِّ صَلَّى اللهُ عَلَيْهِ وَسَلَّمَ قَالَ: يَدْخُلُ الْجَنَّةَ أَقْوَامٌ أَفْئِدَتُهُمْ مِثْلُ أَفْئِدَةِ الطَّيْرِ

*'An Abi Hurairah (ra), 'an anNabiyi ﷺ qala: "Yudkhulul jannata aqwamun afeydatuhum mithlu afeydati attayri."*

*Abu Hurairah (ra) reported: The Prophet (pbuh) said: "People whose hearts are like the hearts of birds will enter Paradise."*

And the attribute of a bird is he's always in praising and *zikr* (Divine remembrance). And the praising and the *zikr* of the bird is so powerful that the angels carry the bird into the sky and fly. Because nobody could believe that it's the aerodynamics of their movement that's actually making them to fly because mankind tried to copy that and they all crashed. You move your arms to see if Allah ﷻ will let you fly. No, but you don't even have to move your arms. If you're pious and Allah ﷻ finds sincerity with you, your soul flies everywhere.

So, be like the birds and make the *zikr* of Allah ﷻ. So, even the dove's *zikr*, 'cooh-cooh,' when in the *ayatul Qur'an* (verse of the Holy Qur'an) where Allah ﷻ said, 'Remember me and I remember you.'

فَاذْكُرُونِي أَذْكُرْكُمْ وَاشْكُرُوا لِي وَلَا تَكْفُرُونِ ﴿١٥٢﴾

*2:152 – "Fadhkuronee adhkurkum washkuroli wa la takfuroon."* *(Surat Al-Baqarah)*

*"So remember Me; I will remember you. And be grateful/Thankful to Me and do not reject faith." (The Cow, 2:152)*

Mawlana Shaykh Nazim ق said, 'The *zikr* of a dove, and why this Earth thinks the dove is a symbol of peace, because it's actually reciting *ayatul Kareem* to remind *insan* (mankind) what Allah ﷻ asked, 'Remember me and I remember you in a higher place.'

And that is the *zikr* of the dove. So, the *zikr* of all these birds are all different secrets but their characteristics, Prophet ﷺ said, 'Be like that.' They are all day long. They are making *zikr*. And as a result, they are flying and the servant also can fly with his soul. He doesn't need his body to fly. And then they look like a magician because they have those fake ones that pretend like they're flying in the air but there's a piece of metal going around into their sleeve. Yeah, because they can't do the *zikr* of Allah ﷻ.

So, do it through *zikr*, that you make your *zikr* praising upon Allah ﷻ. That have a heart which is so powerful, and the mind is that you've battled your mind to shut it off. Because the bird never thinks, 'Oh my God, I'm 5,000 feet in the air and I'm going to die right now because God forgot me.' It has complete reliance on Allah ﷻ and busy itself with his *zikr* and it's flying as a result.

37

So, then when did the bird sing the most? If they came at *Fajr*, they beat you. So, Sayyidina Abu Bakr as-Siddiq ☬ said that, 'If I hear the birds, I know that *Fajr* is already taken place.'

عَنْ أَبُو بَكِرٍ الصِّدِّيقُ عَلَيْهِ السَّلَامُ " إِنَّهُ مِنْ ٱلْعَيِبْ أَنْ تَسْتَيْقِظَ ٱلْطُيُوْرْ قَبْلَكَ فِي ٱلصَّبَاخْ " .

*'An Abu Bakris Siddiq (as), "Innahu min al'ayib an tastayqiza altuyoor qablaka fi alsabah."*

*Abu Bakr as Siddiq (as) said, "It's a matter of shame that the birds should be awake earlier than you in the morning."*

So, they try to get up before birds. The birds are reminding them and reciting at *Fajr* time. And when did the birds recite again? It's *Maghrib* time. Here, there are 10,000 crows in Burnaby. It's the scariest site you can imagine, maybe more than 10,000. But it's a  sign and all over the world that *Maghrib* time, the birds all come, and they face the sun and they start praising and crying unto Allah ☬ to protect them through the difficulty of nighttime.

And in the daytime, they praise Allah ☬ for this beatific day and the glory of what Allah ☬ is about to bestow upon them. So, if we live a life just following the idea and the understanding of even the birds, they're  teaching us. So, most powerful will be the *Fajr* and the *Asr* to *Maghrib*. So right before *Maghrib*, they're meditating on the power that's coming onto this Earth as a death of the day, *inshaAllah*.

## Can We Remain in a State of Meditation Throughout the Day?

It's best to have a respect for that state. It means that's a state in which we're trying to keep a connection in a place that's clean, in an environment that's right. When I'm about to make my *namaz* (prayer) and my *salah*, I'm asking for meditation, I'm asking for support. When I'm about to sit and do my *tafakkur* (contemplation), I ask for support. When I'm about to sit in the *zikr* (Divine remembrance), I ask for the meditation and support. I don't ask for meditation and support on the bus. Why?

Why do you want all that energy to come? Why are you calling them to sit with you on a bus? One, it's not a nice *adab* (manners). Two, if you start to bring those types of energy in a public forum, you'll carry all the energy of the bus. So, whatever is on this bus, whatever type of craziness, whatever they're doing from any type of walk of life, all that energy will come onto that person and they begin to get sick and in difficulties. Not in an airport, not in a bus, not in a mall – those are the not the places to meditate.

Those are the places to go and then come out and take a wash and shower. And then when you're nice again back at home, then you sit and try to meditate because their presence comes. It's a reality that's coming and the more you treat it with respect, and what we call *ihtiram*. With a tremendous respect, we're about to meditate and these *awliya* (saints), *inshaAllah*, are coming into this room and to this environment.

'I want to make it pleasing for them. I put beautiful fragrances, I put all these beautiful symbolic spiritual items I have because these *awliya* are coming.' This becomes like a *maqam*. They're coming and they're praying. They're doing their worshipness there, *inshaAllah*. If  you feel that you're in danger then yes, you make your *madad* (support). You feel something's wrong, some danger on the bus, immediately make your *madad*. You recite your *madad* and their energy comes, again to protect and assist through that difficulty, *inshaAllah*.

# Practicing Meditation

### If You Are a Beginner in Meditation, Where Do You Start?

We have on the websites, we have everything. You have to catch up from the videos on how to do to the *tafakkur*, how to do the contemplation, and then the easy steps of just isolating oneself. Playing some *salawats* (praises upon Prophet Muhammad ﷺ) and just breathing and being conscious and trying to do your *zikr* (Divine remembrance). Visualize that you're in front of the Holy Ka'bah and that you're going to do your *zikr* and that Allah ﷻ dress you and bless you.

And then it keeps going into more and more steps, that we have all the different videos and playlist on *muraqabah* (spiritual connection). So, you go to the playlist on *muraqabah*. The website, NurMuhammad, also has the section on meditation and energy. And how to do the connection and the *madad* (support). Everything, everything is there, *inshaAllah*.

## What Should We Be Aware of During Meditation?

This level of *tafakkur* (contemplation) is to sit in a room and put *salawats* (praises upon Prophet Muhammad 🕮) on so that you can hear this beatific energy and to feel it with your heart. And you feel in yourself

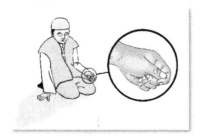

that you are isolated, it's like your grave. You are all alone and that I am sitting, and I am listening to *salawats*. I hold my pulse because I want to feel my heart. That and I am going to put my hand to feel my thumb because the thumb is holding the pulse of my heart [Shaykh holds thumb in his palm]. That is going to be a *tafakkur*, meditation, based on my *qalb* (heart). As soon as I hold that thumb, I feel my pulse is beating. And because my relationship now that I built with my shaykh, I am asking in my meditation, 'Oh Allah ﷻ, don't leave me alone. Your order was *"Ittaqollaha wa kono ma'as sadiqeen."*

يَا أَيُّهَا الَّذِينَ آمَنُوا اتَّقُوا اللَّهَ وَكُونُوا مَعَ الصَّادِقِينَ ﴿١١٩﴾

*9:119 – "Ya ayyuhal ladheena amanoo ittaqollaha wa kono ma'as sadiqeen." (Surat At-Tawbah)*

*"O you who have believed, have consciousness of Allah and be with those who are truthful/ Pious/ sincere (in words and deed)." (The Repentance, 9:119)*

That I was to have a *taqwa* (consciousness) and always keep the company of the pious people, not only physically but spiritually. That I am sitting in my room. I want to be with my teacher. And that I visualize him in front of me and that I say to myself, 'I don't need to see you' because that's from the *nafs* (ego). That, 'Where are you? Where are you? Shaykh, when I close my eyes, I can't see you.' It's not important to see. But just to know that I want to be in your presence and that you are right in front of me and I shouldn't  even be looking at you. Then I just keep myself on a humble path that I am nothing, I am nothing. That put your *faiz* (downpouring blessings) upon me, put your eyes upon me, put your light upon me.

And every day; two, three, four, five minutes, keep that state. And that's best from *Asr* on and you don't try to do meditation at *Zuhr* because that's a busy signal. Everybody is working, everybody is trying to make money. You have to go when the energy field is coming down, like this Earth is dying. Everybody from *Asr* time is going back home, they are tired. This field of energy for *tafakkur* and for the soul becomes stronger from *Asr* all the way up to *Salatul Tahajjud* and *Fajr*, *inshaAllah*.

## Should We Meditate in Silence or With Sound?

Why we don't meditate in silence is because of the danger of *shaitan* (satan) coming through the ear and making *waswas* (whispering). So, as soon as you meditate, you are leaving a very open mic for *shaitan* [Shaykh points to ear]. So, as soon as you make your *tafakkur* and you contemplate, if you leave the mic open, most likely the *tafakkur* will be based upon his whisperings. 'Oh, why did your boss say this? Or why didn't like this or why like that?' That's now an open mic for *waswas* and you've stopped everything to focus. Instead of focusing on a higher reality, you are just focusing on the *waswas* now. So, many people when they start to meditate, they go crazy because they start to hear all the gossip and listen to all this gossip and then they super analyze every single sort of negative issue.

So, the secret for that is put *salawats* (praises upon Prophet Muhammad ﷺ), that it's not about to hear anything from your ears. You got to put *salawats* to take yourself in the mode in which the angels are praising upon Prophet ﷺ. That I am in the presence of Prophet ﷺ in holy Madina. I am nothing, that keep your *nazar* (gaze) upon me and that I just want to breathe. Or I am going to do my different *salawats* and *zikrs* (Divine remembrance), *inshaAllah*.

44

## What Should We Envision During Meditation?

You can envision anything you want. The light coming and just envision at the first phases that you are in the presence of the shaykhs and that,

'*Ya Rabbi*, I'm nothing, I'm nothing, I'm nothing and fill me with the light.' At that time, if you have a *khashf* (spiritual vision), if opening from the shaykh that a light is entering into your heart and entering into your belly, that's all based on what they want to show you. The first step and the most important is that, 'I'm nothing, I'm nothing, I'm nothing and that they're in front of me and I don't have to focus on seeing them.'

Say, 'I can't see your face, Shaykh. I can't see this shaykh's face. I can't see that.' It doesn't matter. Just know that, 'I am in front of them and I'm nothing, I'm nothing. *Ya Rabbi*, I'm nothing. Just under this *ni'mat*, this blessing. Let me to be under their *faiz* (downpouring blessings) and let my heart to believe with all my belief. Their gaze is upon me.'

Because they are servants of Allah ﷻ, this is not about money. This is not about a membership fee. They are servants of Allah ﷻ, of course they have to be. Because they're there to serve Allah ﷻ. If you're calling, they're arriving. If their soul is arriving, then you reach to the *faiz*. Every unique experience is based on the shaykhs, what they want to so there is no description of right and wrong, *inshaAllah*.

## What is Grounding and How Do You Do It?

The grounding, *inshaAllah*. That you're asking to bring in a positive light. At the same time, that every time you breathe and you're bringing in this energy, there has to be a purging and grounding of negative energy. This means that with every breath that's coming in, you have to ground the negative energy to go out. So, like a three-prong system that Prophet ﷺ brought, not the two prongs. It's the third prong that is the grounding. So, that when we're sitting, the *'asaa* (cane) was the grounding. When you're standing, the *'asaa* is the grounding for the shaykh. As he walks on the Earth, whatever energies are coming between his interaction and the electromagnetic force of the Earth. The *'asaa* and the *sunnah* of the cane was the grounding. That the shaykh knows how to push his negative energy back out and whatever positive energies are coming, then they bring in that positive energy.

For those who are meditating, that you're asking to breathe in a positive light but then the negative lights and negative energies have to come out. So, they always put one hand down and begin their meditation and they can shift between the hands. That they're meditating and then one hand down on the ground as they're breathing, so that to ground the negative energy out of their body and out of their being.

One other way was the *sujood* (prostration) and that's why Allah ﷻ had prescribed one of the realities of the *sujood* was an immense grounding. That after you make all your prayer, bring your energy; as soon as you go into *sujood* the body is grounding from the forehead, every negative energy back into the earth. And that's why they feel an immense closeness to Divine Presence in their *sujood*. And that's why anytime you want to talk to the Divine, you feel inspired to prostrate your head to the ground. One, because it purges all negativity, and two, from the reality of the closeness with your Creator in the position of *sujood* (prostration).

Because you're bringing your donkey to be down and your soul is riding. When you show Allah ﷻ that I can ride this body, my soul can ride this body – look, the donkey is down. There are some people who will never put their body into *sujood* cause the donkey's riding on top of them. But those whom Allah ﷻ granted this *ni'mat* (blessing), they show Allah ﷻ that my donkey is under *tarbiyah* (discipline) and its head is down. When its head is down, they feel their closeness to Allah ﷻ because Allah's ﷻ happy with them that they controlled and their soul has a majesty, not the body, *inshaAllah*.

## How Do We Place Our Hands When Grounding?

Visualizing again that there's a tremendous positive light but we have also a tremendous amount of negativity that we collect throughout the day. So, that when you're going to be grounding with either hand, you do your grounding. That you bring an energy and you're breathing in, you visualize breathing in the positive energy. And then you visualize that you're going to be grounding out any type of negativity with the hand. If you're holding the left hand to feel your heart, then put the right hand onto the ground. Breathe in your energy and ask to sort of ground all the negativity. See a light 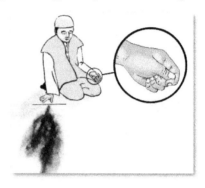 coming in with every breath, and every exhale, pushing out any type of darkness or difficulty, *inshaAllah*.

## What Are Different Types of Meditations We Can Practice?

So, if we are going to do a breathing meditation then you just focus on the breath. Play *salawats* (praises upon Prophet Muhammad ﷺ), make your connection and just breathe for energy and *qudra* (power), that you are just trying to develop now your breathing. You are also trying to develop now the faculty of focusing, which is very difficult for people whose minds are too active. That's why a lot of people in last days don't like to meditate because the active mind is so wound up, and so active, that they can't really sit and focus on one thing. They are thinking a thousand things at a time.

48

So, then this process of sitting for that type of meditation is that I just want to shut my active mind down and I want to breathe. I want to see myself at the Holy Ka'bah in the presence of my shaykh. That I am with my shaykh, that I want to be at the Ka'bah, dress me from the lights of the Ka'bah. Listen to something so that you don't have *waswas* (whispering) in your ear. And make sure that you feel the pulse of your hand so that the focus is on the heart. And then just breathe and just two, three, four minutes a day of your breathing practices to make sure that you are breathing and able to shut your mind and to focus. Then there is meditation which you can do with your *awrad* (daily practices).

You sit down, you connect with the shaykh's light, 'I am nothing, I am nothing, *ya Rabbi*. Let me to be with Your pious people and that I want to do my *awrad*. Sayyidi, that it's not me but I want your blessings and for you to do the *awrad* from the *barakah* (blessings) and *niyyat* and intention that you have, and I don't know. Because you know

a greater intention than what I would know.' And then I sit and do my *awrad*, *inshaAllah*.

## What is the Best Zikr to Do During Meditation?

The *zikr* of *"Hu."* When they're going to do the meditation – either when they're sitting for the meditation and they try a couple times, 'I'm nothing, I'm nothing. Let me to be in the presence of my shaykh. Sayyidi, dress me with your *nazar* (gaze). Just let me become familiar with your  presence. It's always there looking at me.' With your heart's faith, do you see the presence of your shaykh? It's like right now you're looking at him, close your eyes and visualize he's right there. So, anyone looking, close your eyes, can't you see the same image in your heart's eye? And you keep that image, keep that image, that the shaykh is right there. 'Sayyidi just dress me from your *nazar*.'

And then you may, if you're going to be doing your *awrad* (daily practices), you do your *awrad*, *"Ashhadu an la ilaha illallah, wa ashhadu anna Muhammadan 'abduhu wa Rasulu. Ashhadu an la ilaha illallah, wa ashhadu anna Muhammadan 'abduhu wa Rasulu. Ashhadu an la ilaha illallah, wa ashhadu anna Muhammadan 'abduhu wa Rasulu."*

أَشْهَدُ أَنْ لَا إِلَهَ إِلاَّ الله وَأَشْهَدُ أَنَّ مُحَمَّدًاعَبْدُهُ وَرَسُولُهُ

*"Ashhadu an la ilaha illallah, wa ashhadu anna Muhammadan 'abduhu wa Rasulu."*

*"I bear witness that there is no god but Allah, and I bear witness that Muhammad is the messenger of Allah."*

*"Astaghfirullah, astaghfirullah, astaghfirullah, astaghfirullah."* That keep your *nazar* upon me. So, then they do their *awrad* with full *tafakkur* (contemplation) so that it's the *tafakkur* that begins to open these *faiz* (downpouring blessings) and these energies. Then if I have to do my *"Allah"* or my *salawats*, then

I can do my *zikr* of Allah عز وجل. Because this is the source of power. The *tafakkur* is the source of power. You want to be nothing. If you're nothing, that's how to open the *faiz* of the shaykhs.

And that the *tarbiyah* (discipline) of the shaykhs, that they're going to have their *nazar* upon you and begin the *tarbiyah* process; begin to send onto your consciousness what you're doing wrong, begin to send onto

you lights and energies. Only through that dimension, everything opens. That's the real opening. That's the real door when Allah عز وجل say, 'Go through the home, through the proper opening.'

وَلَيْسَ الْبِرُّ بِأَن تَأْتُوا الْبُيُوتَ مِن ظُهُورِهَا وَلَٰكِنَّ الْبِرَّ مَنِ اتَّقَىٰ ۗ وَأْتُوا الْبُيُوتَ مِنْ أَبْوَابِهَا ۚ وَاتَّقُوا اللَّـهَ لَعَلَّكُمْ تُفْلِحُونَ ﴿١٨٩﴾

*2:189 – "...Wa laysal birru bi-an tatol buyoota min zuhooriha wa lakinnal birra manit taqa, wa' tol buyoota min abwabiha, wat taqollaha la'allakum tuflihoon." (Surat Al-Baqarah)*

*"...And it is not righteousness to enter houses from the back, but righteousness is [in] one who fears Allah. And enter houses from their doors. And be Conscious of Allah that you may succeed."*
*(The Cow, 2:189)*

51

The proper opening is *malakut* (heavenly realm) and the soul, not *mulk* (earthly realm). Allah 🕈 didn't care for the *mulk*. So, when you enter through the soul, that's the relationship that Allah 🕈 wants. So, they do their *zikr*, then they do their *salawats*. When they're sitting and asking for the *salawats*, "*Allahumma salli 'ala Sayyidina Muhammad wa 'ala aali Sayyidina Muhammad.*"

اللَّهُمَّ صَلِّ عَلَى سَيِّدِنَا مُحَمَّد، وَعَلَى آلِ سَيِّدِنَا مُحَمَّد

"*Allahumma salli 'ala Sayyidina Muhammad wa 'ala aali Sayyidina Muhammad.*"

"*O Allah! Send Peace and blessings upon our master Prophet Muhammad and upon the Family of our master Prophet Muhammad (pbuh)*"

Dress me from your lights. Put your *faiz* (downpouring blessings) upon me, that I'm nothing. Later in their *tafakkur*, they'll be trained in their *tafakkur* that there can't be two, there can only be one. That, 'I'm seeing you, but I don't want to exist, I don't want to exist. Put your light and your dress upon me.' And those whom rise to that level of understanding, they negated themself and they brought the dress of their shaykh upon themself and they sit and do their *salawats*. "*Allahumma salli 'ala Sayyidina Muhammad wa 'ala aali Sayyidina Muhammad. Allahumma salli 'ala Sayyidina Muhammad wa 'ala aali Sayyidina Muhammad. Allahumma salli 'ala Sayyidina Muhammad wa 'ala aali Sayyidina Muhammad,*" in that state.

That they acknowledge that they're nothing. If they're nothing, then they're in the dress of the shaykh. The dress dresses over them and they find themselves like a piece of dust within his reality. And they're making their *zikr* and their *salawats*, their *zikr*, their *salawats*. Later, when they want to bring the power of their breath, they can do their breathing. They can do the *zikr* of *"Hu."* And then each faculty is something different. That would be the meditation on the breath and how to do the meditation of the breath.

So, you have *muhabbat* (love) of shaykh, the love of shaykhs and the guides. *Hudur ma shaykh*, keeping his *hudur* and keeping his presence. That love makes us to come to the association. The *hudur* means to keep his presence. I love to be in the presence, but I have to be in the presence all the time. If I'm not in the presence, I'm under attack and under difficulty. And that's when Allah 'جل جلاله, *"Kono ma'as sadiqeen."*

يَا أَيُّهَا الَّذِينَ آمَنُوا اتَّقُوا اللَّهَ وَكُونُوا مَعَ الصَّادِقِينَ ﴿١١٩﴾

*9:119 – "Ya ayyuhal ladheena amanoo ittaqollaha wa kono ma'as sadiqeen." (Surat At-Tawbah)*

*"O you who have believed, have consciousness of Allah and be with those who are truthful/Pious/sincere (in words and deed)."*
*(The Repentance, 9:119)*

He didn't say *"kono ma'as sadiqeen,"* only in the daytime, or *"kono ma'as sadiqeen,"* only *Fajr*. No! Allah's ﷻ order is, 'Keep the company of *sadiqeen*.' Allah's ﷻ words are eternal and have no time. And more important, it's not even from the *mulk*. It's from *malakut*, Allah's ﷻ keeping. That keep their company, reach to that reality and never split from that moment, never to be on your own. As soon as you stray, *shaitan* (satan) will grab you. So why would anyone want to be away from their *madad* (support) and their support? Allah ﷻ said, 'Hold tight to the rope.'

$$\text{وَاعْتَصِمُوا بِحَبْلِ اللَّهِ جَمِيعًا وَلَا تَفَرَّقُوا ۚ ﴿١٠٣﴾}$$

*3:103 – "Wa'tasimo bihab lillahi jamee'an wa la tafarraqo…"*
*(Surat Ali-Imran)*

*"And hold firmly to the rope of Allah all together and do not separate…" (Family of Imran, 3:103)*

Not in the daytime and at nighttime, you don't have to hold. Or only on *Jum'ah* (Friday prayer) you hold to the rope. Because now everyone only goes for *Jum'ah*. The rest of Islam, they don't have any understanding. So, no, no, this is a practice that you do all day and night, day and night.

### How Do We Practice the Zikr of "Hu"?

The *"Hu"* is the strongest, and that is a pushing of the sound. You can

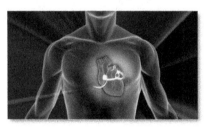

practice first with, *"Hu"* [Shaykh inhales and exhales saying *Hu*]. Once you become comfortable with the breathing practice, then the next level is that it's actually silent, *"Hu"* [Shaykh breathes quietly]. It's the push of the breath with the *zikr* (Divine remembrance) in the heart. But that, you have to sort of practice that, become like a juggling. Understand how to make a *zikr* where you're pushing, *Hu* in your heart,

54

and your breath is just pushing the sound *"Hu."* And they're pushing the *zikr* through their heart and the breath is coming out. But you make the *zikr* through the tongue and practicing even out with that *zikr* *"Hu," inshaAllah.*

## What is the Importance of the Breath in Meditation?

The *Nafas ur Rahmah* (the Breath of Mercy) and the importance of the breath, that the whole *tariqah* (spiritual path) is based on the breath which is *ajeeb* (strange) that no shaykh talks about the breath. *Hosh dar dam*, the consciousness of your breath, and every section of the Naqshbandi book, every Grandshaykh – first comment in the way is based on their *nafas* (breath). That understanding your *qudra*, your power, your gift from Allah ﷻ is your breath. Before anything we want and anything we're praying for, Allah's ﷻ saying, 'Have you thanked me for your breath?'

So, then this *nafas* that's coming in can be a tremendous might and power. This *nafas* that coming in from *Bahrul Qudra* is a power. They  were taught on how to unlock the reality of their breath and they pull the *Hu* out of the atoms. That every atom and its nucleus has a secret of *Hu* and it's the *qudra* and the energy. Like now, they're making ships that go out very far. They can't give them gas, so they make them atomic ships. They have their own reactor because how you're going to put an ice breaker out in the middle of the ocean and keep refuelling it? So, Allah ﷻ giving the same, say, 'How you're going to keep refuelling? You can't be sort of checking in five minutes for refuelling.' So, this means then Allah ﷻ ignite within them how to pull the power out of everything around them.

So, the breath, most powerful. We said before it's like a wi-fi that emanating throughout creation. Every photon carrying that reality. So, Divine wi-fi that broadcasting all upon this creation. Every flower needs it. Every bug needs it. Every animate and inanimate object is in need of it because of its atomic reality.

Within it has the secret of *Hu*. And that's why all the *tariqas* (spiritual paths) they have the *zikr* of *Hu* built into their *awrad*.

So, when they're breathing and they're unlocking and training themselves on how to breathe, they visualize the breath of light that

comes in and asking Allah ﷻ to take out all the negativity. And as they're practicing and making their *tafakkur* (contemplation), the more they efface and become nothing. 'I'm nothing and realize I'm truly nothing but an oppressor to myself.' *La ilaha illa anta Subhanaka, innee kuntu minazh zhalimeen.* 'That Glory be to Allah ﷻ, I'm an oppressor to myself.'

$$\text{...﴿لَّا إِلَهَ إِلَّا أَنتَ سُبْحَانَكَ إِنِّي كُنتُ مِنَ الظَّالِمِينَ ﴿٨٧﴾}$$

*21:87 – "...La ilaha illa anta Subhanaka, innee kuntu minazh zhalimeen." (Surat Al-Anbiya)*

*"...There is no god/diety except You; Glory to you: Indeed I have been of the wrongdoers/Oppressor to Myself!" (The Prophets, 21:87)*

As Allah's ﷻ watching that you really believe that you're nothing, your breath and your breathing will become more powerful. So, it's not something that, 'Oh, I want to unlock the *Hu*.' You just keep breathing and practicing, breathing and practicing until Allah ﷻ determines you're sincere.

## What is the Purpose of Holding the Fingers During Meditation?

There's a system in which they hold their pulse so that their hand and their finger is calling an energy. And for many years they made fun of us,

'Oh, look, he's doing like the buddha sign.' No, they stole it from us, they stole it from Prophet ﷺ. Anyone wants to know spiritual growth, go Google 'baby's hands, baby's hands.' You see every baby's hand is locked like this [Shaykh forms a circle with his thumb and index finger]. They're like this the whole day long. Little babies and they grow from birth to one year like 'whooo.' The fastest growth that a 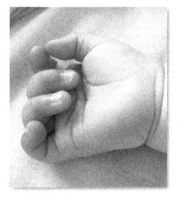 human will grow is from their birth to their first and second birthday. How this little thing popped up like this? Because they're calling their energy. Allah ﷻ inspire them, call upon your energy. All day long, they're making *tafakkur* (contemplation) and *muraqabah* (spiritual connection). That's why you think they're sleeping and they're holding their hand and the energy is coming, energy is coming and they're growing, growing at a speed that Allah ﷻ wants them to grow so that they can survive upon this Earth.

So, everyone's doing it except the people who don't know why they're meditating. Then they begin to teach everything has an energy. As soon as your thumb is your identity and each one has a unique print. In the

spiritual realm, your thumb is what identifies your soul's light in an ocean of light that all in one. Because the ocean of light, we're all one. Nobody knows who you are, I am, we're in one ocean. But this print knows exactly your identity. As soon as this print appears, it pulls you from that reality and begin to send the energy that's necessary for your being. Soon as you touch this [index] finger, the *shahadah* finger with the thumb, you're calling from *Bahrul Qudra* (Ocean of Power).

Your energy, that I'm in need of more energy to come to me. You're signalling an energy to come and then from that like a satellite – 'zhoooo.' It directed to you and begin to send you more of your *qudra* (power), more than you need on a daily basis. So, when they sit to make *tafakkur* (contemplation), they understood that they can. They don't have to do like this [Shaykh joins his thumb and index finger]. They just hold their hand and they're calling upon a signal and an energy that coming. And then Allah ﷻ make them to become more aware of their heart signal that they begin to feel

the movement of their heart. When they meditate with their hands open, the meditation is like flowing everywhere. They're just flying around lost like a kite in the air. Soon as they put their hand to their thumb, they're back on the focus of their heart. Why? Because *qalbil mu'min baitullah.*

قَلْبَ الْمُؤْمِنْ بَيْتُ الرَّبِّ

*"Qalb al mu'min baytur rabb."*

*"The heart of the believer is the House of the Lord."* (Hadith Qudsi)

They want to stay focused on the house of Allah ﷻ. So, it means they

 just learn how to be sincere. Allah ﷻ will begin to open their breath where when they breathe, they feel now an energy coming, like a fire. They breathe like a fire, like a dragon. So, in the spiritual world, the dragons are something very good for the *mu'min* (believer) ones. They breathe like a dragon. They bring in a tremendous amount of energy and they exhale a tremendous amount of energy. And that's Allah ﷻ. The reality of it is Allah ﷻ unlocking for them the *hu*. When they unlock that *hu*, their breath is like a fire, tremendous amount of energy comes from their breathing.

## How Does the Nazar (Gaze) of the Shaykh Affect the Student?

When the *nazar* (gaze) of the shaykh, when they're sitting and they're making *tafakkur* (contemplation), that's why they're making *tafakkur*. Is that when they're praying *Assalamu 'alaika ayyuhan-nabiyu wa 'ibaadillaahis saa'liheen* in the *salah*. You did not close the *salah* (prayer) yet.

التَّحِيَّاتُ لِلَّهِ وَالصَّلَوَاتُ وَالطَّيِّبَاتُ. السَّلَامُ عَلَيْكَ أَيُّهَا النَّبِيُّ وَرَحْمَةُ اللَّهِ وَبَرَكَاتُهُ، السَّلَامُ عَلَيْنَا وَعَلَى عِبَادِ اللَّهِ الصَّالِحِينَ، أَشْهَدُ أَنْ لَا إِلَهَ إِلاَّ اللَّهُ وَأَشْهَدُ أَنَّ مُحَمَّدًا عَبْدُهُ وَرَسُولُهُ

*"Attahiyatu Lillahi wa salawatu wat tayyibatu. Assalamu 'alayka ayyuhan Nabiyu* ﷺ, *wa rahmatullahi wa barakatuhu.*

*Assalamu 'alayna wa 'alaa 'ibadulllahis saliheen. Ashhadu an la ilaha illallahu wa ashhadu anna Muhammadan 'abduhu wa Rasuluhu."*

*"All the best compliments and the prayers/praising and the pure/good things are for Allah. Peace and Blessings be upon you, O Prophet (pbuh)! Peace be on us and on the righteous servants of Allah. I testify that there is no deity but Allah, and I testify that Prophet Muhammad (pbuh) is the servant and Messenger of Allah."*

So, Allah ﷻ is telling us give them *salaams* (greetings). Give Prophet ﷺ *salaams* in present tense, *wa 'ibaadillaahis saa'liheen,* that they may be present or not present but you are to give them greetings. In the *salah* (prayer), then you give your *salaams* and close your *salah*. What secret is

that that you're facing, who are you facing, and why Allah ﷻ wants you to give *salaams*? Because it's the best of manners. For one day you should see in your *salah*, you have been trained with good manners. You're giving Prophet ﷺ *salaams* in present tense and who are *'ibaadillaahis saa'liheen?* So, then the *tafakkur* (contemplation) comes and teaches that, *'Ya Rabbi,* from that reality, let me always to be in the presence of *'ibaadillaahis saa'liheen. Nabiyeen, Siddiqeen, Shuhudahi was Saliheen* and Allah ﷻ says this is the best of company because I am with them.

وَمَن يُطِع اللهَ وَالرَّسُولَ فَأُوْلَئِكَ مَعَ الَّذِينَ أَنْعَمَ اللهُ عَلَيْهِم مِّنَ النَّبِيِّينَ وَالصِّدِّيقِينَ وَالشُّهَدَاء وَالصَّالِحِينَ وَحَسُنَ أُولَئِكَ رَفِيقًا ﴿٦٩﴾

*4:69 – "Wa man yuti' Allaha war Rasula faolayeka ma'al ladheena an'ama Allahu 'alayhim minan Nabiyeena, was Siddiqeena, wash Shuhadai, was Saliheena wa hasuna olayeka rafeeqan."*
*(Surat An-Nisa)*

*"And whoever obeys Allah and the Messenger (pbuh) are in the company of those on whom Allah has bestowed His Favours/Blessings – of the prophets, the sincere Truthful, the witnesses (who testify), and the Righteous, and excellent are those as companions." (The Women, 4:69)*

If you really connect your heart and you're always with *saliheen* (righteous), and always with *saliheen*, and they begin to take you slowly into the associations of *nabiyeen* (prophets), *siddiqeen* (truthful) and *saliheen*. Of course, then Allah ﷻ is with them and you begin to feel that *ruhaniyat* and the Divinely Presence of what Allah ﷻ wants the servant to feel. So, it's like a rope that comes. You can't say I'm going to just connect with Allah ﷻ. That's arrogant. And you can't say I'm just going to connect with Sayyidina Muhammad ﷺ because again we're just in training wheels. So, then Allah ﷻ, *Atiullaha wa atiur Rasula wa Ulil amre minkum*. That keep the company of the *ulema* (scholars) and the *ulul amr* (saints).

...يَاأَيُّهَا الَّذِينَ آمَنُوا أَطِيعُوا اللَّه وَأَطِيعُواْ الرَّسُولَ وَأُوْلِي الْأَمْرِ مِنْكُمْ... ﴿٥٩﴾

*4:59 – "...Ya ayyu hal latheena amanoo Atiullaha wa atiur Rasula wa Ulil amre minkum..." (Surat An-Nisa)*

*"...O You who have believed, Obey Allah, Obey the Messenger, and those in authority among you..." (The Women, 4:59)*

The *ulul amr* whom their practice and their knowledge is real, not they have book knowledge. Whom their hearts are real and their hearts are containers of reality. Not somebody who speaks from his head about somebody else's heart. It is a big danger. Big danger when you talk, and you listen to somebody who's speaking from his head about somebody else's heart and somebody else's achievements. But to keep the company of whom their own hearts, Allah ﷻ made it to be a container for realities. So, when we keep them, meditate and contemplate to be in their

company, that begins to bring the *faiz* (downpouring blessings). So, they're practicing their breath, breathing. Then the *faiz* of the shaykh that I know that you're in front of me and I don't need to see you. I just need to know that I'm always in your presence and that your *nazar* (gaze) is always upon me. The more you believe and perceive, the *nazar* of the shaykh is always looking at you, the more that *nazar* becomes powerful.

And that constriction they're asking about is when the *nazar* comes, it comes *jalali* (majestic), not *jamali* (beatific). So, when the *nazar* (gaze) comes, you feel like you're having a heart attack cause now their *jalali* presence is entering into that space and you feel like your chest is going

to crack. And you just breathe through that, I'm nothing and just keep breathing, breathing. Say, 'It's better for me to die, *ya Rabbi*, it's okay. I die.' Not oh god, it's scary my heart was beating, I stopped. No, because this way was *mawt qablil mawt* (death of desires

before physical death). What are you scared from death for? And why Allah ﷻ wants you dead? You probably better off alive. If you can do more than be dead, you're just another corpse in the ground. So, Allah ﷻ says I don't need you right now. Stay and do what you're doing.

So, then they overcome the fear of death and when the *nazar* (gaze) come they feel a very strong contraction and then expansion. When it eases up, there's an expansion and the contraction and expansion is the growth. With every contraction, they're bringing up a level and then there's an ease. There's a tightening and then an ease.

How to keep it is how to keep the respect of the *nazar* (gaze) that my shaykh is watching me at all times, whatever I'm doing. If you think you escaped his *nazar*, you have lost yourself. There's not a place that their *nazar* cannot enter. And most likely when you're doing something wrong, the angels are sending out emails to them. That  they're doing something wrong, keep your *nazar* and they're watching.

As much as the servant wants and these are *jasoos e qalb* (spy of the heart). If you accompany them, they understand they know a lot of things and they don't say anything. For their students, they may know many things and they're training from Allah 耀, from Prophet ﷺ and  from *awliyaullah* (saints), is there's no permission to say anything. So, you think, 'Oh, he doesn't say anything. He doesn't know anything.' No, he may know lot, but he's trained not to speak at all. It's not his place to reveal what Allah 耀 wants to conceal. So, it's not about you know, go and say something, do this or that. No, no, we're not here to punish people. This is in Allah's 耀 Hand. But to train them that you're being watched, you understand that? The more they keep the understanding, they're being watched. Every time they get angry, an email is sent 'ding,' they're watching. Now I have a nice Ring camera for the Center. If you pass through the camera, it sends me a notification. You think Ring has it and Allah 耀 doesn't have it?

Soon as your temperature goes up, something in your character goes up, they send a notification that his temperature just went up, his *akhlaaq* (character) is changing and something's happening. Then those whom are training for the reality, those who  don't want the reality, they just enjoy the food and the companionship, that's no problem. That's a different group of people. You'll get your training in the grave. It's a bit more intense, I think about 70,000 times more intense in the grave because then everybody's going for *khalwah* (seclusion) and everybody going to be trained in the grave. Those who want the training now, they say, 'No, no, *ya Rabbi*, I don't want the hard stuff. Let me do it now.' Then they understood keep the *nazar* (gaze). My shaykh is watching me. He's watching everything I'm doing and then they have been given technologies to understand.

 They understand and their soul understands. Their soul is from Allah's ﷻ Divinely Secrets. Don't think the soul is not capable. Their soul can be many places and every place as much as Allah ﷻ wants their soul to be. And their soul doesn't even have to physically notify them because it has already a macro code in which it has to do different things. Can you imagine being notified physically on tens of millions of commands throughout the day? You see the person like completely like a lunatic. I think it was, who was the one that played God in the movie and he was doing emails and he started to answer everyone's emails? [Audience says Bruce Almighty]. Yes, Bruce Almighty – when he started to say, 'No, no, no' or 'Yes' on every email that came in, no.

So, the soul has an ability from Allah ﷻ. Allah's ﷻ Divinely Ocean

dressed the soul with Divinely Secrets and Divinely *Qudra*, not anything understood from the physical world. Their physicality is not even in need to know it but these lofty souls, these souls that are *rabbaniyoon*, Allah ﷻ gave the soul *fulkil mashhoon*. They're loaded with realities of what the soul is capable of doing by Allah's ﷻ *Izzah* and Might.

وَآيَةٌ لَّهُمْ أَنَّا حَمَلْنَا ذُرِّيَّتَهُمْ فِي الْفُلْكِ الْمَشْحُونِ ﴿٤١﴾

*36:41 – "Wa ayatul lahum anna hamalna dhurriyyatahum fil fulkil mashhooni." (Surat YaSeen)*

*"And a sign for them is that we have carried their atoms/forefathers in the loaded ship." (YaSeen, 36:41)*

So, yes, no doubt that soul is monitoring and checking and gauging the temperature, the activity. Then the student began to understand like the story of Shaykh Abdul Qadir ق, 'Go kill the chicken where you don't think Allah ﷻ will see.' Everyone went out to kill the chicken. One student stood there and he said, 'Why are you not doing what I asked you to do?' He says, 'Is there somewhere I'm actually going to go that Allah's ﷻ not watching me?' Say, 'Okay, now you're ready.' All the other ones running around looking for a place where Allah ﷻ won't see them. Yeah, it's like that.

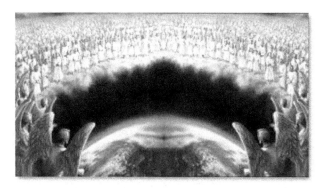

When you truly believe that they're watching, Prophet ﷺ definitely watching. *Awliyaullah* (saints) watching. Angels are watching. The *jinn* are watching, everyone's watching. It's just you don't know it. So, then your life is like the 'Truman Show' where he's in a bubble and everybody else is on television. So, your life is like that. Even your descendants in heaven are watching because this life and one of the realities of this life, you're like the Truman Show. All your descendants are sitting up like that, 'Wow, what is he's doing? Oh my God! Look at that.' So, they're watching.

When I truly understood that then my *khuluq* and my character would then be based on that. I can't do like that; I can't say like that; they are watching. I can't do like that and they start to correct themselves, correct themselves. The more they correct themselves, the more they enter into the oceans of Allah's ﷻ Sincerity and Allah's ﷻ Gift on sincerity. Then He bestows from His bounty and His treasures upon the soul, *inshaAllah*.

## What is Hosh Dar Dam and How Do We Practice It Consistently?

*Hosh dar dam* is to be conscious of the breath. That, later in the states of *tafakkur* (contemplation), the most important first is to establish the presence of the shaykh. So, that

you have the love, you're coming with the *muhabbat* (love), the *hudur* (presence) is your *khidmat* and being of service and doing all that you can to get their attention, their *nazar*, their gaze upon you. Then you sit and begin to practice how that, 'I want to see that energy there and that the shaykh is there and I am nothing. The shaykh is there and I'm nothing. Sayyidi, dress me from your light.'

And we have an *awrad* (daily practices), a daily *wazifa* (spiritual practice) that we are supposed to do. So, I sit and I make three *shahadah* (testimony of faith), 70 *istighfar* (seeking forgiveness) and all of this is on the app. So, the app is there for all the *du'as* (supplications), all the *salawats* (praises upon Prophet Muhammad ﷺ), all the *awrads* and everything that we are supposed to be doing in the *tariqah* (spiritual path), it is all compiled on the app. So, you sit and meditate and do your connection, do your *awrad* and visualize the shaykh in front of you. And then you say your three *shahadah* and your 70 *istighfar*, but first make the connection.

As soon as you are starting to make the connection, that you feel the presence of the shaykh is there, you feel an energy come. You feel your heart is constricting because when his energy comes, it comes with a might. And you feel your heart pumping, and something is happening. Like a constriction in

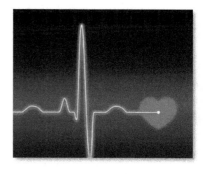

your heart, their energy is present with you. And if you can reach to that state, so we have to go step by step. First is to make the connection. Somebody who has made the connection, they feel the presence of the shaykh, feel the shaykh is in that room. Then they'll ask the shaykh, "Dress me from your presence. Dress me from your light and from your energy.'

And then begin to take a way of breathing. Every time they meditate, they immediately go into their dress of the shaykh and they begin to breathe the *zikr* "*Hu.*" They hold their thumb and breathe [inhaling] and breathe out [exhaling]. And asking the shaykh that, 'Send the energy

and *qudra* (power) into my breath and all my badness to be pushed out and all goodness to be dressed within me.' And then you practice that every day – two, three minutes – just hold the thumb and the *madad* (support) of the shaykhs that they are dressing you. You reached a state in which you feel like their energy is coming. And then you say that, 'I want to open up the power

of breathing and then by *zikr Hu,* I want to release all my bad energy and breathing in all the positive energy into the heart.' And then it goes deeper and deeper but that is just for an introduction because we don't know that who is at what state and who is asking.

## What Happens When You Forget to Breathe During Meditation?

It's really hard to truly forget to breathe. But what's happening is there's

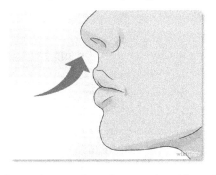

a euphoria that's happening, an excitement within that energy. And the state of like dying, that just so much energy is coming that they feel they're entering into a state of death. You just have to push yourself just to breathe from your nose. Don't open your mouth to breathe. Learn how to breathe, restricted breathing through your nose.

And if the energy becomes too much, *jalali* and *jamali* energy. *Jalali* energy is the Ocean of Munificence or Might. When that energy of might comes, it's crushing. So, there's crushing and expanding, crushing and expanding. For every crush, when the servant enters into these oceans of energies, and they're breathing and Allah ﷻ is crushing something and

lifting. So, it's like a rocket. You ever see the rocket that's just going 'khhh' [referring to rocket taking off], coming. The state of crushing is Allah ﷻ is lifting the servant with the *tajalli* (manifestation).

When *jamali* comes, it's now a *maqam*. That they're on a plateau, it's now beatific again. And this could be

happening daily as they're meditating. That they meditate and again, an energy comes onto their heart. They're crushing their heart, they can't breathe. They think they're going to have a heart attack and just breathe through it, breathe through it. And you know, if Allah ﷻ wants you dead, you're dead anyways. So, what are you running from?

69

If He doesn't want you dead, you're not going to die. You keep just keep getting that energy, learn how to breathe through it, through your nose, not to open the mouth. And release the energy. And begin to bring the power of your breath coming in through your breath. Because the more restricted in your breathing, the breath becomes like a fire and a flame, that begins to give a fuel to the energy. And then the constriction comes, and then it goes. 'After difficulty, comes ease.'

As soon as the ease and the *jamali tajalli,* then there's a softness that dresses the servant, *inshaAllah.*

إِنَّ مَعَ الْعُسْرِ يُسْرًا ﴿٦﴾

*94:6 – "Inna ma'al 'usri yusra." (Surat Ash-Sharh)*

*"Indeed, with hardship [will be] ease." (The Relief, 94:6)*

### What if Nasal Problems Affect Your Breathing Practices?

You get a stuffy nose medicine. If you're not capable of that and there's actual medical problems, then you breathe through your mouth. Whatever you can do, not a problem. But don't suffocate and you say, 'I can't breathe. I'm going to pass out, hyperventilated.' No. So, you try your best if you can, to  breathe through the nostrils and you take some medicine to clear up your sinuses if that works. If not, then medically you can't, then no problem. You can breathe through the mouth and maybe restrict your breathing, *inshaAllah.*

## How Do We Know We're Progressing in Our Meditation?

*InshaAllah,* how to know you're progressing in your meditation – when your meditation gets stronger. Your character gets better, and your meditation gets stronger because as soon as you want to make *tafakkur* (contemplation) then *awliyaullah* (saints) will begin to pray that, '*Ya Rabbi,* that they want to be tested. They want to reach towards your heavenly stations and they want to be tested.' If you look at the lives of the shaykhs, they have been extremely tested with every type of possible difficulty and only through the endurance and good character they can reach towards Allah's ﷻ Satisfaction. When Allah's ﷻ happy with you, He opens hearing. When Allah's ﷻ happy with you, He opens seeing. When Allah's ﷻ happy with you, He opens everything that Allah ﷻ wants to open. So, the servant would know, *inshaAllah.*

## How Do We Feel the Realization that the Quality of Our Meditation is Getting Better?

*Atiullaha wa atiur Rasula wa Ulil amre minkum.*

﴿٥٩﴾ ... أَطِيعُوا اللَّهَ وَأَطِيعُوا الرَّسُولَ وَأُوْلِي الْأَمْرِ مِنْكُمْ ...

*4:59 – "...Atiullaha wa atiur Rasula wa Ulil amre minkum..."*
*(Surat An-Nisa)*

"*...Obey Allah, Obey the Messenger, and those in authority among you...*" *(The Women, 4:59)*

The meditation in Islamic understanding is the last phase, last phase of perfection but because of *dunya* (material world) and the condition it is, they're allowing to be taught almost at the beginning of this way of *ma'rifah* (gnosticism). It is the hardest step in the way of realization because the *nafs* (ego) is not interested in people sitting and trying to realize their potential. It is the biggest battle against the *nafs* to achieve that type of energy.

So then, to be consistent in the practice and the understanding of the *madad* (support). That it's not able to do by myself, this discipline and to control, but to have a strong understanding of the *madad* and support that I'm asking continuously from Allah 'ﷻ for Divinely support, the support of Sayyidina Muhammad ﷺ, and the support of these authorized *ulul amr* (saints). That they be with me, their *nazar* be upon me, their dress be upon me and that they support me through my path and my way of realization.

Then the whole system of this *tafakkur* (contemplation), on how to and the importance of listening. So, when we want to make our *tafakkur*, see the beatific sounds that we're producing with these *salawats* (praises upon Prophet Muhammad ﷺ) and these *na'ats* (prophetic praising) and these *mehfil* (association) and the *zikr* (Divine remembrance); we keep that all the time. So, in the room that we're going to meditate has to have beatific *salawats* always playing, beatific fragrance.

So, you set the whole environment, you change your clothes. Don't use your work clothes for your appointment with Allah ﷻ. You make a

whole set of different clothing that you don't wear for *dunya* (material world) and then you sit and begin to make your *namaz* (prayer). And at the end of your *namaz*, you sit, you play your *salawats* and begin to connect your heart and the whole system of how to connect the heart. And we try to for just a few minutes every day until you feel that you're understanding the *madad* and the support.

And you feel that you're true to your understanding that, 'I'm asking for your presence. I'm asking to be nothing and that I want to feel the presence of my shaykh is in front of me. I don't have to see anything because that's too *nafsani* (egocentric), that's too much from my *nafs* (ego). But I know that I'm not worthy of seeing you, but I know that you're seeing me and that your soul is there and present with me.' That's from *iman* and faith. And that's when we begin to really build and establish our faith. It's one thing to say you believe, now put it into action. When you believe, of course my Shaykh is looking at me, the

angels are looking at me, Prophet ﷺ is looking at me. In my *salah* (prayer), I say *'Assalamu alaika ayyuhan Nabi wa ibadillaahis saliheen.*

التَّحِيَّاتُ لِلهِ وَالصَّلَوَاتُ وَالطَّيِّبَاتُ، اَلسَّلَامُ عَلَيْكَ أَيُّهَا النَّبِيُّ وَرَحْمَةُ اللهِ وَبَرَكَاتُهُ، اَلسَّلَامُ عَلَيْنَا وَ عَلَى عِبَادِ اللهِ الصَّالِحِيْنَ، أَشْهَدُ أَنْ لَا إِلهَ إِلَّا اللهُ، وَأَشْهَدُ أَنَّ مُحَمَّدًا عَبْدُهُ وَ رَسُوْلُهُ

*"At-tahiyyatu lillahi, was-salawatu wat-tayyibatu, as-salamu 'alayka, ayyuhan-nabiyyu wa rahmatullahi wa barakatuh, as-salamu 'alayna wa 'ala 'ibadil-lahis-saliheen. Ashhadu an la ilaha illallahu wa ashhadu anna Muhammadan 'abduhu wa Rasuluh."*

*"Salutations to God and prayers and good deeds. Peace be upon you, O Prophet, and the mercy of God and his blessings. Peace be on us and on the righteous servants of God. I bear witness that there is no god but Allah, and I bear witness that Muhammad is His servant and His messenger."*

Allah ﷻ making me to give them *salaams* (last part of prayer) so no doubt there; if I'm giving them *salaams*, they must be there. But behind a veil of my ignorance and bad character. When I begin to burn that veil then they become more apparent to me. I feel them in the room. I feel the energy in the room. And that's what Allah ﷻ wants for us is to become more subtle and more conscious of our surrounding, *inshaAllah*.

## How Can We Learn and Progress in Body, Mind, and Soul Meditation?

Go to the website on how to meditate. The articles on Sufi Meditation on sufimeditationcenter.com. Go and click on how to meditate. We have

it all written there. How to breathe, how to make the steps, very simple. Just close your eyes and sit for five minutes, six minutes every day. And contemplate and breathe and play some nice *salawats* (praises upon Prophet Muhammad ﷺ) so that you're not distracted with your mind and begin the process of meditation. Later, you'll understand on how to meditate and then to keep the presence of the shaykh in his spiritual form. Then, making your connection, your *rabita* with these *awliyaullah* (saints) so that you're not meditating alone. And then you keep progressing in this ocean of meditation.

Then, in the "In Pursuit of Angelic Power." So, we put a whole book on how to pursue angelic power. That was a whole sort of summarization of all these hundreds of articles condensed down. And what we're trying to pursue is an angelic *qudra* (power), not the magnetic earth frequency of this *jinn* (unseen beings) world and their electricity, but angelic *qudra*. How to raise the character, raise the frequency with *zikr* (Divine remembrance), with meditation, contemplation so that we resonate at an angelic frequency. Through that angelic frequency and that light, that energy, then

everything becomes clear – especially in Naqshbandiya. How to meditate into the heart, how to meditate with the soul, how to close off the mind.

The first *zikr* is, *"La ilaha illAllah."*

$$\text{لَا إِلَهَ إِلاَّ الله}$$

*"La ilaha illAllah."*

*"There is no deity but Allah."*

*'La' is on the head,* that this way towards the Divine is not through your head. So, don't use your head with the shaykh. Don't try to think what he's saying, because this *La* is here that cut your head. Your head is of no importance into that reality. Anything that you're being taught, let it come into the heart and that's the end. If it leaves the heart and goes, and starts to move towards the head, it's already lost because *shaitan* (satan) resides within *insan's* (mankind's) head. His *nafs* (ego) and *shaitan,* they're up there partners together in this piece of meat that's in a closet.

It has never seen the light. It's seen nothing, your brain. And *shaitan's*

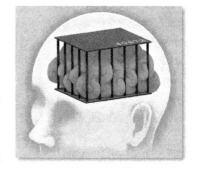

up there and everything, contemplating, thinking, 'Let me see, let me question. I just want to know.' Why you want to know? This *tariqah* (spiritual path) was not about you have to know. Because you're saying your head has to know, it means your ego and *shaitan,* they want to be educated in what you're talking about. Why? Why does your head have to know what the shaykh is talking about? He said it, you believe it. Put it into your heart. That is the way of the *tariq* (path) and the way of reaching towards realities. If you don't take that and you keep saying, 'I'm not going to do it that way,' then no problem. You're handicapping yourself and you will never reach to the reality and they'll sit with you 100 years, it doesn't matter. In the grave, they'll try to teach you.

But the system they had, you cannot customize them. So, sometimes people come say, 'I want to ask. I want to ask.' You're feeding your head and your head will never be satisfied and it will never take you towards your reality. And as much as you feed your head, they want more. 'I want more, I want more.' Now he opened a door into which to question everything. That's not faith. Faith is to hear it as long as it's good and clean we're talking about, not crazy things. It's good and clean –

it's faith; comes into my heart true; it's a *haq* (truth) and I'm going to do it. I'm going to try to fulfill that prayer, to fulfill that obligation. As soon as it enters my head, it's lost with *shaitan*. You learned it and understood it through your head, it has now absolutely no value to you.

## How Can We Speed Up Our Spiritual Progress?

It's a university without walls, *inshaAllah*. That you can watch the YouTube channel, you can watch the videos. This time that Allah's ﷻ giving us and Prophet ﷺ described that every time that Allah ﷻ gives to us we're accountable for. So, this is like an isolation and a *khalwah* (seclusion) that we have a time to ponder and think of what's important in our life. And *alhamdulillah*, watch the YouTube. Watch the channel, watch the teachings, take a playlist and play the videos from beginning all the way to the end, several. Instead of people doing binge video watching on Netflix, turn on the YouTube and learn the realities.

Read from the books, make your *salawats* (praises upon Prophet Muhammad ﷺ), spend your time in *tafakkur* (contemplation). If you can, to meditate and contemplate and to connect the heart. Allah ﷻ will hold us accountable for the time He's given. So, it means this is an

immense *ni'mat* (blessing) from Allah ﷻ that, 'I've given you this time, what are you going to do with it?' And those whom they want to build themselves and they move towards excess positive, they should be very content from what Allah's ﷻ going to be dressing upon their souls. Those whom their reality is more towards negativity then they move towards the negativity. What was once grey will clearly become black and white, *inshaAllah*.

## Should We Continue After Becoming Consistent in Our Practices?

Of course. You have to be regular with the meditation and keep meditating and keep reaching a state in which you are nothing. Say that,

'I'm nothing, I'm nothing I'm nothing,' and that you visualize the energy and the dress of the shaykhs to be present. As much as you find yourself to be present, as much as you're away from that reality. So, it means there's a way in which to say, 'I'm nothing and I'm visualizing that I'm in the dress of their light and asking their light to dress me.' If I can keep that and understand

that, and begin to feel that *qudra*, that power, and that energy begin to come. So, it becomes very real that they have to feel the energy; they feel that presence and that dress upon them, *inshaAllah*.

## How Do We Make Our Spiritual Connection (Muraqabah) Stronger?

Practicing every day, *inshaAllah*. Just like we talked last week is to

practice on a daily basis on how to make the connection. That, how to visualize yourself. The *awrad* (daily practices) is the *awrad*. To sit at the end of your *salah* (prayer), put *salawats* and Qur'an on, visualize yourself at *Madinatul Munawwara*, visualize yourself with *awliyaullah* (saints) and saying, 'I'm nothing, I'm nothing. *Ya Rabbi*, I'm nothing. That just let me to just breathe in this ocean of power.' And see yourself as nothing in the presence of *Rauza e Sharif* (holy burial chamber) in the presence of *Madinatul Munawwara*, in the presence of these *awliyaullah* that, I'm nothing. And learn how to breathe. Learn how to feel the energy. But again, everything that we're teaching it's built upon a system.

So, people who tune in and say, 'Well, how do we do meditation?' Yeah,

that's a whole system. That's why email us because then we will send a reply form. That once all of this is based on understanding your *wudu* (ablution), understanding energy, the importance of sanctifying your energy,

purifying your energy, making sure your energy is strong, and then you sit for your *tafakkur* and your contemplation on a daily basis on just breathing and feeling the presence of these *awliyaullah*. That, 'I want to be with you. I want to be dressed by your lights of what Allah ﷻ has given to you. Dress me.' Don't expect to see them and just feel them.

Everybody was given a basic package. And we described many years ago in training, 'You are like a computer that came with a basic software.' So,

right now close your eyes – wherever you are and whoever is hearing this at whatever time you are hearing it – just close your eyes. Gently hold your thumb, relax your heart, and I want you to visualize Mickey Mouse. I don't know if in Pakistan you have Mickey Mouse. He's that mouse, looks like a rat, has two big ears and a smile. It's so easy to see Mickey Mouse and he's right there. Why? It's in your basic package, came in your basic software.

Now through your practices and training your software has to be upgraded. Right? You don't just get a basic phone and now you're going to download 264MB apps. Your phone is going to crash. So, the whole process of learning and slowly, slowly trying to build your energy. Listen to the *zikr* (Divine remembrance), listen to the teachings. There are 1,000 videos and somebody says, 'Oh, I need a *wazifa* to do.' No, no, you should actually be sitting down and watching a video. Put

headphones on wherever you are. Watch a video so that you become very familiar with the Shaykh, very familiar with those teachings, very familiar with that understanding so that you are entering into his ocean of

reality. You hear him, you sense him, you understand how he talks, the reality that he is talking about. It's like something that you are eating from. It's not something you occasionally get involved in. It's you immerse yourself in anything that you want to learn.

As a result, when you're meditating, your package will begin to slowly upgrade. Upgraded so that, '*Ya Rabbi*, let me to be with them and then  with my heart, I know that they are in front of me. *Ya Rabbi*, I see a picture of *Madinatul Munawwara* and *Rauza e Sharif*, that let me keep that image in my mind's eye.' And as your software is being upgraded and the energy being sent to you is becoming more and more. And every *zikr* you make your *madad* (support), you keep yourself in *wudu*, you come to the *zikr*.

If you need, put headphones so that you can isolate from every other external sound so that you bring yourself to be wholly present with the shaykh. See yourself right on the carpet with them. That, 'I'm present with them and that bring me into that presence.' Shaykh will lift you and bring you in an instant into their presence. Then you're closing the eyes and visualizing I'm with them, "*Wa kono ma'as sadiqeen.*" Allah's command, 'Have a consciousness and keep the company of these *sadiqs*.' Not in physicality, Allah doesn't care about your body. But in your spirituality that you are always with them.

يَا أَيُّهَا الَّذِينَ آمَنُوا اتَّقُوا اللَّهَ وَكُونُوا مَعَ الصَّادِقِينَ ﴿١١٩﴾

*9:119 – "Ya ayyuhal ladheena amanoo ittaqollaha wa kono ma'as sadiqeen." (Surat At-Tawbah)*

*"O you who have believed, have consciousness of Allah and be with those who are truthful/ Pious/ sincere (in words and deed)."*
*(The Repentance, 9:119)*

'*Ya Rabbi*, let me always to be with them. I'm with You, I don't see You, I don't deserve to see You. I'm not yet clean.' And your vision with your

faith is that, 'I'm with them. I'm with them, I'm with them, I'm with them' until Allah ﷻ begin to grant sincerity, your software is upgraded, and you begin to feel and see that you are in Madina and Mecca. And that you feel in your heart, in your heart's eye, not your physical eye. The eye of your faith, that, 'I see Mawlana Shaykh ق. I see *Madinatul Munawwara*. I see *Rauza e Sharif* and I'm breathing in that presence. I'm asking to be dressed from that presence. I'm nothing, I'm nothing,' and just breathe. And say, '*Ya Rabbi*, I just came to get the *faiz* (downpouring blessings) and the energy of that association and that reality.' And that's *tafakkur* (contemplation) – keep doing every day, every day until the beatific fragrance of that reality opens.

The beatific energy of that presence begins to open in which I'm sitting there and I begin to play the *salawats* and say, '*Ya Rabbi*, I wish I could recite these *salawats* at *Rauza e Sharif* for the presence of Sayyidina Muhammad ﷺ. Let these

beatific recitations be my praising upon that reality.' And visualize when these *salawats* are playing these all *malaika* (angels) that are coming and moving around that *Rauza e Sharif* (holy burial chamber). And that these *malaika* are coming and dressing upon that reality and Prophet ﷺ is sending his divinely *faiz* (downpouring blessings) upon the soul. And every time this meditation you keep doing, you keep doing consistently until it catches. So, it means they keep practicing, keep practicing.

Every student has a little candle in their heart. Every *insan* (human being)  was given a little light like a candle. Your life's responsibility was to manage that light. Defend and protect that light. Don't think that faith is something you can do anything you want. Attack the shaykh however you want, speak however you want, yell and scream however you want. Do any type of thing that you want. You're blowing out your candle! Faith is very fragile. And Sayyidina Muhammad ﷺ described, 'It's like a shirt, it will be worn out. Ask Allah ﷻ in every prayer to renew your faith,' so that this candle becomes lit.

عَنْ عَبْدِ اللهِ بْنِ عَمْرٍ قَالَ۞، قَالَ رَسُولُ اللهِ صَلَّى اللهُ عَلَيْهِ وَآلِهِ وَسَلَّمَ: إِنَّ الْإِيمَانَ لَيَخْلَقُ فِي جَوْفِ أَحَدِكُمْ كَمَا يَخْلَقُ الثَّوْبُ الْخَلِقُ فَاسْأَلُوا اللهَ أَنْ يُجَدِّدَ الْإِيمَانَ فِي قُلُوبِكُمْ. [المستدرك على الصحيحين ٥]

*'An Abdullah ibn Amr qala: Qala Rasulullahi* ﷺ: *"Innal Imana layakhlaqu fi jawfi ahadekum kama yakhlaquth thawbul khalequ fasaloo Allaha an yujaddedal Imana fi qulubukom."*
*[Al-Mustadrak 'alal Sahihin 5]*

*Abdullah ibn Amr reported: The Messenger of Allah, peace and blessings be upon him, said: "Verily, the faith of one of you will wear out within him, just as a shirt becomes worn out, so ask Allah to renew faith in your hearts." [Al-Mustadrak 'alal Sahihin 5]*

The candle, when you practice the meditation, 'Let this light to grow, *ya Rabbi.*' When I'm receiving their *faiz*, their *faiz* is building this light, building this light, building this light until the point you will become 'lit.'

When you are lit, it means an energy hits you and you went from a candle into the beginning formation of a star. And the first level of sainthood and the formation of sainthood is a *najm* (star), in which you are becoming a sun. You are being granted a Divine Light that is eternal. Your heart is now lit. You're heating up all the time. Your hands are hot. The back of your neck heats up. If they take your temperature, all your clothes are wet from the heat that you are producing. That servant is lit. That servant is on the process of sainthood to achieve these lights and these realities.

That which is lit is eternally lit. Then through all their training, they're going to develop that light to become stronger and stronger, stronger, and stronger until it begins to make *salawats* and become super powerful. As a result, that sun –
it feeds off of difficulties. It takes the waste in the galaxy, brings it into its atmosphere and gravitational pull. And as a result, it uses that garbage as a fuel. And what happens when the sun is burning a fuel, it produces a *diya* (divinely fire).

It produces immense lights that are coming out. And Sayyidina Muhammad ﷺ described, 'My *Sahabi*, they are like stars, *najm*, on a dark night.'

أَصْحَابِيْ كَالنُّجُـــوْمْ بِأَيِّهِمْ أَقْتَدَيْتُمْ اَهْتَدَيْتُمْ

*"Ashabi kan Nujoom, bi ayyihim aqta daytum ahta daytum."*

*"My companions are like stars. Follow any one of them and you will be guided."* (Prophet Muhammad (pbuh))

So, anyone should understand the reality of a star formation. That until you achieve that your faith is very frail. Don't live life trying to blow it out. And these *awliyaullah* (saints) come into our life to teach us how to nourish it, protect it, and begin to try to spark it. So that to take it from a temporary to an eternal reality. Mawlana Shaykh ق would describe,

'The word *daayim* is so beautiful.' *Daayim*, that which is eternally because they are lit. That you achieved your eternal light and eternal reality, *inshaAllah*.

## How Can We Accelerate Our Spiritual Growth?

The *muraqabah* (spiritual connection). We've talked about that before

for the *muraqabah*, how to do the meditation. You do the *wazifa* (spiritual practice), do the *awrads* (daily practices), do all the practices that you can. Do as much *salawat* on Sayyidina Muhammad ﷺ as possible, making *istighfar* (seeking forgiveness), keeping your *wudu* (ablution), keeping your energy practices, and then a strong adherence in *tafakkur* and contemplation.

They call it meditation in the west and Islamic terminology is *tafakkur*, to contemplate. There's a light that Allah ﷻ has given into the heart. We have to every night contemplate that light, that I'm in the presence of these lights and asking, '*Ya Rabbi*, dress me and bless me from these lights and let this light within my heart to grow.' And as I'm breathing and meditating and listening to *salawats*, listening to Holy Qur'an and breathing, trying  to make that meditation powerful for myself and trying to dress myself from that reality.

The more you become stronger, the more your *salah* (prayer) will be your meditation. Because every time you pray, it's the same. That you're in a connection and that you're asking to be dressed by the lights of  Allah ﷻ, dressed by the holy lights of the Ka'bah. '*Ya Rabbi*, dress me from these lights, bless me from these lights.' And as soon as you give your *attahiyat* and close and *salaams* and close your *salah*, at that time you're asking to communicate with Divinely Presence, and you go into *sujood* (prostration) for long periods of time.

This means this is a whole practice, a whole way of life. There's no accelerant. There's no shortcut, no fast way. This not about being fast but being slow and consistent. It means this is a way in which you do all the time. Not McDonald's where you get, you know, three dollars and drive thru. Send ten thousand and you become reiki master, maybe eleven thousand and you become Sufi master, but no. So, it's a long and consistent life. Take the beatings and let's go.

Take the path and the path will begin to open. There's no way of escaping the path. Anyone whom Allah ﷻ has destined on a path and he says, 'You know I'm not ready to do it.' That's a wrong choice, cause you're going to get the angel with the stick on one side and an angel with a stick on another side. And every time you go left and right, he's going to beat you this way and he's going to beat you that way. Nobody escapes Allah's ﷻ  plan. It's not the shaykh, it's not any human being. You've only tuned in because it came to your heart. You say, 'I don't know what the shaykh is talking about. I'm not going to take the path.' But if Allah ﷻ loves you, you're on the path and there's no escaping that.

Then you find the people who didn't really understand that, they had a really difficult time coming to this understanding because Allah ﷻ, when He wants the servant to submit, they're going to submit. And easier to  submit by yourself. We said many times before, you're inspired to give something in the way. You say, 'I'm not going to give.' You get in a car; you get a ticket for $300. Because Allah ﷻ, when He says, 'You give that night,' and you say, 'No,' Allah ﷻ say, 'I'm going to take it.' You go home, the oven explodes. It's $500. It's probably by that way, even Allah ﷻ made it to go up because every few minutes you're progressing, the expense is going up.

So, pay attention in your life that these are signs from Allah ﷻ. Do things by the inspiration in your heart. The more you're inspired, and you act on the inspiration, you're getting closer to *taslim* and submission. The more you deny the inspiration and now the inspiration left the heart we said, and went to the *maghz*, went to the brain and *shaitan* (satan) is up there chewing on that. 'Oh! You don't have to do, you don't, don't like that, don't listen, don't do like that.' And before you know it, your life is through very difficult testing.

So, *tariqah* (spiritual path) comes and inspires, 'Why you have to have difficult testing. Just *taslim* and begin to submit.' We say your *tariq*, it's not all the way from here to heaven. 'Oh! I got to do this, I got to reach to that, I'm going to do 10,000 of this, 20,000.' Your *tariq* is about this long. What? Your will and the shaykh's will. If you can match 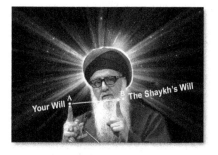 the will of the shaykh and listen to his advice, you're going to reach your *tariq*, your path. And that's what's happening now on the internet. Nobody wants to find a shaykh that they have to listen to.

So, then their *tariq* (path) became huge, long. 'I have Baba Ji back home and as a matter of fact he passed away, so I don't listen to anyone.' So, then your *tariqah* became huge. There's no way to reach *taslim* (submission). There's no way to reach, how to bring your desire, your want, and your will down. So, *tariqah* comes and says, 'No, must be a living guide that can communicate with you.' So, when these channels of communication are opening, it's to bring you into the *tariq* (path). That come, ask a question, and slowly begin to build the relationship and you'll begin to get answers that are not pleasing to you. If you move away from it, it becomes more difficult from you.

The more you can understand it and move towards that direction, the more you're entering into the ocean of *taslim* (submission) and that's what Allah ﷻ wants. *Atiullaha wa atiur Rasula wa Ulil amre minkum.*

...أَطِيعُوا اللَّه وَأَطِيعُوا الرَّسُولَ وَأُوْلِي الْأَمْرِ مِنْكُمْ... ﴿٥٩﴾

*4:59 – "...Atiullaha wa atiur Rasula wa Ulil amre minkum..."*
*(Surat An-Nisa)*

*"...Obey Allah, Obey the Messenger, and those in authority among you..." (The Women, 4:59)*

So that the more the servant is submitting, submitting, submitting, the more the appearance of Sayyidina Muhammad ﷺ will begin to manifest within the eye of that servant's heart, *inshaAllah*.

# Chapter 2
## Connecting the Heart and Accompanying a Guide

# Connecting the Heart to a Guide and Importance of the Bayah

### What is the Best Way to Be Introduced to the Spiritual Teachings?

It's the websites. The easiest is to take the articles from the Sufi Meditation site. If they have no Islamic background, then our website sufimeditationcenter.com is all entry-level for people who are not exposed to Islam, but you're exposed towards energy and meditation. Because you have to have an equal denominator. You're not going to talk in religious terms because then somebody already has preconditioned religious understandings. So, the equal denominator in math that they taught us is energy. Everybody is equal in energy and their understanding. Are you building it or losing it? So, then you talk to them in general sense.

If they have an Islamic background, then the NurMuhammad website has all the articles on *tafakkur*, contemplation or guidance. If they have difficulty in their life and say, 'Are you trying to really take this path by yourself?' And you guide yourself, and you prescribe the *zikrs* (Divine remembrance) that you have to do, the *awrads* (daily practices) you have to do. And then anyone who comes to them and says that, 'There's no need for a shaykh,' well, that's a shaykh. Because the one who's telling you there's no need for a shaykh, he's actually the shaykh who tells people to be misguided. So, everyone's a shaykh. When your mom says, 'You don't need a shaykh,' your mom is the shaykh. So, everyone plays the role of guiding someone. So, there is no, 'No guidance.' It's just what are they going to guide you to. Some guide you to go off the cliff and the other ones are trying to guide you towards Allah 'ﷻ, *inshaAllah*.

## How Can We Be Sure This is the Right Path?

How can you be sure? Because we are not a people by the mind; we are a people by our heart. So, this path is for a seeker. And the seeker must be hungry to seek the knowledges. So, everyone has to review themselves, 'Am I seeker of the way, a seeker of realities and a seeker of the sacred knowledges?' Because this path is not meant for everyone.

You know, everyone has a flavour and a desire they want. And *inshaAllah*, with their true intention, they find what they're looking for. But if it's realities, good character, perfection of character, and the love of Sayyidina Muhammad ﷺ, then I recommend that you seek that reality out. And whomever your heart is attracted to, you follow your heart. And Allah 'ﷻ will lead you according to your intention, *inshaAllah*.

## How Do We Know Which Shaykh and Spiritual Guide to Follow?

By just saying, 'I love these six shaykhs online, I like this shaykh, I like this shaykh, I like this shaykh, I like this shaykh, I like this shaykh.' No problem, but which shaykh likes you? That's what you should be really

worried about. It's not like rock-stars, you like ten of them online and you go click, click, click, click – 'I like this shaykh, I like this shaykh, I like this shaykh.' Find out which shaykh likes you? That's your lock, that's your bond! If you can answer that, that shaykh likes you, you're set, *alhamdulillah*. You're good with Sayyidina Muhammad ﷺ because that's his descendent and there is a relationship. So then, our life is how to be good with the shaykh. Find the one that your heart is connecting to. That their knowledges connect like a puzzle into your heart.

Some of them you listen to, they're teaching things like reading an encyclopedia and really slow. I clicked online and literally like someone picked up an encyclopedia, 'Page one, hmm.' Said, 'Oh my God I can't take it more than two seconds, that's it, forget it!' You know, the heart is not connected to that. Some people actually like to join in and read the encyclopedia, some people will join in.

So first you find whom your heart is connected to and then now this line opens, then email. Email and begin to communicate! 'This is me. This is

what I'm doing, this is what I'm watching, I'm following. I want to be known by you, by interacting with your community, with the email.' Not personal, there's not

95

10,000 people emailing the shaykh personally and he's going to sit there and stop his whole life just to send 10,000 emails back. But they try to develop a system in which the staff, and all of the people who are being of service, can contribute and support that. Then you build that relationship with the shaykh, you're asking, you're getting answers. You're asking and you're getting answers. That's called guidance!

Then you begin to support, you begin to read, and study the knowledges. If you see the shaykh has this many books, this many websites, this many articles, this many YouTube videos; have you finished all the thousand videos that you need to click on ten other websites? If you did, wow *subhanAllah*. There is so much information there. So, it means take a course and go deep into it. If you find your heart connected to it, then be from it and build that relationship with the *tariqah* (spiritual path), *inshaAllah*.

## Can We Follow Any Guide in the Naqshbandi Tariqah?

Sure, wherever your heart is. Every stream, and every river, and every ocean, however big and small, it leads to Sayyidina Muhammad ﷺ. So, whomever your heart is feeling that connection. Shaykh Abdullah al-Faiz Ad-Dagestani ق, Mawlana Shaykh ق, all of these big shaykhs of the Naqshbandiya, whomever your heart feels that affinity and that love, you close your eyes and you try to connect. If you don't feel the connection with that shaykh, then go to the next shaykh until you feel the connection. Many, many, many feel a strong attraction to  Shaykh Abdullah al-Faiz Ad-Dagestani ق *Naqeeb ul Ummah* (the Leader of the Nation), *Wa'yez ul Ummah* because of the amount of *qudra* (power) coming from his holy eyes. As soon as you look at his face, and stare and stare at the face, and then close your eyes and meditate, that, 'I want to be under your *nazar* (gaze) and your *tajalli* (manifestation).'

Or Sultanul Awliya Shaykh Muhammad Nazim al-Haqqani ق, and all those great representatives, whomever your heart feels that affinity and that connection with. And they, when you truly connect with them, they dress you, bless you, and they eagerly want to take you to the presence of Sayyidina Muhammad ﷺ. Nobody wants to keep you for themselves. They are also shy to represent and to keep themselves to be present. As soon as you learn how to do that meditation, they are the doors towards the reality of Sayyidina Muhammad ﷺ, *inshaAllah*.

## How Will I Know Who My Shaykh Is?

When the student is ready, the shaykh will appear. And I think we talked about a more easier understanding is that Allah ﷻ laid the track down. That this creation is not something random. Allah ﷻ has laid all the track. You know when you want to build the choo-choo train, you put all the tracks where you want it to go, everywhere it's supposed to go. He's already laid the path for every *insan* (human being); where the ideal path, what that person would go through, all their experiences.

If they would go through spiritual experiences, if they would meet towards guidance – all of that has already been written and that path has been laid. Then Allah ﷻ created your form. As a result, that destiny has already been written. Through a series of incidences in life and destiny, Allah ﷻ takes the student to become a seeker. Whom Allah ﷻ guides is truly guided and there is no guidance without Allah ﷻ.

...وَقَالُوا الْحَمْدُ لِلَّهِ الَّذِي هَدَانَا لِهَذَا وَمَا كُنَّا لِنَهْتَدِيَ لَوْلَا أَنْ هَدَانَا اللَّهُ ۖ لَقَدْ جَاءَتْ رُسُلُ رَبِّنَا بِالْحَقِّ...﴿٤٣﴾

*7:43 – "...Wa qalo Alhamdulillahi al ladhee hadana lihadha wa ma kunna linahtadiya lawla an hadana Allahu, laqad jaa at Rusulu Rabbina bil Haqqi..." (Surat Al-A'raf)*

"... And they will say, Praise be to Allah, who has guided us to this [joy and happiness]; and we would never have been guided if Allah had not guided us. Certainly the messengers of our Lord had come with the truth..." (The Heights, 7:43)

That nobody can guide anybody or bring anyone to guidance if not Allah ﷻ writing it. So, it means then in my life, all of my experiences were meant to prepare me for a day when I would be ready, and I would want the guidance within myself.

That I had guided myself towards disaster and I had made all my choices that were wrong because I was driving the train and trying to make a left when it's going right, make a right when it's going left. And those whom Allah ﷻ guides, they have similar understandings. They've been through many difficulties so that they stopped trying to drive their own train. And when they reach to an understanding of submission, 'I'm just going to submit, *ya Rabbi*, I want the guidance. I want to reach towards this reality.' Then what does that mean? The shaykh will appear.

Along the way, there may be bandit shaykhs. That you're trying to reach your destiny and somebody jumps on your tracks and says, 'You come with me.' And you're going to go through many sour experiences. So, the day that you're again, really ready, you'll understand guidance. Some people have come directly to the shaykh and they were thinking everywhere they go, there's going to be beatific *salawats* playing, food laid out for you in abundance and every type of nice talk with a happy smile. That, you're lucky. But most have experienced all the crazy, different types of associations, different Centers and all of the sour experiences. So that in a state, you're ready. 'Oh! I've tasted everything sour. I've heard all their garbage.' At that point, your heart is ready.

When Allah ﷻ want to send you to sunshine, you know because you've been through the rain. And you know exactly what sunshine is. You know what that beauty is. You know what that fragrance is and at that

time you heart tells you. If the teaching of that shaykh – and you're ready, and you think you're ready – and the teaching of that shaykh resonates within your heart, means then there's a bond happening, and we talked about that before but that's a very deep subject. The bond that is happening is based on the reality of your form, energy, and sound. Your form is existing by the power of an energy. And when you break this energy down, it's a sound. And this sound is not the audible sound only of our tongue. This sound that Allah ﷻ wants and its understanding is being conveyed is a resonance on your soul.

There's a sound that you make, 'Laaa,' that's different. There is a sound that your soul makes. That's  from Allah's ﷻ power oceans. And Allah ﷻ makes the soul of that guide because He lifted them, dressed them, lifted them, lifted them – the resonance of their soul has a frequency. Let's say 92.1, the frequency of that shaykh's soul; it's resonating from Allah's ﷻ power oceans. When you come into their ocean of vibration because the shaykh's soul is everywhere.

The soul is not something people understand. If he releases his soul, he can hold the moon and the sun in his hand. The vastness of the soul is not something small. Allah's ﷻ creation is something of an immense size. It's not contained in this little body that is in a little Earth in a little galaxy in the midst of billions of galaxies. The vastness and the power of the soul is something unimaginable. And when Allah ﷻ wants to release the frequency of that soul, it means the soul of those guides, they're out. Allah ﷻ, 'Don't deem them to be dead, they're very much alive.'

وَلَا تَقُولُوا لِمَن يُقْتَلُ فِي سَبِيلِ اللَّهِ أَمْوَاتٌ ۚ بَلْ أَحْيَاءٌ وَلَٰكِن لَّا تَشْعُرُونَ ﴿١٥٤﴾

*2:154 – "Wa la taqolo liman yuqtalu fee sabilillahi amwatun, bal ahyaon wa lakin la tash'uroon." (Surat Al-Baqarah)*

*"And do not say about those who are killed in the way of Allah, 'They are dead.' Rather, they are alive, but you perceive [it] not."*
*(The Cow, 2:154)*

Their whole life was to surrender, surrender, surrender. When Allah ﷻ brought them into surrender, Allah ﷻ gave them *Hayat al Barzakh* (the

Abode of the grave). That the reality of their *barzakh* reality, the dress of their *malakut* (heavenly realm) is dressing them. As a result, their soul is free. Their associations are filled with their soul. Wherever their heart, their soul is flowing. Anyone watching them is calling and drawing a portion of the soul to be present with them.

This means you put all these teachings like a *tasbih*, like beads together.

As soon as you look at their picture, their soul – whoosh – is right there present with you. Because the soul is not one, it's a light. They have these little games of lasers where you hit the laser and it goes in a thousand directions and a laser with just a little battery is able to do that. Imagine the power oceans of Allah ﷻ. It means then their soul, their light is moving everywhere. Imagine then the frequency of that soul. With what frequency and energy that soul is resonating? And it comes into your presence.

Then you open the oceans of attuning. As soon as his soul comes into your presence, it begins to attune your soul to his frequency and that's what guidance is. Guidance is not through your *nafs* (ego). That's the

playing part. If they had to guide humanity through the two eyes and two ears and the nose that doesn't listen, the guidance and we would all be dead. Nobody would listen. Everybody more interested in

their hamburger and french fries, drive thru. If Allah's ﷻ talking about, 'There is no guidance except through Allah's ﷻ guidance and permission (Holy Qur'an, 7:43). Those whom been granted a light, have a light. Those whom have no light but not granted a light, have no light.

﴾٤٠﴿ ...وَمَن لَّمْ يَجْعَلِ اللَّـهُ لَهُ نُورًا فَمَا لَهُ مِن نُّورٍ

*24:40 – "...Wa mal lam yaj'a lillahu lahu noora famaa lahu min noor."*
*(Surat An-Nur)*

*"...And he to whom Allah has not granted light – for him there is no light." (The Light, 24:40)*

This means Allah ﷻ saying that, 'These guides, this reality has a power.' As soon as it enters in, it begins to dress your light. Change the frequency of your light to resonate at their frequency. And as a result of resonating at your frequency, the true guides. Imitated guides, that's like plastic fruit. They can sit and nobody will be changed. They can sit for years and nobody changes. Real guidance, they can sit for five minutes and begin to change everyone. Right?

The master of that was who? Sultanul Awliya Mawlana Shaykh Muhammad Nazim Haqqani ق. We said many times before; says he was given a secret from the light of *sifat ar-Rahman* (attribute of the Most

Compassionate). That when you came into his presence, he would throw that light into your heart and you went back and immediately, you grew a full beard, you became full *sunnah* (traditions of Prophet Muhammad ﷺ) and forty people following your way. That was a power. And that power even more powerful now because the physicality got out of the way; the sickness and limitation of the physicality went away. His soul is much more powerful now. So, it means just he says, 'Think about me for five minutes; my soul is entering towards you. It's coming with my frequency, my resonance and I begin to change all of your imperfections so that you resonate on my light.'

And that's when Grandshaykh ق, because then talks one way to you but its *haqqaiq* (realities) is of a deeper understanding. He said, 'Sit with us for five minutes, I take you to my *maqam*.' What does that mean? Like I'm taking you to an elevator and I'm taking you somewhere? It's that my soul will dress your soul. What Allah ﷻ put upon my soul, it will come with every truth to every falsehood of yours and shatter it. And when it shatters it, it rebuilds it back as a duplicate of his own light.

103

وَ قُلْ جَآءَالْحَقُّ وَزَهَقَ الْبَطِلُ، إِنَّ الْبَطِلَ كَانَ زَهُوقًا ﴿٨١﴾

*17:81 – "Wa qul jaa alhaqqu wa zahaqal baatil, innal batila kana zahoqa." (Surat Al-Isra)*

*"And say, Truth has come, and falsehood has perished. Indeed falsehood, [by its nature], is ever perishing/ bound to perish." (The Night Journey, 17:81)*

This means he takes the frequency of that *insan*. If they were at ten and he was at 10,000, he raises the frequency of their soul like 10,000, puts it in a trust. Allah ﷻ puts that reality in a trust because they're not capable of handling that reality on their physicality. Many things are happening. All of guidance is  happening behind the scenes. It's not the guidance in the front. But as a result of these lights and these emanations coming upon the soul, dressing upon the soul, it begins to completely change the form of that person in which they begin to exhibit all of that *nurani* (luminous) characteristics.

Naqshbandiya tul 'Aliya and the students of Sultanul Awliya Mawlana Shaykh Abdullah Faiz ad-Daghestani ق, Sultanul Awliya Shaykh

 Muhammad Nazim Haqqani ق and all the subsequent shaykhs after that, they have an exact characteristic. Anywhere on Earth you go, you'll know this is Shaykh Nazim's ق Naqshbandi students. They have a beautiful light upon them. They carry the *sunnah* (traditions of Prophet Muhammad ﷺ) upon themselves. They carry this love within their heart

and their character and their light. Even you may find problems in their actions but the light and the trust that was deposited upon them is of a very unique ocean of realities. So, it means guidance is from the soul.

## Can We Join the Subhah (Discourse) if We're Following Another Way?

The *suhbah*, definitely! That was the answer from the other question is that we are all representing the way to the heart of Sayyidina Muhammad ﷺ. Anyone is welcome to take from that fountain, it's a fountain coming from the heart of Prophet ﷺ. It's asking like, 'Can I take from this *Kawthar* (The Fountain of Abundance), or from that  *Kawthar*, or from this *Kawthar*?' Whatever *Kawthar* you think you find, because anything coming from the heart of Prophet ﷺ is *Kawthari*, it's a *Kawthar*, It's a fountain. That if you drink from that knowledge, it brings you to life. If you feel that, drink from it!

But what they ask is that when you take those knowledges, you have to understand there's a responsibility. And these knowledges are like breastfeeding. As soon as you've been fed from somebody, that person  is your mother. So, in Islamic law, you can't take your children around to be fed by every lady in the village. Because then that child can't marry anyone in that village because everyone becomes his mother. So, it's very specific on who's going to feed that child. If Allah ﷻ has that requirement for a child, imagine then for the *shuyukh*, who are feeding you from the reality of their knowledges.

*Ilm e Laduni wa hikmati bis Saliheen* (Divinely Knowledge and Wisdom of the Righteous). Where Allah ﷻ give them from the two milks of their reality to dress the servant. They give you *Ilm e Laduni,* heavenly knowledges, and a *hikmah* in their training. They train you on how to have *hikmah* so that you don't use the knowledge incorrectly and understand it incorrectly. So, anyone whom you're taking that source of knowledge, you owe something to them. You can't just bounce around. So, then if you have too many mothers, you're going to have difficulty.

But if you're just watching YouTube on how to make *wudu* (ablution) then that's a thousand people you can watch. But once you start to take *Ilm e Laduni,* then you have a responsibility and a lock with those people, *inshaAllah.*

## What Are the Best Manners in Asking For a Prayer?

We go through all of these questions and *du'as* (supplications) and try our best to pray for everyone, and everybody be safe and try to follow the guidance and teaching. More than ever, that's when people are following 500 different directions asking 500 different people for *du'a,* but this way is based on loyalty and they monitor. They understand whom and how many you're asking, and they just stand back and watch.

You ask the whole world, that's okay, but you have to build a relationship with the Shaykh. If you have a relationship with that shaykh, that you're listening, you're following, you're doing all the practices, then you're *istiqam* and firm on that belief. If you don't believe that person has an ability to reach to you and that their teachings are not of benefit to you, go somewhere else until you do and then you're committed with loyalty. That way your *du'as* and your remedy is not going to be a soup, where you just add it from everywhere. You follow the guidance, they give you an *awrad* (daily practices), you do the *awrad*. They give you the *du'as*, you do the *du'as*.

We have put out an app for Naqshbandiya tul 'Aliya, it has all the *du'as* of Shaykh Abdullah Al-Faiz ad Dagestani ق, Mawlana Shaykh Muhammad Nazim al Haqqani ق, all approved. Read those *du'as* if you're under the Naqshbandiya tul 'Aliya way, *inshaAllah*. We pray that everybody to be safe, be calm, do your practices, watch the live broadcasts, watch the video playlists when you're sitting at home doing your seclusion. Take the books to read from the *ma'rifah* (gnosticism) and the way and, *inshaAllah* you should find a peace and tranquillity.

Their teachings and this *Haqiqatul Muhammadiyah* (The Muhammadan Reality) brings a tranquillity into the home. As soon as you play the video, all of the *jinn* (unseen beings) and *malaika* (angels), they want to hear those realities, so they all come. Their energy brings a peace and *sakinah* (tranquillity) into the home. As soon as you play the *salawats* (praises upon Prophet Muhammad ﷺ), the *zikrs* (Divine remembrance),

they come. By them coming they bring all of their energy and their happiness and you find your heart to be at peace. If your house is devoid of spiritual energies who's going to be there? All the *shayateen* (devils) they come, they come  until you're nervous and you're a wreck and all under their control because there's a party in your house and you just don't know it. So, try to make the home a *maqam*, everything beatific in the way of Allah ﷻ and Sayyidina Muhammad ﷺ.

## What Are the Manners to Ask the Shaykh a Question?

*InshaAllah*, anything that your questions that have to do with like inspirations and to prove your knowledge, don't show your knowledge to the shaykh. Because then they won't open for you anymore. You ask your question on clarity, 'I want to know about this, I want to know about that.' But if he teaches you a knowledge and then you want to show yourself that you know something that's *tark al adab* (leaving manners). So, don't show that you know anything.

Anything that's being revealed to your heart is for your heart, so write it in your notes and for your understanding and to keep the way of *tariqah* (spiritual path). Otherwise if the shaykh wanted to raise everybody with knowledges and all day long they wanted to challenge the knowledge back to him, they would have a school of chaos. So, anything that you're being inspired is good, write it down, keep it, contemplate, meditate on it, *inshaAllah*. Anything that you need

clarity that, 'How do I do this? How do I recite this?' Then no problem.

## What is the Importance of the Bayah and Can We Take It From Any Shaykh?

The most important concept of the *bayah* is to your allegiance to
Allah ﷻ and Sayyidina
Muhammad ﷺ. That I'm trying to
reach the satisfaction of Allah ﷻ
and to the heart and satisfaction
of Sayyidina Muhammad ﷺ.
These *ulul amr* (saints) are
facilitators for that reality and they
have schools of knowledge. To
enroll oneself in that school so
that you have an opportunity to show your *khidmat* (service).

So, the *bayah* was not that you take *bayah*, 'I'm going to take something
from him,' because the words they're using is incorrect. And that's
specifically because the *nafs* (ego) wants to use those words. But it's, 'I
gave *bayah*.' Take and give are different. Take, you're coming to get
something. Give, he's coming to take everything from you. That's why
then this is Surah Tawbah. It's verse 103, Surah Tawbah, 103, 'That I'm
coming to give *bayah* to this shaykh.'

$$ خُذْ مِنْ أَمْوَالِهِمْ صَدَقَةً تُطَهِّرُهُمْ وَتُزَكِّيهِم بِهَا وَصَلِّ عَلَيْهِمْ ۖ إِنَّ صَلَاتَكَ سَكَنٌ لَّهُمْ ۗ وَاللَّـهُ سَمِيعٌ عَلِيمٌ ﴿١٠٣﴾ $$

*9:103 – "Khudh min amwalihim sadaqatan tutahhiruhum wa
tuzakkeehim biha wa salli 'alayhim, inna salawataka sakanun lahum,
wallahu samee'un 'aleem." (Surat At-Tawbah)*

*"Take, [O, Muhammad (pbuh)], from their wealth a charity by which
you purify them and Sanctify them and Pray on their behalf. Indeed, your
Prayers are a source of Peace/security/reassurance for them. And Allah
is Hearing and Knowing." (The Repentance, 9:103)*

I feel that I want to be under Naqshbandiya. I want to be under the *tarbiyah* (discipline) of Sultanul Awliya Mawlana Shaykh Abdullah Faiz Dagestani ق, Sultanul Awliya Mawlana Shaykh Nazim al Haqqani ق and the Naqshbandi shaykhs. And I want to serve them. I want to now give from myself, from whatever Allah عز وجل gave to me, and I want to be of *khidmat* and service to them. *InshaAllah*, they accept me in their service. And then I study from their knowledges, I begin to give support, and then I begin to serve.

This is then somebody who is *muhibbin* (lovers of the way). Naqshbandiya *muhibbin* can be millions. That they love the way, love the path. Naqshbandi *muridin* (devoted disciples) they have to have reached the station of *irshad* (guidance). So, the shaykh on this Earth may only have four or five, six *mureeds*. And they reach the station of *Murshid* (Authorized Spiritual Guide) and then there are degrees of *ijazah* (authorization) and *irshad*. So *muhibbin*, many.

And you want to succeed in being *muhibbin*, then the first category we described, be of service. Come to give, come to support. Come to learn, not take anything. You're going to give everything. You're going to give your way, your time, everything to reach towards that reality. And we have many other talks about that. If you truly believe that your head is on the feet of Sayyidina Muhammad ﷺ, '*Ya Sayyidi, ya Rasul e Kareem, ya Habib e Azeem* ﷺ, I won't lift my head. Don't let me to lift my head. Put your *qadam* on my neck and keep me in this place.' Then you will truly believe that, 'I don't want to do anything other than to be of service to you.' So then your whole life was, 'How I can serve you, *ya Sayyidi ya Rasul e Kareem* ﷺ.'

Then you would quickly try to find these *shuyukh* and say 'I want to serve. I want to do the Mawlid, I want to do those programs, I want to support those programs, I want to propagate your teaching, I want to support your books, your internet, your social media, your videos. So that every night I see my head still under the feet of Sayyidina Muhammad ﷺ.' And then Prophet ﷺ become happy with you. Because he's the ultimate master of this entire orchestra.

He knows he is not going to give everybody a tongue and say, 'Oh, I want to talk like him.' No! But if he gave you a skill why aren't you supporting him? Then it becomes like an amazing ensemble. That the one whom has this skill, he gives his skill. The one whom has this ability, give his ability. The one who can orate and talk, he talks. The one who can support, they support.

And that becomes the power of *tariqah* (spiritual path). It's all these skills are coming together.

*MashAllah*, how many of these IT men are online and doing all these things? It was not about everybody giving a *suhbah* (discourse). It's one

person who's talking, okay good for him. But everybody else, all these people who are supporting, and making that talk to be out. Because they came, they did their part, so that today people could be enjoying this in the middle of a pandemic. They're sitting on their couches and this message is nicely coming to them like a *kebab*. And they have apps to read, they have books to get, they have internet and social media, everywhere conveniently brought to you by the Naqshbandi first responders.

## Can We Do the Awrad Without Having Bayah?

It's like buying a cellular contract without a phone. You can do whatever you want, right? You say, 'I'm going to buy a nice phone, but I don't want to have a cellular contract, *ahlan wa sahlan*. What are you going to do with that phone? Or say, 'No, shaykh I don't want a phone I just want to get a cellular contract!' You can do whatever you like, but why not the *bayah* (allegiance)? It's in your heart; nobody needs to touch your hands. Everything is wireless now, put into your heart that you want to be of

service, that you accept Sultanul Awliya Shaykh Muhammad Nazim al Haqqani ق as your Shaykh and all the other shaykhs and representatives and that you love them. And that you want to be under their guidance and under their *nazar* (gaze); read your *bayah* to yourself and it's a matter of fulfilling your contract. If you feel your *bayah* is with someone else, then you should be listening to them.

## Do We Need Permission for Bayah From Our Family?

If you feel that that's a concern, then wait until your heart feels a sense of peace. That if there's going to be an issue with your husband, then wait until your heart has a sense of peace and that he's comfortable and the family's comfortable with the practices. Because the *tariqah* (spiritual path) doesn't want to come and make disturbances within the household. If it's between the understanding of the parents following a different *tariqah*, then you have to use your diplomacy and your *bayah* (allegiance) is something that you read in between you and Allah ﷻ and His Rasul ﷺ. It can be something very hidden and just for your personal understanding and satisfaction to your heart. It's not something that has to be publicized and told to the whole world, especially if your situation is of a concern to you. The one who has no concern and is free to do pretty much what they want to do, no, then they take their *bayah* and join the *tariqah* and *alhamdulillah*.

The *bayah* for Naqshbandiya tul 'Aliya is to Sultanul Awliya Mawlana

Shaykh Muhammad Nazim Haqqani ق through his representatives and the 41st shaykh of the *tariqah* now is Mawlana Shaykh Muhammad Adil ق, who is heading the Naqshbandi *tariqah*. Your acceptance of ourselves is a sign of

love that I accept and I want to learn from your teachings and that *inshaAllah*, Shaykh Nazim ق to raise you, Shaykh Daghestani ق to raise you into their presence and to dress and bless you, *inshaAllah*.

## Can Unintentional Actions Cause Disconnection Between Student and Shaykh?

You know, like a legal contract, you have to define unintentional. So, the leaving of a shaykh's hand is very difficult, if not impossible. That when Allah ﷻ destines guidance, it's again from an ocean of *malakut* (heavens). That what Allah ﷻ has written for guidance is going to be guided. And the hand that is guiding is not the hand of an ego but is the hand of the Divine guidance that comes from Allah ﷻ to the hand of Sayyidina Muhammad ﷺ to the *ulul amr* (saints) who are inheriting.

So, it means the actual guidance *"Innal ladheena yubayi'oonaka innama yubayi'on Allah."* The *bayah* (allegiance) is always only to Allah ﷻ. There are intermediaries in the process. The *bayah* is always to Allah ﷻ.

إِنَّ الَّذِينَ يُبَايِعُونَكَ إِنَّمَا يُبَايِعُونَ اللَّـهَ يَدُ اللَّـهِ فَوْقَ أَيْدِيهِمْ ۚ فَمَن نَّكَثَ فَإِنَّمَا يَنكُثُ عَلَىٰ نَفْسِهِ ۖ وَمَنْ أَوْفَىٰ بِمَا عَاهَدَ عَلَيْهُ اللَّـهَ فَسَيُؤْتِيهِ أَجْرًا عَظِيمًا ﴿١٠﴾

*48:10 – "Innal ladheena yubayi'oonaka innama yubayi'on Allaha yadullahi fawqa aydeehim, faman nakatha fa innama yankuthu 'ala nafsihi, wa man awfa bima 'ahada 'alayhu Allaha fasayu teehi ajran 'azheema." (Surat Al-Fath)*

*"Indeed, those who give Bayah (pledge allegiance) to you, [O Muhammad] – they are actually giving Bayah (pledge allegiance) to Allah. The hand of Allah is over their hands. So, he whoever breaks his pledge/oath, only breaks it to the detriment/Harm/loss of himself. And whoever fulfills their covenant (Bayah) that which he has promised Allah - He will grant him a great reward." (The Victory, 48:10)*

Right? Because Allah ﷻ is the only one who can give guidance and destine you for guidance. Then when Allah ﷻ want to give you guidance, sends an *isharat* (sign) to Sayyidina Muhammad ﷺ because, 'This is a creation that you are in charge of. Tell your creation this one will be guided.' The *nazar* (gaze) of Prophet ﷺ begin to hit upon that servant. And then he dispatches from the station of the *ulul amr*, the people of authority.

This means their steadfast station is in the heart of Prophet ﷺ, in the soul. Those souls then are dispatched with the command that this one,

Allah ﷻ has assigned guidance for. That from *malakut* is locked. It's already been written. Now does your physicality and your *nafs* (ego) understand that guidance? And was it written for your physicality and your *nafs* to actually meet your guide? Some 'yes', some 'no.' Some were not physically guided in this world. They never met the physical guide, but they have been guided and they'll reach their destination.

Can they do something completely by accident to break their connection? No. *InshaAllah*, no. It's not so petty that you make a mistake, and they get angry and say, 'Get out now and take your five dollars with you.' It's not cheap like that. It has an immense Divine Grace. But when you intentionally keep doing things wrong, you're taking your hands off. It means you're going a thousand feet high and you're trying to cut them but, in actuality, *shaitan* (satan) is convincing you to cut yourselves.

So, there are some wonderful blooper videos that the guy is cutting a tree and he has a chainsaw. And you're looking at him cut that tree and it's like, 'Can anyone tell this man that if he cuts a little bit more, he's actually going to fall?' You know, you see the guy with a chainsaw and a big tree and he's cutting the wrong part of the tree. If he clears that cut, he's going to fall and that's all *shaitan* wants in our life. Keep telling you, 'Cut it. Cut it. Cut the relationship.'

As soon as you cut that relationship, that *faiz* (downpouring blessings) and that blessing no longer can reach to you. And a life of difficulty and hardship and we gave a talk on Allah ﷻ says, 'Hold fast to your *tariq*' (path). *"Istiqaamo fi tariqat."* 'Hold firm onto your *tariqah* (spiritual path), hold firm until Allah ﷻ dress you from oceans of abundance, waters of abundance flowing, oceans.'

﴿ وَأَن لَّوِ اسْتَقَامُوا عَلَى الطَّرِيقَةِ لَأَسْقَيْنَاهُم مَّاءً غَدَقًا ١٦ ﴾

*72:16 – "Wa alla wis taqaamoo 'alat tareeqati la asqaynaahum maa'an ghadaqaa." (Surat Al-Jinn)*

*"And [Allah revealed] that: "If they had only remained firm on their tariqa (straight path), We would have bestowed on them Rain/water in abundance." (The Jinn, 72:16)*

It means that hold fast through all your testing so that these blessings and these *faiz*, these dressings can dress upon you. You don't lose the *bayah,* but you lose the emanations and the blessings because you've

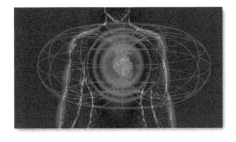

given yourself to the commands and to the whims of *shaitan* until Allah ﷻ if again wants to bless you, guides you. And then we talked before, guidance is like a magnet. And when Allah ﷻ wants the servant to be guided, He puts your polarity and your magnetism to that shaykh. So, who can make somebody a magnet? Allah ﷻ. Who can make your heart to be attracted to that shaykh, that, 'I want to follow that shaykh?' That is only from Allah ﷻ and that is also the reality of love.

You can't force anybody to love you. And you can't be forced to love anyone because Allah ﷻ is the one whom brings that magnetism. If Allah ﷻ sends this magnetism, you find your entire being attracted to

that reality. Every time you make a bad characteristic, the polarity of your magnet is shifting. Right? So, how did we change the polarity in magnetism in school? Because I was really bad in science. You hit the magnet, right? You take a magnet – if you

hit it with an iron rod, you can reverse the polarity of the charge. So, *shaitan's* role is what? Keep hitting us with a bad character until this person that we're attracted to is no longer attraction. Because he hit us, the polarity changed. You're no longer attracted to them; you are actually being repelled. You can't stand the presence of that person. You begin to repel away from them.

Allah's 🕮 *rahmah* (mercy) – one, is that you're guided and He flips the magnet again and brings you back. Because He's not going to let *shaitan* to win. *Shaitan* tests you, make you to 'whooo,' go like that, reverse your polarity. But when Allah 🕮 says, 'You are guided' He reverses it again and you keep coming back, you keep coming back, you keep coming back. By that reality, the testing can occur because if every time you tested the students and they got angry and ran away,  there would be no *tariqah* (spiritual path). But because Allah 🕮 reverses that charge and still makes you to be attracted to them, you keep coming, you keep coming, you keep coming.

And that's why we say the good manners makes Allah 🕮 to always save us, '*Ya Rabbi,* don't let my polarity to leave and all of a sudden, I repel and I walk away.' If you walk away from the shaykh, you walk away from  Sayyidina Muhammad 🕮. You walk away from all the *tariqah.* If *shaitan* lets us to come in and start exhibiting crazy characteristics, you'll be repelled from everything and just out, adrift in the abyss of nowhere. So, it means faith is something delicate and Allah 🕮 has to continuously dress it and bless it, *inshaAllah.*

# Accompanying a Guide and Importance of the Madad

## Can We Be in the Company of the Shaykh All the Time?

You're physically accompanying or spiritually to know? Everyone knows Allah ﷻ is watching them and that Sayyidina Muhammad ﷺ is watching them. The two angels – two eyes on one side, the angel [Shaykh points to right shoulder], two eyes on the other side of angels [Shaykh points to left side]. So, you have four set of eyes, five, six set of eyes of Prophet ﷺ and two angels. And Allah ﷻ above them watching. And no doubt if you have belief in the shaykhs, and the *nazar* (gaze) of the shaykhs, and the *arwah* (soul) of the shaykh is watching. And it's not something that can be understood. That, you know, to think through your mind, but their vision is not like the physical vision.

That when they get an email that something is happening, they can direct their *nazar* (gaze) into what's happening for the servant. That Allah ﷻ send an announcement into their hearts that there is a situation happening. At that time, they can make a *nazar* to find what's going on. Other than that, Allah ﷻ has attached their soul to the soul of that student and that is not something difficult.

The soul and the light can be in infinite amounts of places. And we said that's how they would teach before. All of this technology – they darken the room, put a box, and put a candle. As soon as you make a hole in the box, the light will escape from the candle in one direction. If you put a hundred holes for the hundred students, turn off the light, a hundred lights will come out. Because light is not a form, it's a wave. That light wave will go through every hole, out. That was to show the soul can be wherever Allah 'ﷻ wants the soul to be. Their soul can accompany the student wherever Allah 'ﷻ wants the soul to be.

Now all that information, is it coming to the shaykh? No. It's going through a processor to his soul. His soul is not in need of giving that information to the body. That is an information overload. No need, 'He had a hamburger, he had fries. He walked down the street. He had this, he had that.' That information is not necessary. What information comes to the body is when something is important happening. And *awliyaullah* (saints) teach that at least three times a day, the *nazar* of these *awliya* – can be from any of the Grandshaykhs of the Naqshbandi Golden Chain – are watching over the students. When their *nazar* comes, when their vision comes onto the student to raise the student with their *faiz* (downpouring blessings). This means when we say *nazar* in the spiritual world of light, that when they direct their light onto your soul, this is what is the *haqqaiq* (realities) of the *faiz*.

The *faiz* and emanation that begin to dress from them. Why? This is how they give their gift that Allah ﷻ gave to them. When you go to a wealthy person, if you come to their home, they give you a gift, especially if they are generous. As much as you come, they give you, they give you. You never go away empty handed. Imagine then the generosity of the heavens where they are asking Allah ﷻ, 'What You gave of my soul, what am I going to do with it here for myself?' It's not like a bank here where you're going to go cash it in.

The reason Allah ﷻ gave to them was to be of service. So, they are saying, '*Ya Rabbi,* can I give from my soul onto this servant?' As soon as they are going to put their *nazar* onto the *insan* (human being), it's the *tajalli* of *jalali*. It's a majestic *tajalli* (manifestation) in which the energy, when it comes into the room, most likely you begin to argue and fight and yell and scream. At that time, you should know their *nazar* is on you. Their *nazar* caused that, understand?

If they look at you in a 'smiley' way, you feel so happy, you start to cry. It's a different *tajalli,* right? If Prophet ﷺ is looking at you, and you're doing something good, or making *salawats* (praises upon Prophet Muhammad ﷺ), you start to cry. You say, 'I don't know why I'm crying.' Because Prophet ﷺ is looking. And he is looking with the *jamali,* a beatific *tajalli* that dresses the

soul in which it remembers everything it did wrong, and the love that it has for Divine Presence, and the soul begins to cry. But the *tajalli* that raises you is the one that crushes you. It's like a fire on your rocket. It comes and hits you to lift you up because they want to lift through

121

difficulty. So, that *tajalli* comes and the person is going to, most likely, some sort of event is happening where it's going to be a fight. There is going to be an argument. How much can you control it? How much can you use your tools? How much you remember? 'My shaykh is looking right now. I'm just going to cool down. Hold it, hold it, hold it.' And then he's lifting you, lifting you, lifting you, lifting you. You didn't explode. You got to where he wanted you to get. And now, he'll lift you up and leave you at that place and give you *jamali*. You can have your donut at that time or something sweet, right? Because you have to have something sweet after difficulty. After every difficulty, you put something sweet so the *nafs* (ego) is going to be, you know, leave you alone. And that way, you can have a more blissful state at that time, *inshaAllah*.

**What is the Power of the Shaykh's Nazar (Gaze)?**

The *nazar* (gaze) of *awliyaullah* (saints) is a gentle breeze. And better to talk in reference to Allah 'ﷻ and Sayyidina Muhammad ﷺ. That when the gaze of Prophet ﷺ, by his *awliyaullah* is going to come into our lives, they say three times a day, they'll be looking into our lives. When they come with that *nazar*, it's a *jalali*, not *jamali*. So, when someone says, 'Oh, it's like so  beautiful, the breeze. The birds were all coming.' No, that was not what they were talking about.

122

The *nazar* of Prophet ﷺ coming, by command of Prophet ﷺ, the *awliyaullah* look with their *tajalli*, it become *jalali*. That's usually when the energy hits and you're sort of exploding. You're having some sort of a reaction because the *jalali* and might. When the energy of might enters into an area, it begins to attack every type of falsehood. So, that's usually when we're yelling and screaming, and getting angry, and arguing.

That's when they're watching. And that's why the teaching is 'Walk away. Wash. Go wash yourself.' Walk away because it's only your grave that you have to worry about, not anyone else. And you learn your training, you stay quiet, you walk away, you go do your washing because, 'My shaykh is watching me now.' And the other one wants to yell and scream and do everything. Then the shaykh is also watching them and they're being marked down.

So, that's important in the *nazar* (gaze) and to always think that when I'm meditating and contemplating, then I'm bringing the light of the shaykh to be with me and to continuously accompany me. *"Ittaqollaha wa kono ma'as sadiqeen"* Have a consciousness of Allah ﷻ. And *taqwa* (consciousness) is really the opening of all your five senses and accompany the truthful servants.

123

يَا أَيُّهَا الَّذِينَ آمَنُوا اتَّقُوا اللَّهَ وَكُونُوا مَعَ الصَّادِقِينَ ﴿١١٩﴾

*9:119 – "Ya ayyuhal ladheena amanoo ittaqollaha wa kono ma'as sadiqeen." (Surat At-Tawbah)*

*"O you who have believed, have consciousness of Allah and be with those who are truthful/Pious/sincere (in words and deed)."*
*(The Repentance, 9:119)*

And Allah ﷻ doesn't care for *dunya* (material world). So, it means that in our world of light, we should always be accompanying them. So, it's not something we do only once a year when we go to visit them, but that was the whole concept of the *muraqabah* (spiritual connection). It's that to bring their light into my life and to always be with that light. And that, from these talks in the last few nights, is we said that, 'We found Allah ﷻ' and everything is now reflective reality.

When Allah ﷻ wanted to be found, we were searching in Islam and we came to *La ilaha illAllah.* Leave everything but Allah ﷻ and make the *zikr* (Divine remembrance) of Allah ﷻ and in this journey for the love of Allah ﷻ, Allah ﷻ introduced us to Sayyidina Muhammad ﷺ and put within our hearts Muhammadun RasulAllah ﷺ.

لَا إِلَهَ إِلاَّ اللهُ مُحَمَّدًا رَسُولُ الله

*"La ilaha illallahu Muhammadun Rasulallah."*

*"There is no deity but Allah, Prophet Muhammad is the messenger of Allah."*

When Allah ﷻ loves the servant and guides the servant, He puts a love in their heart for where He is. Like hide and go seek, 'I'm here.' He doesn't want two hearts where you'll be searching, you know, from here to the moon. Allah ﷻ keep inspiring within our hearts, 'I'm here.' And then we begin to love Prophet ﷺ more and more and more, and realize that Allah ﷻ is a hidden treasure within the soul of Prophet ﷺ.

كُنْت كَنْزاً مخفيا فَأَحْبَبْت أَنْ أُعْرَفَ؛ فَخَلَقْت خَلْقاً فَعَرَّفْتهمْ بِي فَعَرَفُونِي

*"Kuntu kanzan makhfiyya, fa ahbabtu an a'rafa, fa khalaqtu khalqan, fa 'arraftahum bi fa 'arafonee."* (Hadith Qudsi)

*Allah said, "I was a hidden Treasure then I desired to be known, so I created a creation to which I made Myself known; then they knew Me."*

Now that reflects back out because, *"Atiullaha wa atiur Rasula wa Ulil amre minkum."*

﴿٥٩﴾ ...أَطِيعُوا اللَّه وَأَطِيعُوا الرَّسُولَ وَأُوْلِي الْأَمْرِ مِنْكُمْ...

4:59 – *"...Atiullaha wa atiur Rasula wa Ulil amre minkum..."* (Surat An-Nisa)

*"...Obey Allah, Obey the Messenger, and those in authority among you..." (The Women, 4:59)*

So, then the *ulul amr* (saints) who are *ahbab* and lovers, they're also are the secret of Sayyidina Muhammad ﷺ. Where Prophet ﷺ is saying, 'I'm a treasure and I want to be known. Have you found me yet?' So, when you come and say, 'Yeah, I want to see Prophet ﷺ. I want to see Prophet ﷺ. I want to go to Madina. I want to do all these things.' But that was like at the first stage.

When the one keeps saying, 'I want to be with Allah ﷻ. I want to make *zikr* of Allah ﷻ. I want to see Allah ﷻ. I want all these things.' Allah ﷻ asks, 'But did you see Me? When you're asking for Me, you should have seen Me in Sayyidina Muhammad ﷺ.' And the clever one realizes, 'Oh my, *ya Latif, ya...* I found you.' All these expressions of love and beauty and tears and passion, that's all the light of Allah ﷻ in Sayyidina Muhammad ﷺ.

So, the same in the reflection of Prophet ﷺ. Where Prophet ﷺ comes to you and says that 'You're yearning so much. You're from these people of *ahbab* (lovers), like the flame.' We said, 'You're the moth who's gathering around all these flames. Don't you see me in them? What makes them to be beatific to you, is me.' Prophet's ﷺ talking to us. 'Why

you enjoy their company? It's me.' Don't give that person the credit. It's the reflection of Prophet ﷺ that coming out.

That's why the *tariqah* (spiritual path) is all about *adab* (manners). That when you give, you're giving to the hand of Prophet ﷺ. When you do and you serve, you're serving to the lovers of Sayyidina Muhammad ﷺ who are manifesting that love for you. That you should be able to see Prophet ﷺ through their face, through their actions and through their kindness, through their gestures and though their entire *akhlaaq* (character) on how they deal with you.

So much so, that if you're good and clever and sincere, you may have dreams as if you're eating with Prophet ﷺ. And it becomes like a reminder of when you're eating with your shaykh. And Prophet ﷺ, 'Yes, I'm with you. When you're eating, I'm there with you. You're eating with me. You are praying with me. You are fasting with me. You are struggling with me.' Because what makes that one to be attractive to you is he carries the light of Sayyidina Muhammad ﷺ. It's not the one from his mother. That one died a long time ago. What he represents and what these *awliya* (saints) represent is the love of Sayyidina Muhammad ﷺ. *Nurul anwar* (light of every secret), there are *Muhammadiyoon* lights that are flowing from them. That's what attracts humanity.

They are the roses from the garden of Sayyidina Muhammad ﷺ. And then Prophet ﷺ will ask you, 'Don't you see me? Don't you feel me? Don't you feel that expression of love?' And then the clever ones whom are

reaching to be *awliya* (saints) say, 'Yes, I found you. And when I found you, I did everything to treat that one as if it was you.' And that's why

127

it's such a big *ghunah* (sin) for shaykhs to do something bad and even

someone who's a shaykh in training. You're abusing the power and the light of Sayyidina Muhammad ﷺ. When that love fills you and the light of Prophet ﷺ emanating from your ears and from your eyes and from your breath and from your tongue – people like you, attracted to you, have a magnetism to you not because of you. You are merely just a mirror, but what's reflecting through you. So, get out of the way and let the reflection dress to people, not to take it as an abuse for yourself.

So, it's not the same. The sin of a common man is not the same as the sin of a shaykh where you just forgive the faults. No, they were representing a Muhammadan reality. And based on that reality, people are attracted and love them. They're held to a much more higher standard and their punishment from Allah ﷻ is much more severe. So, it's a responsibility for those whom taking that path. That that light that coming, that love that coming – not simple *istighfar* (seeking forgiveness), I'm sorry. Allah's ﷻ going to punish severely. It's a responsibility that this *Nurul Muhammadi* ﷺ (Light of Prophet ﷺ) when it begins to reflect out to people. Then Prophet ﷺ asks, 'Don't you see me in them? Don't you

feel me in their companionship? Don't you feel that light and that love in the expression of their love in their hearts?'

That's *tariqah* (spiritual path). It means everything that they're teaching about the reality towards Allah ﷻ, it reflects in our understanding of the reality of Sayyidina Muhammad ﷺ. And then Prophet ﷺ becomes so much more accessible. You don't have to have a ticket to go to Madina. You find one of these *Muhammadiyoon* and accompany them. Be with them, love them, and every day should be a Madina for you.

And when Prophet ﷺ calls you to Madina, 10,000 times more powerful. Because you trained, you trained with that love, you trained with that

respect, you trained with all that character. That's what *tariqah* (spiritual path) comes to teach. That's why it's a school of manners and not a school of *fiqh* (Islamic jurisprudence). Because manners. Why? Because Prophet ﷺ is present there and how are you going to conduct yourself in the presence of Sayyidina Muhammad's ﷺ light?

*InshaAllah.* And to each *wali* (saint) and to each *awliya*, their *darajahs* (spiritual ranks) and those whom love them, their *darajah*. All of them carrying that love of Sayyidina Muhammad ﷺ, *inshaAllah.*

## How Can We Keep a Constant Connection to the Shaykh?

*InshaAllah,* that we're human and that we're very weak. And Prophet ﷺ was praying, 'Don't leave me for the blink of an eye.'

اللَّهُمَّ لَا تَكِلْنِي إِلَى نَفْسِي طَرْفَةَ عَيْنٍ وَلَا أَقَلَّ مِنْ ذَلِكَ

*"Allahumma laa takilnee ila nafsee tarfat 'aynin wa laa aqala min dhalika."*

*"O Allah! Don't leave me to my ego for the blink of an eye or less."*
*(Prophet Muhammad (pbuh))*

If Prophet ﷺ is saying not for like a fraction of a second to leave me under my *nafs* (ego), then of course we're completely lost under the *nafs*. We're 90% under our *nafs*. There are very few people who can reach to not be under the influence of their *nafs*. And then to be in the *hudur* (presence) of their shaykh, to be in the *fana* (annihilation) and the *muhabbat* (love) of their shaykh. The *hudur* and then the *fana* of the shaykh, these are levels of *awliya* (saints). So, that's not easily achieved.

But we took a path in which to keep trying, keep trying, keep trying, and that Allah ﷻ open. So, it's a matter of we put in the struggle, Allah ﷻ declares the victory, but not to think we're ever going to be victorious. It's like an ocean. We're just sort of struggling in this ocean waiting for Allah's ﷻ victory to come. Now they should be more encouraged because looks like the whole world is collapsing, so victory should be very close.

## Is It Too Late to Build a Strong Connection?

No, Allah's ﷻ reason for difficulty is to bring people. Because this is really not that difficult, this is just the beginning. So, Allah's ﷻ shaking

up the Earth and taking away all these distractions. We see everything crumbling. We see that whatever people were running after thinking everything would be abundant, everything would be great, they're running for toilet paper. So, then it makes everybody think, 'What was I running for?' And those whom Allah ﷻ guides, they have been guided. Whom Allah ﷻ has not guided, all my talking in the world and anyone else talking is for their entertainment purposes.

...وَقَالُوا الْحَمْدُ لِلَّهِ الَّذِي هَدَانَا لِهَٰذَا وَمَا كُنَّا لِنَهْتَدِيَ لَوْلَا أَنْ هَدَانَا اللَّـهُ ۖ لَقَدْ جَاءَتْ رُسُلُ رَبِّنَا بِالْحَقِّ...﴿٤٣﴾

*7:43 – "...Wa qalo Alhamdulillahi al ladhee hadana lihadha wa ma kunna linahtadiya lawla an hadana Allahu, laqad jaa at Rusulu Rabbina bil Haqqi..." (Surat Al-A'raf)*

*"... And they will say, Praise be to Allah, who has guided us to this [joy and happiness]; and we would never have been guided if Allah had not guided us. Certainly the messengers of our Lord had come with the truth..." (The Heights, 7:43)*

If Allah's ﷻ guiding, then the person will begin to see the *isharat* and the signs, that, 'Oh my God everything is collapsing. Maybe it's time that I should really make that connection.' Any type of spiritual connection has a spiritual umbrella. As soon as you make the *madad* (support) and the understanding of the *madad* is that, *"La ilaha illa anta Subhanaka, innee kuntu minazh zhalimeen."*

131

﴾٨٧﴿ لَّا إِلَٰهَ إِلَّا أَنتَ سُبْحَانَكَ إِنِّي كُنتُ مِنَ الظَّالِمِينَ ...

*21:87 – "...La ilaha illa anta Subhanaka, innee kuntu minazh zhalimeen." (Surat Al-Anbiya)*

*"...There is no god/diety except You; Glory to you: Indeed I have been of the wrongdoers/Oppressor to Myself!" (The Prophets, 21:87)*

I admitted to myself that, 'Ya Rabbi, You're the Supreme, and I'm an oppressor.' If I'm an oppressor I have no ability to protect myself, I have no ability to protect my children. And that's why Prophet ﷺ wanted you to be married. Because when you're single and by yourself, you probably don't care for other people. You're worried about yourself. You say, 'Oh, I grab my  backpack and I go.' Poor people who have children. Their only thought is that if some harm comes to me okay, I'm going to go. But what about my children? Who's going to take care of them? Who's going to feed them? Who's going to keep the oppressors away from my wife and kids? If you don't feel like that, something's already wrong with you.

 And if you do feel like that, then that was the motivating factor. 'Ya Rabbi, I don't know how I'm going to do any of this.' Then they began to cry at night and meditate at night. And that's why the shaykhs then taught them, that why you're not go into the presence of *Sultanan Naseera* (Victorious King)?

وَقُل رَّبِّ أَدْخِلْنِي مُدْخَلَ صِدْقٍ وَأَخْرِجْنِي مُخْرَجَ صِدْقٍ وَاجْعَل لِّي مِن لَّدُنكَ سُلْطَانًا نَّصِيرًا ﴿٨٠﴾

*17:80 – "Wa qul Rabbi adkhelni mudkhala Sidqin wa akhrejni mukhraja Sidqin waj'al li min ladunka Sultanan NaSeera."*
*(Surat Al-Isra)*

*"Say: O my Lord! Let my entry be by the Gate of Truth and Honour, and likewise my exit by the Gate of Truth and Honour; and grant me from Your Presence a Victorious King to aid (me)."*
*(The Night Journey, 17:80)*

Why aren't you able to reach to the presence of Sayyidina Muhammad ﷺ? And say, 'I'm begging you, *ya Sayyidi, ya Rasulul Kareem*. My head and my eyes upon your feet. That grant me your satisfaction and sign for me, *Sultanan Naseera*, that I'm reaching to your satisfaction.' And with everything in their life, they motivated themselves for that. What they're teaching is not a hodge-podge of, you know, just making a soup and throwing everything into the pot. Everything they were teaching, breathing practices, *zikr* (Divine remembrance) – everything so that when you understood, you begged at the presence of Sayyidina Muhammad ﷺ.

That everything is collapsing, difficulty everywhere, oppression is everywhere. And yet I'm not able to reach to you in which my heart feels satisfied. Grant me from the authorized king of Allah ﷻ, the *sultan*. That if you sign for me, that you're *rida* and satisfied with me. Your support is upon me and they didn't stop. And that's why then they do *mawlids*, they do *zikrs*. They give, they contribute, they're of service. They're doing everything because they know. And they ask Prophet ﷺ, 'Look

133

upon me.' 'What I want to look upon you for? You're not doing anything.' You just make yourself fat and do nothing for the way. Then Mawlana Shaykh ق gave now a *suhbah*, the real death is not this plague. The real death is whom Allah ﷻ gave a life and he did absolutely nothing with it. You came on this Earth, you made it a little bit dirtier, a little bit angrier, and you left and you're already dead – walking dead. That's why all the teaching. You're just walking, backbiting. You're a walking flesh eater on this Earth.

The real life was the one who woke up and understood, 'I have a purpose, *Ta'zim un Nabi* ﷺ.' My purpose was to glorify the magnificent status of Allah's ﷻ most beloved servant. With my life, with my wealth, with my possessions, with my time, with my breath, with my family, and teach my family that is what I lived on this Earth for. If you don't inherit it, you lost my way. Of whatever I give to you in life, whatever I taught you in life, our life was about *Ta'zim un Nabi* ﷺ (honouring the Prophet ﷺ).

If you really think like that, then your whole life is to be of service. And

do everything you can, so why? That next time we're kissing the holy feet of Prophet ﷺ, you have something in your account. You're not coming with nothing. Say, 'I came. I'm doing everything I possibly can. Give me more. Give me good health. Don't let me to become sick now when I can do so much more. Give me wealth and I can spend in your way. Give me time and I put in your way. Give me an ability, an ability and I put that ability in your way. Just give me something to be of service to you.'

They turn their whole life's focus around and that's what a real shaykh does. Make our focus and everything about them is *Ta'zim un Nabi* ﷺ. Are you doing that now? Are you following a shaykh in which he made your whole life to be about Sayyidina Muhammad ﷺ? That your money is spent in that direction? Your time is spent in that direction? The knowledges that you read were not political books, not books about himself, but about the reality of Sayyidina Muhammad ﷺ? Then *alhamdulillah,* you are guided. Then *tafakkur* and meditation is that door. We're going and begging Prophet ﷺ, 'Please, I see it more.'

We said it before in many calamities, put yourself in the calamity. That they're abusing and what if they come to my door to abuse, '*Ya Sayyidi, ya Rasulul Kareem,* will you answer? Will you answer?' And then they cry every night, begging Prophet ﷺ. And then they're inspired by Allah ﷻ, 'Do something at least so that you have a *hisaab* (account).' Don't you feel shy you've done nothing? And that's why these *rijal* (people of maturity), they have a *himmah* (zeal). They spent everything of what Allah ﷻ gave to them to do

*da'wah* (religious propagation); to go, come do things. They even sacrifice from trying to get more from *dunya* (material world) and they come to be of service. And their only concern is, 'Why no one else serves?'

 Because Allah ﷻ didn't grant them guidance. If everybody served, then the sky would be daylight. But the sky is dark and only a few stars shine. And that's what Allah ﷻ wants. You're a shining star in an ocean of darkness. Nobody wants to serve. If you're the only one serving, congratulations for you. If you're the only one cleaning, brooming and trying to do something good, congratulations for you. You got all of the reward. When many should have been doing, nobody did. Say in the last days, few will represent many. They become, *"fulkil mashhoon."*

وَآيَةٌ لَّهُمْ أَنَّا حَمَلْنَا ذُرِّيَّتَهُمْ فِي الْفُلْكِ الْمَشْحُونِ ﴿٤١﴾

*36:41 – "Wa ayatul lahum anna hamalna dhurriyyatahum fil fulkil mashhooni." (Surat YaSeen)*

*"And a sign for them is that we have carried their atoms/forefathers in the loaded ship." (YaSeen, 36:41)*

What Allah ﷻ will give to their soul of power, of might, of blessings, and knowledges and realities, *alhamdulillah.*

### How Can We Achieve Presence of the Shaykh All the Time?

That's the whole goal. That we go step by step – it is how to make the connection, how to feel, so you will enter from the *muhabbat.* It's the love. You have the love of the association. That this stage of *muhabbat,* it has to be a very clean and respectful love like the love for pious people. So, it is usually denoted with green hearts and regular flowers, nothing to insinuate anything romantic and incorrect.

You keep the love of the shaykh. Then learning how to make the *hudur*

(presence) of the shaykh means that, 'I want to see you and I want to meditate. And I always want to be with you, so that I am always in your presence.' And then based on the good character, the good actions and a daily *muhasabah*. That it's a daily accounting of myself. As much as I am bringing this Muhammadan Light, Allah ﷻ wants us to make an accounting. That if we live with *haq* (truth) and we are doing correct, that light becomes stronger and stronger. Everything that we do of falsehood and incorrect, the light begins to dissipate and go away because that light of Sayyidina Muhammad ﷺ, the truth and falsehood, they don't mix.

وَ قُلْ جَآءَالْحَقُّ وَزَهَقَ الْبَاطِلُ، إِنَّ الْبَاطِلَ كَانَ زَهُوقًا ﴿٨١﴾

*17:81 – "Wa qul jaa alhaqqu wa zahaqal baatil, innal batila kana zahoqa." (Surat Al-Isra)*

*"And say, Truth has come, and falsehood has perished. Indeed falsehood, [by its nature], is ever perishing/ bound to perish."*
*(The Night Journey, 17:81)*

So, it means that every time I try to do good, I feel that light. As soon as I do bad things and bad actions, that light goes. And then the student becomes like *"Thumma amano, thumma kafaro."* One day, they are doing good and they believe, next day they are not doing good and they don't believe. The light goes away.

إِنَّ الَّذِينَ آمَنُوا ثُمَّ كَفَرُوا ثُمَّ آمَنُوا ثُمَّ كَفَرُوا ثُمَّ ازْدَادُوا كُفْرًا لَمْ يَكُنِ اللَّـهُ لِيَغْفِرَ لَهُمْ وَلَا لِيَهْدِيَهُمْ سَبِيلًا ﴿١٣٧﴾

*4:137 – "Innal ladheena amano thumma kafaro thumma amano thumma kafaroo thumma izdado kufran lam yakuni Allahu liyaghfira lahum wa la liyahdiyahum sabeela." (Surat An-Nisa)*

*"Indeed, those who have believed then disbelieved, then believed, then disbelieved, and then increased in disbelief – Allah won't forgive them, nor will He guide them on a path/way." (The Women, 4:137)*

Because Prophet ﷺ doesn't stick with something that is incorrect. So, then as much as we can keep the goodness, good character and that's

why the shaykh teaches you good character. That if you see a shaykh who is yelling and screaming and angry and smoking, and is doing every type of crazy thing, no, he doesn't have the Muhammadan light. Prophet ﷺ never would attach with something incorrect and bad. So, then our whole way is based on how to keep the good character, good manners, *muhabbat* (love), *ihtiram* (respect), keeping the *shari'ah* (Divine Law) to the best of their ability. And that that light of Prophet ﷺ dresses them, blesses them. So, it is about building the energy and keeping the energy. Many people build the energy and they have like a leaking house where it just goes everywhere due to all their bad actions.

## Can the Student Become Annihilated in the Presence of the Shaykh?

Yes, we have a whole article on that. These are high levels of keeping the *muhabbat* and the love for these *awliyaullah* (saints). Going deep into their knowledges and into their practices,
into their *tafakkur* (contemplation) until they are trained on how to keep the *hudur* (presence) of the shaykh. That at every moment, they are trying to keep the *hudur* and the presence of the shaykh upon themselves. And by their good character, their knowledges, their training, they're entering into that *hudur* where the shaykh's replicating his light upon the light of that person. As much as that person goes inside and not coming out to show themselves, the more his light can shine through them.

The more he comes out or she comes out, the less the light of the shaykh will come until they reach a state of *mawt qablil mawt* (death of desires before physical death). When they begin to die and not show themselves, the light of their shaykh is reflecting through them. And the hearing of the shaykh will dress him. The seeing of the shaykh will dress him. The breath of the shaykh will dress him. The hands and the power of the shaykh will dress his hands and his *qadam* and his feet will be under the *madad* and support of the shaykh, and then they become *muqaddam*.

And then they have trained in isolations, they have done all the practices of Rajab and Sha'ban, they've been for seclusion. These are high levels of *muhabbat* (love), *hudur* (presence) and *fana* (annihilation). And they keep that state until the shaykh takes them into seclusion, into the *muhabbat* and the *hudur* and the *fana* of Sayyidina Muhammad ﷺ and then after, *inshaAllah*.

## Can We Receive Guidance From the Shaykh Through Meditation?

The meditation is not for the guidance at that level. That's at a much higher level, you know. That's when your whole cellular network is running. You're talking about the introduction to meditation by connecting your heart, making your *muraqabah* (spiritual connection), and you're doing your *awrad* (daily practices). So, it's already written awrad authorized by the shaykhs and Grandshaykhs. You recite the *awrad*, you make the meditation, you make the *zikr* (Divine remembrance) of Allah ﷻ. Enter into a state in which you can get your heart to feel the energy that's coming,  that the shaykh is in front of you that, 'I'm nothing, I'm nothing.' Make yourself to be in a state of nothing to enter into the *muhabbat* (love) and the *hudur* (presence) and the *fana* (annihilation).

So, it means then all these things that have to be accomplished and then as far as actual guidance, from the articles, from the talks. A lot of the questions that people have are probably already answered before they even ask them. Because the guidance is what comes to your heart is like a signal being sent out. It's their responsibility to begin to sort of answer that signal. So, the  guidance is coming by the sheer amount of talks and lectures, and SoundCloud, and every format imaginable.

Anything specific to a life choice, then they can email the society or the shaykh that they're dealing with. They email and say, 'I have a specific question.' But the guidance is on a day to day. The talk gives us a guidance, 'I shouldn't fight with anyone. I should be following that.' Did you follow that? Because immediately tonight and tomorrow, you'll be in conflict with all sorts of testing. Let's see if you follow that.

**Should We Follow the Guidance Given to Us in Our Dreams?**

 Pay no attention to that. Our understanding from Mawlana Rabbani Alf Thani ق, describes that, 'Don't take a way of focusing on dreams.' Naqshbandiya is more the living guidance. If you rely on dreams because your *nafs* (ego) is big, and you need to be told something when the *zalim* (oppressor) is out of the way. That's what the dream is. It's that the *zalim* had to get out of the way to convey a message to you. So, if you live a life by always trying to get a dream, there is something wrong. And the dreams can be affected by what you eat, what you do,

141

what's the condition of your mind, what's your struggles, and many different factors that can affect that. And that's not important for your guidance.

Your guidance is to come from a living shaykh, in which you can communicate, and then the coordinance are given to you. And as soon as you begin to do your *tafakkur* (contemplation), do your meditation, do all your practices, you should be getting your guidance live flowing through your heart and understanding. You don't have to see everything, just understand from your heart what you need to be doing on a daily basis. If you don't develop that skill, don't practice that skill and keep saying, 'How come I'm not seeing anything, I want a dream, I want a dream,' they close that channel so that you don't do that. They don't want you to take your guidance from dreams.

They want you to build your relationship in the living state, which is a much higher state for information, for guidance, you need it for everything. Imagine if you're trying to help somebody, give guidance to somebody and you say, 'Wait till I take a nap, I'll be back.' How are you going to help somebody? 'No, I need to know, I need to know shaykh,'

'Wait let me take a nap, I'll be back.' No, you should have been able to train yourself to connect your heart and feel what your guidance is coming to your heart, and what you understood. And that can take years and years of practice, and fine tuning your coordinance, not through your own desire and *nafs* upon that guidance.

142

So, no. They don't take any interest in dreams and interpretation. They don't like to hear anybody's dreams. So, there is no need to convey a dream unless you feel something is urgently dangerous that, 'I felt this, and this, and this,' then no problem.

But usually when people convey their dreams, they're trying to show off. 'I saw this, I saw that, I walked on water, I went to the Ka'bah and then I flew around the Ka'bah five times; shaykh what do you think that means?' That means you're trying to show off. Who talks like that, who would tell you what happened and what Allah ﷻ wants to show them? Then they don't disclose that to anyone else, it's something hidden. If Allah ﷻ gave you a good experience, you don't need somebody's *tafsir* (interpretation) on it. So, it can become *nafsani* (egocentric). Then you told it to somebody to make yourself like important to them and to you, diminish the value that was actually sent for you, *inshaAllah*.

## Can You Tell Us About the Muhammadan Government and Shaykh Abdul Qadir Jilani ق?

Shaykh Abdul Qadir ق, *alhamdulillah*, Shahmatul Fardani ق, Abdul Rauf al-Yamani ق, that these are big, big *awliyaullah* (saints). And that their

eternal station is like a pyramid. That they have their *Ghawth*, they have a *Sultanul Awliya* (King of Saints) above, they have *Warith ul Muhammadiya* (Muhammadan Inheritor), they have *Qutub* (Cardinal Pole); they have a whole system of a Muhammadan Government. And these *awliyaullah*, they're shaykhs of the past, and their seat is never vacant. It means their station in *akhirah* (hereafter) is their station. And Allah ﷻ gives them thrones in which that blessing.

143

But on this Earth, there must be living inheritors of that reality. There must be at all times. Can you imagine an Earth with no *Ghawth*? It means that *shaitan* (satan) is in charge of everything? There must be a king on this Earth, on this universe, on this galaxy, every position must be filled.

Whoever sits on this position now, and on this Earth now on, and on their seats now, they must have inherited from these *awliya*. Because this is the gift from these *awliyaullah*, whatever they receive, they give as an inheritance to sitting *awliya*, they receive all the inheritance of the past and they receive everything new coming from the heart of Sayyidina Muhammad ﷺ.

What may have taken years in the past to achieve or for a student to achieve, can be achieved in minutes if not seconds now because of their power, and *izzah* and might. Whatever Allah ﷻ gave to them, whatever Allah ﷻ dressed upon them, when they left the physical confine of this physical Earth imagine then the immensity of their power. They have tremendous power.

Whomever sitting on those positions now in that Muhammadan Government, with all His *Izzah*, and all His Might, they know there is no more time.

In the midst of everyone's paying for apartments and homes, and cars, there is nobody who can do isolation and *khalwah* (seclusion). And now Allah 'ﷻ made the whole world to go into isolation. So, it's very difficult for them to achieve like old times. Now within an instant, in less than an instant they can shoot everybody up into that presence, dress their souls from that reality, and bring them back, and they don't even know what occurred. This is the gift of their souls, are giving. *InshaAllah*.

Sayyidina Abdul Qadir Jilani ق and Sayyidina Ibn Arabi ق have an importance in this Earth. That under the *Wuzara* and the deputies of Sayyidina Mahdi ﷺ. Sayyidina Shahmatul Fardani ق is a secret from Sayyidina Ibn Arabi ق and Abdul Rauf al-Yamani ق is a secret from Sayyidina Abdul Qadir Jilani ق. And when *awliyaullah* want knowledges, they ask from Shahmatul Fardani ق, Ibn Arabi ق from those Divinely Knowledges into

Sayyidina Ibn Arabi (as)   Shaykh Abdul Qadir Jilani (as)

their hearts. So, knowledge was Shahmatul Fardani ق, from *Wuzara* of Sayyidina Mahdi ﷺ. And *izzah* and might, and struggle and fight was Shaykh Abdul Qadir ق, and through the name Abdul Rauf al-Yamani ق, where he's dressing this name of Abdul Rauf al-Yamani ق from an eternal reality of the soul. So, calling upon Sayyidina Mahdi ﷺ and the *Wuzara* of Sayyidina Mahdi ﷺ has an immense dressing and blessing. And that their support and *madad* (support) to be upon us and to dress us, *inshaAllah*.

145

## What is the Naqshbandi Tariqah's Relation to Sayyidina Khidr ﷺ?

Sayyidina Khidr ﷺ is the 11th Shaykh of the Naqshbandi Way. Sayyidina Khidr ﷺ is the connection with *barzakh* (purgatory), with the dimension of the physical reaching over to the oceans of *malakut* (heavens). And that he facilitates for the servant to take them into the oceans of *malakut*. So, it's like a bridge between the *mulk* (earthly realm) and *malakut*. And Sayyidina Khidr ﷺ gives the knowledges and the oceans of *al-hayat* (ever-living) onto the servant. That's when we said that in their studies and in their progress, 'I won't stop until where the two rivers meet.'

وَإِذْ قَالَ مُوسَىٰ لِفَتَاهُ لَا أَبْرَحُ حَتَّىٰ أَبْلُغَ مَجْمَعَ الْبَحْرَيْنِ أَوْ أَمْضِيَ حُقُبًا ﴿٦٠﴾

*18:60 – "Wa idh qala Mosa lefatahu laa abrahu hatta ablugha majma'a albahrayni aw amdiya huquba." (Surat Al-Kahf)*

*"Behold, Moses said to his attendant, I will not give up until I reach the junction of the two seas or (until) I spend years and years in travel." (The Cave, 18:60)*

Those two rivers meet at the point of *hu*, the *hey* of Allah ﷻ to the *waw*, hitting to the *meem* of *Muhammadun Rasulallah* ﷺ. So, in this cave of *hu*, when they are progressing with the love of Sayyidina Muhammad ﷺ, and Prophet ﷺ begins to open for them that reality to reach towards the reality of *La ilaha illAllah*. Because they understood that everything exists within the ocean of *Muhammadun Rasulallah* ﷺ.

لَا إِلَهَ إِلاَّ اللهُ مُحَمَّدًا رَسُولُ الله

*"La ilaha illallahu Muhammadun Rasulallah."*

*"There is no deity but Allah, Prophet Muhammad is the messenger of Allah."*

This means they are *Muhammadiyoon* at that time; they have an immense love for Prophet ﷺ. In this love of Prophet ﷺ, they are seeking out the reality of Allah ﷻ. At that time, Sayyidina Khidr عليه السلام begins to appear to them and begins to teach them the realities of *malakut* and becomes a teacher for them, a source of inspiration into their hearts and has different *maqams* (stations).

He has a *maqam* in Damascus Sharif at the Umayyad Mosque. There is a *maqam* for Sayyidina Khidr عليه السلام, that when they sit in *tafakkur* (contemplation), then a door opens and Sayyidina Khidr عليه السلام appears for them there. And there was that *maqam* in Turkey, when we went to that *masjid* in Turkey, there was a big *waw*. And that was a door for Sayyidina Khidr عليه السلام there. And that mosque was for Sayyidina Mahdi عليه السلام and doing the *Jum'ah* (Friday prayer) at that mosque with Sayyidina Mahdi عليه السلام. So, it means there's many different realities and *tajallis* (manifestations).

But for us is to make your connection with the shaykh, the living shaykh. Make your connection on how to make your *tafakkur* and your contemplation. And then calling the *madad* (support) of the *silsila* (spiritual lineage). All the shaykhs are in there and then everything will open according to how they want it. You don't have to worry about, 'Oh, I didn't know, I should call on this.' You're not supposed to call on anything. You're supposed to do your *madad*, do your practices, make

your connection. They do what is necessary from their side. You don't have to start calling upon Sayyidina Khidr عليه السلام when you didn't even make your connection with your shaykh.

### What is Sayyidina Ali's عليه السلام Importance in Sufism?

Sayyidina Ali عليه السلام, not only in Sufism, it's all of Islam. Its importance is in the *khalifas*. And you have to go back to some of our earlier videos and that's a reality of Prophet ﷺ in Muharram. So, go back into the 'Muharram Videos' and click on 'Muharram' and the 'Secrets of

148

Muharram.' Muharram is the *hijrah* (migration) and the movement and opening the door of Islam. Two events happened in that *hijrah*. One, Imam Ali ؏ laid in the bed and surrendered himself to die because they were coming to kill Prophet ﷺ. And so, he gave himself as a young child, this young boy, 'I'll die, and you continue your message.' That's called chivalry. When you say *"La fata illa Ali,"* that there is no one in the school of chivalry like Imam Ali ؏.

لا فَتى إِلاَّ عَلِى لا سيف، إِلاَّ ذُو الفَقار

*"La fata illa Ali, La saif, illa Zulfiqar."*

*"There is no victory except with Imam 'Ali (as). There is no sword of justice like zulfiqar, the sword of Imam 'Ali (as)."*

So, that example of laying your life for the sake of Prophet's ﷺ mission and this is a *khidmat* (service) beyond any *khidmat*. So much so that Allah ﷻ was asking the angels, 'Look at this young boy, how he's willing to die for

Prophet ﷺ at this young age.' So, it has a tremendous reality.

فِي لَيْلَةِ الْمَبِيتْ أَمِيرْ الْمُؤْمِنِينْ عَلَىٰ فِرَاشِ النَّبِيِّ ﷺ .
أَوْحَىٰ اللهُ عَزَّ وَجَلَّ إِلَىٰ جَبْرَائِيلْ وَمِيكَائِيلَ: أَلَا كُنْتُمَا مِثْلِ عَلِيِّ بْنِ أَبِي طَالِبٍ ؟
آخَيْتُ بَيْنَهُ وَبَيْنَ مُحَمَّدٍ (صلَّى اللهُ عَلَيْهِ وآله) فَبَاتَ عَلَى فِرَاشِهِ يَفْدِيَه بِنَفْسِهِ ،
وَيُؤْثِرُهُ بِالْحَيَاةِ .اهْبِطَا إِلَى الْأَرْضِ فَاحْفَظَهُ مِنْ عَدُوِّهْ۞

*Fi Laylat al Mabeet, Amir al Muminin 'ala ferashi anNabiyi* ﷺ. *Awha Allahu 'Azza wa Jalla ila Jibrayilu wa Mikayilu: "Alla kuntuma mithli 'Aliyi ibn Abi Talib? Akhaytu baynahu wa bayna Muhammadin fabata 'ala firashihi yafdiyah benafsihi, wa yuthiruh bil hayati. Ahbita/ihbeta ilal Ardi fahfazhahu min 'adowwihi.*

*On the night when Amir al Muminin (the Leader of the Believers, Imam 'Ali (as)) slept in the place of the Prophet Muhammad (pbuh), Allah told the angels Jibreel (as) and Mikhayil (as): "Have you seen anyone like 'Ali the son of Abi Talib? The brotherhood between him and Prophet Muhammad (peace be upon him and his family) is as such that Imam 'Ali (as) slept in the place of Prophet Muhammad (pbuh) to sacrifice himself and give his life. Go to the Earth and protect him from the enemies."*

Next part of the *hijrah* was with Sayyidina Abu Bakr as Siddiq ﷺ accompanying Prophet ﷺ to the cave. So, Sufism and *tariqah* (spiritual path) is about this whole relationship. These two companions are coming to teach us how to accompany Sayyidina Muhammad ﷺ because our way, our *tariq* is the way of Prophet ﷺ. That we have to take a life in which we're going to follow Prophet ﷺ. Have a *Siddiqiya* (truthful) character like the 'Friend ﷺ' and the 'Great Friend' of Sayyidina  Muhammad ﷺ. Enter the cave means enter the heart of Prophet ﷺ. Give everything for that love and all that remains in your heart is *"La ilaha illAllah Muhammadun Rasulallah* ﷺ*."*

لَا إِلَهَ إِلاَّ اللهُ مُحَمَّدًا رَسُولُ الله

*"La ilaha illallahu Muhammadun Rasulallah."*

*"There is no deity but Allah, Prophet Muhammad is the messenger of Allah."*

And then every secret that happened within the cave. At the same time, the 'Great Siddiq' that lays within the bed comes to teach us that, if you want to perfect your character, also live a life in which you sacrifice yourself for that reality. That every time you come against a bad character, 'I'll come against it for my love of Sayyidina Muhmmad ﷺ. I'll stay quiet and not argue with this person for the sake of Sayyidina Muhammad ﷺ. I'll take the difficulty of this path for the sake of Sayyidina Muhammad ﷺ.' So, these companions are coming to teach great characteristics, great characteristics. So, the love of the Companions and then love of *Ahlul Bayt* (Holy Family of Prophet ﷺ). You'll inherit a *Siddiqiya* dress if Sayyidina Abu Bakr as Siddiq ؓ destines you to be sincere or deems you to be sincere by order of Allah ﷻ. He'll grant you an inheritance from his companion reality, that you'll be *Siddiqiya* and be dressed with the truthful servanthood dress.

And if your love for Imam Ali ؓ is sincere and following the example of Imam Ali ؓ, he has an option to grant you from his 'Prophetic Family' dress, two different secrets. He can grant you from what Prophet ﷺ granted as his family. And not every companion is authorized to give that, but the family companion is. The one whom is from the family of Sayyidina Muhammad ﷺ can grant you from the Prophetic realities and the secrets of Sayyidina Muhammad ﷺ. Then these two companions are like the moon.

One is the known face of the moon and one is the unknown face of the moon. And the moon is symbolic of guidance. That to be *kamil* and perfected is to be granted from the two realities. The *Siddiqiya* character

that they are truthful in their words and in their actions. And the prophetic inheritance that Prophet ﷺ dressed them of realities and inheritance upon their soul. And these are the *Ulul al Baab* (Gatekeepers of the Reality). That Imam Ali عليه السلام give them a *zulfiqar* and they are owners of the secret of *laam alif.* And they hold the sword and a key to the door of realities when Prophet ﷺ is the reality, the City of All Realities, and Imam Ali عليه السلام is *Baaba Hu,* is the caretaker of the door to that realities.

أَنَا مَدِيْنَةُ الْعِلْمِ وَ عَلِيٌّ بَابُهَا

*"Ana madinatul 'ilmin wa 'Aliyyun baabuha."*

*"I am the city of knowledge and 'Ali (as) is its door/gatekeeper."*
*(Prophet Muhammad (pbuh))*

We pray that Allah ﷻ dress us and bless us from these immense realities, immense characters, immense love. That Allah ﷻ increase our love for all the Holy Companions, all the *Ahlul Bayt* عليهم السلام, all the *awliya* (saints) *fis samayi wa fil ard* (in the heavens and on earth); above all, our love for Allah ﷻ and our love for Sayyidina Muhammad ﷺ.

### How Should We Ask For Madad and Make Rabita (Connection) With the Shaykh?

*Rabitat ash-Sharif* (Noble Connection) is to keep the way of holding the rope. Where Allah ﷻ describes, 'Hold tight to the rope, and *tafarraq.*' Don't make a separation from the rope.'

وَاعْتَصِمُوا بِحَبْلِ اللَّـهِ جَمِيعًا وَلَا تَفَرَّقُوا ۚ ﴿١٠٣﴾

*3:103 – "Wa'tasimo bihab lillahi jamee'an wa la tafarraqo..."*
*(Surat Ali-Imran)*

*"And hold firmly to the rope of Allah all together and do not separate..." (Family of Imran, 3:103)*

It means our life was like a golden chain, not even a rope, is chain yourself to that reality! That *'Ya Rabbi, kono ma'as sadiqeen.'* You said, 'Have a *taqwa* (consciousness) and keep the company of truthful servants.' And I'm with these shaykhs. I'm asking to be under the *rabita*, under their hands and tied to that reality.

يَا أَيُّهَا الَّذِينَ آمَنُوا اتَّقُوا اللَّهَ وَكُونُوا مَعَ الصَّادِقِينَ ﴿١١٩﴾

*9:119 – "Ya ayyuhal ladheena amanoo ittaqollaha wa kono ma'as sadiqeen." (Surat At-Tawbah)*

*"O you who have believed, have consciousness of Allah and be with those who are truthful/Pious/sincere (in words and deed)."*
*(The Repentance, 9:119)*

Then the app we have, and everybody has the different *madad* and support. Asking for the *madad* of the shaykhs, calling upon their names, asking for their *madad*. Visualizing that you're in their association and that always acknowledging *'Ya Rabbi*, I'm a weak servant.' When Allah ﷻ says, "*Wa kono ma'as sadiqeen*." That, 'Have a *taqwa* (consciousness) in life and keep the company of My truthful servants.' Allah ﷻ doesn't care for the material world.

This was not keep a physical company with the shaykh and go have hamburger with him. This was the spiritual company. Is that are you keeping their company spiritually? Are you envisioning that you're always with them? Are you visualizing that they're in front of me? I remember them. I

see them, *ya Rabbi*. Let me to always be in their association. If I can visualize that I'm sitting with them and that I'm making my *zikr* (Divine remembrance), I'm making my *salawat* (praises upon Prophet Muhammad ﷺ), I'm asking to be under their *nazar* (gaze).

This was the order of Allah ﷻ, 'If you truly have a *taqwa* and consciousness.' *Taqwa* means that, 'Are your senses open?' The

*muttaqeen*, whom have a high level of *taqwa* (consciousness) means that Allah ﷻ gave them a *taqwa* on all their senses. That's why Allah ﷻ in that holy *ayah* (verse) is saying *"Ittaqollah"* because these are *muttaqeen*. That their *taqwa*, they have a fear in their ears not to lose their connection with Allah ﷻ. As soon as they're listening to something wrong, their heart begins to beat, 'Something is not right!' Allah ﷻ is warning them, 'You're going to lose My hearing!'

If they – *muttaqeen* – if they have eyes that are conscious. They're not looking at everything *haram* (forbidden). And Allah ﷻ says, 'I'm about  to shut off your vision and it's going to take a long time for you to bring it back.' They took a life in which to '*Astaghfirullah* (seek forgiveness from Allah ﷻ) [Shaykh closes eyes and looks down]. They close that vision from what they're looking at. And they keep their vision into their heart and down where *shaitan* (satan) is now playing with all of them. *Shaitan* want to bombard your ears with every type of horrific sound, bombard your eyes with every type of horrific vision to block so that you never become *muttaqeen* (those with high level of consciousness).

If their hearing has been perfected, their seeing is being perfected, Allah ﷻ perfect their breathing in which they breathe with a *qudra* (power). And an energy perfects their hands and their senses, their feet and their *qadam*. Then Allah ﷻ from the holy *Hadith* that we were talking the other week is then, 'I'll be the tongue in which you speak.'

...وَلَا يَزَالُ عَبْدِي يَتَقَرَّبُ إِلَيَّ بِالنَّوَافِلِ حَتَّى أُحِبَّهُ، فَإِذَا أَحْبَبْتُهُ كُنْت سَمْعَهُ الَّذِي يَسْمَعُ بِهِ، وَبَصَرَهُ الَّذِي يُبْصِرُ بِهِ، وَيَدَهُ الَّتِي يَبْطِشُ بِهَا، وَرِجْلَهُ الَّتِي يَمْشِي بِهَا، وَلَئِنْ سَأَلَنِي لَأُعْطِيَنَّهُ،. [ رَوَاهُ الْبُخَارِي]

"..., *Wa la yazaalu 'Abdi yataqarrabu ilayya bin nawafile hatta ahebahu, fa idha ahbabtuhu kunta Sam'ahul ladhi yasma'u behi, wa Basarahul ladhi yubsiru behi, wa Yadahul lati yabTeshu beha, wa Rejlahul lati yamshi beha, wa la in sa alani la a'Teyannahu, ...*"

*"...My servant continues to draw near to Me with voluntary acts of worship so that I shall love him. When I love him, I am his hearing with which he hears, his seeing with which he sees, his hand with which he strikes and his foot with which he walks. Were he to ask [something] of Me, I would surely give it to him..."*
Hadith Qudsi (Sahih al-Bukhari, 81:38:2)

And at that time, Allah's ﷻ Might and *Izzah*, the *nazar* (gaze) and *izzah* of Prophet ﷺ is moving upon their tongue. Their tongue can revive the dead. It's not a tongue that entertains the brain. That's when you go to school and the professor, he talks, he can make the whole room to sleep in five seconds. Because he talks complete nonsense. He may not even understand what he's talking about. Brain to brain will shut off everybody's head, right?

So, if you talk from the heart, it's an energy that immediately hits the heart and people come to life. Their energy is now vibrating within their  being. As soon as their body goes out of the way, they will ask Allah ﷻ tonight, 'What I heard from Your servant, let me to swim in that ocean and that reality.' And Allah ﷻ says' You heard it? Then swim in it.' The ocean is free to enter. There is no fee. There is no money for these courses. Allah's ﷻ way is free. Allah's ﷻ knowledges are free. Only thing Allah ﷻ is that have you been given the grant in which to hear it? Because Allah ﷻ says 'I allow My name to be mentioned in their home.'

فِي بُيُوتٍ أَذِنَ اللَّـهُ أَن تُرْفَعَ وَيُذْكَرَ فِيهَا اسْمُهُ يُسَبِّحُ لَهُ فِيهَا بِالْغُدُوِّ وَالْآصَالِ ﴿٣٦﴾

*24:36 – "Fee buyotin adhina Allahu an turfa'a wa yudhkara feeha ismuhu yusabbihu lahu feeha bilghuduwwi wal asal." (Surat An-Nur)*

*"(Lit is such a Light) in houses, which Allah has permitted to be raised to honour; and that His name be mentioned therein: In them He is glorified in the mornings and in the evenings, (again and again)."*
*(The Light, 24:36)*

Allah ﷻ has to allow His name to be mentioned in your heart. Because His home is where? *"Qalb mu'min baitullah."*

قَلْبَ الْمُؤْمِنْ بَيْتُ الرَّبْ

*"Qalb al mu'min baytur rabb."*

*"The heart of the believer is the House of the Lord."* (Hadith Qudsi)

So, it's a *ni'mat* (blessing), it's a grant. Don't take what Allah ﷻ gives as a grant and as a favour and say, 'I can always go to *zikr.*' No, because if Allah ﷻ gets tired of you He says, 'No, tomorrow your name will not be mentioned in my heart, in My house.' It's a

gift from Allah ﷻ. I allow, in Surah Nur, 'I allow my name to be mentioned in their homes.' (Holy Qur'an, 24:36) So, it means this is a gift from Allah ﷻ. We keep it, we nourish it, we safeguard it. And then Allah ﷻ says 'Since you have an *ihtiram* (respect) and respect for My name, you cherish it. The ability to come and do your *zikr*, to mention My name, I begin to release the power of My name.' Then they do their *zikrs*, they do their *awrads* (daily practices), they do all their practices, *inshaAllah.*

## Why is the Concept of Madad Important?

Let's put it this way. The *madad* is important. The *madad* – if Allah ﷻ give to a servant an opening – without *madad*, the servant is *fir'aun* (pharaoh). So, it means that if Allah ﷻ open to a servant reality and that servant is not trained in the whole *aqidah* (belief) of *madad*, they are *fir'aun*.

So, then Allah ﷻ describes these servants of this *haqqaiq* (realities), and Sayyidina Khidr ﷺ is the 11th Shaykh of the Naqshbandi Golden Chain, who his *madad* reaches to us. That Sayyidina Khidr's ﷺ example was for Nabi Musa ﷺ who wanted to reach a reality that was a Muhammadan *haqqaiq*. He told him go to one of our servants who attained a *rahmah*, attained a mercy and then we taught him. So, it means he attained his mercy and then we taught him knowledges.

فَوَجَدَا عَبْدًا مِّنْ عِبَادِنَا آتَيْنَاهُ رَحْمَةً مِّنْ عِندِنَا وَعَلَّمْنَاهُ مِن لَّدُنَّا عِلْمًا ﴿٦٥﴾

*18:65 – "Fawajada 'abdan min 'ibadinaa ataynahu rahmatan min 'indina wa 'allamnahu mil ladunna 'ilma." (Surat Al-Kahf)*

*"So they found one of Our servant from among Our servants, on whom We had bestowed Mercy from Ourselves and whom We had taught [unseen/heavenly] knowledge from Our own Presence..." (The Cave, 18:65)*

So, it means anyone whom goes to a school and learns knowledges and thinks that because of their knowledge they don't need *madad*, they don't need a shaykh, they don't need anything. 'I know, I'm *hafiz* (one who memorized Qur'an), I did this' – they became a *zalim* (oppressor) and they became a *fir'aun* because they think they achieved something on their own.

The concept that Allah ﷻ wants from this servant is that this servant attained a *rahmah*. How do you attain a *rahmah*? It's not an *ilm* (knowledge); how did you attain a mercy? It's by Allah ﷻ crushing. Allah ﷻ sending through *tarbiyah* (discipline), Allah ﷻ sending through difficulty these servants. What type of difficulty Sayyidina Khidr ﷺ had to endure to find that fountain of realities? What type of difficulty was put upon and crushing, and what type of system of crushing and crushing and crushing until the servant gives up. Says, '*Ya Rabbi*, I think I'm going to die on this path.'

Many times, they would go through jungles and deserts and oceans and rivers to reach to something. We said before they would sit in isolation and tell you that they're going to sit in a jungle and do *khalwah* (seclusion). You think, 'Oh! This must be very easy. Just put your chair and go in the jungle.' We said, 'Put your chair in the backyard and see if you last a half an hour.' Allah ﷻ will send every bug in this backyard up the chair and into your ears, your nose, your eyes. If you go sit out there, Allah's ﷻ not leaving you alone to sit out there. He's going to make all that creation come after you and to see your level of *taslim* (submission).

Shaykh Abdullah Faiz ad Daghestani ق,
with the beatific character, five years
ordered into seclusion. The first minute
arriving he says, 'A snake appeared and
wrapped himself all around me with a face
right at my face. And my Shaykh
whispering in my ear, 'If you focus on this
snake, he will kill you in this *khalwah*
(seclusion). You'll be dead.' He said, 'For
40 days I prayed.' We have the Naqshbandi
book of all the Grandshaykhs online. You
can listen to the audio book, very beautiful.

Shaykh Daghestani's ق life – amazing. Listen to these and then make
your *tafakkur* (contemplation) and say now that, 'You're my beloved
grandfather.' Anyone listening to us is Naqshbandi. Anyone
Naqshbandi, these are your grandfathers. Not only your baba and mama
who brought you here. Your spiritual grandparents that they're sending
their inheritance of Naqshbandiya to you. Listen to your grandparents,
their life stories and meditate. The snake facing the face and for 40 days
praying and every time I make *sujood* (prostration, this snake would
move. I'd go back up in my worshipness. It means what type of difficulty
put upon the servant until the presence of Sayyidina Muhammad ﷺ.

That's what we just described. You're crushed and go down. Who begins
to appear? *"Wa maa arsalnaaka illaa rahmatal lil'aalameen."*

وَمَا أَرْسَلْنَاكَ إِلَّا رَحْمَةً لِّلْعَالَمِينَ ﴿١٠٧﴾

*21:107 – "Wa maa arsalnaka illa Rahmatal lil'alameen."*
*(Surat Al-Anbiya)*

*"And We have not sent you, [O Muhammad (pbuh)], except as a mercy
to the worlds/creation." (The Prophets, 21:107)*

When attaining a *rahmah* is what? It's that you attained the presence of Sayyidina Muhammad ﷺ. That holy presence of Sayyidina Muhammad ﷺ is what makes you to be sweet. *Khuluqal azheem*, give you the best and the most magnificent of character.

وَإِنَّكَ لَعَلَىٰ خُلُقٍ عَظِيمٍ ﴿٤﴾

68:4 – *"Wa innaka la'ala khuluqin 'azheem." (Surat Al-Qalam)*

*"Truly, You (O Muhammad!) are of a magnificent character."*
*(The Pen, 68:4)*

Because the one whom had the best character is the one who's teaching ﷺ. So, they have a beatific character. Then Allah ﷻ, *"Ittaqullah wa 'aleemukum Allah."*

...وَاتَّقُوا اللَّـهَ ۖ وَيُعَلِّمُكُمُ اللَّـهُ ۗ وَاللَّـهُ بِكُلِّ شَيْءٍ عَلِيمٌ ﴿٢٨٢﴾

2:282 – *"...Wat taqollaha, wa yu'allimukumullahu, wallahu bi kulli shayin 'Aleem." (Surat Al-Baqarah)*

*"...And Be conscious of/Fear Allah, And Allah teaches you. And Allah is the All-Knower of everything." (The Cow, 2:282)*

That they have such a consciousness, such a beauty in Allah's ﷻ presence because of the presence of Sayyidina Muhammad ﷺ. Then every knowledge opens into that servant's heart. The treasure of Allah ﷻ is the soul of Prophet ﷺ. If Prophet ﷺ is accompanying you, and Allah ﷻ happy with you, *uloom ul-awaleen wa 'l-akhireen* (knowledges of the beginning and the end) is dressing upon your tongue because it's not you. It's the tongue of Sayyidina Muhammad ﷺ that's using you as a vehicle to address his audience and those whom love him. So, the *madad* is everything.

## Do Our Senses in the Heavenly Realm Show We Have Little Control Over Ourselves?

It is not something that can be understood and it's not your soul that has any ability. Your soul is merely a drop in the reality of the soul of Sayyidina Muhammad ﷺ. That's the holy *Hadith al-Qudsi*. That they did their *fard* (obligatory worship), they came to me with voluntary worship, I became their hearing.

...وَلَا يَزَالُ عَبْدِي يَتَقَرَّبُ إِلَيَّ بِالنَّوَافِلِ حَتَّى أُحِبَّهُ، فَإِذَا أَحْبَبْتُهُ كُنْتَ سَمْعَهُ الَّذِي يَسْمَعُ بِهِ، وَبَصَرَهُ الَّذِي يُبْصِرُ بِهِ، وَيَدَهُ الَّتِي يَبْطِشُ بِهَا، وَرِجْلَهُ الَّتِي يَمْشِي بِهَا، وَلَئِنْ سَأَلَنِي لَأُعْطِيَنَّهُ." [ رَوَاهُ الْبُخَارِيُّ]

*"... Wa la yazaalu 'Abdi yataqarrabu ilayya bin nawafile hatta ahebahu, fa idha ahhabtuhu kunta Sam'ahul ladhi yasma'u behi, wa Basarahul ladhi yubsiru behi, wa Yadahul lati yabTeshu beha, wa Rejlahul lati yamshi beha, wa la in sa alani la a'Teyannahu..."*

*"...My servant continues to draw near to Me with voluntary acts of worship so that I shall love him. When I love him, I am his hearing with which he hears, his seeing with which he sees, his hand with which he*

*strikes and his foot with which he walks. Were he to ask [something] of*
*Me, I would surely give it to him…"*
*(Hadith Qudsi, Sahih al-Bukhari, 81:38:2)*

If Allah's ﷻ your hearing, there's no limitation on your soul's hearing.
Then I became your seeing. So, what they can see is far beyond anything
you can imagine. They can see to the depth of your body. They can see
on the street everything that will happen on Judgement Day as what this
street looks like on Judgement Day. And they can see into the seven
heavens and into the presence of Sayyidina Muhammad ﷺ because it's
not your soul's seeing.

It's *Hadith al-Qudsi* that Allah ﷻ
describing upon Prophet ﷺ, 'I
will be your seeing.' Is there a
limitation on Allah's ﷻ seeing? I'll
be the tongue in which you speak.
Is there a limitation on what that
tongue can speak? There's
*darajahs* (spiritual ranks), how
much Allah ﷻ going to be on
their tongue? How much Allah ﷻ

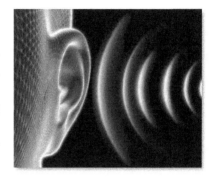

going to be on their hearing? Based on how well they heard and how
well their *dunya* (material world) went down and their *malakut* dressed
their hearing.

So, every binary code on all of these faculties. That's why we started with
the Ramadan. How is the binary code of your hearing? If your hearing
is strong in *dunya*, but you don't hear anything from *malakut* (heavenly
realm), so means what? Then you're going to fast with this ear. I don't
want to hear this music; I don't want to hear these things. So, that this
one become like a *nuqt* (dot). When the ears are clean, when the ears did
their *siyam* and their fasting, what type of inspiration going to start to
hear? It's going to hear now the inspiration of *malakut* (heavenly realm).

163

So, the same for the fasting of the eyes. If the eyes are looking at everything, looking at everyone, looking at everything forbidden and not *halal* (permissible) for you. Even the *halal* for you not to be looked at. Then the eye becomes to fast and fast and fast in which they don't care for the *dunya* (material world) anymore. The *zikrs* (Divine remembrance)

for them is like a time of death. They can enter in and feel like they died and go back into heaven. This eye becomes nothing. The eye of your soul becomes from that reality where Allah ﷻ say, 'I'm the seeing in which you see. I'm the tongue in which you speak. I'm the hand in which you touch.'

What kind of hand is that that this person would have that Allah's ﷻ hand is upon their hand? Hand of Sayyidina Muhammad ﷺ is upon their hand. That what Allah ﷻ gave to their hand – the whole control of *mulk* (earthly realm).

تَبَارَكَ الَّذِي بِيَدِهِ الْمُلْكُ وَهُوَ عَلَى كُلِّ شَيْءٍ قَدِيرٌ ﴿١﴾

*67:1 – "Tabarakal ladhee biyadihil mulku wa huwa 'ala kulli shay in qadeer."*
*(Surat Al-Mulk)*

*"Blessed is He in Whose hands is Dominion/kingdom; and He has Power over all things." (The Sovereignty, 67:1)*

164

So, it means the soul is not something that we understand from your faculties. It's if you inherit from Prophet's ﷺ soul to dress upon your soul, finish. What kind of *qadam* and foot move is with that? That when they move and the step of Prophet ﷺ is upon them, can anybody stop what Allah ﷻ wants? Impossible! Can anybody understand the *qadam* of Prophet ﷺ? No. That's why they don't

care what anyone thinks. They do what they have to do because it's the footsteps of Prophet ﷺ supporting them.

So, it's not from our soul's understanding and small things that we can achieve. It's you becoming non-existent. When you don't exist and you're 0, there is 1. So, we said many times Sultanul Awliya Mawlana

Shaykh Muhammad Nazim Haqqani ق said, 'I'm nothing, nothing, nothing, but I had achieved 124,000 nothings. It means I went to the negative 124,000. I showed myself as nothing, nothing, talked as nothing, wore clothes of nothingness.' All of those teachings were Shaykh Nazim's ق teaching. 'Don't show yourself, don't wear fancy colours. Don't wear stripes. Don't wear all of these things that are like clown outfits. Be nothing. Blend in with everything.'

As much as you can achieve a state of nothingness, if Allah ﷻ turn you on, he says, 'I have a power of 124,000 *awliyaullah* (saints). But in my day to day life, I'm nothing, nothing.'

165

So, it means this reality and this *haqqaiq* (reality) of taking a path of nothing to achieve that reality of the dress. When Allah ﷻ wants the servant on, the binary code comes, those *nuqts* (dot) move the other way in one shot and that person becomes 124,000. But not everyone's going to achieve that, but this is the understanding. Be nothing, be nothing, until Allah ﷻ flips the binary switch so when they're 'ON,' they're 'ON' with support. When they're 'OFF', they took a path of being nothing, show themselves as nothing.

**What Can We Recite if Under Demonic Attack?**

A demon attack is spooky. Demons don't deal with humans. If a demon, if it's truly a demon, he would've taken your head off by now and eaten you. You're talking about just naughty *jinns* (unseen beings). Demonic attack is something that you can't even be typing or watching our face right now; it's not something you understand. The naughty *jinns* are being sent by people. Email us at helpme@nurmuhammad.com.

Because there is a whole system again. It's not just one thing you recite. Everybody wants now the McDonald's version of, 'Let me just drive thru, and give me this, and I'm on my way.' There is no more drive-thru help and there is no drive-thru *tariqah* either. Everything is a series of being locked in and studying. Understanding the *wudu* (ablution), understanding the energy, and most important supporting. You know support is a sign of your faith. If you go to a  doctor, and you go from doctor to doctor to free clinics, you probably won't really get any help. Because you know, you're just going around sort of left and right. But once you engage with a physician, you start to pay the bills, you're a patient of that physician, you're locked in.

More, *awliyaullah* are *wakeels* (representatives), so they're attorneys in  law firms. If you're going to hire the Naqshbandi law firm, it's a big retainer. And once you are involved with Naqshbandiya, then the whole team of these *awliyaullah* (saints) are supporting you. So, it's no different than *dunya* (material world). You go to *dunya* and try to get free advice. Free advice is just as good as the free-ness that you got from it. But you want real support, lock your foot with them.

Tie yourself in with them, and begin to do the practices, begin to do the *awrads*, begin to do the *zikr*, it becomes a way of life. You know, to give someone a fish has no value to Prophet ﷺ, but to teach them to fish with you, by the time you've trained and by the time you've disciplined, and why the giving is that you're not going to go anywhere. If you're planning

on bouncing around to twenty different shaykhs on the internet, good luck for you. And if you want to give them all donations, then you know, you must be super wealthy. But if you're going to dedicate yourself to one shaykh and learn and be a student of that shaykh, you're locked. Because they said, 'I'm enrolled. I'm years with this person. I've developed a relationship with them. I'm studying, I'm doing my *awrads*, I'm doing the knowledges.' Now you're somebody who knows how to fish.

You not only acquired the ability, you fought off all these difficulties and all of these satanic influences. At the same time the shaykh has replicated himself in you. He's made you a replica of himself so that wherever you go on this Earth, you're like an image of him. You teach what he teaches, you know what he knows, you act like he acts. And hopefully you're doing a good job and not ruining that representation. And that's what we have other talks of being an ambassador for this reality. We represent Prophet ﷺ. You can't go out and molest and humiliate and steal and cheat from people.

You're representing Sayyidina Muhammad ﷺ. And you're representing your shaykh, and the shaykhs who have been giving all their *faiz*, and all their teachings so that you become exemplars of faith. That's what is important. Not just the windows of the *zawiya* and handing out fish to people, '$1 fish, $1 fish, $1 fish, $2 fish, $2 fish,' yeah. But teach them no, no, bring them in and make them duplicates of yourself. What you learnt from your shaykhs, teach them so that they all have now your characteristics. When you come see any of these

students, they better be really loving, and very kind, and very good, and very generous. That means then they learned from their shaykh good character, and a good example and a good way, *inshaAllah*.

## How Does the Madad Protect Us From Attacks at Night?

Remember always say your *madad* (support) and in your meditations it's

important to do the *tafakkur*, do the contemplation, do the meditations, build the relationship in the spiritual world. Become familiar with the spiritual energy and that at this time, at any time you feel frightened at night, feel something around, you have to

move your energy. Don't succumb to something and feel that you're going to be shy – that's exactly what they want. That you be shy, that you be like, 'It's not happening.' No, it's happening.

You have to push yourself and train yourself on how to bring your energy out, 'Raah! Push yourself out and don't let anything to get near

to you. The energy that you use and bring your force out has a tremendous energy and light, and that many times will scare away many different beings. Don't just succumb to *shaitan* (satan) to ride all over you, take your breath and then begin to suffocate you. So, it means that you do your *madad* and your training and your *madad* is because you're training, training, 'Madad, madad, 'I'm nothing I'm nothing.' And then as soon as you become frightened or something is coming and you become hyper-alert when you're sleeping, push your energy to wake up, to push something off. And that you're in a state of *madad*.

As soon as you're frightened in life you should have trained to be in *madad*, that you don't resolve the issue yourself but that you call upon those whom are in authority. When you train to be in *madad*, that at the moment something is wrong, your intuition that you're trained yourself is a *madad*. Immediately their energies come, their energies come into the room to resolve whatever issue needs to be resolved. We pray Allah ﷻ give us more and more understanding and more and more resolve to reach to our reality of what Allah ﷻ wants for us.

## What Can Be Recited for Protection Against Evil and to Remove Fear?

We have a protection against evilness. That if you go to the website or the app, that you click on the meditation or even in the search engine. That protection against evilness, it's a whole system. This means that you learn through the *tafakkur* (contemplation), that you keep your *wudu* (ablution) at all times, that you keep yourself covered. You entered teachings of meditation and *tafakkur*, that you've been taught how to make the *madad* (support). Everything you're doing is a *madad*. As soon as I sit, I'm asking support. I'm asking the support of all my teachers, all the way up to Sayyidina Muhammad ﷺ. I live and die by that understanding; always in a state of *madad*, always in a state of *madad*.

Then they learn from them, and read all of the different recitations, keep themselves in a state of *wudu* (ablution), and then they sleep. When they sleep, they sleep with their head covered. Their body parts are covered, and they sleep in a state of *wudu*. And they try not to break their *wudu* unless they have to get up, wash again, and then enter into the *wudu*.

Then there's *ayatul Qur'an Kareem,* four Surat al-Falaq, three Surat an-Nas, two Surat al-Ikhlas, and one ending *du'a* (supplication). That's on that article of wickedness; that it adds to nine. They recite and blow upon themselves before they sleep. And then there are other *du'as* on that article if they're experiencing more and more energies.

As soon as they enter into their *tafakkur* and contemplation, they may have many dreams in which they're trying to defend themselves. Because now the shaykhs want to test that, 'Are you trying to defend yourself with yourself? Or are you calling upon *madad?*' If you're not making the *madad,* then there is still something wrong in what you understand. You think that you can fix the problem instead of asking for the *madad* and the support of Allah ﷻ.

## How Can We Control Our Fear?

This is our greatest danger. What's happening right now is *shaitan* (satan) ruling by fear and we talked, and the website has and the NurMuhammad, everything is tagged. If you go in NurMuhammad and type the word 'fear,' it will pull all the videos and articles in the search. So, any subject that you have deeper concern, go to the website, put the word. Most articles – even from the thousand videos from the first ones – I think have been retagged. But fear is how *shaitan* is operating now in last days because fear is the opposite of faith.

Fear is the opposite of faith and faith is a light and a guidance that comes into the heart. That light that comes into the heart when we begin to teach the meditation, teach the *tafakkur* (contemplation). It's the anger and the ignorance that makes a fire within people's hearts. It means if people have anger in their heart, they have an ignorance on their being. Then everything ruled by them is fire. The *tariq* (path), Islam, Sayyidina Muhammad ﷺ came to take away ignorance. So, it means the reality of *deen* (religion) is to conquer  ignorance and bring guidance. As soon as guidance begins to come into the heart, the teachings, the way comes into the heart, a light will begin to enter into the heart. That guidance begins to take down that anger and the *ghadab* that's entering into the heart.

We described many times it's like walking in a crowded room but with your eyes closed. If you hit the table two times, you're going to be screaming angry because you're bumping into everything and hurting. The guidance, the religion, the teaching is a way in which to take the veils off. And a guide is essential because you can't see, but he sees. That's why guides should be open-hearted, not the blind leading the blind.

## How Do We Overcome Childhood Fears?

Again, these are general. There may be specific issues; that's why you have to email. But fear in general is to build our faith. The counter to

fear is faith. And what *shaitan* (satan) wants to put into us is fear. So now everything is fear. Everything on television is about bringing fear into the heart of the believer. And we talked last week on that; that's the first psychological

step in conquering the believer, is to psychologically put a fear on him so his whole immune system and his whole system, his or her system, drops. Their defence mechanism drops. And all the practices that they are propagating and teaching now is to counter fear.

That you counter fear by making your connection. When your connection is strong and you feel the presence of *awliyaullah* (saints), you feel the presence of what

Allah '꙳ wants you to feel, what you have to be scared from? You're doing your *zikr* (Divine remembrance), you're doing all your practices, you're keeping your *wudu* (ablution), you're

keeping all the requirements that Allah '꙳ wants from you, then the *iman* and the faith becomes strong.

That the *yaqeen* (certainty) of the meditation and *tafakkur* and contemplation grants a *yaqeen*. You feel the connection; again, this is countering the fear. Then specific issues of phobia of things that have happened to you, events that have occurred in life, then you email helpme@nurmuhammad.com, and then we'll go over how to deal with those. That's about *taslim* (submission).

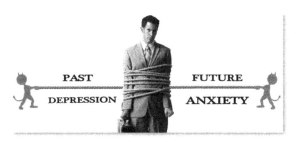

As much as you can cut the rope; *shaitan* throws two ropes on you – one from behind and one in front. He has a rope on you about everything from the past and this rope holds you from levitating and moving into the Divinely Presence. And the strongest rope is in the front, of what's going to be coming in your life, fearing what's coming in your life, fearing what's going to open for you in life, what's not going to open for you. All of these fears of what was in the past – regrets and things that you did wrong – it's in the past.

The only thing you should understand from regret is that, 'I should have done more.' Whatever choice you made is done, nothing you can do to change that but when you *tafakkur* and contemplate, 'I wasted all the time Allah ﷻ gave me. I wasted all the money Allah ﷻ gave me. I wasted every opportunity that Allah ﷻ gave me.'

Put it in your *muhasabah* and accounting. Put it in your writing and say, 'Bad boy.' If Allah ﷻ gives me again money, I should be spending it in the way of Allah ﷻ. If Allah ﷻ gives  me time, I should be spending that time in the way of Allah ﷻ. If Allah ﷻ gives me good health and long life, I should be spending it in the way of Allah ﷻ. So, there's no regret from the past. You can't go back and change the past but with the *muhasabah* and writing, don't repeat it, because history seems to repeat itself. That's why Allah ﷻ says that when the dead comes before him and they have a regret, '*Ya Rabbi*, please send me back; I'm going to give everything away so that I can become from *saliheen* (righteous).'

وَأَنفِقُوا مِن مَّا رَزَقْنَاكُم مِّن قَبْلِ أَن يَأْتِيَ أَحَدَكُمُ الْمَوْتُ فَيَقُولَ رَبِّ لَوْلَا أَخَّرْتَنِي إِلَىٰ أَجَلٍ قَرِيبٍ فَأَصَّدَّقَ وَأَكُن مِّنَ الصَّالِحِينَ ﴿١٠﴾

*63:10 – "Wa anifqoo mim maa razaqnaakum min qabli any-ya'tiya ahadakumul mawtu fa yaqoola rabbi law laaa akhkhartaneee ilaaa ajalin qareebin fa assaddaqa wa akum minassaaliheen." (Surat Al-Munafiq)*

*"And spend something (in charity) out of the substance which We have bestowed on you, before Death should come to any of you and he should say, "O my Lord! why didst Thou not give me respite for a little while? I should then have given (largely) in charity, and I should have been one of the doers of good." (The Hypocrites, 63:10)*

And in reality, if Allah ﷻ sends them back they go back exactly to their character. When they come back again, 'Oh *ya Rabbi*, one more time.' And this is the nature of mankind.

And says that, 'When I put them on a boat and the storm comes and everything is upside down, 'O my Lord save me. If You save me, You save me; I'll dedicate my life to You.' Allah ﷻ eases the storm.

The boat lands and says, 'What you're talking about, I never promised these things.' And walk off the shore like nothing ever happened. Yes, the storm came; how many people think they're going to die? Their children going to die, they're all going to be in a morgue with masks on their face. You didn't die. Now where is your commitment and your promise to Allah ﷻ and his Rasul ﷺ? Nobody stepped forward. Then what, you're waiting for the next time? Then Allah ﷻ takes you the next time.

It means the *rijal* (people of maturity) and the people of faith understood, '*Ya Rabbi*, I'm going to do it, I'm going to do it and I have no regrets. I understood from my past and what the future brings I'm going to try to be committed into what Allah ﷻ wants.' Then I don't fear the future of what's going to happen and how everything is going to collapse. Why everything going to collapse? And these are the two ropes that *shaitan* throwing on to the believer to tie them down. If they can cut the past and cut the future, cut these two ropes, they live within the present and in every moment they're in a *haal* (spiritual state).

Because they're not thinking of the past and they don't care about tomorrow. If Allah جل جلاله want them dead by nighttime they're happy with that too. So, every moment is a *haal* for them. Because they're not tied, they're continuously floating away. We pray that Allah جل جلاله open more and more understandings of these and we're coming through big difficulties.

Don't think the game is over. Whatever they tell you of everything is ok, it's just the beginning, *"Yaaa aiyuhal lazeena aamanooo, aaminoo."* Those who believe; believe.

يَا أَيُّهَا الَّذِينَ آمَنُوا آمِنُو ﴿١٣٦﴾

*4:136 – "Yaaa aiyuhal lazeena aamanooo aaminoo." (Surat An-Nisa)*

*"O ye who believe! Believe." (The Women, 4:136)*

These 90 days that Allah جل جلاله gave to everyone because He loves all His creations, you can't go around saying this is *kafir*. Allah جل جلاله put everybody into isolation to show how much He loves all His creation. Everybody went into isolation. Some are going to come out very demonic, and don't worry about what they call themselves. The ones who call themselves with nice names they're probably the most evil. But the ones who come out and something opened of an awakening in their heart, and they think that there is a higher power and they want to dedicate their lives to that power. So, it means then the next test will be coming. And *Ahlul Bayt* (Holy family of Prophet ﷺ), and *hadith* of Nabi ﷺ for *qiyamah* (resurrection) and *akhir zaman* (end of time) is that, 'The white death is coming. Red death is coming. Death by wars is coming, death by plagues and pandemics are coming.

178

قَالَ أَمِيرُ الْمُؤْمِنِينَ إِمَامْ عَلِي ابْنُ أَبِي طَالِبٍ عَلَيْهِ اَلسَلَامْ: "بَيْنَ يَدَيْ اَلْقَائِمِ مَوْتٌ أَحْمَرُ وَمَوْتٌ أَبْيَضْ. فَأَمَّا اَلْمَوْتُ الْأَحْمَرُ فَبِالسَّيْفِ وَأَمَّا الْمَوْتُ الْأَبْيَضْ فَبِالْطَاعُونْ. (الْمَصْدَرْ: اَلنُّعْمَانِيَّ ص٢٨٦)

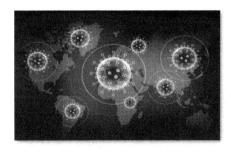

*Qala Amirul Mumineen Imam 'Ali ibn Abi Talib (as): "bayna yadai alqaayimi mawtun ahmar wa mawtun abyad. Famma almawtul ahmar fabeyssayif wa ammal mawtul abyad fabil taa'oon."* [Annu'maniya Safha 286]

*The Leader of the believers Imam 'Ali Ibn Abi Talib (as) said: "Before the arrival of the Qaayim (uprising) of Imam Mahdi (as), there will be the 'red death' and 'white death'. The 'Red death' is by the sword, and the 'white death' is by plague."* [An Numani Page: 286]

So, it means then Allah ﷻ (says), 'It's just the beginning.' So that to keep our faith strong, our practices strong, our connection strong. The love for Sayyidina Muhammad ﷺ very strong so that you identify as being *Muhammadiyoon.* Which those other *mazhab* they really get angry with that term. It means then an immense blessing. Before people used to say, 'Oh, those are Muhammadans.' This was an honourable name, this was an honourable title, that they represented the reality of Sayyidina Muhammad ﷺ. When they see them and their turban, they look at their face, they say these are *Muhammadiyoon.* And that's exactly what the angels are

looking for. They're looking for who are the Muhammadans on this Earth. That they honour and love their King and they want to serve and live their life in service to the King, the one whom Allah ﷻ has made the most praised throughout His heavens. We pray that Allah ﷻ open more and more understanding.

### Can We Take Advice From Anyone?

Don't ever ask anyone a question other than your shaykh. You've opened and broken your *a'uzu* (protection). That you ask somebody blind a question, it's the blind leading the blind. And now the children and teenagers, that's all they do. They ask fellow crazy people, 'What should I do? What should I do? What should I do with this? What  should I do with that? How should I do like that? How should I do like that?' Why would you open yourself to ask all of those things? Most of your friends are crazier than you and you want them to give you guidance? Imagine then what type of garbage people are collecting. They sit, they think that's a good thing. I'll ask my friend, 'Now what should I do? What should I do? What should I do? What should I do?'

One, you've lowered yourself, showed yourself as weak and put upon somebody else now the role of being a shaykh for you. You change your  relationship. That's no longer a relationship of friendship. That's a relationship of somebody always wanting to see you and tell you what to do. So, *tariqah* comes and teaches, 'Don't ever do that. Don't ask anyone anything other than your shaykh,' so that you don't give the perspective or the point of being weak. And that you don't want to have 15 opinions coming into your mind and becoming

180

schizophrenic. Imagine schizophrenia is *waswases* (whisperings). Some people have multiple personalities like five different *waswases* at a time talking to them. Imagine if you made that into actual *insans* (human beings). Ten times worse, thousand times worse. That five people are continuously telling you all the time what to do? And each coordinance, a different direction until your mind just splits and says, 'I don't know.' I become anxious, depressed and all sorts of sicknesses.

*Tariqah* comes with the perfection of character. No, why you have to ask? You pray to your Lord, you make *salawats* upon Sayyidina Muhammad ﷺ, read Qur'an for your guidance and if Allah ﷻ inspire you to a guide, then ask the guide. 'What are my coordinance for my life? What should I do on a daily basis?' And we said before the guidance they give, you'll know your *tariq* by this guidance is this way and your

opinion is that way. So, your *tariqah* is what? It's just this distance on how to shift what you think into what they're teaching. When you're meeting the understanding of what the guide is teaching you, the coordinance that the guide is suggesting for you and you've come to the *taslim*

(submission) that, 'You know, I don't know.' And if Allah ﷻ inspiring within you the coordinance for me because the real guides who *Atiullaha wa atiur Rasula wa Ulil amre minkum*, they have a file on who you are.

﴿٥٩﴾ ... أَطِيعُوا اللَّه وَأَطِيعُوا ٱلرَّسُولَ وَأُوْلِي الْأَمْرِ مِنْكُمْ ...

*4:59 – "...Atiullaha wa atiur Rasula wa Ulil amre minkum..."*
*(Surat An-Nisa)*

*"...Obey Allah, Obey the Messenger, and those in authority among
you..." (The Women, 4:59)*

Like a doctor's clinic. Now it's all electronic. You don't even have to...
in old times the doctor had to have your actual file. He had to actually
 fax it to somebody else. Now it's
all electronic. You go to the
doctor; he's been dedicated to
you from your insurance
company. You walk in, he knows,
'Hello, how are you. Just tell me
your date of birth and oh, these
are all the medications you're on.' He already has everything there. You
think if Allah ﷻ did that for *dunya* (material world), He doesn't have that
for *akhirah* (hereafter)? Your electronic file is already flowing. He merely
makes the connection; that file is downloaded its guidance. It's
coordinance is already there. Every guidance they're giving is based on
that file that's there to take you to that destination.

And *taslim*; before you can submit, is tend to hear the coordinance and
say, 'Yeah, I don't agree with you.' Then your whole life is about how to
bring it back, bring it back, bring it back until you feel that you feel, and
you think and you understand like he understands. And it's all based on
the love of Sayyidina Muhammad ﷺ. Not based on the love of that
person. We're not making an idol out of a person.

182

He's merely like a life coach. He should play an invisible role in your life. That you ask a question, he gives an answer and guidance, suggestions to you, never command. Nobody's capable of carrying any command. He gives a suggestion, 'I think like this.' And your whole life is to chew on that and think that in my heart, 'I should be trying to accomplish maybe closer to that.' I want to conquer the Earth and he's telling me to conquer myself. And that becomes the whole path and that whole reality. That's it. So, it means this light comes in. This guidance comes into the heart. When the guidance comes, your eyes can see. I've seen the Glory of my Lord. 'It's coming down, it's coming down.' Because you can see now. When you see, you're not angry. What's there to be angry about?

You know the people on the street, they're angry. Why? Because they don't see. If they could see that this is a time in which Allah ﷻ said, 'This world is coming to an end and very holy people are coming.' Why are  you on the streets screaming then? You should be in your house, 'Wow, *subhanAllah, ya Rabbi*, let me to see these magnificent souls. They look like they're going to be arriving really soon.' But when they're ignorant, they want to go out and throw bricks and anger. Did you not understand last days where there would be no justice on Earth? You don't see what time this is? You're just surprised it's here now. If you don't know the time, then you become angered.

If you know the time and you meditate and contemplate and say, 'This is exactly what my Lord has decreed. This black cloud is moving. My job – stay out. Pray that I have good character to see these blessed souls.' That's why meditation is not an entertainment but is a life-saving ability. To meditate and contemplate, so that you never make the wrong choice to  be at the wrong place at the wrong time and all of a sudden find yourself in immense grief and difficulty that you can't take yourself out of.

## How to Live Amongst Family Who Don't Have an Understanding of Spiritual Practices?

*Alhamdulillah*, Allah ﷻ wants it that way. That's from the talks of Sayyidina Yusuf ﷺ. That he lives with a father who is a Prophet, eleven brothers who many *ulama* (scholars) say were prophets, but some argued on the internet and said they're not prophets. Whatever you want to call it. Eleven highly blessed brothers. And the brothers wanted to kill him.

So, Allah ﷻ is teaching you, 'Your path is uniquely for you.' It's not meant for anyone else. Keep a path of silence. So, the first step of the  way is *samt,* silence. You're not supposed to explain it to anyone because you don't even know it yourself yet. You're not supposed to describe it to family and friends and everyone else because you'll get confused, and you'll confuse people. So, the way wasn't about propagating.

Unfortunately, there are many people now of – no need to, we don't want to make a whole group of people to be angry with us. But people who don't get attention at home now become copy-paste shaykhas on the internet, right? They don't get the respect and the feeling they want from home. The internet became like a *masjid* for them. They copy this shaykh, post it out, and then get two likes. They copy this shaykh, and they post this out, get five likes. Before they know it, they feel like they're shaykhs now. Copy-paste shaykhs. They copy-pasted this *awrad*, they put it out. Copy-pasted this *awrad*, they put that out. That's not guidance.

And for us, it's like a medical office. Always refer back to a medical office because their degrees are high. You know, their degrees are higher than your highest Harvard law school, medical school. To be granted a degree from Allah ﷻ, the Creator of all the universes, through the order of Sayyidina Muhammad ﷺ, down to the order of their shaykhs. When they come out with an *ijaza* (permission), it's beyond the understanding of a med degree and a law degree. It's a clinic. So, when they start giving out prescriptions and *wazifas* (spiritual practices), their soul stands behind that. And they ask Prophet ﷺ that to give it it's *barakah* and give it its blessing. Even if it's deficient in something, make it to work because they did it so Allah ﷻ doesn't disappoint his *awliya* (saints) and embarrass them. So whatever they put out, Allah ﷻ blesses it. If it's incorrect, they make their *istighfar* (seeking forgiveness), pull and add to whatever has to be added.

But copying and pasting some shaykhs prescriptions isn't the same as the shaykh posting that. And then his authorized students are re-posting that information. That's a *nuskhe;* it's a prescription that has a power. So, when they give you an *awrad* and a *zikr* to do for a condition, a time, or whatever's happening on this Earth. And in every era may be different, and Prophet ﷺ has different prescriptions for  different shaykhs. Not all shaykhs are the same. None of them are the same, and Prophet ﷺ may want to see your belief in your shaykh. A different shaykh has a different prescription because this is also testing. If one shaykh says, 'Here, recite this whole thing.' And another shaykh says, 'No, just drink this water.' Say, 'Oh, he doesn't know'; no, he knows. Maybe your belief in him and that water, it will be the healing that you needed. This means every prescription is coming by order of Prophet ﷺ towards that shaykh to test your belief.

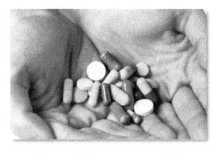 Don't mix and match. And don't copy-paste everybody's prescriptions all over the internet because those can also be toxic. If you're giving to the wrong person, the wrong *zikr* and they start to lose their mind, that's on you. So, it means these are like medicines; you can't just go around telling everyone 'You take these antibiotics.' What if they're allergic to amoxicillin and you didn't know they were allergic. Because you're not a shaykh, or a shaykha.

So, better just to use the internet as source of information from authorized representatives. To watch it, read it, say, 'I like, *alhamdulillah*.' But copy and pasting and putting out, and then mixing with ten different peoples, ten different shaykhs, ten different prescriptions. Then that's where the problem lies and then that becomes *nafsani* (egoistic) because the person wants attention.

# Importance of Being of Service
# and Attaining Sincerity

### How Can We Be of Service?

Whatever skill you have, email us at helpme@nurmuhammad.com and
they'll get back to you. If you
can type, you type. If anything
you can be of service, then
*alhamdulillah.* *InshaAllah,*
they'll try to find something to
be of service or something
locally. We have people in
Pakistan who are serving, trying
to put food out. And anywhere

in the world, people can find a way to be of service. Just coordinate with
the office and they'll get back with you, *inshaAllah,* on how to do that.
Allah ﷻ bless you and forgive me. And the *tariqah* (spiritual way) – join
and follow.

And if you don't want to join, then
*alhamdulillah,* keep following.
Don't despair from the mercy of
Allah ﷻ and love of Sayyidina
Muhammad ﷺ. Everything points
its way back to the love of
Sayyidina Muhammad ﷺ and love
for all *awliyaullah, inshaAllah.*
And all those whom are striving towards goodness and good character.

## What Can We Do if We Feel Our Service Isn't Enough?

The *khidmat* (service) the shaykh is teaching is not to serve him, but to serve Prophet ﷺ. So, serving your family in a good way and a happy way.

If you're the female, making your husband happy and your children to be lovers of Sayyidina Muhammad ﷺ is immense. If you're the male in the family – the same, making your wife happy, making your children happy and because you're the *imam*, guiding them to the love of Sayyidina Muhammad ﷺ and

the love of *awliyaullah* (saints). This is the best of service. And if Allah ﷻ gives you extra, and then you share. Of whatever time, ability, wealth, whatever Allah ﷻ has given to you. So, there is nobody who cannot be of service.

Even if you're in jail, in the bottom of the jail, and somehow you're hearing this message, pray for people. Be good, pray, and give that prayer

and the *ihda* (dedication) of that prayer as a gift to the soul of Sayyidina Muhammad ﷺ, *Ahlul Bayt Nabi* ﷺ (holy family of Prophet ﷺ), *Ashab Nabi* ﷺ (holy companions of Prophet ﷺ), and *awliyaullah fis samayi wa fil ard*. Your *salah* (prayer) and your good actions are an immense gift. And that's why the key for all our actions when you read our *awrads* (daily practices) and *zikrs* (Divine remembrance) is *ihda*. "*Ila sharifin Nabi* ﷺ *wa ila aalihi wa sahbihil kiram. Wa ila mashayikhina fit tariqatin Naqshbandiyati 'aaliyah.*"

190

إِلَى شَرَفِ النَّبِيِّ ﷺ وَإِلَى آلِهِ وَصَحْبِهِ الْكِرَام. وَإِلَى أَرْوَاحِ مَشَائِخِنَا فِي الطَّرِيْقَةِ النَّقْشْبَنْدِيَةِ الْعَالِيَّة

*"Ila sharifin Nabi ﷺ wa ila aalihi wa sahbihil kiram. Wa ila arwahi mashayikhina fit tariqatin Naqshbandiyati 'aaliyah."*

*"Honour be to the Prophet (Muhammad (pbuh)), and his family, and his distinguished Companions, And to our honoured Shaykhs (spiritual guides) of distinguished Order of Naqshbandi."*

That is the whole secret. That, '*Ya Rabbi*, if You saw anything of what I did good, give to the honourable and noble soul of Sayyidina Muhammad ﷺ.' Because our way was what? To gift everything. If we give a gift to them, imagine they take that blessing up into the heavens. And then that *ni'mat* (blessing) is that, 'We're now going to give you from our blessings.' And your whole life is then the raining of their *rahmah* (mercy) upon our souls. You didn't want for yourself that, '*Ya Rabbi*, I'm going to do this for my beloved Sayyidina Muhammad ﷺ.' Dress with that light. And Prophet ﷺ, no doubt, takes that gift and dresses it back eternally upon our souls. So, everything in our life is a *hediah*, a gift in the way of Allah ﷻ.

Anybody panicking – don't panic. Anybody reading too many formulas of cures and sumac and all sorts of sweets and desserts, enjoy, no problem. It's all *halal* food. Try to follow the advice of *awliyaullah* (saints). Try to do your *salawats* (praises upon Prophet Muhammad ﷺ). Make sure that your *hisaab* (account) is good with Allah ﷻ, good with Prophet ﷺ. If you're sinning, then you must not be giving. If what you're doing is not cleaning you, give! Give in the way of Allah ﷻ. That *zakah* (charity) is a *zaki*, is a purification. That which you give purifies and cleanses you. It cleans you of all the badness and bad character. That badness that's within somebody that doesn't allow them to pray, that badness within the somebody that makes them to be aggressive and angry. Every bad character – it's like an infection within the body.

The concept of *zakah* – why they link *zakah* to the purity of the soul was to be of service. It takes away the sickness. It takes away all the bad characteristics. Those are the real remedies. Not what you're going to put on the kebabs, and you know, make this kind of tea and make all these things. This is all very nice. It's good, appetizing for you. But the real painful medicine is giving, not what you're going to douse your kebab with and have chai with your paneer and the chai is going to be your *shifa* (healing). Allah ﷻ wants something a little more substantial than that, 'Give until it hurts.' Be of service. Do your prayers. Do your *salawats*. Do all of your *'ibadah* (worship) and actions. Make sure your account is good with *Sultanan Naseera*.

وَقُل رَّبِّ أَدْخِلْنِي مُدْخَلَ صِدْقٍ وَأَخْرِجْنِي مُخْرَجَ صِدْقٍ وَاجْعَل لِّي مِن لَّدُنكَ سُلْطَانًا نَّصِيرًا ﴿٨٠﴾

*17:80 – "Wa qul Rabbi adkhelni mudkhala Sidqin wa akhrejni mukhraja Sidqin waj'al li min ladunka Sultanan NaSeera." (Surat Al-Isra)*

*"Say: O my Lord! Let my entry be by the Gate of Truth and Honour, and likewise my exit by the Gate of Truth and Honour; and grant me from Your Presence a Victorious King to aid (me)." (The Night Journey, 17:80)*

That, '*Ya Rabbi,* let me to be under the *sultanate* (kingdom) of Sayyidina Muhammad ﷺ, under the guidance of your *awliyaullah.* And let me to reach to the threshold of Sayyidina Muhammad ﷺ to feel that security and feel my sense of security.' That, 'I'm reaching.' That clarifies everything. If that is your goal and that is your target, then all of what we taught will make sense to you. If that's not your goal and it's about entertaining yourself with what you want to have in your seclusion, then that's something different. That's just a description of a menu for eating.

## What Other Ways Can We Support if We Have No Income?

That *alhamdulillah,* through your prayers and *du'a* (supplication) and to be of service. If there is time that is available and there is a service that you can provide, then *alhamdulillah.* You email the helpme@nurmuhammad.com on what your abilities or your God-given

gift. We have so many people now translating and trying to be of service to translate in their native tongues, in Spanish, in French. We need more Spanish, we need more French, we need every language possible; Bengali, we need Hindi, we need Russian. So *alhamdulillah,* there is always a way to be of service and *inshaAllah,* Allah ﷻ open a way in our hearts in which to make us to be of service to Prophet ﷺ, *inshaAllah,* Sayyidina Muhammad ﷺ, *inshaAllah.*

## How Can We Be of Service if We Have No Means?

That's impossible unless you got no hands, no feet, no eyes, and no ears. Because *khidmat* (service) can be anything. We have people all over the world. It's not only these gentlemen that are sitting here. We have people all over the world that are transcribing. They take the talk, they immediately start to write it out into their language, they send it in for review. They start to sort of put it together. They compile books from that. So, there is always a way of *khidmat*.

We even have people who are in Pakistan who get together. They collect money in Pakistan and they go give the food out at a *maqam*. So, there always has to be a way in which to give from our life, from our time, from whatever Allah ﷻ gave of an ability, *inshaAllah*. And if not, then *alhamdulillah*, the shaykh knows best that you have absolutely no way of being of service and Allah ﷻ bless you and give you more, and open an opportunity for you to have those abilities, *inshaAllah*.

## How Do We Reach the Station of Sincerity?

Sincerity is the whole way. That when you give, when you do, when you study, when you believe and practice to the best of your ability, you are becoming sincere. So those whom are sincere, they practice with all earnest, with all their zeal in their heart. They give with all their heart. They try to do with all their heart. They try to be of service with what Allah ﷻ gave to them and all their heart.

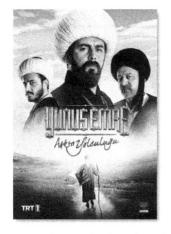

The shaykh is a – what do they say the one for the orchestra? Conductor. 'Yunus Emre,' again is a wonderful show on Netflix and recommend everyone to sit with their families and watch. You have a beautiful programming of how the *adab* (manners) of *tariqah* (spiritual path) is. That when everyone knows their reality and their station, it means the shaykh is merely the conductor. That's his job by Allah ﷻ and Allah ﷻ gives him all these instruments. His responsibility is to teach everybody what their role in this orchestra is. It's not an orchestra for everyone because every shaykh has his own orchestra. That's why you don't drum here and drum there, and drum there, and drum there.

You find the maestro that you feel your heart is connected to. You feel the conductor that your heart is connected to and say, 'I want to be in his orchestra.' His life then is to inspire you on, 'You play drums. You play this, you play that.' This is all an analogy. It means play the role that Allah ﷻ wanted for you. It's not for him to hire and fire and kick people out of the orchestra. His job was to do his job by Allah ﷻ. And his job was merely, 'Inspire them to do their best for Me.' Who owns the orchestra? Allah ﷻ. Not the shaykh, not the conductor. He's

merely doing his job. When he dies, another conductor will come. And that's his job then given, 'Can you make them play?' Because you know the human nature is the drumming guy, he wants to do violin. The violin guy wants to do trumpet. The trumpet guy wants to sing, 'But you don't have a voice to sing.' 'It doesn't matter, I will be very upset.'

So, the job is what? Make everybody happy. Make everybody try to do what their role is. This is *tariqah* (spiritual path). 'Have I met someone in my life that inspires me to my God-given role and to bring out my God-given best? To do good, to practice good, to give in charity, to give from what Allah ﷻ has given to me? Am I learning *Ilm e Laduni* (Divinely Knowledge)? I'm not learning videos of only *wudu*

(ablution).' My children learned that a long time ago. 'But am I learning knowledges of the heavens that will improve the power of my soul and reality of my soul?' If so, practice those ways. And if you practice those ways, you should reach towards the oceans of sincerity.

And in these days of difficulty, avoid certain situations. There is a psychology of what's happening. When people are not feeling good and confident in themselves, you know what type of people they are attracted

to? What's the polite way? I'm trying not to be aggressive in my talk. Outlandish people, right? Somebody who is too outlandish, like a big peacock, want to give everything, say they're everything, say they're everything – be like this. The psychology of someone who doesn't feel good about themself, they are attracted to these peacocks. Why? By virtue of being with the peacock, they feel better about themselves. And that's why you are in a danger of falling into misguidance. *Tariqah* is to avoid all the peacocks.

If you are looking at a peacock and thinking, 'This person is like this. They're so big. This guy is so huge. He sees this, he sees like that, he does like this.' That peacock is going to get you into trouble and you're not going to grow from that. And you're not going to grow the way that

Allah ﷻ wants you to grow and that is how cults are born. Why the reason of a cult? You watch the 'David Koresh Show' on Netflix and these different shows? It's that people are not feeling good about themselves. And they're attracted to a person who says he is Jesus and he walks on water. That, 'Oh my God, I know Jesus. This is great!' Avoid that in life.

The *tariqah* and the real *tariqah* is the one who says he is nothing, *"Ana abdukal 'ajeez, wa dayeef, wa miskin, wa zhalim, wa jahl."* 'I'm but nothing.' If you want to keep sitting there, that's up to you. Then you are sitting there for Allah ﷻ, not for me. And our shaykh was like that, Mawlana Shaykh Nazim ق, humblest example you can imagine; never spoke of anything, never spoke that he sees this, he's this; he controls this, he controls like that, but took a way of being nothing. And anyone who came to him in his last days, he was crying and praying for them. A whole bunch of ladies came, and he told them, 'Pray for me' and they started to pray, and he started to cry. This means he gave and left us, 'This is my example.'

And Mawlana Shaykh Muhammad Adil ق, same way – not an expression on his face to show you that he's anything, and that he's going to do this, he's going to do that, he's going to work miracles for you. No, no, the *tariqah* came to say, 'You're nothing.' The only miracle is the knowledge. That knowledge flows from the heart of Sayyidina Muhammad ﷺ. That's important.

197

Those whom are scanning for everything, if you are not feeling good about yourself, watch out for the peacocks. Oh, you think, 'Oh, I met

Jesus. Now I'm going to be a big shot too.' No, stay away from that. That's the difficulties of the last day. Meet those who say they're nothing. And in your nothingness is how you'll be gained access into the presence of Allah 'ﷻ and Sayyidina Muhammad ﷺ because that door is the door of nothingness. You can't come to Prophet ﷺ saying, 'Oh, I know Sayyidina Isa ﷺ. I'm with this, I'm with that. We are kings. We are walking with feathers.' They come to the door of Prophet ﷺ and say, 'I'm absolutely nothing,' crying to

Prophet's ﷺ door that, 'I'm nothing, I'm nothing. Forgive me my wrongs and my sins.' We pray that Allah 'ﷻ help us through these days of difficulties when too much deceit enters upon this Earth.

### How Can We Honour the Shaykhs of The Golden Chain?

To honour the shaykhs of the Golden Chain, *inshaAllah*, good character. This is the example of the shaykh. If you follow the example

of the shaykh, all those types of questions would be answered because he must be doing something to honour his shaykh. That's why his character is like that. It means that if you follow their example and live by that example, then you should be showing how to honour the shaykh. One, by having good

character in the midst of all the different testings, that if you have good character and you're a good exemplar of faith, then that brings a

198

happiness to the shaykh because the students are presented to Sayyidina Muhammad ﷺ. And said, 'This is your student and this is his actions.'

So, we pray that always it's the best of examples and that we live a life of showing the love for Sayyidina Muhammad ﷺ. So, good deeds, good actions, good character, and exemplars of faith. And this way, we said before, is to set the way for Sayyidina Mahdi عليه السلام and that's by love. That's by love and *muhabbat* (love). That nobody left on Earth except those whom they are extremely sincere, and their sincerity is based on the immensity of love  and kindness that they have within their heart. Or they're extremely evil. These are the two polarities which will become black and white, and grey will vanish from the Earth.

## How Can We Increase Our Love for the Shaykh?

To take the teachings, to have good characteristics. That not to have doubt. That continuously trying to figure out or doubt that, 'I'm with the shaykh, am I with the right shaykh, I should be with another shaykh.'  And then keep thinking every time you have a dream of a different shaykh, 'Does it mean this, or does it mean that?' All of them are Muhammadan representatives if they are these true shaykhs. And the understanding that one has to have is, 'I have to be perfecting myself.' And every time an *isharat* (sign) or guidance, or something comes from a shaykh, is it to perfect myself and notify me that I am off course? And that's all I have to worry about. Don't look to the station and the *maqam* of the shaykh, and is this the highest shaykh? Is this like this?

You're doing the wrong *tafakkur* (contemplation); you're trying to figure out the station of the shaykh. And that one we talked about in the mirror.

You have to worry about your grave, and did you complete what you needed to complete. Are you perfecting yourself to the best of your ability? If you are perfecting yourself, doing the best that you can, then you are making Prophet ﷺ happy, and that's what you have to focus. Forget about all these – the shaykh names, and who's this shaykh and that shaykh. Are you making Sayyidina Muhammad ﷺ happy? Are you following the way of Prophet Muhammad ﷺ? Are you accountable for the time you have? Are you heedless with your time? Are you taking Prophet's ﷺ way with a reverence?

Whatever Sayyidina Muhammad ﷺ brought, we put it like on a royal pillow and we carry it with an *ihtiram* (respect). That he brought for us a holy turban. We wear the turban as if it's the crown of paradise. Not something small; it multiplies your *salah* (prayer) by 27 times, and be granted the *maqam* of the martyr, of seventy martyrs. The *ajer* and the reward of someone who wears a holy turban, as if he has the reward of seventy martyrs because he is *Muhyil Sunnah*, he is one whom is reviving the *sunnah* of Sayyidina Muhammad ﷺ upon this Earth. And

every *salah* he makes is 27 times his *salah*. So, if you were worried about your *qadha* and made up *salah*, if you followed the shaykh you'd have nothing to worry about because every *salah* counted for 27 times, right?

If you followed the shaykhs and saw that, 'Oh look, they use a *siwak*  (teeth cleaning twig), and they never do anything without their *siwak*, and they multiply their *salah* by 27 times. And they got the *ajer* and the reward of seventy martyrs.' Because why? They are *Muhyil Sunnah*. Why? Because they keep a reverence that Prophet ﷺ brought this *siwak*. We don't compare this to Crest and toothpaste. It has nothing to do with toothpaste. It has nothing to do with brightening your teeth. This has to do with the key to your heart. When you, "*Nifaq e Qalbi, wa shirk Khafi.*" That, 'Don't let hypocrisy enter my heart, and that don't let me to fall into hidden *shirk* (polytheism) and judging Allah's ﷻ creation.'

اَللّٰهُمَّ طَهِّرْ قَلْبِي مِنَ النِّفَاقِ والشِّرْكِ اَلْخَفِي.

"*Allahumma tahhir qalbi minan nifaaqi wash shirki al khafi.*"

"*O Allah! Purify my heart from hypocrisy and the hidden polytheism.*"

They were keys, and *ihtiram*, and love, and respect for Sayyidina Muhammad ﷺ. Am I making Prophet ﷺ happy? You know they don't break their Ramadan (fasting) unless they're dying. And if they're very sick they cry the whole time that Allah ﷻ give them health to pray and to give their Ramadan. They don't feel like they have a headache and they don't do Ramadan that day. Every day that you intentionally miss in your fasting is a $600 penalty, for every day. Or  feed 60 people per day, or fast 60 consecutive days, for every day. We say by thirty, 1,800 consecutive months. You have to fast two months for every day that you miss. So, in 30 days you have to fast 60 consecutive months, for one day. It's not something small but means that this love is all from love. Nobody can force anyone to do anything. Nobody is even watching. It's what we do is from love. Are you thankful with Allah ﷻ? Then we try to do what we do. Are you thankful with *Rasulul Kareem* ﷺ (The Most Generous Prophet)? That Sayyidina Muhammad ﷺ – I know personally for myself – Prophet's ﷺ *nazar* (gaze) and love is dressing and blessing. And that love gives me the sweetness of my *deen* (religion). No doubt I want to make Prophet ﷺ happy with me in Allah's ﷻ presence.

Or the reverse – if I start to do bad, the shame I would feel if Sayyidina Muhammad ﷺ has to go to Allah's ﷻ presence and ask my forgiveness because Prophet ﷺ loves me. I know he loves me. When I know that he loves me, he has to ask Allah ﷻ, 'Please, *ya Rabbi*, don't punish him, don't punish her.' Why I want to put them into that type of position? I want it to be the other way, where they keep asking, '*Ya Rabbi*, can you bless him more because they're doing this. Can you give him more because they are doing this?'

We try to stay out of the dirty water in our lives and enter only into

oceans of goodness and *khair*. In which everything we're doing, we're hoping Prophet ﷺ is happy with it, and present it to Allah ﷻ. Imagine a gift coming from Prophet ﷺ to Allah ﷻ, where He hears from Prophet ﷺ something good from you. This is the cream of our existence, that if Sayyidina Muhammad ﷺ is happy with us, *inshaAllah.*

## How Do We Know Our Connection to the Shaykh, Prophet ﷺ, and Then to Allah ﷻ Exists?

We said that how do you know if Allah ﷻ loves you is to know your own love. And how do you know that Prophet ﷺ loves you and how do you know that the shaykh loves you is that how much do you love? It's not a one way, it's a two way. I love, *ya Rabbi*, I love You with all my heart, but I have absolutely no action that would quantify that. So, that's an empty love. That's just something somebody would say through their mouth. We meet many people like that. 'Ah, don't worry about me. I'm good with God. I love God.' But they don't do anything for it.

So, love is something real. It's when I'm immensely in love with Allah ﷻ, immensely in love with Sayyidina Muhammad ﷺ, that my life and everything about it is to show that love. I want Allah ﷻ to know how much I love Allah ﷻ, how much I love Sayyidina Muhammad ﷺ. If you

feel that and think that, then *awliya* (saints) come and teach you that you must understand they feel that about you. If you are of that nature in which your love is sincere and your actions match your love, you're doing the most you can to show that love, you have truly gotten their attention. And then know that Prophet ﷺ loves you like that, then you are reaching towards *ahbab* (lovers of Prophet ﷺ) because you put your life and your love where your mouth is.

It's not something you just say but it's something you say and you do with your actions. And the actions are important. And that's why they come to teach then do *khidmat* (service). *Khidmat* they taught us all in our homes; *khidmat* brings a *rahmah* (mercy), why? Because it shows your love. Can you love something? We said you can give without love; all your life you can give to all the different things you want in your life.

But can you love without giving? It's impossible. This love that Allah's ﷻ talking about no, no, *"Qul inna salaatee wa nusukee wa mahyaaya wa mamaatee lillaahi Rabbil 'aalameen."* For verily my prayers, my life, my family, my *rizq* (sustenance) everything for Allah ﷻ.

قُلْ إِنَّ صَلَاتِي وَنُسُكِي وَمَحْيَايَ وَمَمَاتِي لِلَّهِ رَبِّ الْعَالَمِينَ ﴿١٦٢﴾ لَا شَرِيكَ لَهُ ۖ وَبِذَٰلِكَ أُمِرْتُ وَأَنَا أَوَّلُ الْمُسْلِمِينَ ﴿١٦٣﴾

*6:162 – "Qul inna salati wa nusuki wa mahyaya wa mamati lillahi Rabbil 'Aalamin." (Surat Al-An'am)*

*"Say, 'Indeed, my prayer, my services of sacrifice, my living and my dying are for Allah, Lord of the worlds.'" (The Cattle, 6:162)*

So, then they come and teach, no if you really love, you give everything for that love. Why? Because you know it's going to begin to open and it's going to blossom, and you struggle for that love and you do for that love. Then you must know that Allah ﷻ loves you like that, Prophet ﷺ loves you like that and no doubt *awliyaullah* (saints) love you  because you're of service. You're doing things in that way to accomplish that mission of love and that spreading of love.

We are now in oceans of ignorance everywhere. Can you imagine the one who's going to complain about *zulumat* and all these oppressions coming onto the Earth, but didn't lift a finger? Didn't put a dollar, didn't do nothing to stop the oppression and then you're surprised that you're in the middle of a fire burning? No, you made it, you live with it. But those whom they give their whole life to spread the light and spread the love, why Allah 'ॐ want to put  them into oppression? Allah 'ॐ says you lived a life in which you spread the light and spread the love. I'll keep you in a pocket of love; even if the whole world is burning, you won't be burning.

## Can We Build Our Love For Prophet ﷺ By Praying?

*Alhamdulillah*, praying is beautiful, that it's required from us. But following the *tariqah* (spiritual path). Most important is to follow their example, read the daily *awrad* (daily practices), and like we said, email for the guidance. The Sufi 101 step, how to make your connection.  Everything that they're giving you is to make that connection with Sayyidina Muhammad ﷺ. Attending the *zikrs* (Divine remembrance) and the *salawats* (praises upon Prophet Muhammad ﷺ), the live broadcast – all of that is to increase the love to Sayyidina Muhammad ﷺ. So that is the medicine and that is the objective, is to connect humanity back to the love of Sayyidina Muhammad ﷺ, *inshaAllah*.

## How Do We Lower Our Ego and Remain Humble?

We just gave that advice before you asked that. The hardest advice is to be of service and to give from what Allah ّ gave you because you worship that. That's the hardest thing to pull from you like teeth. What Allah ّ gave to you, they're going to pull it, *"Khudh min amwalihim"* – we have on the wall is the *qiblah*. Take from them and pray for them.

خُذْ مِنْ أَمْوَالِهِمْ صَدَقَةً تُطَهِّرُهُمْ وَتُزَكِّيهِم بِهَا وَصَلِّ عَلَيْهِمْ ۖ إِنَّ صَلَاتَكَ سَكَنٌ لَّهُمْ ۗ وَاللَّـهُ سَمِيعٌ عَلِيمٌ ﴿١٠٣﴾

*9:103 – "Khudh min amwalihim sadaqatan tutahhiruhum wa tuzakkeehim biha wa salli 'alayhim, inna salawataka sakanun lahum, wallahu samee'un 'aleem." (Surat At-Tawbah)*

*"Take, [O, Muhammad (pbuh)], from their wealth a charity by which you purify them and Sanctify them and Pray on their behalf. Indeed, your Prayers are a source of Peace/security/reassurance for them. And Allah is Hearing and Knowing." (The Repentance, 9:103)*

Allah ّ didn't ask, 'Ask from them' because He knows they're not going

to give. So, when they take it's going to be a big enemy against your *nafs* (ego). As soon as you support, as soon as you give, and you give, and you give, and you give until it hurts. That you're attacking your *nafs*. If you have a service and you have a time, give your time. If you have *rizq* and sustenance, give your *rizq* and sustenance. If you have *aqel* and ability, give it and be of service until it

206

hurts. That is what is the fastest defeat of your *nafs* because it's most against that.

What, what can you give to your *nafs* – like a shower? That's not going to do anything. But what's real and what it truly hates is that – it hates to be of service. It only wants to serve itself and *shaitan* (satan). So then, when you enrolled and you gave and you gave and you did and you did, your foot is locked onto that shaykh. Where you going to go after all that? You're going to re-establish yourself somewhere else? It's like pay your whole Harvard tuition and say now, I'm quitting. No, nobody does that, unless your parents paid for it and you didn't care. But if you did it yourself with your blood, your sweat and your tears, you enrolled in that and you supported that, you're locked onto their feet; you're not going anywhere.

And that brings the fight of the *nafs* (ego) down, that brings like a flame upon the *nafs* (ego). Everything that you gave and every action of *khidmat* (service) is a fire against the *nafs* and that's what brings the *nafs* down. That's what bring the *nafs* into control because you're locked onto that reality. You're locked onto the shaykhs, you're locked onto the love of Sayyidina Muhammad ﷺ, you're committed to it. And that's what brings that ego down so that you can do your practices and do all  the *zikrs* that you have to do. If the *nafs* is wild, it becomes impossible to do anything. Every time you want to sit, it's all over the place.

And take a path of humility. That keep silent when people talk and someone fighting with you – keep silent, don't answer back. Put a lollipop in your mouth. We said a rock, but people might swallow it and then get in trouble. So, kinder, gentle is just put a lollipop in your mouth and don't answer back to people. So, that you can come against yourself. You don't have to vindicate yourself; Allah ﷻ will vindicate you, *inshaAllah*.

# Chapter 3
## The Daily Awrad
## and
## General Recitations

# The Daily Awrad (Practice)

## How Should We Begin the Daily Awrad and What More Can We Recite?

Everyone wants to recite more because they think, 'If I take two it'll be faster, three, it'll be really fast. 'No, no, no, it's just you are going to open up something that you are not prepared for. So if you become more subtle and feel more energies and you didn't build your connection with the shaykh to build yourself, to shield yourself with that light that the shaykh is bringing on behalf of *"Atiullaha wa atiur Rasula wa Ulil amre minkum,"* they are like a 'cable-man.

...أَطِيعُواللَّه وَأَطِيعُواْلرَّسُولَ وَأُوْلِي الْأَمْرِ مِنْكُمْ... ﴿٥٩﴾

*4:59 – "...Atiullaha wa atiur Rasula wa Ulil amre minkum..."*
*(Surat An-Nisa)*

*"...Obey Allah, Obey the Messenger, and those in authority among you..." (The Women, 4:59)*

So, when anyone says, 'Is this *shirk* (polytheism)?' Again, this is not the mind of a correct understanding. They are merely a cable-man. That Allah ﷻ give an authority because they are trustworthy. Who would you give it to? You have to give it to an executor of your trust. If you are not entitled, and not of a mindset and character to receive your grant from

211

Allah ﷻ – don't you have to go to an attorney before you get your inheritance. Because you are still out there partying and doing bad things and not of a sound mind. How could they give you your inheritance, you'll lose it. So, they are like a cable company, like a law firm. You go to them, they teach you, teach you, teach you; the authorization is given by them to begin to teach. When the student is being taught then what has already been destined for them is coming. Because Allah ﷻ then approves the teaching, approves the character, approves their understanding and from their inheritance is now flowing to them, flowing to them.

If you don't take that path, then you don't reach your inheritance until the *qabr* (grave). Because remember we said the diamond was already given. If Allah ﷻ wants you to reach that diamond to take your inheritance, you'll get it in the grave. But the grave unfortunately is 70,000 times more difficult. If you are worried about seeing something here during your *zikr* (Divine remembrance) then taking a break and having some fresh air, what do you do in the grave when

there is no break? And you see exactly what Allah ﷻ wants you to see, and they eat you and bite you and this is the *'azab* (difficulty) of the grave.

So, this is a *ni'mat* (blessing) and a blessing from Allah ﷻ when He inspires them that, 'Do your grave time on Earth.' So that forty days, everybody does forty days in the grave, that's why our mourning and *Khatmil Qur'an* (complete recitation of Holy Qur'an) and all our practices for forty days when the person dies. Because they are doing a *khalwah* (seclusion), they're doing their *chilla* (forty-day seclusion). But if we do our forty days on Earth it's much easier when we are alive. And that's why we have a specific recitation *"Nawaytul Arba'een, Nawaytul 'itikaf, Nawaytul Khalwah."* Every time you recite that, the time you recite and enter into your *'ibadah* (worship) takes away from these forty days.

نُوَيْتُ الْأَرْبَعِينْ، نُوَيْتُ الْإِعْتِكَافْ، نُوَيْتُ الْخَلْوَة، نُوَيْتُ الْعُزْلَة، نُوَيْتُ الرِّيَاضَة، نُوَيْتُ السُّلُوكَ وَالصِّيَامْ لِلَّهِ تَعَالَى فِيْ هَذَالْمَسْجِدْ

*"Nawaytul arbaeen, nawaytul itikaf, nuwaytul khalwa, nuwaytul uzla, nuwaytul riyada, nuwaytus sulook wal siyam, lillahi ta'ala fi hadhal masjid."*

*"I intend the forty (days of seclusion), I intend seclusion in the mosque, I intend seclusion, I intend isolation, I intend discipline (of the ego), I intend to travel in God's Path, I intend to fast for the sake of God in this mosque."*

So like when we are doing *zikr* (Divine remembrance), and it's four hours of *zikr* and we started with *"Nawaytul Arba'een, Nawaytul 'itikaf, Nawaytul Khalwah, Sulook wa Siyam fee hadhal masjid"* it begins to click until the time our practices are finished. That four hours will be

subtracted from your forty days you owe Allah ﷻ. So many achieved way beyond, just on that *du'a* (supplication). And then all your training, all of your practices are going towards that reality of the grave, that Allah ﷻ will begin to allow you to clean, once you're being clean and dressed by your reality. So, what's there to fear from people, they're going to do it in the grave where it's 70,000 times more difficult.

213

## Can We Do the Daily Awrad With Video if Needed?

If you're a beginner, no problem. Every action is based on intention.

إِنَّمَا الْأَعْمَالِ بِالنِّيَّتْ

*"Innamal 'Amaalu bin Niyyaat."*

*"Every action is according to (its) intention."*
*(Prophet Muhammad (pbuh))*

Allah's ﷻ is not expecting you to be perfect in Arabic. You can split and just take a few minutes of the beginning of the day to do the beginning part of the *awrad* (daily practices). Then when you get to the *"Allah, Allah"* 1,500 (times) and the *salawats* (praises upon Prophet Muhammad ﷺ) 300 times, you can split that throughout the day. That you sit for the 25 minutes to do the beginning part of the *awrad* and recite by looking at the book and reading it seven times, 70 times *istighfar* (seeking forgiveness), make your *du'as* (supplication) and finished. Then you do your *"Allah,"* 1,500 times and say, 'I'm going to do it on the bus going to work.' And then every day on the bus coming back, 'I'm going to make my 300 *salawats*' and then *alhamdulillah*.

Never leave the *awrad* for the nighttime because that's the trick *shaitan* (satan) plays with you. You stop doing it in the day, you don't do it in the afternoon. Before you know it, it's 12 o'clock and you haven't done it. And then just sleep on it. If you miss one day, it's as if you've lost your insurance for that day. There's an umbrella of protection. How we started first that the concept of the *madad* (support) is if I haven't the ability to protect myself and my family and I've admitted to that, Allah ﷻ

inspire with you the understanding of the *madad*, 'Be conscious of God, and keep the company of truthful servants.'

يَا أَيُّهَا الَّذِينَ آمَنُوا اتَّقُوا اللّه وَكُونُوا مَعَ الصَّادِقِينَ ﴿١١٩﴾

*9:119 – "Ya ayyuhal ladheena amanoo ittaqollaha wa kono ma'as sadiqeen." (Surat At-Tawbah)*

*"O you who have believed, have consciousness of Allah and be with those who are truthful/Pious/sincere (in words and deed)."*
*(The Repentance, 9:119)*

As soon as you keep their company and they train you, that ask for *madad*. As soon as you ask for *madad*, their lights are all around that *insan* (human being). They are like an umbrella of protection because what Allah ﷻ gave to them of *barakah* and blessings, Allah ﷻ inspires, 'Go and be with that servant because they call upon you.' And that's why *"Tanzilur Rahma."*

عِنْدَ ذِكْرِ الصَّالِحِينَ تَنْزِلُ الرَّحْمَةَ

*"Inda dhikres Saliheena Tanzilur Rahma."*

*"In mentioning the names of the pious people, Allah's Mercy descends."*
*(Prophet Muhammad (pbuh))*

By calling upon these pious souls, it brings the *rahmah* (mercy) of Allah ﷻ. That becomes like the insurance of energy around you. I keep calling upon them. I keep meditating to connect with them. Then they begin to teach that you don't have any power. When you make your *tafakkur* and contemplation, negate yourself to be nothing, their energy comes with their shaykh, their energy comes with their shaykh. Their energy comes with their shaykh all the way to the presence of Prophet ﷺ. And then imagine the presence of Prophet ﷺ and what type of energies come with that reality? Then before you know it, their field of protection is huge for themselves, for their families, for their children, for everyone. And that's what makes these real shaykhs the real shaykhs; it's their field of

protection is so immense. And Allah ﷻ make them to be a guide so that people fit under their umbrella of protection for their soul.

**What's the Minimum Awrad We Can Do When Busy?**

Actually, if you do the *awrad* consistent – the beginning of the *awrad*, before you get to the *"Allah"* and the *salawats* – that the three *shahadah*,

70 *istighfar*. That one if you have that memorized – Surat al-Ikhlas, Surat an-Nas, Surat al-Inshirah – if you have that memorized, it doesn't take more than twenty minutes. So, that has to be done, then the *du'a* (supplication) has to be made and sealed. Then the *zikr* of Allah ﷻ and the *durood sharif*, the *salawats* on Prophet ﷺ, can be split that you can do on your way to work. Your 1,500 *zikr* of Allah ﷻ, *"Allah, Allah, Allah, Allah, Allah"* – you do the minimum, not the 5,000, but to admit that we're weak servants and 1,500. And I do 1,500 *"Allah,*

*Allah, Allah, Allah"* on the way to work and then with the discipline, I'm going to do my 300 or 500 *salawats* (praises upon Prophet Muhammad ﷺ) on the way coming back.

216

And it's a matter of time management like everything else in life. That if you manage the time and have the discipline in which you write it and

religiously stick to it that I'm going to do this at this time, it should never be something difficult. If you don't have that discipline and then you just say well, I'll just wait, wait, wait and then everything at the end of the night trying to do it right before you fall asleep, then you begin to pass it and miss it. So, you

can do the beginning part before you leave the house up to the *Ihda* and the *du'a* (supplication), and then the *zikr* of Allah ﷻ and the *salawats* on Prophet ﷺ, split it. That shouldn't be left out, *inshaAllah*.

Where we talked about before that, you know, that people are paying to their home and thinking their home is going to protect them. When we first came here, we described that a day is coming of immense difficulty

that people won't imagine what type of difficulties, but they'll begin to test you. And they test you in your faith and your *istiqam*, firmness in your belief, that you could be sitting in a home and begin to hear scratching coming from everywhere. Where you think the house is under attack

from rodents, from raccoons, from creatures and you begin to panic and begin to have fear. That box that you live in is not as secure as you think it is without the *barakah* of Allah's ﷻ *Nazar* (Gaze), Prophet's ﷺ *nazar* and the *nazar* of *awliyaullah* (saints). That you begin to hear scratching and noises and you feel like the house something going to be coming in to eat you. And they begin to test on your faith that why do you believe like that?

Make your *du'as* (supplications), make your *salawats* (praises upon Prophet Muhammad 鐌), make your *zikrs* (Divine remembrance), make your *tafakkur* (contemplation) and your meditation asking Allah 㐅 to

push away, push away. For you may think it's a rodent but it could be spiritual beings playing with you by permission of Allah 㐅 to test you. Because a day coming where, wherever you are, there may be screaming outside the door that they're trying to get in. Nowhere will be safe except by Allah's 㐅 permission. If your faith is firm at that time and you know that you are good and your *hisaab* (account) is good with Allah 㐅 then *alhamdulillah*, nothing.

That was in Surah Tawbah, verse 51. *"Qul lany-yuseebanaaa illaa maa katabal laahu lanaa Huwa mawlaanaa; wa 'alal laahi fal yatawakka lil mu'minoon."* For verily nothing can happen to me that not written in Allah's 㐅 book and Allah's 㐅 my Mawlana, Allah's 㐅 my Protector and Allah 㐅 is the best of those to protect His *mu'mineen*. But didn't mean that you reached to be a *mu'min* (believer), you merely accepted Islam.

قُل لَّن يُصِيبَنَا إِلَّا مَا كَتَبَ اللَّـهُ لَنَا هُوَ مَوْلَانَا ۚ وَعَلَى اللَّـهِ فَلْيَتَوَكَّلِ الْمُؤْمِنُونَ ﴿٥١﴾

*9:51 – "Qul lany-yuseebanaaa illaa maa katabal laahu lanaa Huwa mawlaanaa; wa 'alal laahi fal yatawakka lil mu'minoon."*
*(Surat At-Tawbah)*

*"Say: 'Nothing will happen to us except what Allah has decreed for us: He is our protector' and on Allah let the Believers put their trust."*
*(The Repentance, 9:51)*

It means that these *ayatul Kareem* (the generous verse of Holy Qur'an) will begin to come alive with power for the believer. That based on that verse they'll have a power in which nothing is approaching them, and that Allah's ﷻ hand is firmly above them. But that requires sincerity, that requires a faith in which you put your faith and you put your faith to be real. What you have is real, you should be preparing for it. If you're preparing to pay off your home and you think your home is going to protect you, good luck with that. But if you believe your faith is true and you want the attention of Sayyidina Muhammad ﷺ, you want to do your *da'wah* (religious propagation),  you want to do all these things to get the *nazar* (gaze) and the attention of Sayyidina Muhammad ﷺ, that's what's important in our life.

That's why when you follow these *awliyaullah* (saints), they lead by example. They're not sitting at home just playing. They can play video games too and just sit at home. But they're continuously moving, moving, moving to the point of exhaustion. When people look at them, they say, 'Shaykh, you look like you're going to be dead.' The beginning of our journey was nice. We're all fresh and hello, we're leaving. By the end of the journey we didn't even broadcast it. It was ten kilometers a day of intense walking.

Why we do things like that? Why do they continuously go, continuously do events, continuously do? Because they want the *nazar* (gaze) and the *barakah* (blessings) of Sayyidina Muhammad's ﷺ *nazar* upon them that Prophet's ﷺ happy. With what

I gave you, you are using it in that way to save souls, to do your *da'wah*, to be of service and *khidmat*. That's the whole purpose of our life. My whole life was to be of service. If what Allah ﷻ gave me of knowledge and I dispense it. What Allah ﷻ gave me an understanding of character and I dispense it. Not to take what Allah ﷻ gave to you and to sit upon it. But to give, to give, and to be of service.

If what you have sitting in your bank could be opening a Center and people be coming and saving lives. What you think going to save you –

your bank account or the fact that you opened up a Center and the people are sitting on a carpet doing *zikr* (Divine remembrance) from your generosity? People don't seem to have an understanding. They pay more towards their car than towards their faith. So, this is the day that we live in. But turn on the news and you see what's happening all around and things are coming in very fast and very difficult now. *InshaAllah*, Allah ﷻ *nazar* (gaze) be upon us and the *rahmah* (mercy) of Prophet's ﷺ *nazar* be upon us, *inshaAllah*. And the support of *awliyaullah fis samayi wa fil ard* be upon us, *inshaAllah*.

## How Can We Manage Our Time?

*InshaAllah*, you'll be accountable for your time. So, *alhamdulillah*, Mawlana ق breaks the day into eight, eight, eight. Eight hours of worshipness, eight hours of sleep, eight hours of work. And all of them can be under worshipness. Because when

you work in the way of Allah 'ﷻ and support your family and support your *tariq* (path), your way and your faith, that becomes immense *'ibadah* (worship). Because that *'ibadah* is flourishing and nourishing many different realities. When you sleep and you sleep with *wudu* (ablution), you sleep with cleanliness, you sleep with all your *du'as* (supplications) – that is again an immense state of worshipness. If you are an oppressor and you sleep, even better – that is a state of worshipness. The sleep of an oppressor is *'ibadah*. So, if you're mean, go to bed. It becomes a state of worshipness. And then the other eight was what? Worshipness, *inshaAllah*. Try to manage your time to the best you have.

Now everybody has a lot of time in their homes. So, it's best to try to do your *zikr* (Divine remembrance), have your *tasbih* (prayer beads) in your

hand. Try to do the *zikr* while you're with your family and watching television. Try to be soft on everything, try to be moderate in everything, and *inshaAllah*, Allah 'ﷻ inspire everyone to their level. Now again, don't be too hard on

yourselves but take a medium path, a middle way in which to be soft and gentle and continue, or consistency. That to be consistent at something is dear to Allah 'ﷻ; not to take a lot and then dump it, but to be consistent, *inshaAllah*.

## On the Spiritual Path How Many Hours Should We Sleep?

The rule that Mawlana Shaykh ق teaches is eight hours. Get your good eight hours of sleep and keep struggling against one's self. Eight hours of worshipness and eight hours of work, and your eight hours of sleep. Your worshipness includes your *salah* (prayer) and the time you spend with your family and loved ones so that they can feel the presence of that person and that reality. And as they progress and progress, it's not a matter of  you sleeping less. It's the energy will become so intense it's difficult to sleep. So, it's not a matter of trying to keep yourself awake and then I have to have coffee and fall and stumble around the house.

The energy is coming so heavy onto that servant that they just can't sleep. And that's then by Allah ﷻ and not by you. So, it's not a matter of something you have to *tarbiyah* (discipline) yourself so much. Now to  go too deep into sleep and miss all your prayers then the result is that before you sleep – your *Fajr* – before you sleep the nighttime prayer, drink lots of water, lots of water. And then train yourself to keep making *wudu* (ablution). Get up and then wash, pray your *Salatul Wudu* (Prayer of Ablution) on the side of your bed and then go straight to bed. You do this throughout the night so your sleep is very light. That way you are more attentive and ready for your *salah* (prayer) and not going into such a deep sleep. Some people sleep like they're in a coma. *InshaAllah*.

## How Do We Become Regular in Waking Up For Fajr?

*InshaAllah,* drink a lot of water before you sleep; it's not difficult. Just train yourself not to sleep deep. Put a big pitcher of water and drink that water before you sleep, and you have to wake up every few hours to wash. And you train yourself to wake up, wash and go back to bed. Wake up,  wash, and go back to bed, so that the sleep is not so deep that you're completely knocked out. Before you know it, one of those times you have to get up is going to be your *Fajr* time; then you get up, wash, and pray your *Salatul Fajr.* But discipline yourself not to have a very deep sleep, *inshaAllah.*

## If Chanting Inwards "Allah" is Difficult, What Should We Do?

Difficulty in doing the *"Allah"* only is that to do *khafi zikr* (silent Divine remembrance), is just to close your eyes, see yourself at the  Ka'bah or in the presence of these *awliyaullah* (saints), and then just making *khafi zikr, "Allah, Allah, Allah"* [Shaykh recites in low voice]. And doing your *tasbih* (prayer beads) in a silent, *"Allah, Allah, Allah."* Basic – just almost the sound of your breath coming out, *"Allah, Allah, Allah"* [Shaykh recites with his breath]. And later as you progress, then you don't even have to move your tongue. At first, it's not easy just to do the *khafi* without the tongue moving. So, people are not trained to do and to make their *zikr* (Divine remembrance) without their tongue. Later, you'll learn that your finger is acting like your tongue. This means if you just sit and try to say *"Allah"* in your heart, it's very difficult unless somebody's been trained on how to move their *zikr* in their heart.

So, your finger becomes with your *tasbih* like your tongue. Every time it moves, you're making *"Allah"* into the heart. But for now, the first phase would be, *"Allah, Allah, Allah"* with a barely audible voice, saying, *"Allah, Allah, Allah,"* *inshaAllah*. Now if it's difficult through energy, that's something different. If you're feeling an energy when you're saying that and difficulty coming to you, that's something different. But difficulty in the ability is then what we described, *inshaAllah*.

## How Do We Deal With Anxiety Attacks Even When Doing Our Awrad?

Anytime we are doing our spiritual practices, *A'uzu Billahi Minash Shaitanir Rajeem*, that you're dealing with energy. And when there is energy around and you're not familiar with something, your soul sees but you don't. So, if your soul is sensing something from an energy while

you're meditating and practicing or your soul senses something, a difficulty, an issue, something happening. Remember the body is in a state of heedlessness and the soul is hyper-alert. And that's why when the practices are too heavy, and too often or too much, then the soul can become hyper-alert. And the physicality is not ready for that. So, then it depends on

what issues are happening, when they're happening. If you're doing the *awrad* (daily practices) and feeling the anxiety coming or you're not doing the *awrad* and you're feeling, so everything has to be very specific to your condition. Then we can prescribe, *inshaAllah*, based on what you're describing as far as, 'Is it during your meditation, is it during the practices, is it because of too many practices and energies.' And these are all things that you can email. So, you can email the helpme@nurmuhammad.com, describe what's happening, and then we try out best to address that, *inshaAllah*.

## Should Zikr Be Done Loudly or Silently?

Depending upon on what *zikr* (Divine remembrance). You do your *zikr* in not a loud voice. You'll come across people, *"Allah, Allah, Allah, Allah"* [Shaykh recites in a loud voice]. It's entertaining maybe for a few people who are watching

you. But the correct *adab* (manners) is, *"Allah, Allah, Allah"* [Shaykh recites in a low voice], so that I'm hearing it. I'm hearing it and I'm meditating, *"Allah, Allah, Allah, Allah"* [Shaykh closes eyes and recites in a low voice]. At a higher level of energy, Naqshbandiya is built on *khafi zikr* (silent Divine remembrance). But that's a place where somebody has to understand. They got to that place in which their meditation is so strong that when they train in their meditation, they don't move. And they enter into a state of death where nothing is moving on them. As soon as they even want to breathe or make a sound, it causes their soul to come back into their body.

To avoid that, and that's why Mawlana Shah Naqshband ق, *Fardul Alam, Fardul 'Arsh,* in the *khatm* of his shaykh would walk out and go into another room. And many of the students were being angered, 'Why he leaves, he thinks he's...what is he doing?' When the shaykh was giving a *zikr,* he was leaving. That doesn't mean everybody leave when we're doing *zikr.* But his state was so high that his shaykh gave him permission because he has to go somewhere where he's completely silent, and he's not going to make any sound.

It means that you enter into a state of death, so that his heart is making the *zikr*, not his tongue, and he doesn't even bring the *zikr* to the

tongue. It's all through his living heart. The heart is alive and it's going, *"Allah, Allah, Allah."* And through their breath, their breathing in that *zikr* and that power. But for now, to imitate, it's a voice in which I can hear, *"Allah, Allah, Allah, Allah"* [Shaykh recites Allah silently], so that the angels are hearing, and I'm hearing. And the energy around is also

hearing that *zikr*. It doesn't have to be so loud that it's disruptive for other people, *inshaAllah*.

### Should We Reduce Our Zikr if We Start Seeing Things?

Please follow the *awrads* (daily practices) and the *wazifas* (spiritual practice) of the shaykhs. And don't prescribe for yourself anything right now, because anybody who becomes hyper-alert, they don't have the dress of that protection. So, it's like we said in the other talk, I think a few weeks ago. That, if you take medicine, medicine is good for you, but doesn't mean that you take ten tablets. It can have a different effect upon you. If you're not one who's been built up, the *zikr* (Divine remembrance)

may open up something that you haven't prepared yourself to defend or to push away, and then can begin to have problems.

So, the Naqshbandi *awrad* is on the app, and Ramadan is a time where you appreciate it the most. That please, download the Muhammadan Way app, click on Ramadan, entire *wazifa* and etiquette is there.

Anybody who wants the attention of the shaykhs, support the shaykh! You know, just calling and all the time texting and emailing, emailing, emailing, at least support their mission and their *da'wah* (religious propagation). And we have people who even have offices and businesses, and they are familiar with that concept. Why would it be different for Allah's servants? If you're going to take their office time, going to take their time away from them, want to have their attention – support their mission! That shows that you have an *ihtiram* and a respect.

And that's why Allah says, 'When you go to Sayyidina Muhammad ﷺ, don't go empty handed.' This was the *adab* (manners) of Islam. When you go somewhere, don't go empty handed. Allah is teaching the people, 'Don't keep going to Prophet ﷺ and then take all his time and talk all the time. Say your thing and go. And don't come empty handed, come with a gift!' Why? To show the *ihtiram* and the respect. This is the Islamic *adab* and the Islamic way, *inshaAllah*.

## Can We Recite Different Salawats Than the Ones Recited During Zikr?

Yes, but if you go to a doctor and they give you antibiotics and you say, 'Thank you so and so; I think I want to take Tamiflu,' and take their own pills, then you can do whatever you want. Now whether we recite here as far as the *mawlid*, you can recite any *mawlid* you want. But whatever Mawlana Shaykh ق has given in the *awrad* (daily practices) and in the *zikr* (Divine remembrance) and in the *salawat* books (praises upon Prophet ﷺ), it's best to follow their prescriptions.

That, we talked about few weeks ago. That when you start to add too many things, then side effects from the medication can begin. Some people would say, 'I'm experiencing all these things. I'm seeing all these things. All these things are attacking me. All these types of horrific dreams are coming at night,' and they don't tell you what exactly  they're doing. They say, 'No, no, I'm following what the *wazifa* (spiritual practice) the shaykh gave. I'm reciting that on daily basis.' Later they come back and say, 'You know, as a matter of fact, I recite 10,000 such and such *salawats.*' But you may not have the ability to carry that. And as a result of making you even more hyper-alert, maybe the opening in your heart is opening to see, but you haven't been spiritually built to defend. So, then you have a problem.

That's why there's a system, very simple, follow it. If the shaykh feels that you're doing more and more and you're consistent and your spiritual training, your character, your *akhlaaq* (character) is of a nature that they feel you can carry more, don't worry, it will come to you. But by virtue of just taking more pills doesn't make you more healthier. You can open up different problems.

# General Prayers, Recitations, and Praisings

### Can We Do the Fajr Awrad and What Can We Recite for Barakah (Blessings)?

I don't know if you have opened the app yet – that *Fajr awrad* is a good hour for you. So, if you can complete that with all of the *Fajr namaz*

(prayer) twenty *rakahs* (cycles of prayer) in the *Fajr*. There is *Tahajjud*, you can go eight, ten *rakahs* of *Tahajjud*, *Salatul Najat*, *Salatul Shukr*, *Salatut Tasabih*, you will be there for a couple of hours, and then the *surahs* (Qur'an verses)

to recite after that. Just first let's go slowly, slowly.

If you start to see the gargoyles and all the demons and the difficult things, and you start to scream, then you are going to complain. So again, everything in life is just slowly, slowly.

Slowly, slowly. Anything you do too much of and you are not built up for that level and that understanding, and you open up – you know a *pardeh* – you open up a veil that you are not prepared to be open, you are going to have problems. So, we have talked on those issues before, That you want to do too much and say too many things, then you are going to have

problems with what's opening, so just try to do the *awrad* from the book. This is the *wazifa* from the Shaykhs and that is from Grandshaykh Daghestani ق, Shaykh Mawlana Shaykh Muhammad Nazim Haqqani ق to all the living shaykhs right now that is the Naqshbandi, and that's the authorized *wazifa*, so do that. *Alhamdulillah*, that should be enough and the *muraqabah* is most important. *Muraqabah*, your connection, all your practices. In other talks we have given it is not your *zikrs* that are opening anything.

If you think that you do a hundred thousand and you going to open something, like reach into the heavens, it is actually your good manner, good characteristics, and your level of *muraqabah*. That, the shaykh is flying like a rocket throughout the heavens. And the minute your good character and your *muraqabah* can connect, you can feel how quickly they are lifting the student; that is what is important. Not that, 'I am relying upon myself that I am going to do all these practices, I am going to exaggerate the count of these practices,' then it is not about lifting myself up.

It is about the good characteristics and mastering the understanding of *muraqabah*, what we talked about at the beginning of the discussion. Your path is about two inches long – can you follow that? And then from this A to B you don't have to add anything. Somebody comes, 'I want to add this, I want to add that.' Okay, but you are diverting from the cause; just get to the A and the B. If you are able

| POINT A | POINT B |
| :---: | :---: |
| ◎ | ◎ |
| Your Will | Shaykh's Will |

to match the guidance that comes to you, you get an award. That is B to C then. Now you are ready – from B to C is a little bit more bumpier.

**Can the Fajr Awrad Be Performed Throughout the Day?**

Sure, there's not a problem for that. If you have to do your *Fajr* quickly

and you want to recite the *awrad* (daily practices), you copy and paste it in your notes and you can recite it throughout the day. It's a *du'a* (supplication) and a prayer that has tremendous blessings and takes away every type of difficulty,

*inshaAllah*. Not a problem, *inshaAllah*; Allah's, *"Innamal A'malu Binniyat."*

إِنَّمَا الْأَعْمَالِ بِالنِّيَّتْ

*"Innamal 'Amaalu bin Niyyaat."*

*"Every action is according to (its) intention."*
*(Prophet Muhammad (pbuh))*

**What Can We Recite While Travelling?**

*"Astaghfirullahal 'Azim, wa atubu ilayh."*

أَسْتَغْفِرُ اللهَ الْعَظِيمِ وَأَتُوبُ إِلَيْه

*"Astaghfirullahal 'Azim, wa atubu ilayh."*

*"I ask forgiveness of Allah the Magnificent, and I turn to Him in repentance."*

They can make *istighfar* (seeking forgiveness) because that *istighfar* will clean them, clean their loved ones and at least, clean the energy that is trying to attach itself to the person. So, if you're going to make a *zikr* (Divine remembrance), the journey is long, then *istighfar,* and "*Astaghfirullahal 'Azim, wa atubu ilayh.*" The "*Azim,*"because you're asking for forgiveness by asking Allah's سبحانه وتعالى *sifat al-'Azim* (attribute of the Magnificent). That, 'Your Might and Your Majesty that nobody can comprehend, and my sins are small in comparison to Your greatness, *ya Rabbi.* Wipe it away.' And it's not something difficult for Allah سبحانه وتعالى.

"I seek the *forgiveness* of Allah, the Mighty."

## If You've Done Nothing Wrong That Day, What Should You Recite?

You are home all day, you weren't lazy, you did all your *zikr* (Divine remembrance), you did all your *awrads* (daily practices), make *istighfar* for yourself always. Then make *istighfar* for the family because when we are making *istighfar* always as a means in which the power of *istighfar,* "*Astaghfirullahal 'Azim, wa atubu ilayh,*" it opens Allah's سبحانه وتعالى *rahmah* (mercy).

أَسْتَغْفِرُ اللهَ الْعَظِيمِ وَأَتُوبُ إِلَيْه

"*Astaghfirullahal 'Azim, wa atubu ilayh.*"

"*I ask forgiveness of Allah the Magnificent, and I turn to Him in repentance.*"

By you asking for Allah's ﷻ forgiveness, Allah ﷻ says, '*Bismillahir Ar-Rahmanir Raheem*, in the name of My Generosity and My Compassion, I am forgiving you.' So, one, Allah's ﷻ *zikr* upon you, then you make *istighfar.* So, every time you are saying "*Astaghfirullahal 'Azim, wa atubu ilayh,*" Allah ﷻ replies with, "*Bismillah Ar-Rahmanir Raheem.*" So, by washing and *istighfar* is like a cleansing, '*Ya Rabbi,* I am cleansing, cleansing. If everything is clean off of me today, now I am asking *istighfar* for my children, for my community, for my loved ones.' And then you become one whom, if you are excess positive, you can become of benefit to society. So, it's a means in which to clean. Clean ourselves and clean all the homes around us, and all the people that we love and care for, *inshaAllah.*

## What Zikr Can We Recite Throughout the Day?

You'll find the Naqshbandi *awrad* (daily practices) on the app. And it's highly recommended in this time, making *istighfar* (seeking forgiveness) all day long, "*Astaghfirullahal 'Azim, wa atubu ilayh.*"

أَسْتَغْفِرُ اللهَ الْعَظِيمِ وَأَتُوبُ إِلَيْه

"*Astaghfirullahal 'Azim, wa atubu ilayh.*"

"*I ask forgiveness of Allah the Magnificent, and I turn to Him in repentance.*"

233

So, we go from morning time till afternoon *"Astaghfirullahal 'Azim, wa atubu ilayh."* That *sifat al-'Azim* (attribute of the Magnificent), Allah's Azimah (Magnificence) to wipe away all my sins and that *istighfar* is a shower and a cleansing. Soon as we ask Allah *"Astaghfirullahal 'Azim, wa atubu ilayh."* Allah's reply is *"Bismillah Ar-Rahmanir Raheem,"* *inshaAllah.* That from the oceans of mercy and compassion they dress us and bless us and take away every type of difficulty.

Once we've washed and showered with *istighfar*, then the remaining time of the day *salawat* on Sayyidina Muhammad , *"Allahumma salli 'ala Sayyidina Muhammad wa 'ala aali Sayyidina Muhammad. Allahumma salli 'ala Sayyidina Muhammad wa 'ala aali Sayyidina Muhammad. Allahumma salli 'ala Sayyidina Muhammad wa 'ala aali Sayyidina Muhammad."* *InshaAllah.*

اللَّهُمَّ صَلِّ عَلَى سَيِّدِنَا مُحَمَّد، وَعَلَى آلِ سَيِّدِنَا مُحَمَّد.

*"Allahumma salli 'ala Sayyidina Muhammad wa 'ala aali Sayyidina Muhammad."*

*"O Allah! Send Peace and blessings upon our master Prophet Muhammad and upon the Family of our master Prophet Muhammad (pbuh)."*

234

## Are There Salawats For Uplifting Ailments?

Yes, all the *salawats* on the app. That the Salawat al-Nariyah is to take away many calamities and difficulties. Salawat al-Fatih is the one that Mawlana ق most prescribing, and most being recommended now for openings. Because you're asking from the *haq* (truth) of Prophet ﷺ to open; through that *haq* everything that is closed and that the realization that Prophet's ﷺ key must open everything.

All these *salawats* when we look at the English, and look at the Urdu, the Arabic – whatever language we're looking at, it's teaching us with the shaykh's teachings that you're not going to Allah's ﷻ door. If you think you're going to Allah's ﷻ door, yet your character is not correct. If you think, 'I have a problem. I have to go to *Mushkil Gusha*, the one who takes my problems away. So, I go to Prophet ﷺ, I go to *Ahlul Bayt* (Holy family of Prophet ﷺ), I go to *Ashab an Nabi* ﷺ (Holy companions of Prophet ﷺ), and say that, give me an audience with Sayyidina Muhammad ﷺ.

الله الله نبی کا گھرانہ، یہ گھرانہ ورا الوریٰ ہے
اس میں حسنین ہیں فاطمہ ہیں، اس گھرانے میں مشکل کُشاء ہے

*Allah Allah Nabi ka gharana, Yeh gharana wara-ul-wara hai*
*Iss may Hasnain hai Fatima hai, Iss gharany may Mushkil Kusha hai*

*O Allah, the household of Prophet (pbuh), it's highest of the highest, It has Hasnain (as), Fatima (as), it has the Solver of all Difficulty (Ali (as)).*

235

As soon as they inspire, 'Make this *durood* (praising on Prophet Muhammad ﷺ),' that is your audience with Prophet ﷺ. Because you are greeting him with a beatific greeting. 'O the one who takes away calamity, the one who takes away difficulty,' it's like a praising. You're not asking in a regular language; you're asking in a beatific way. Of course, Prophet's ﷺ then listening.

And then you're giving, and doing, and supporting, of course then every difficulty opens, every *mushkilat* (difficulties) opens. Now the medicine is intense amounts of *salawats* to the level that you can and what's written onto the *awrad* (daily practices). And any time you're sitting at home, open up your Mawlid Book, and do your *mawlid* in the home. Get your children to recite the *mawlid*, play the *mawlid* in the house. The house becomes a beatific energy of angelic forces that stops the *shaitans* (satans) from entering into that precinct, *inshaAllah*.

## Are There Specific Recitations For Healing Body Pains?

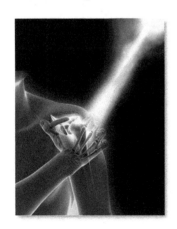

For pain everything is going to be something different. There's a different *salawat* (praises upon Prophet Muhammad ﷺ) for different ailments and different difficulties that are coming. But the most important is that when they're in a state of *tafakkur* (contemplation), they're meditating, they're breathing, it's to visualize where that pain is and asking Allah ﷻ to send a light, to send an energy to take away that difficulty.

236

So, this means the whole dialogue in *tafakkur* or in contemplation is that, *'Ya Rabbi,* grant me Your power, Your light. Grant me Your energy, Your *qudra* (power). That grant me a light in which my light is not sufficient, not strong enough to protect me. Grant me Your satisfaction.' That Allah 'ﷻ bestow lights and energy upon the soul that is resolving everything. That is the knowledge, that is the healing, that is the sustenance.

If Allah 'ﷻ grants a power to your soul, why would you need to ask for

money? Because He gave the most premium part of you a reality. You don't ask for the side pieces, 'I need some cash. I need like this. I need like this.' No, no, you say, *'Ya Rabbi,* grant me a light and *rida* (satisfaction) upon my soul.' And if Allah's 'ﷻ satisfied, and He begin to send a *qudra* and a light upon your soul and you feel it. You feel an energy coming. You feel an energy while breathing. You feel yourself heating up, that Allah 'ﷻ is giving your access to now a Divinely source of lights and energies that begin to dress your soul.

If those lights dress you, they take away the sicknesses that Allah 'ﷻ wants to be taken away because of deficient energy. The rest Allah 'ﷻ wants to stay and you can't take away what Allah 'ﷻ wants there to be in your

character. If any *rizq* (sustenance) and sustenance that's not coming, where it will be taken away by the light that's dressing upon your soul. So, the most premium request from Allah 'ﷻ is, *'Ya Rabbi,* grant me a light and energy upon my soul that You'll be pleased with me.

Take away any darkness and fill me with every light.' So, that Allah ﷻ sends the best of blessings and they resolve every type of difficulty.

After the meditation, then the *zikr* (Divine remembrance) throughout the day should be *salawats* on Sayyidina Muhammad ﷺ. That for you to recite a *du'a* (supplication) and for you to recite something, that's the assumption that you're already in a correct place with Allah ﷻ. Because you think that your *Ismullah* is going to count. You think all these recitations are going to count. The more perfected understanding is that I am in this because of my deficiency. So, the *zikr* that's most powerful for me is *salawat* on Sayyidina Muhammad ﷺ, *"Allahumma salli 'ala Sayyidina Muhammadin wa 'ala aali Sayyidina Muhammad."*

اللَّهُمَّ صَلِّ عَلَى سَيِّدِنَا مُحَمَّد، وَعَلَى آلِ سَيِّدِنَا مُحَمَّد

*"Allahumma salli 'ala Sayyidina Muhammad wa 'ala aali Sayyidina Muhammad."*

*"O Allah! Send Peace and blessings upon our master Prophet Muhammad and upon the Family of our master Prophet Muhammad (pbuh)."*

Immediately, Prophet's ﷺ *nazar* (gaze) is upon you sending ten *salawats* upon you.

عَنْ أَنَسِ بْنِ مَالِكٍ رَضِيَ اللهُ عَنْهُ، قَالَ: قَالَ رَسُولُ اللَّهِ - صلى الله عليه وسلم -: "مَنْ صَلَّى عَلَيَّ صَلاةً وَاحِدَةً، صَلَّى اللهُ عَلَيْهِ عَشْرَ صَلَوَاتٍ، وَحُطَّتْ عَنْهُ عَشْرُ خَطِيئَاتٍ، وَرُفِعَتْ لَهُ عَشْرُ دَرَجَاتٍ."

*Qala Rasulullah* 🖼: *"Man Salla 'alaiya Salatan wahidatan, Sallallahu 'alayhi 'ashra Salawatin, wa Huttat 'anhu 'ashru khaTeatin, wa ruf'at lahu 'ashru darajatin."*

*Prophet Muhammad (pbuh) said:* "*Whoever sends blessings [Praises] upon me, God will shower His blessings upon him ten times, and will erase ten of his sins, and elevate [raise] his [spiritual] station ten times.*" *(Hadith recorded by Nasa'i)*

It means Prophet 🖼 is resolving your case through your *salawats*. And that, 'I'm a weak servant.' And what Allah ﷻ ordered, the only *zikr* that Allah ﷻ ordered, "*InnAllaha wa malayikatahu yusalluna 'alan Nabiyi.*"

إِنَّ اللَّهَ وَمَلَائِكَتَهُ يُصَلُّونَ عَلَى النَّبِيِّ يَا أَيُّهَا الَّذِينَ آمَنُوا صَلُّوا عَلَيْهِ وَسَلِّمُوا تَسْلِيماً ﴿٥٦﴾

*33:56 – "InnAllaha wa malayikatahu yusalluna 'alan Nabiyi yaa ayyuhal ladhina aamanu sallu 'alayhi wa sallimu taslima."*
*(Surat Al-Ahzab)*

"*Allah and His angels send blessings upon the Prophet [Muhammad (pbuh)]: O you that believe! Send your blessings upon him, and salute him with all respect.*" *(The Combined Forces, 33:56)*

And that's enough that Allah ﷻ and the angels are praising and praying upon with the secret of that reality. That *salawat* is enough to take away every type of difficulty and deficiency, *inshaAllah*.

## What Zikr Can We Do to Overcome Constant Fear?

Constant fear – again, because there's some other issues too. If you have to take medicine, continue your medicine. Never leave your medicine and this way is based on mind, body, and soul. If your mind is not well and that's Allah 󰐨 put the servant in every type of condition. There can be servants with broken legs, sickness. Allah 󰐨 gives the difficulty for you to walk on a crooked path. Don't try to fix people's problems. It's not for you to compete with Allah 󰐨. You're merely here to fix the person's faith.

Allah 󰐨 gave everybody a difficulty in life. Say if everybody complains, let's get a bucket, everybody writes their problem, put it in the bucket and take somebody else's problem. You say, 'No, no, no, I'm happy with my problem. I know how to deal with my problem. I don't want your problem.' Everybody has something. This makes the quality of your life. There has to be a squeezing, there has to be a crushing.

How are you going to be patient and persevere through the difficulty Allah 󰐨 sends? And that's what Allah 󰐨 wants. It wasn't about you declaring victory for everybody, healing everybody, everybody to be great. As a matter of fact, if you ask the shaykhs, everybody's sick. And that's the way Allah 󰐨 wants it.

Said, 'I want to put a difficulty on you, and I want to see your ability to keep struggling through your difficulty.'

240

Use your *zikr* (Divine remembrance), use the medicines so that your mind is well. Use good health and good nourishment and not to be excessive in which your diet becomes your religion. Your body is dying anyways. Don't say that these cherries are organic and that it comes from a very special farm that nobody ever touched it. As a matter of fact, the organic is

they take the feces and they put the feces back into the field and they put the waste of humans on those very expensive tomatoes which Prophet ﷺ forbid the use of your bodily function on any fruit. You're not allowed to urinate near a tree. You're not allowed to defecate near a tree because all of the toxins, Prophet ﷺ taught, will go into the fruit.

عَنْ أَبِي هُرَيْرَةَ رَضِيَ اللهُ عَنْهُ، أَنَّ رَسُولَ اللهِ ﷺ قَالَ " اِتَّقُوا اللَّعَانَيْنِ "
قَالُوا: وَمَا اللَّعَانَانِ يَا رَسُولَ اللهِ ﷺ ؟ قَالَ: "الَّذِي يَتَخَلَّى فِي طَرِيقِ النَّاسِ أَوْ فِي
ظِلِّهِمْ ." [اَلْمَصْدَرْ: مُسْلِمْ وَ أَبُودَاوُد ٢٦٩/٢٥]

*'An Abi Hurairah (ra), anna Rasulullahi* ﷺ *qala,*
*"Ittaqul la'aanayni."*
*Qalo: wa mal la'aanaani, ya Rasulullahi* ﷺ*?*
*Qala* ﷺ *:"Allazi yatakhalla fi Tariqin nasi aw fi zhellihim."*

*Narrated Abu Hurairah (ra), that the Messenger of Allah (pbuh) said:*
*"Beware of those two acts which cause others to curse." They asked,*
*"What are those two acts, O Messenger of Allah?"*
*He (pbuh) replied, "Relieving oneself in the people's walkways or in their*
*shades." [Source: Muslim and Abu Dawud (269/25)]*

So, what *shaitan* (satan) gives to all of these organic rich people? Fruit filled with feces. Sorry, organic people. They're paying big money for those things and they're taking human waste and putting it onto the fields and say, 'This is grey water. The water that we recycled, throw this water onto all the flowers.' Yeah whatever *shaitan* is doing, he's trying to kill everyone.

The only thing that has a *barakah* and a blessing; take any orange you can find and make *du'a* (supplication), mention Allah's ﷻ name upon it, "*Ila sharifin Nabi* ﷺ, *wa ila aalihi wa sahbihil kiram, wa ila mashayikhina fit tariqahtin Naqshbandiyatil 'aaliyah, khasatan ruhi imamit tariqah.*" You start mentioning your shaykhs, mentioning Allah ﷻ, mentioning Prophet ﷺ, mentioning your shaykhs, anything you eat – if it's even a rock, it will be golden for you.

إِلَى شَرَفِ النَّبِيِّ ﷺ وَإِلَى آلِهِ وَصَحْبِهِ الْكِرَامِ. وَإِلَى أَرْوَاحِ مَشَائِخِنَا فِي الطَّرِيقَةِ النَّقْشْبَنْدِيَةِ الْعَالِيَّةِ، خَاصَةً إِلَى رُوْحِ إِمَامِ الطَّرِيْقَةْ

"*Ila sharifin Nabi* ﷺ *wa ila aalihi wa sahbihil kiram. Wa ila mashayikhina fit tariqatin Naqshbandiyatil 'aaliyah, khasatan ila ruhi Imamit tariqati.*"

"*Honour be to the Prophet (Muhammad (pbuh)), and his family, and his distinguished Companions, And to our honoured Shaykhs (spiritual guides) of distinguished Order of Naqshbandi. especially the leader of the Way.*"

In times of *mushklilat* (difficulties) and many *awliya* (saints) know and many people who have survived war on this Earth, they have nothing. And *awliyaullah* will bring something for them, begin to make a *du'a* (supplication) and they all eat it, they can be full for a week. If Allah ﷻ want to open, Allah ﷻ opens and it's by *du'a* (supplication). You can have the most expensive fruit and food, think that your chicken never touched the ground, and everybody tickled your chicken all day long [Laughter]. It's farm fresh and tickled the whole time and you get sick like a dog by it. And Allah ﷻ make somebody else eat from something else but they're sincere. They make a *du'a* on it and they're full for seven days.

## Can You Explain More About Durood Sharif and Salawats?

*Durood sharif* (praising on Prophet Muhammad ﷺ), that's the whole *tariqah* (spiritual path). That would be whole hours and hours of talking, but the immensity of *durood sharif* and its blessings is something that can't be even understood. What type of power, what type of reality, what type of blessings are dressing and blessing the servant. The way is to the heart of Sayyidina Muhammad ﷺ, and the magnificent power of *durood sharif* to be dressed by the *nazar* (gaze) of Sayyidina Muhammad ﷺ.

But most important for this month's *tajalli* (manifestation) is to understand *istighfar* (seeking forgiveness), and to shut off, and to dress ourselves to flow upon that track of reality into the heart of Sayyidina Muhammad ﷺ. The *durood sharif*, we have the whole website is on the power of *salawats* (praises upon Prophet Muhammad ﷺ) and reaching towards the Muhammadan reality, *inshaAllah*.

243

## Are Big Sins Forgiven With Durood Sharif?

*InshaAllah*, all sins forgiven. What's big and what's small? There are physics and science apps now that you can look and say look into the universe. You take this leaf and then begin to zoom out, zoom out, zoom out. It goes outside of the Earth, goes outside the galaxy, goes out to the milky way, goes out into space. You can no longer even see the dot of the Earth. Allah ﷻ – how many billions of galaxies and universes Allah ﷻ has? Aren't you astonished that He even knows who you are? Right?

This, *Allahu Akbar* that, 'Ya Rabbi, the vastness of everything – are You sure you know who I am? Did anybody forget me up there?' He says, 'Not a single breath you make, I forgot. Not a single step you make, I have not written for you.'

So, when Allah ﷻ says, 'Everything is in a *hisaab* (account)' but with that vastness and greatness Allah ﷻ want to rip you to pieces for what? Why Allah ﷻ created you? He wants you to make your *istighfar* (seeking forgiveness), want you to understand that, 'You are of a sinning nature. Your nation sins and never tires from sinning and I'm not tired of forgiving them.'

عَنْ أَنَسِ بْنِ مَالِكٍ رَضِيَ اللهُ عَنْهُ قَالَ رَسُولُ اللهِ ﷺ : "إِذَا أَذْنَبَ الْعَبْدُ ذَنْبًا كُتِبَ عَلَيْهِ"

فَقَالَ أَعْرَابِيٌّ : فَإِنْ تَابَ عَنْهُ ؟ قَالَ " مُحِيَ عَنْهُ "

قَالَ : فَإِنْ عَادَ ؟ قَالَ النَّبِيُّ ﷺ " يُكْتَبُ عَلَيْهِ "

قَالَ الْأَعْرَابِيُّ : فَإِنْ تَابَ ؟ قَالَ " مُحِيَ مِنْ صَحِيفَتِهِ "

قَالَ : إِلَىٰ مَتَىٰ ؟

قَالَ " إِلَىٰ أَنْ يَسْتَغْفِرَ وَيَتُوبَ إِلَى اللهِ عَزَّ وَ جَلَّ إِنَّ اللهَ لَا يَمَلُّ مِنَ الْمَغْفِرَةِ حَتَّى يَمَلَّ الْعَبْدُ مِنْ الِاسْتِغْفَارِ . "

*'An Anas ibn Malik (ra) qala Rasulluahi* 🌸*: "Iza aznabal 'abdu zanban kutiba 'alayhi."*
*Faqala 'Arabiyun: Fa in taba 'anhu? Qala: Muhhiya 'anhu.*
*Qala Fa in 'ada? Qalan Nabi* 🌸*: "Yuktabu 'alayhi."*
*Qalal 'Arabiyun: "fin taba?" Qala: "Muhhiya min sahifatihi."*
*Qala: ila mata? Qala: "Ila an yastaghfira wa yatubo ila Allahi 'Ajza wa jal, inAllaha la yamallu min al maghfirati hatta yamallal 'abdu minal isteghfari."*

*Narrated Anas Ibn Malik (ra), that the Messenger of Allah (pbuh) said:*
*"When a servant commits a sin, the sin will be written in his account.*
*So, a Bedouin man asked: "What if he sought forgiveness?*
*The Prophet (pbuh) said: He will be forgiven.*
*The Bedouin asked: What if he did it again?*
*The Prophet (pbuh) said: "It will be written for him."*
*The Bedouin asked: What if he asked for forgiveness again?*
*The Prophet (pbuh) said: "That will erase the sin from his book."*
*The Bedouin asked: Until when?*
*The Prophet (pbuh) said: "Until he asks for forgiveness again, as Allah does not get tired of forgiving, until the servant lose hope/gets tired of asking forgiveness."*

And this way is a way of *muhabbat* (love) and *rahmah* (mercy). And this is what makes the greatness of Allah ﷻ. Otherwise, what would make Allah ﷻ great? Where the angels were astonished that, 'How come they do so many bad things and you forgive them?' And

that's when you say, '*SubhanAllah*, Allah ﷻ is *Kareem* (The Most Generous). Allah's ﷻ generous because the servants are sinning. If all the servants were good, how would you know the greatness of Allah ﷻ?

But it's because we're bad, because we're doing wrong things, and because Allah <sup>﷾</sup> forgiving us and raising us.

The game is stacked in our favour. Allah <sup>﷾</sup> manipulated the game for you to win. Why? Your *hasanat* (goodness) is ten and your *sayyiat* (sin) is one. So, every time you go out and sin. Right? Tomorrow you go out, sin, it's one. Come in the next day, say *'Tawbah, ya Rabbi,'* you got ten. Oh so, I'm now nine ahead (*subhanAllah* from the audience). As long as you're keeping good count because you don't want to go ten times bad and then you only got one. No doubt – so *alhamdulillah*, Allah <sup>﷾</sup> stacked the game in our favour. And that, that which we can't clean, that's why we talked last night on *istighfar*, making *Astaghfirullahul 'Azim* (I ask for forgiveness, O Magnificent).

When *awliyaullah* put these words together for us, it's by *sifat al-Azim.* That, *'Ya Rabbi,* Your Might and Your Magnificence – I'm asking *isitghfar* from that power, *ya Rabbi* – which all universes are in Your command. I'm so small, blow away my sin.' Allah <sup>﷾</sup> says, 'Yes, *alhamdulillah, Bismillahir Rahmanir Raheem.'* Every time we make *istighfar*, the *zikr* of Allah <sup>﷾</sup> back upon us is *"Bismillahir Rahmanir Raheem."* In My name of Compassion and Mercy is forgiven. So, busy yourself

all day long asking *istighfar* so that Allah <sup>﷾</sup> make *zikr* of *Bismillahir Rahmanir Raheem* upon your soul in which you be dressed from every knowledge of *Bismillahir Rahmanir Raheem. Bismillahir Rahmanir Raheem* is the *baab* and the door of all *uloom* and all knowledges.

So, that *istighfar* actually is opening the secrets of knowledges. Until every cell in you has made a sincere *istighfar* – because every cell is its own universe in you – every cell in you, you've made so much *istighfar*. Every cell in you has made an *istighfar* and which we call a zero-point energy where you have reduced your energy so much on to  the horizon of death in which Allah ﷻ going to raise you into these oceans of *baqa* (subsistence). It has its own complete reality.

And we said before, you want to be washed before you make *salawats* (praises upon Prophet Muhammad ﷺ). You know, you don't go as a dirty person running into the presence of Sayyidina Muhammad ﷺ. Although  we're all dirty, but at least take a shower. When people don't understand that, then you think, 'Oh my God, how are they coming to this *zikr* (Divine remembrance)?' You know, in time of Mawlana Shah Naqshband ق – three times a week, they would do *muraqabah* (spiritual connection) and all his *majlis'* (associations), they have a *hamam* (washroom) outside, shower outside, and you put your white clothes there. From wherever you come, before you can enter in his presence, you had to shower. You showered, you put your clothes and then you came into the presence of that Shaykh so that every reflection of energy would be dressed upon you. He wouldn't be spending the whole time just trying to clean himself from all of the *sayyiat* (sins) of people flying towards them.

247

If that is an *adab* (manners) for Mawlana Shah Naqshband ق, imagine the *adab* for Sayyidina Muhammad ﷺ. But people are heedless now. When we talk on *adab*, they make *salawats* – it's real. As soon as they're making *salawats*, they're soul is entering into the presence of Sayyidina Muhammad ﷺ. They feel ashamed and shy that that dirtiness is with them. So, all day long they're making *istighfar. Astaghfirullahul 'Azim, Astaghfirullahul 'Azim* until they feel that dirtiness to be lifted from them, their children, their family and their communities. And then they're coming now, '*Ya Rabbi,* is let me to be sweetened by that presence of Sayyidina Muhammad ﷺ.'

*Alhamdulillah.* Don't despair in the mercy of Allah ﷻ – immense. There's not a *ni'mat* (blessing) that you cannot find. When we did in Ramadan, so many people worried about their *salah* (prayer). 'Oh, I came into Islam at 40. I came into Islam at 30. Imagine that when you came, Allah ﷻ wiped away all your sins. And then we had that *salah* that  counted for a thousand years of *salah.* The game is so much in our favour, it's ridiculously amazing.

Why people then have to make it hard? So, Shaykh Nazim ق would say what? 'Make the doors of paradise as wide as possible.' And why? Why  the wisdom of that? And they said that a man had a dream and he was doing good and saying good and doing lots of *da'wah* (religious propagation). He had a dream of his resurrection that he dreamed that he had died and that he was being brought in Allah's ﷻ

Divinely Presence. And Allah 🕌 was judging him and began to say everything that he was doing wrong and judgment. And then the servant was starting to cry, cry because he was a good person and he had done good all his life. Then Allah 🕌 says, 'Why are you crying?' He said, 'I expected more. I expected something different.'

And immediately Allah 🕌 changed the whole scenario that, 'You'll see me as how you envisioned me.' Allah 🕌 wanted to see something in his heart and he was firm that, 'I tried my best, *ya Rabbi*. All these

judgements that you're passing upon me, I told everybody about Your *Rahmah* (Mercy), about Your love.' How Allah 🕌 wants to punish the servant who talked about love? So, you talk from love and *muhabbat* to save your own soul. '*Ya Rabbi*, I don't know what I've done wrong, but I told people about Your *Rahmah*. Don't grab me to throw me into fire.' That Allah 🕌 be pleased upon how you presented Allah 🕌 to His creation. And Allah 🕌, 'Judge not for you shall be judged.' All prophets came and warned that how you're judging? Allah 🕌 will judge you. So, give people the best of news and Allah's 🕌 *Rahmah* will dress and bless all of you because I'm counting on it the most, *inshaAllah*.

## Do We Have Permission to Recite the Naqshbandi Zikr?

*InshaAllah*, there's always *ijazah* (permission) to recite the *Khatm e Khawjagan* and to do the *zikr* (Divine remembrance) for yourself. There's no *ijazah* to lead a *zikr* and to do a *majlis* (association) of *zikr* without the authority of the shaykh knowing who you are and what your

character is. I recommend that anyone out there who was trying to do a *zikr* in their home and somebody came by and told them, 'Oh, you can do a *zikr* now,' you're going to have a lot of problems.

If you're not somebody who's been built up, and somebody who's been trained, as soon as you do a *Khatm e Khawjagan,* it's the cleansing of

burdens. Those people who come, their burdens will be coming, their burdens will be staying. And if you're not trained with an energy that's enough to take that away, those burdens stay there, and you become somebody loaded with difficulties.

So, it means those are by the authorized shaykh. They know who they're going to authorize and that their *madad* (support) and their support reaches to that person. But it's not recommended just to start doing whatever you want, and you invite five people to come and do it with you because you're carrying all their burdens and all their difficulties. You're taking a responsibility that you may not know or that you want.

But the *ijazah* to do anything on the app. All of the *salawats* (praises upon Prophet Muhammad ﷺ) are by permission. All the *du'as* (supplications) are by permission. Any of the *awrads* (daily practices) are by permission. And if you're doing it and you're finding the blessings of it then

include the Naqshbandi shaykhs in your *du'a* because at least you're using their blessings. You might as well pray for them too, *inshaAllah.*

250

## How Do We Maintain the Spiritual Momentum From Ramadan?

*Inshallah, A'uzu Billahi Minash Shaitanir Rajeem Bismillahir Rahmanir Raheem.* That the feeling and the euphoria from Ramadan is uniquely Ramadan. Because of the fasting and entering a state of fast and the feelings, the energies, all these experiences are meant to be uniquely in Ramadan. But it gives us like a head-start to continue that *himmah* and the zeal in which

to attend the *zikrs* (Divine remembrance), do the *awrads*, do all the practices, keep the connection, so that Allah 🕋 can continue to send that *faiz* (downpouring blessings) and that energy.

And know that from Mawlana Shaykh's ق teachings, 'Every night is *Laylatul Qadr* (the Night of Power).' Don't think these are once in a lifetime events. That, for these *Qadiri* souls, and the souls in which they operate in this reality, they're continuously teaching their students every night is *zikr*, *"Salamun, hiya hatta matla'il Fajr."* There is a *tajalli* (manifestation) coming every morning. Every *Tahajjud* all the way till *Fajr.*

سَلَامٌ هِيَ حَتَّىٰ مَطْلَعِ الْفَجْرِ ﴿٥﴾

*97:5 – "Salamun, hiya hatta matla'il Fajr." (Surat Al-Qadr)*

*"Peace it is until the emergence of dawn." (The Power, 97:5)*

251

As much as you can attend their associations, watch on live, do their practices, these *faiz*, these lights and these dressings should be coming upon the soul, feeling, feeling a lot more energy. So, we pray that Allah ﷻ give an opening. That's why we said, 'These ninety days of this difficulty upon the Earth is like an opening for an awakening.' Many people are experiencing. And we said that these difficulties are not diminishing, they are all going to be increasing. So, now we hope we have more of the tools to survive them. Keep your supplies, keep your practices, don't run on empty, make sure your home has supplies.

## What Do We Recite for Laylatul Qadr?

*Surat Al-Qadr.* And that we have on the study of the months the,

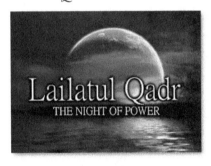

"*Subhana man taqarrab bil qudrati wal baqa.*" That continuously "*Subhana man taqarrab bil qudrati wal baqa.*" You open the Muhammadan Way App – you can copy and paste now from the app. So, you can copy that month, you go into the *awrad* of the month and then "*Subhana man taqarrab bil qudrati wal baqa,*" you copy, paste, and push it into YouTube.

So, it means anybody who has the app, they go to the months, they click on Ramadan, they go to 'General information' and that has the reality of the *hijabs* (veils) of every month. That's the *zikr* (Divine remembrance) of that month and in Ramadan, "*Subhana man taqarrab bil qudrati wal baqa.*"

سُبْحَانَ مَنْ تَقَرَّبِ الْقُدْرَةِ وَالْبَقَا

*"Subhana man taqarrab bil qudrati wal baqa."*

*"Glory to Him who draws nigh to His Omnipotence and Immortality."*

That they're entering into this lightning and that it is the ocean of *fana* (annihilation) in which the lightning hit and destroy everything from form. And that they enter in through this ocean of *fana* that its other side is *baqa* (eternal existence). That they be resurrected in their true reality. That this world of form and the mirror in which they appear in this *dunya* (material world) to be smashed, to be crushed, and what comes from the other side to be resurrected as something new and something real, and something that is eternal, *inshaAllah*.

## Can Angels Listen to Our Recitations if We Recite Quietly?

Yes, everything is heard by them. The intention is understood even by *awliya* (saints). That you can be silent and make an intention, they can pick up the vibration. They are *jasoos* (spy) of the heart. Definitely angels have the ability

and definitely malignant beings have that ability to figure your intention and what's moving in the first levels of the heart, not as it goes deeper into the reality of the heart.

But definitely to clean the tongue, clean the mind and then the *zikr* (Divine remembrance) and all the spiritual practices begins to clean the heart and seal the heart. That these bad *khater* and thoughts that are moving in the heart want to clean them. Most have the thought in their heart and then they begin to voice it through their tongue.

So, the *zikr*, the practices is to begin to stop that. Bring that fire down so that thought is not even coming into their heart, because there are many beings that are picking the signal up of that heart.

It's not something difficult, it's the vibration that's emanating and they pick up that vibration to understand it. When you email – how delicate energy is – that if you email or text the shaykh, the energy of what you were thinking will come to him before the words of the email have to be read. That's when Allah ﷻ says that, 'We seal up their tongue and we question their hands.'

الْيَوْمَ نَخْتِمُ عَلَىٰ أَفْوَاهِهِمْ وَتُكَلِّمُنَا أَيْدِيهِمْ وَتَشْهَدُ أَرْجُلُهُم بِمَا كَانُوا يَكْسِبُونَ ﴿٦٥﴾

*36:65 – "Al yawma nakhtimu 'ala afwahehim wa tukallimunaa aydeehim wa tashhadu arjuluhum bima kanoo yaksiboon."*
*(Surat YaSeen)*

*"That Day, We will seal over their mouths, and their hands will speak to Us, and their feet will testify about what they used to earn."*
*(YaSeen, 36:65)*

So, means they don't need to talk to you, whatever you're doing, you're putting an intention into that. There is an energy into that. That energy  is moving with that document. That's why that, when people are angry or disappointed or upset with people, don't write anyone. Because what happens is the energy of what you're upset about will contaminate what you write. By the time it goes to the person, it can create a big *fitna* (confusion). And people will misunderstand each other and didn't understand because *shaitan* (satan) comes into that energy and through that text.

So, when people are angry don't text, call! So, it's voice to voice with somebody. You're disappointed at a friend, you want to talk to somebody, it has to be through the voice. *Shaitan* is less likely to play with that. But when you text somebody and you think it was mellow, they can pick up a different signal because *shaitan* plays with them.

But for the shaykhs and for the understanding of energy, they pick up the energy of what people are even writing. So, means keep yourself in *wudu* (ablution), keep yourself in a state of goodness and happiness, and write only good things. If you start to try to use this channel towards bad, they probably put  you on a spam block. So that you can't come in and keep trying to put that type of fire into that.

255

# Chapter 4

# Energy

# Understanding Energy
# and Practices for Protection

### How Do We Identify Positive and Negative Energy?

You'll feel it. Negative energy is negative energy. Positive energy is

positive energy. And negative energy, you can put your tongue on a nine-volt battery, the square ones. I wouldn't put it too long. You just tap your tongue 'zzz,' that feeling is negative energy. Because the frequency of the battery and the frequency of your being is clashing. So, anytime you are resonating at a higher frequency, the lower frequency when it comes near you, it has a 'zzz' because it's a lower frequency and your field of energy is pushing that away. So, when it clashes with your field of energy is hence the discomfort. Because it's coming into your frequency, your area of energy that you've built.

When you lower your frequency and you resonate at a very low frequency, all the low energies and bad energies come around the person. That's why we said, 'They are not awakened.' So, there's a movie called 'Odd Thomas' that somebody sent to us. 'Odd Thomas', like the name 'Thomas' – and just for the symbols and the images – we don't know about the story plot that's not

important, but the images. That people walk around with all these

creatures all around them. Because that's the low frequency that they emanate. And that's exactly why *shaitan* (satan) is propagating what he propagates, right? So, he puts out the bad music so that really bad energies can accompany you. He puts bad movies so real bad energies can accompany you. So everything he uses, he knows the frequency fields. He knows that he has to contaminate the ears so that his demons can approach you. He knows he has to contaminate your eyes so that these demons can come and approach you. So, he knows what he's doing and because it's harder to learn from angels, and easier to learn from demons because they're more prevalent.

So, when you watch this demonic world, what it's doing, you begin to be aware, 'Oh look they're going after everybody's ears, with these horrible songs,' because why? To attach beings onto them. They go after all these demonic movies. And now the movie is at your fingertip. Horrific things that you could be watching and inappropriate things on the fingertip of every child holding a phone. Why? To again, contaminate.

And if you resonate and build your energy with *zikr* (Divine remembrance) and *salawats* (praises upon Prophet Muhammad ﷺ), and the *awrads* (daily practices) that they're giving, your soul now is emanating at a higher frequency. So, there are devices now that are on the phone. They're frequency emulators. I showed the guys, there's a thing where they tap the glass, and there's an app that can hear the frequency of the glass, let's say 13,000 mega-watts, I don't know the numbers.

Then they have another app that replicates that sound, that frequency, and it puts out that pitch 'zhhhh.' So, the one hears the pitch and another app replicates the pitch. And they can take the app that replicates the vibration of this glass, and they put it next to it, and in a few seconds the glass shatters. Because it's emanating at a sound. If you take the frequency of something and reverse it back to it, you can disrupt its structure and bring everything down. This is the power of *hamd* (praise).

So when your *hamd* is strong, your praise is strong, your *zikr* is strong, your *muraqabah* (spiritual connection) and connections are strong, because *muraqabah* is how you're going to get energy, more than what you have, upon yourself? You need to take a breath, but you only have one lung. How do you go swimming and diving in an ocean that's deep? You have two little lungs; you think it's meant to go down deep? Or they put a whole pipe onto you, a mask onto your face, and say, 'Now go down 300 feet, 200 feet.' It's not your own lungs, but now there's a support coming. So, there is a whole machine breathing for you and sending a lifeline of breath for you.

Same as in the *madad* (support). 'That with my energy, how am I going to defend myself against this onslaught of *shayateen* (devils)?' And Allah 'ﷻ says, 'No problem, put the mask on, learn how to do the *madad*. This energy field will begin to approach and make its way to you. To begin to dress you and bless you with

261

energy and begin to surround you from its energy.' And enough of this energy begins to build upon you, your energy becomes stronger. So, in elementary school they taught us magnetism. You go back to your elementary school classes. And magnetism is they would get the battery, one of those bigger batteries with the two slots on it, and they would take a wire and they would put it on the positive and negative, and say, 'Look, you put this wire onto something and try to attract paper clips.' And it would attract very little.

Then they tell you the concept of coiling the wire. So, they would take this wire and put a nail and coil it. You put it many times, like ten, twenty times, they would coil it and then make the connection; this would then magnetize. And when it would magnetize, it would collect, 'Err' (attaching sound), all the paper clips coming. The coiling is *madad*

(support). You're trying to connect and coil yourself with these *awliyaullah* (saints), that they come, they come, they come. And they are from the *jinn* (unseen beings) and *ins* (human beings).

That they're coming by support, you're asking for support from Allah ﷻ. He's teaching, 'How to coil yourself and magnetize yourself.' And then you become magnetic character, and you become magnanimous. All these phrases, 'Oh you are of a very magnanimous character.' Yeah, because they're coiling themselves with all of these energies. And as a result, their charge becomes very strong, and this is the reality and *Haqqiqatul Juzba* (reality of attraction). Very simple science courses that we all took in fourth, fifth, sixth grade. You don't have to think of it as it's so, 'Oh my God, this like so heavenly stuff that doesn't exist!' No, no, we took it all in school. It's called magnetism and how to create a magnetic charge.

How to take the iron within your body and create a magnetic charge. Once you become charged as a magnet, you have magnetism. And that's

the same word for good character, or people are attracted to you – from the magnetism. This is then the *faiz* (downpouring blessing). These *awliyaullah*, they are continuously coiling around you, all around you, and they're sending their *faiz*, their energies, their *du'as* (supplications), their blessings upon you. And this becomes a source of all their *barakah* and blessings. From Allah ﷻ to Sayyidina Muhammad ﷺ, because this is always the same. *"Atiullaha wa atiur Rasula wa Ulil amre minkum."*

...أَطِيعُوا اللَّه وَأَطِيعُوا الرَّسُولَ وَأُوْلِي الْأَمْرِ مِنْكُمْ... ﴿٥٩﴾

*4:59 – "...Atiullaha wa atiur Rasula wa Ulil amre minkum..."*
*(Surat An-Nisa)*

*"...Obey Allah, Obey the Messenger, and those in authority among you..." (The Women, 4:59)*

Allah ﷻ wants to send all these blessings, always through the heart of Prophet ﷺ. From Prophet ﷺ, it cannot come directly to you. It would blow you up. So, it comes then to his *ulul amr* (saints), then moves down this mirroring system, and each time step lower, step lower, step lower, until they can dress you with this *faiz* (downpouring blessings). If they dress you too hard, again you 'out.' That's why Nabi Musa ﷺ wanted, 'Let me see you.' Says, 'I don't think you can see Me, but I send you My Glory.'

وَلَمَّا جَاءَ مُوسَىٰ لِمِيقَاتِنَا وَكَلَّمَهُ رَبُّهُ قَالَ رَبِّ أَرِنِي أَنظُرْ إِلَيْكَ ۚ قَالَ لَن تَرَانِي وَلَٰكِنِ انظُرْ إِلَى الْجَبَلِ فَإِنِ اسْتَقَرَّ مَكَانَهُ فَسَوْفَ تَرَانِي ۚ فَلَمَّا تَجَلَّىٰ رَبُّهُ لِلْجَبَلِ جَعَلَهُ دَكًّا وَخَرَّ مُوسَىٰ صَعِقًا ۚ فَلَمَّا أَفَاقَ قَالَ سُبْحَانَكَ تُبْتُ إِلَيْكَ وَأَنَا أَوَّلُ الْمُؤْمِنِينَ ﴿١٤٣﴾

*7:143 – "Wa lamma jaa Musa limeeqatina wa kallamahu Rabbuhu, qala rabbi arinee anzhur ilayka, Qala lan taranee wa lakini onzhur ilal jabali fa inistaqarra makanahu, fasawfa taranee, falamma tajalla Rabbuhu lil jabali ja'alahu, dakkan wa kharra Musa sa'iqan, falamma afaqa qala subhanaka tubtu ilayka wa ana awwalul Mumineen."
(Surat Al-A'raf)*

*"And when Moses arrived at Our appointed time and his Lord spoke to him, he said, "My Lord, show me [Yourself] that I may look at You." [Allah] said, "you will not see Me, but look at the mountain; if it should remain in its place, then you will see Me." But when his Lord manifested His glory on the mountain, He made it as dust, and Moses fell unconscious. And when he awoke/ recovered his senses, he said, "Glory be to You! to You I turn in repentance, and I am the first of the believers."
(The Heights. 7:143)*

Whatever he ﷺ saw was so much for him, that it killed him. And this is *Kalimullah* (speaks to Allah ﷻ). That he was like dust, out. Allah ﷻ had to revive him back. So, then for us then it's always step down, slow, step down, step down. And this is moving through mirrors to reach to us to a level in which we can contain it and not have harm from it, *inshaAllah*.

## What's the Importance and Reality of the Ta'weez?

The purpose of the *ta'weez* (prayer for protection) is to take a sign of humility. That, 'I am nothing *Ya Rabbi*, and that I'm seeking a path of humility and that you watch over and protect me.' And the names of holy people and *ayatul Qur'an* (Qur'anic verses) has a power, *"Allahu Haqq"* (Allah is the Absolute Truth) has a power, the names of *awliyaullah*, *"Tanzeelur Rahmah,"* bring a mercy and a *rahmah*.

عِنْدَ ذِكْرِ الصَّالِحِينَ تَنْزِلُ الرَّحْمَة

*"Inda zikris saliheena tanzeelur rahmah."*

*"In mentioning the names of the pious people, Allah's Mercy descends."* (Prophet Muhammad (pbuh))

*Ruqya* (blessing) is well known in Islam. That when they write *Ayatul Kursi* or *ayatul kareem* (the generous verse of Holy Qur'an) and different *ayat* of Holy Qur'an, they put it for *barakah* (blessings) and *tabarak*. But the *Wahabi mazhab* that came to destroy Islam, that they'll be leaving soon, were not able to do that. That was all Islamic history, that this was the way of protection. Islamic Armory was all the names of Allah ﷻ, the name of Sayyidina Muhammad ﷺ, all the swords had all calligraphy, all their armour had *"Muhammadun Rasulallah," "La ilaha illAllah."*

لَا إِلَهَ إِلاَّ اللهُ مُحَمَّدًا رَسُولْ الله

*"La ilaha illallahu Muhammadun Rasulallah."*

*"There is no deity but Allah, Prophet Muhammad is the messenger of Allah."*

*"Hasbunallah." "Innaa fatahna laka fatham mubina,"* everything.

﴾١﴿ إِنَّا فَتَحْنَا لَكَ فَتْحًا مُّبِينًا

*48:1 – "Inna Fatahna laka Fatham Mubeena." (Surat Al-Fath)*

*"Verily We have granted you [Muhammad (pbuh) a manifest Victory." (The Victory, 48:1)*

Because there are angels; with everything written there are angels and *malaika*. Every verse or word, if you mention just, *"Allah,"* and write it, what angels are accompanying those *kalaam* (words). And what is the responsibility of those angels to

watch over that *kalaam*, and whoever wears it. What type of difficulty to take? And then it's a protection from unseen.

That Prophet ﷺ gave his *awliyaullah* flags, gave each of His *awliyaullah* a flag from the kingdom. And the flag is the *ta'weez* in which Prophet ﷺ told them, 'That your people write this, they should be under Allah's ﷻ protection, under the protection and *nazar* (gaze) of Sayyidina

Muhammad ﷺ, under the *nazar* of *ulul amr* (saints). And then from the *ulul amr* there are the *budala, nujaba, nuqaba, awtad, wa akhyar, ghawth, jinn wa malaika*. It means these categories of *rijal* (people of maturity) and saints, and *jinns*, and *ins* that are responsible, and they come as a protection with that flag. So, it has to do with a kingdom, that who wears that *ta'weez* is under the flag of those shaykhs. And they're known in the

Divinely Kingdom. And the *shaitans* (satans) know those flags.

So, it's like in your house when you put a sign, and you say 'ADT' (security company), and your house is protected by ADT, why? Why don't you just let the people come and rob your house? And they can find if the door is ringing or not, or the alarm is going off. Say no, because it's a protection. You sign up, you get your contract with ADT, and more important is the signs on the outside. So the burglar comes and look and says, 'Oh, this is going to be a headache, soon as I hit this glass, a noise is going to go off, the police are going to come, let me go to the neighbour's house, he has no sign in his house.'

This means the *shaitans* - they see, we don't see. When they look at *insan* (mankind) they see something is shining through their chest when they're wearing their *ta'weez* (prayer for protection). They see something is shining on their home and on their car. When they see that *ta'weez* they say, 'We don't need that fight, we're out of here, we'll go to the next person who doesn't have these things.' Many, many different realities.

And this bad *mazhab* that came and made everything to be *shirk* (polytheism) and everything because they work for *shaitan*. When you work for *shaitan*, no doubt you want the *ta'weez* off. No doubt you don't want any of the *ta'weez* on the wall because the *shaitan* is coming to tell them, 'Tell them to take these things off, so we can possess their people better.' That's why they work for *shaitan*. They work for *shaitan* and they took away a thousand years of history.

That there was never a time, that's why look at all the *masjids* of Allah ﷻ, they are all with *ta'weez* and calligraphy everywhere. *Ta'weez* is something that you put. Every calligraphy, every *masjid* has calligraphy. This is a *ta'weez* [Shaykh points to picture behind him]. Why they put the calligraphy in *masjids*? To glorify Allah ﷻ and to bring a safety and an energy, and a positive energy because everyone coming with all their garbage

into the *masjid*. So, then these energies take away every type of difficulty.

All the *mu'min* (believer) beings are coming because of the energies of what was written, and they pray in there. The Taj Mahal had the entire Surah YaSeen written all over it. It was a huge *ta'weez*, immense power, why? They knew what they were doing.

Now they want to make *masjids* like an insane house. Have you seen an insane house? 'Coo-coo' house; it's white walls, nothing, nothing. That is not the *Masjid* of Allah 'أ, Allah 'أ, even His Holy Ka'bah He's putting full *kiswah* (cloth draped upon Ka'bah) and put all the writings on it. That *mazhab* comes and says, 'Make a house like a coo-coo house, all white walls,' so in case they wanted to like grab themselves and go bang into the walls; that's not the way of 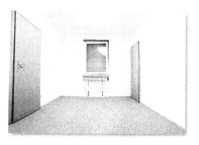 Allah 'أ. Allah 'أ, to glorify Allah 'أ is every moment. And what secrets and powers has in all of these *kalaams*.

We pray that Allah 'أ inspire us and guide us towards goodness. And to forget about these people and what they're teaching. They work for devils, so that the devils can possess people. We pray that Allah 'أ guide and protect us.

## Why Do We Lose Energy or Get Sharp Headaches Around Certain People?

Oh, that's good. Then you understand the reality of energy. That we are  a very powerful energy being. As soon as you build your energy or if Allah 'أ given to you an energy, you're like a light bulb. Wherever you go, the positive will always pull the negative. So, it means a

269

positive force by its nature will attract the negative force. So, every movement that you have as a positive force of your faith and practices, it begins to attract all the negativity.

And that's why then the importance of all of the *usool* (principles) and everything that Prophet ﷺ brought for us was for the perfection of energy. It means that keep your *wudu* (ablution) at all times. *Wudu* is not only for *salah* (prayer); *wudu* is to be at all times. It's never to be outside of your *wudu*. As soon as you lose your *wudu*, you lost your energy force field and you can come under severe attacks especially if your progress is high. So, that *wudu* is like a shield.

The *sunnah* of Prophet's ﷺ ring is again another shield. That they have a turquoise ring as a way of protection against that eye and you see many times if they wear a turquoise, it will crack because of the *nazar* of people and other people are energy forces. When they have an envy and a desire that they can't control, their eyes send out. So, then the *sunnah* of ring of Prophet ﷺ had a power. Keeping the head covered from all sorts of negativities and energies that are coming upon the head. Everything

that Prophet ﷺ brought for us was like a shield for a warrior, that protect them against negative energy. So, when they go out and they feel that negativity then they go home and they wash, and they try to wash away all the negativity of where they were, and they begin to manage where they go.

Unnecessarily, they don't go places where their energy will be pulled and when they go out, they try to keep their *Nazar bar Qadam* (gaze upon the feet), their eyes upon their *qadam*. Because as soon as you put your eyes up, the window to your soul are your eyes and every type of devil and 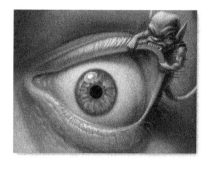 arrow will be shot into the eyes in which the eyes become red, again from all the negative energies that are all around.

So, then they become experts in energy – how to preserve their energy, how to safeguard their *qadam*, their way, in which not to be affected, and by the end result of the energy they pick up throughout their work and all their actions, they go home and they shower. As soon as they enter into the shower, it's like a meditation for them. They ask Allah ﷻ that through the power of *mai* (water) – when Allah ﷻ said, 'My Throne is upon this *mai*.'

وَهُوَ الَّذِي خَلَقَ السَّمَاوَاتِ وَالْأَرْضَ فِي سِتَّةِ أَيَّامٍ وَكَانَ عَرْشُهُ عَلَى الْمَاءِ ... ﴿٧﴾

*11:7 – "Wa huwal ladhee khalaqas samawati wal arda fee sittati ayyamin, wa kana 'arshuhu 'alal maa ..." (Surat Hud)*

*"And it is He who created the heavens and the earth in six days – and His Throne had been upon water ..." (Hud, 11:7)*

*Ya Rabbi*, by the power of this water and the secret that you have within it, wash away my difficulties and that *ghusl* (shower) and that wash, it washes away the sins and difficulties and the burdens of *insan* (mankind), *inshaAllah*.

271

## Can People's Energy Reach Us Through Eye Contact?

Definitely! We are energy beings. That's why *nazar bar qadam* (gaze upon the feet) is one of the principles of Naqshbandiya – is that in our lives, train ourselves to keep our eyes upon our *qadam*, our feet. One, the reality is that my eyes carry my desire. So, out of the four enemies of the self: the *nafs* (ego), the *hawa*, the desire, the *dunya* (material world) – all of these are in the eyes. The *dunya* desire is coming through the eyes. What the eyes see, the eye wants. That's why they call 'eye-candy.' And *shaitan* (satan) knows the game too.

If I put it where my eyes are, and you know where your eyes see the most

in the market is the most expensive part of the market because you're at eye level. So, it means that whatever your eyes are seeing, it's wanting. So, Mawlana Shah Naqshband ق was teaching, 'Keep this desire on your *qadam*, on your feet.' Walk in life looking at your feet. Then you won't be surprised where you ended up in life. If your whole life was that I walked and I looked at my feet and I always prayed, '*Ya Rabbi*, take me to good places that You're happy. That this *qadam* to match the *qadam* of Prophet ﷺ, *Sahabi* (Holy Companions of Prophet ﷺ) and my shaykh. And I become a *muqaddam* and I become a person of the footsteps.' *InshaAllah*.

## What Are the Leaks in Energy That One Might Overlook?

Yes, not following the *sunnah* (traditions of Prophet Muhammad ﷺ). The *sunnah* of Sayyidina Muhammad ﷺ is a great defence. It's an immense weapon, it's an ancient pyramid. If you look at the ancient pyramids, those were the power plants. These were not tombs. There's nobody buried in those. Those big pyramids were brought onto this Earth from a technology that these men don't understand, and it was about insulation and the production of power.

Prophet's ﷺ *sunnah* is more powerful. He brought the *sunnah* and the garment, the ring, the *'asaa* (cane), the *topi*, the hat, the turban – all of that are energy. And all of those are to produce the energy, secure the energy, and then the person becomes a sealed energy plant. That any *nazar* comes, their ring is a defense against them. Their *'asaa* is a grounding for them, because they have two prongs of their feet and this energy is

continuously conflicting. From negative energy coming from the earth, and the heavenly coming upon their soul, the third is a grounding. So, it's the grounding line that pushes all the negative energy back into the earth.

The ring is a gift from Prophet ﷺ that he gave to Sayyidina Suleiman عليه السلام, that controls a *mulk* (earthly realm) and a majesty, if Prophet ﷺ energizes that reality. So, it means everything from Prophet ﷺ is a power. The beard is a power, it has the power of protection against these *lataif* (subtle energy points), for talking and for healing and for everything.

There is nothing that Prophet ﷺ brought that didn't have an immense reality. They say even the hair to be short to take away the wild energy. So, everything that Prophet ﷺ brought is of an immense reality. As much as we can keep that, keep the concept of *wudu* (ablution), pray the two *rakahs* (cycle of prayer) of *Salatul Wudu* (prayer of ablution) to seal the energy, then you're sealing more than what you are losing. And then the mouth; how to control the mouth and the character.

So, there's nothing like that you'll fill up from the *zikr* (Divine remembrance) you get all this good energy, and no doubt that *shaitan* (satan) is waiting outside the door. Soon as you get in the car, something is going to happen, an argument's going to happen by the time you're home because *shaitan* wants to pull that *barakah* (blessing) out. He doesn't want the person to be excess and begin to make a positive charge.

So, it's like those solar dishes. What's the point of having a solar dish if you can't store the power coming in? You're just putting it there for design? Putting $20,000 worth of cells on the roof. So, then the storage technology was more important than the cellular technology that, 'How am I going to store this energy that's coming on my roof, so I have a benefit? If I'm going to put that  type of money into it, I better store it.' So then now some of the top, more smarter people came up with very powerful storage.

Where enough people store it, they're giving back to the power companies and charging them, that, 'You want to use my power.' It means the [Elon] Musk technology; put ten-thousand homes with the cellular storage, and now he becomes a power company – more powerful than the power company. Because these 10,000 homes that are working with him are producing an immense amount of energy from the sun free, not the power plant that's running with gas and turbine engines.

This was the old knowledges. This is what the pyramid was doing. It was using water and sunlight and they were running the water under the  pyramid. And the electrons and the energy that the water would give off from the natural sun in that region that was so intense, this energy would be released, the pyramid structure would hold that energy. And every energy and vibration was happening inside. Why *Fir'aun* (Pharaoh) didn't want Nabi Musa ﷺ to leave? Musa ﷺ meant like lightning, that his secret for that nation was he had the power. When he left, he took the technology and cast them into darkness. And that's why he didn't want him to go. Power's gone.

## How Do We Protect Our Energy During Sleep?

The energy teaching we have on the power of the *sunnah*. I think there are a couple of videos on the reality of the *sunnah* of Sayyidina Muhammad ﷺ and that we are like a pyramid. That all the energy that we are building with the *sunnah* is a protection. Every type of practice that we are doing is to achieve and to bring that energy within us, insulate

the energy that's being produced, not to lose it. So, one reality is building our energy, next problem is how quickly are we going to lose our energy.

Nighttime is a time of great difficulty. Nighttime is a time of great attacks because *insan* (human being) has lowered his defense. He's lying in bed

and every type of difficulty is trying to come to them. There is a whole *sunnah* of how Sayyidina Muhammad ﷺ has described for us to sleep. It means to keep yourself covered, never sleep uncovered. Keep yourself in *wudu* (ablution), that pray and go wash for your *wudu*, pray your two *rakahs* *Salatul Wudu* (Prayer of Ablution) and then sleep.

When you are lying in your bed recite four Surat al-Falaq, three Surat an-Nas, two Surat al-Ikhlas while blowing upon yourself for protection and lie onto your sleep. Sleep on your back and sleep on your right side. That is your protection and common sense because my heart is exposed and guarding me. So, when I sleep on the right, my heart is guarding me. When I sleep on my heart, I am creating a stress upon my heart which is my energy protection. And because I am sleeping on it, it's not

energizing as a shield around me, so I come under attack if I sleep on the left. If I sleep on the right, I have a shield of protection. And definitely don't sleep on your stomach because then you are completely exposed; your shield of protection is then suffocated because you are sleeping on the heart – it is bad for your stomach, it is bad for your physiology, it is bad for your heart, and your rear end is exposed to every type of devil and demon above you.

Then with this energy, Prophet ﷺ recommended that you sleep covered. If you know that much attack is happening at nighttime, keep your head covered when you sleep. They have now either the sock that people can put on – the mask that we made is multi use; you can pull it back for like a sock over the head, and you pull it a little bit over for the eyes. But either way put something upon your head so that the head is covered as a protection.

And Mawlana Shaykh ق would recommend that a little cup of salt by the bed and *siwak* (teeth cleaning twig). And as soon as you wake up, you put the salt in the mouth because we are not understanding that when we lie in bed the unseen world is ten times more populated than our world. If you think there are bugs in the physical world, the unseen world is ten times more and all those creatures,

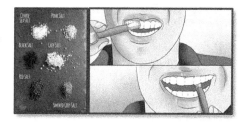

they are free to roam to everywhere. So, they are all over *insan*. So, as soon as you put salt you are cleaning away every type of negative energy and waking up with a positive energy, and the first breath you are going to breathe, even a cup of water you are going to drink, the salt should purify that reality, *inshaAllah*.

And if you have to wash for *wudu*, then again you make your *Salatul Wudu* and go back to bed after you made your *Salatul Wudu*. Those whom are not praying on time, try to wash often. Try to do your practices, wash often, and try to drink lots of water before you sleep so that the sleep is light. Doesn't need to be a super deep sleep. Keep your sleep to be light; wash often so that to *tarbiyah* and train yourself and punish yourself. Learn to punish yourself.

All *awliyaullah* (saints) would inflict a punishment that was great and difficult against themselves. Since we have a lower threshold of that understanding, is that if you did something wrong make a penalty and adhere to that penalty. 'I am going to donate every time I miss my *Fajr*. Every time I do this wrong, miss this, speak bad way'; make there to be a repercussion, make there to be a consequence. Just saying, 'Sorry, *astaghfirullah*,' that is not going to help anything; there has to be a consequence of every bad action. So, make a donation, make an action. Say, 'I am going now to the food bank and do this.' Or make something that will motivate you not to do that. Like when we said that if we anger and talk bad to people, immediately go and ask their apologies. The embarrassment of asking people, 'I am sorry I was belligerent again and was wrong.' That process of continuously asking and seeking people's forgiveness is humiliating for the *nafs* (ego). It begins to inspire you, 'Look, don't do this because I am not going to say another sorry!' And it will begin to help you to stop passing that limit. But if there is no repercussion, there is no punishment – why the servant will stop at

anything? So, make your own laws and punishments – that way to discipline the self and control the self, *inshaAllah*.

## Is There Any Remedy For Insomnia?

Insomnia, yes, are you experiencing a lot of energies and you can't sleep? Because again these are servants who are watching this (the lecture), they are in that training whether they wanted it or not. This means that in that training of what we talked in the beginning of the talk of *Qiyamul Layl* (Nightly Devotion), there are servants whom Allah ﷻ sends a lot of energy to them. And by their nature, they're not going to sleep often and they're not going to sleep too much. Their souls are more of a vigilant reality.

That they stay awake and they're vigilant. And they should be learning how to do their *zikrs* (Divine remembrance), watch entertaining things

that have a message, a reality within them. Read, read your Qur'an, do anything that you can do positive, and just be comfortable with whatever condition Allah ﷻ puts you in. You don't need to seek out medicines and all sorts of

different things. If it's the energy that is coming to you, and Allah ﷻ doesn't want you to sleep, then you don't sleep. And you do your *zikr*, your exercises and practices and pray your *Salatul Fajr*. After *Fajr*, if Allah ﷻ grants you a little bit of rest, then rest after your *Fajr* for one hour, two hours, three hours, and then go on with whatever Allah ﷻ wants, *inshaAllah*.

## Should We Avoid Touching People When Trying to Build Our Energy?

When we meditate, you're entering now into an energy world. And that in itself is an even – some advanced meditation people, they don't really get the concept of energy. That everything you build is an electrical field.

And there are some scientists now that come and say, 'What's the charge on every cell?' Like one something percentage of a volt but you have seven trillion or five trillion of these cells. It means you're a very powerful energy being. If you could harness all that energy, imagine what type of energy would come out of a person and it's not even a battery. It's being made eternally by Allah ﷻ.

So, it means that love, hate, *hasad* (jealousy), these are very strong energy conductors. So, once you begin to understand that you meditate and you contemplate, you're building very positive energy fields. Your whole energy field is moving. No doubt that any positive energy is going to conduct negative energy. Just very basic. If I put a positive charge,

anything negative will be attracted to it. It's like a light bulb on a dark night, all the mosquitoes come. That's why you don't meditate and open up your energy and then sit in the mall and start to meditate in the mall. You'll now pick up all the negative charges of all the people and all their actions.

If that's what you want to do, then you can do that, but it's not recommended. So, you try to preserve your energy. You preserve it and keep it secure by *wudu* (ablution), by washing and unnecessary touching.

## When Someone Else Has a Temperature Why Can I Also Feel It?

You could have an affinity with people in your heart. So, there can be such a connection and such a bond, and such a love that the feelings and the emotions of one can be felt by another. And those whom are training their hearts, the heart is a fine-tuned instrument, in  which we described 'tuning.' So, the purpose of being loyal with the shaykh is the whole subject of tuning. If you come into the *zikr*, (Divine remembrance) the shaykh is vibrating with a frequency. And let's say for your understanding to put into words, he's vibrating at a ten, another shaykh is vibrating at a nine, another shaykh at an eight, not in powers but different frequencies.

The reality of what the shaykh is doing is that when you come into their association – whether live or online – they're going to negate you, they're going to teach you, they're going to bring down all of your frequencies, and then they're going to resonate with their frequency onto you. So then, you become like a tuning fork. Where you put it up and you go  'bowowo' [indicating the vibration of hitting a tuning fork]. I have my own special effects [Laughter]. And then the other thing goes, 'wowowo' [indicating replication of frequency]. You can actually tune something because it's all based onto your frequency; as soon as you hit the one thing, the other thing's vibrating the same. What do you think then is the power of the heart which is the most delicate instrument from Allah's ﷻ creation.

When you're in tune with the shaykh and you're doing the practices they're telling you, keeping the way of what they're telling you, they're negating your frequency. As soon as you attend their associations you're vibrating at their frequency. Their energy is dressing your *zikr*, their frequency is dressing your frequency. And that's why Shaykh Abdullah al-Faiz Ad-Dagestani ق said, 'Just sit five minutes with me and I take you to my station.' They're inheriting from that reality. That as soon as they're on their frequency they're uplifting the servant to where they are.

So, it means these realities of attuning, as soon as you begin to train in *tafakkur* (contemplation) train in the way of *tariqah* (spiritual path), your heart becomes very sensitive. And you may go somewhere and feel that your heart is beating very fast as if you feel agitation but it's not you

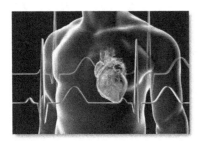

that's agitated. You could be talking to someone who's very angry, and you feel their heartbeat moving very fast. That you feel uncomfortable, you think something's wrong with you. What's wrong? It's not you but it's a tuned piece of equipment (the heart). If it goes somewhere where someone is resonating very angry, very aggressive, you can feel it.

And there are many students who will begin to feel. That's why we said then, 'Pay attention to your heart.' When you enter into somewhere and your heart's telling you 'Something's not right, something's not right, get out!' When you go somewhere and someone's talking a certain way and you feel in your heart something's not right, something is not right. So yes, this is the beginning of understanding attuning.

And this is the beginning of the understanding of the realities of sound. Sound is something that it's not imaginable. How important sound is and how the sound can manipulate everything? So, the frequency in which they resonate and that's Allah's ﷻ gift. It's not that they're acappellas and they practice a certain sound, it's not that reality, 'Ohhh' [Shaykh makes low pitch sound], and then you start to change. It's the reality of their soul because their light is an energy; energy is a sound. So that *"Yusabbihu bihamdihi,"* for everything is praising.

تُسَبِّحُ لَهُ السَّمَاوَاتُ السَّبْعُ وَالْأَرْضُ وَمَن فِيهِنَّ ۚ وَإِن مِّن شَيْءٍ إِلَّا يُسَبِّحُ بِحَمْدِهِ وَلَٰكِن لَّا تَفْقَهُونَ تَسْبِيحَهُمْ ۗ إِنَّهُ كَانَ حَلِيمًا غَفُورًا ﴿٤٤﴾

*17:44 – "Tusabbihu lahus samawatus sab'u wal ardu wa man fee hinna wa in min shayin illa yusabbihu bihamdihi wa lakin la tafqahoona tasbeehahum innahu kana haleeman ghafoora." (Surat Al-Isra)*

*"The seven heavens and the earth and whatever is in them exalt [praises] Him. And there is not a thing except that it exalts [Allah] by His praise, but you do not understand their [way of] exalting. Indeed, He is ever Forbearing and Forgiving." (The Night Journey 17:44)*

So, the praise that Allah ﷻ gives their soul is by Allah's ﷻ power. So, He's not saying something at a sound level that people don't understand. It's the gift that Allah ﷻ gave to his soul, that Allah ﷻ has written a *hamd* (praise) within their soul. That soul has the power to influence other souls. So, you see it as light and the lights are influencing. In reality it's an energy, so the energy is influencing. Its highest reality is actually, it's a sound. And the sound of that shaykh is influencing your soul, *inshaAllah*.

## How Do We Control Body Vibrations and the Feeling of Electric Current?

Anytime we're dealing with energy there's going to be an energy. It means there's going to be those vibrations because everyone's at a different level of attuning. Everyone's at a different frequency. That's when we talked before – when you're vibrating at a certain frequency, every lower frequency is going to have a clash.

So, when we're doing a lot of *zikr* (Divine remembrance), a lot of purification, a lot of these practices, the resonance is much higher, the *zikr* is much higher. That soul's clarity and purity is much higher. Any lower light is going to cause a difficulty onto the light which is like the equivalent of if you take a little battery and stick your tongue, you get a little bit of a shock, those nine-volt batteries. I wouldn't recommend holding it too long to your tongue because that can hurt. Just little bit – 'Oww.' So that you feel that okay, that's uncomfortable and that's the understanding that  an uncomfortable energy comes, you become more attuned to understanding. That way you feel, you feel like energies that are not good or are coming around, they come around your feet. Your feet begin to itch.

Then that's why the importance of these energy people and people whom practice energy, they live by the *sunnah* of Sayyidina Muhammad ﷺ. Others may take it as an entertainment, but they have to live by it. This means that if they're outside of *wudu* (ablution), they begin to burn – have itching, problems, everything because all negativity is trying to come onto them.

Everything that Prophet ﷺ brought for them was advanced realities for purification. Knowing that his nation he wants them to be the most purified nation, living upon a satanic island in which every type of devil is surrounding us. How would anyone survive if not for the Grace of Allah ﷻ sending the *rahmah* (mercy) of Sayyidina Muhammad ﷺ? That's the way his nation would survive that cover your head, wear your ring, put your modest clothing, protect your skin.

We said before in other talks, only now we're understanding that when you cover your skin, look how many viruses you're protecting yourself from. When people are not understanding, they put a mask and they're running with no clothes on. What are they protecting? This is the greatness of Prophet ﷺ, like a father who loves you so much that he set an entire inheritance for you. That a day would come, 'I'm going to leave you all these tools so that you be safe.' Then

you know how much, why *Rasulul Kareem* ﷺ. How much Prophet ﷺ loved his nation, loves his nation that he sent all these tools for us to be protected and how much the nation doesn't show their gratitude to Sayyidina Muhammad ﷺ by not using what he left behind for them.

## Are Negative Energies Attracted to Some More Than Others?

Yes, some whom Allah ﷻ gave as a gift more positive energy. There are people whom Allah ﷻ has given as a gift to be of a subtle nature and they

have a tremendous positive energy. As a result of that energy, they pull in and are sensitive to every negative energy. And as a result of that, they have to be extra careful. Don't expose themselves. Don't put their face on the internet. Don't put any of your body parts on the internet. Nobody should see anything from your body on the internet because then every energy that they look is going to make you sick.

Learn how to keep yourself in *wudu* (ablution). Keep yourself under their *tarbiyah* (discipline) under their *nazar* (gaze). Keep yourself making *salawats* on Sayyidina Muhammad ﷺ to defend that energy and to build that energy, *inshaAllah*. And that's why Allah ﷻ, for every, "*Ya Musabbibal Asbaab*," Allah ﷻ puts us in that condition, "*Ya Mufattihul Abwab*", and then gives us a door to go to.

...يَا مُسَبِّبَ الْأَسْبَابِ، يَا مُفَتِّحُ الْأَبْوَابِ ...

"...*Ya musabbibal asbab, ya mufattihul abwab*...

"...*O Originator of causes! O Opener of doors!...*"

Because the person is in that condition, they found this channel. If you're a person who hasn't had spiritual experiences, you probably tuned out a long time ago from our talks. Our talks are a completely different level of understanding. All those people online are people who have had spiritual experiences. Otherwise, this teaching is not of interest to other people; most of them think it's crazy. But if they had a spiritual experience, these are people who are tasting what the Shaykh is talking about, and they searched all their life.

They asked *imams* (religious leaders), and the *imams* said, 'Oh, you're a crazy person, maybe you should go to hospital.' And I've told you every time, when *Wahabis* would fight us, they would fight the *aqidah* (belief) day and night. As soon as someone would walk into their mosque and say, 'We have a problem with this and this,' they would say, 'Go to that Sufi down the street'. They know. It's out of the realm of their understanding because they're very *zahiri* (external understanding). You know, they give you a video on how to wash and that's it, and only wash your hands and feet and toes. They don't know even the secret of the washing. So, if they're tuning in, most likely they're having experiences and Allah ﷻ inspiring them that to understand these experiences, we have schools for that. And they're understanding of that, *inshaAllah*.

## What is the Best Approach When We See Shaitans in Public?

*Bismillahir Rahmanir Raheem.* Anytime you see *shaitan* (satan), run.
That any type of negativity that people carry, we try to stay away from. The energy that you build within yourself, the practices that Allah ﷻ give for you to do to build your connection and focus on the connection. So, not to focus on seeing a *shaitan* in someone, and that could be

imaginary, and it could be real, but to focus on the positive and building your energy, building your practices, and not focusing on the negativity. And any time you feel a negative energy is to be cautious.

The reason for the sensitivity within the heart is to live a life of caution. If you go somewhere in the woods and you feel uncomfortable and you keep going, something wrong with you. Because you're putting yourself in a place that's very dangerous. So, it means the heart is receiving an

*isharat* (sign). You practice, you build your energy, you build your sensitivity. Then you take yourself to an environment that could have a lot of wild energy all around you. If your heart is telling you that you're uncomfortable and you begin to feel an immense amount

of negativity, it means it's a sign for you not to be there. That don't put yourself in that type of environment. There's a protection for you somewhere else.

So, it means all of these are the practices in understanding guidance. That we talked many times before, if you go to the mall and you're not feeling good with that energy because it's a sign from Allah ﷻ, don't be there.

It's draining your energy. So, then you begin to not only take the advice of the shaykhs but through your training, your heart is going to be trained on how to advise you. And that's the ultimate. It's the shaykh begins to teach the student for you to develop what Allah ﷻ wants you to have within yourself as your internal guidance system. And that's a part of what we call faith.

When you begin to believe, when you begin to practice and you believe in your practices, Allah ﷻ makes it to be real for you and that becomes the reality of faith. So, this *ilm*, the knowledges of reality – *ilm ul yaqeen* (knowledge of certainty), and the *ayn* (vision) and the practices of visualizing and sensing these realities, it becomes a *haq* (truth) for people.

Now because that *haq* is developing, you don't want to look at everything bad and say, 'Oh, this was a *shaitan*. This was a *shaitan*.' Everyone is a *shaitan* and everyone has a *shaitan* assigned. Allah ﷻ says, 'We have assigned upon every *ins* (human), a *jinn* (unseen beings) from the *shayateen* (devils) who his purpose is to distract you in life.'

عَنْ عَبْدِ اللَّهِ بْنِ مَسْعُودٍ، قَالَ رَسُولُ اللَّهِ ﷺ:
" مَا مِنْكُمْ مِنْ أَحَدٍ إِلاَّ وَقَدْ وُكِّلَ قَرِينُهُ بِهِ مِنَ الْجِنِّ ". 
[المَصْدَرْ: صَحِيحْ مُسْلِمْ ٢٨١٤، كتاب ٥٢، حديث ٦٢]

*'An 'Abdullah Ibn Mas'oodin, qala Rasulullahi* ﷺ, *"Ma minkum min ahadin illa wa qad wukkela behi qarinuhu minal Jinni."*
*[Al Masdar: Sahih Muslim 2814, Kitab 52, Hadith 62]*

*'Abdullah Ibn Mas'ood reported that the Messenger of Allah (pbuh)
said, "There is no one amongst you who doesn't have a companion that's
appointed to him/in charge of him, from the Jinn."
[Authentic by Muslim 2814, Book 52, Hadith 62]*

Now are you going to give into him and follow him or you're going to
follow Allah ﷻ? And that becomes this game of life that we live. So, it
wasn't supposed to be free from *shayateen*. It was supposed to be that
you don't listen to *shayateen*, *inshaAllah*.

## What is Nazma and How Do We Protect Our Energy?

What's important for right now is this
*qudra* (power), this *nazma* (energy field) to
be increased. That for us in the training,
when you train with energy, you're making
your *du'as* (supplications), you're making
your *tafakkur* (contemplation), learning the
process, 'I'm nothing. I'm connecting with
the shaykh and that I visualize the shaykh.
Say, 'Send me energy because I'm weak
from what Allah ﷻ has given to you.'

Then they begin to train you on how to bring your breath, your energy
onto yourself, and begin to bring that energy and radiate that energy all
around you. That energy that you radiate around you is your shield of

protection. So, what more do
we need in this life right now is
this *nazma* and this *qudra*. That
your practice is strong, your
character is correct. Then you
understand in the videos that
we have on the *sunnah*
(traditions of Prophet Muhammad ﷺ). The *sunnah* is what do they call
in the wire, electrical wire? The seal of the wire? The insulation. The
*sunnah* is our insulation. The wire is us, the soul. You're now trying to

build this energy. One thing is to build it and waste it all day long. You went through all that effort for what? So, then the *sunnah*, the *shari'ah*, the *hijab* (veil), the hat, the clothes, the beard, the ring was all of the insulation of this magnificent wire.

Then when you make *wudu* (ablution), you seal this energy so that what? You're very powerful. It's not escaping. You keep it, you keep it, you keep it until when you begin to practice, you can feel the energy is coming out. And that energy coming out is then your safety and safeguard. When you practice and you practice and you practice, this energy begins to emanate into your home. And then your home has a shield of protection. And that's then the protection for your wife, children and loved ones. So, it's not something only personal. It becomes a protection for everyone.

Imagine then *awliyaullah* (saints) and shaykhs when they've been trained, their energy is a shield that is everywhere. Because as soon as you make

a *madad* (support), if you don't have a shield, make a *madad* to someone who has a shield. As soon as you make a *madad* and ask for them to come, their shield of energy is all around. Like when you call the police, they have a shield, right? You don't have a shield. So, when you're scared and a burglar's coming, you call 911. *Madad* is your 911. With this *madad,* you can call all the time, not like 911. If you're a very paranoid person – all day long you call 911, they give you a $100 fine and police say, 'We are not coming anymore.' And they come with a shield. Why? Because they're *shareef* (sheriff). Where they got these? Because you know it's a program;

Allah ﷻ wrote the program and Allah ﷻ has a sense of humour. This is for people who have eyes to see. So, why call those *shareef*? Call real *shareef*? Right? You do your *madad*. It's a 911 and this one, you can call all day long, all day long, *"Madad, madad."* Why? *"Tanzil ar-Rahmah."*

عِنْدَ ذِكْرِ الصَّالِحِينَ تَنْزِلُ الرَّحْمَةُ

*"Inda zikris saliheena tanzeelur rahmah."*

*"In mentioning the names of the pious people, Allah's Mercy descends."*
*(Prophet Muhammad (pbuh))*

You're sitting at home, *"Madad."* You're sitting somewhere, you're not comfortable, *"Madad!"* And you bring all their presence always with you until you do it so much, they say, 'This guy is bothering us. Why we have

to come and go? Just stay with him. He's going to be making *madad* all day long.' So, then your *awliya* (saints) are following you everywhere you're going. Right? We try to make it light and simple, but it sticks into your mind. Use the *madad*. Keep them, keep calling upon them. Begin to feel that presence. If you don't have the energy, they do. Call upon them and they come with all the power and all the blessings, *inshaAllah.*

## Can We Be of Service Spreading Light While Meditating?

You can't give what you don't have. The whole process of trying to have is that, '*Ya Rabbi*, I want to build my energy, build my energy.' When we feel that the energy is coming then, 'My Lord, I am praying for all these people.' Pray for all the people

you know, all the people that you love and that then you become like a light worker. That you work in the world of light, that you try to build yourself and know that wherever you are going, you are making *du'a* (supplication) for people. They don't have to know who you are. They don't have to know anything about you. When you go to the grocery store or you go to your favourite places, you can make *du'as* for people. '*Ya Rabbi*, just send that light upon them and take away their difficulties and their sadness.'

So, as much as we can build, as much as we can give. The most important in these days is for your family. That you know that your children will become sick from the parents. So, imagine the children are like little sponges, pure from paradise. They just landed from paradise. You know how they become sick is from the parents. Every time the parent touches and kisses the child, this law of energy is that the positive energy will collect negative energy. So, whoever is more negative will be sending their energy. Whoever is more positive will be carrying the energy in any association.

293

So, in a home, the child is the most positive in energy unless it's a shaykh or a developed student. And that's why so many difficulties in the home. As soon as they have children, all the energy is going onto the child because the child is not protected. The parents are not doing the proper actions and deeds and all that energy goes. So, the more we think of our belief in regards to energy and that's the importance. So, when we wash, when we pray, when we give our *zakah* (charity), when we give our *mawlid*, we are taking and giving away many burdens. You know these burdens are going away instead of going onto the child and kissing the child and then touching the child, and all these energies go onto the child. So, it is important for us take a way in which we build ourselves, build our energy, build our practices. And that find the way in which to extinguish the negative charge from ourselves so that we become now 'plus,' in the home.

If the person who meditates and contemplates, he will become excessively positive. He begins to save his family because he begins to send a positive charge to the child, a positive charge to the spouses, and the environment becomes net positive instead of negative and like a whole black hole, everything is just going into it, it's now radiating out a power. And that's why when you enter in some of these homes and you feel a sense of peace. Like the shaykh's home, the *zawiyah* (spiritual school of Sufism) or the *khaneqah* (the house of a Sufi master); it has a tremendous amount of energy and a sense of peace. Because within that house is built the *zikr* (Divine remembrance) and the love of Sayyidina Muhammad ﷺ. That's why people walk and when

they are in, they say, 'Oh, I feel a tremendous amount of energy and peace.' And that energy is so positive that it pulls away all the negative of anyone who enters, *inshaAllah*.

## Should We Carry Others' Negativity if We Are Excess in Positive Energy?

You carry the excess positive energy and that you seal yourself and your energy with your practices. Allah ﷻ will release it the way He wants the

soul to release it. I wouldn't advise going around thinking, 'I want to bless everyone, dress everyone,' because you may empty yourself too fast. And there may be somebody that you're not aware of that

has a tremendous amount of burdens that can make you sick very fast. Right now, we have to worry about building ourselves and not others. They say that, 'You can't give what you don't have.' Everybody wants to be a spiritual healer, but they don't want to heal themselves. Because this is a sickness, they want to be something, but the whole way is to be nothing! Once you're nothing, you don't want to be anything, you don't want to help anyone – you want to help yourself first to be nothing.

So, they teach you on the plane, when the place is about to go down, 'Put the mask on yourself and then work on your child.' For, if you are busy putting the mask on your child and you lose altitude, you're going to pass out and the child is not going to have a mask on their face. So, they say, 'First secure yourself.' Once you're all secure then you start to work on other people. But you go out and try to do *da'wah* and healing and this and that and you're not *pukhta*, you're not cooked, you're not ripe, you're going to make everyone sick. What did we use to say about the uncooked turkey? Because you're not cooked, right? On the outside you look like you're brown, 'Mmm, that looks delicious.' You bite in and what you get is salmonella poisoning. Because it's not cooked on the inside.

So it's one thing when the nation is more of an outside cooked; they wear nice white, they put all these outfits on, they put all these things, and they look like, 'Oh, these are real cooked guys you know, they look very pious.' But inside empty, no time, inside is poisonous. Because they didn't want the way of *tazkiyah* (purification). So, the inside is more important. Better to cook the chicken for a long time; the browning and roasting you can do in a few minutes. Just put it near the boiler and it roasts really quick. The outside you can fix right away, but the inside is the one that has the work and the difficult part, inshallah.

## Is There Advice for Women Relating to Meditation or Energy?

Women have the ability to have very powerful and strong meditations because they have two spiritual points. They have not only the heart, but they have the holy womb which Allah ﷻ brought the secret of creation within their womb. They have a softer outside and a harder inside. So, it means their subtlety and softness will allow them to pick up energies much faster, much more powerful. They're more sensitive to energies, therefore they have to be very careful of satanic attacks. And that's why 99% of *jahannam* (hellfire) is filled with women, of holy *hadith* of Prophet ﷺ.

عَنْ ابْنِ عَبَّاسٍ رَضِيَ اللهُ عَنْهُ: قَالَ رَسُولُ اللهِ ﷺ: " اطَّلَعْتُ فِي الْجَنَّةِ فَرَأَيْتُ أَكْثَرَ
أَهْلِهَا اَلْفُقَرَاءَ، وَاطَّلَعْتُ فِي النَّارِ فَرَأَيْتُ أَكْثَرَ أَهْلِهَا اَلنِّسَاءَ. "
[المَصْدَرُ: صَحِيحٌ مُسْلِمٌ ٢٧٣٧ ]

*'An ibne 'Abbas (ra), qala Rasulullahi* ﷺ: *"Attala'tu fil jannati fara
aytu akthara ahleha alfuqara a, wa attala'tu fin naari fara ayatu akthara
ahleha annisaa a." [Sahih Muslim 2737]*

*Ibn 'Abbas (ra) narrated that the Messenger of Allah (pbuh) said, "I
looked into Paradise and saw a majority of its people were poor. I looked
into Hellfire and saw a majority of its people were women."
[Authentic by Muslim 2737]*

Not against – we're not saying bad about women. But you can imagine
in the last days when the energy is horrific, and the energies are flowing,
they're describing now the most susceptible to energy is going to be
women. She's picking up the energy from all directions. If that energy is
coming negative and she makes choices by emotion, then imagine the
amounts of difficulty, amount of horrific energies that can quickly dress
the woman.

So, she's in a danger. And that's what we
said today like no other time in our history,
women are all now tattooed. Everywhere
you go, they're all fully [tattooed]. What
used to be only for sailors on a ship, is all
tattooed because whatever energy is now,
they're coming and picking up. They're
thinking this is okay. This is peaceful. This
is green. This is a part of the Earth. I want
to put butterflies all over my head and my
face and because of the subtlety of her
energy she's very susceptible to picking up all qualities of energy. And
she has a hard inside that she can endure a tremendous amount of pain.
And that's why they are capable of giving birth.

Man is the reverse. He's like a walnut on the outside, has no emotion but his inner core is very soft and sweet. And the role of the shaykh is to crack the nut and bring out the fruit and bring it out. So, what's inside the man, if the outside can be cracked and the hard shell of this world teaching the man just to be tough and hard and hard. If that light hit and cracks that person, their inner core is soft and can be brought out, *inshaAllah*.

## Are There Special Practices for Women During Their Cycle?

Yeah during all times, *A'uzu Billahi Minash Shaitanir Rajeem, Bismillahir Rahmanir Raheem.* Don't be too particular on the *awrads* (daily practices). Remember the basis of the teaching, and the door of this teaching, *"La ilaha illa anta Subhanaka, innee kuntu minazh zhalimeen."*

$$...لَّا إِلَهَ إِلَّا أَنتَ سُبْحَانَكَ إِنِّي كُنتُ مِنَ الظَّالِمِينَ ﴿٨٧﴾$$

*21:87 – "...La ilaha illa anta Subhanaka, innee kuntu minazh zhalimeen." (Surat Al-Anbiya)*

*"...There is no god/diety except You; Glory to you: Indeed I have been of the wrongdoers/Oppressor to Myself!" (The Prophets, 21:87)*

That I admitted to myself, I'm an oppressor to myself. And as an oppressor, I don't believe that the actions I do will actually do anything. I'm doing them out of imitation. When I truly believe that, then I don't have to worry about all these different *awrads,* all these different recitations as if they're going to do anything for me. The most important for you to do is the basic *awrad* from the Naqshbandi practices and then be a supporter.

Build the relationship with the shaykh. It's the shaykh that will be doing.
The shaykhs will be pulling us and
lifting us. Wherever their shaykh
is taking them, wherever their
shaykh is taking them all the way
up to the connection of the heart
of Sayyidina Muhammad ﷺ,
they're moving. The magnet that
moves all of this is *muhabbat*
(love). 'You'll be with whom you love.'

قَالَ رَسُولُ اللَّهِ صلى الله عليه و سلم: الْمَرْءُ مَعَ مَنْ أَحَب

*Qala Rasulullah ﷺ: "Almar o, ma'a man ahab."*

*Prophet Muhammad (pbuh) said: "One is with those whom he loves."*

Not by your actions and by your character, but by your love and
*muhabbat*. It's not the actions that we do make us to go on this *mi'raj*
(ascension). The real, only action is the good character, *muhabbat*,
loyalty, and adherence to the way. When I love them, they love me. This
love locks on and shoots up as they're going on a *mi'raj* into the heart

of Sayyidina Muhammad ﷺ at
every moment. So, the shaykh is
lifting and taking everyone on
their journey. Now you want to
do your basic *awrad* so that you
feel the connection, you feel the
inspirations coming, and you feel
the benefit of being in their
rocket ship. You don't want to be
a blind passenger in the ship
where your eyes are bound and put into the bag. They say, 'No, I want
to be in the ship and looking out the window. I want to enjoy this beatific
journey to the Lord of Power.' So, then they begin to teach and then do
the *awrads*. Try the best you can do to your ability.

Whether you're on your cycle or not, keep yourself in *wudu* (ablution). Never lose the state of *wudu*. So, don't think with your mind. Just listen

to the understanding, keep yourself in *wudu*. Anything that you can do by *hafiz* (one who memorized Qur'an). You're not allowed to touch the Qur'an by hand, but somebody who's *hafiz e Qur'an* and memorized, they can't shut off their mind. So, anything that you do by your mind, you're free to recite your *awrads*, your *zikrs* (Divine remembrance), everything that you have to do. Keep yourself

in *wudu* and recite. That is a protection during every type of difficulty. If you lose your state of *wudu* and do nothing, you will come under severe attack as a result of the cycle. And the cycle opens up for difficulties of negative energy, so highly recommended that keep your state of *wudu* because *"Kulu Innamal A'malu bin Niyyaat."*

$$\text{إِنَّمَا الْأَعْمَالِ بِالنِّيَّتْ}$$

*"Innamal 'Amaalu bin Niyyaat."*

*"Every action is according to (its) intention."*
*(Prophet Muhammad (pbuh))*

That, you're making intention, 'Ya Rabbi, to keep myself in a state of purity,' and try to do the best that you can. You cannot enter the *masjid* for the *salah* (prayer), but you can do the *zikrs* and anything that you do by heart and memorize and not touching the Holy Qur'an, *inshaAllah*.

## Are There Any Specific Practices for Women During Pregnancy?

During pregnancy is a very powerful time. There's this tremendous amount of angels, a tremendous secret of creation is entering within the womb; the meditation should be very powerful. That connecting your heart with the shaykh, connecting with Prophet ﷺ, asking to be dressed from the lights of Holy Qur'an. You may begin to hear the Holy Qur'an being recited to the child. That the Qur'an is recited within the womb to develop the child in its development phases.

So, the meditation for women could be very positive and very powerful. And meditation, generally by women, is more powerful than the men because Allah ﷻ gave them these two openings. Because Allah ﷻ gave within their heart a secret and gave within their womb a secret. So, because of these two secrets they can reach much faster. And the nature and sensitive nature makes them to be again, more softer towards the approach of realities. Where men have become hardened and become more difficult and more stubborn to reach towards their reality. With their denying it, denying it, denying it.

But because of their sensitivity, that's why in the last days, many women can fall prey to *dajjal* (system of deceit) and the whole system of difficulty. Because they're sensitive in their nature, their energy is easily hijacked. The *shaitan* (satan) can play with their sensitivity and flip all their switches. So, the man who's insensitive, he has a harder time *shaitan* to play with him to that extent. So, it goes both ways. If they're going to meditate and contemplate, they have to build their faith and their practices and understand the energy world and understand how *shaitan's* playing, *inshaAllah*.

## Are Children Protected by Beings and How Do We Protect Their Energies?

Yes, for the children they have – if their character is good – they have an angelic reality that's around them. But they inherit the sins of the parents. So, there's also things coming towards them. That's why the family is like an *imam* (religious leader). The leader of the family is responsible for his practices, his actions, his character. As he's learning these realities, he's bringing an energy into his home, like a shield. Just like you buy ADT or security services for your house because you say, 'Oh my God, in the middle of the night, I don't want to get robbed.' Well, this is a spiritual security system. And how you buy insurance policies, make sure your insurance never lapses because in the middle of the lapse, that's when difficulty comes. Your insurance is your support. Your energy is your security system.

As soon as you're meditating, there's an energy coming, an energy building, an energy coming all around the home. And many times, children want to come into that room that you're meditating, and they learn your system of watching you when you breathe and you're connecting. That *barakah* (blessings) dresses them. Then watching the *zikr* (Divine remembrance), having a life of raising the children within the *zikr*. Then again, they'll be dressed by those lights and dressed by those blessings. And then all the other practices.

When the children are screaming and yelling too much, then you should do a *wudu* (ablution) upon them. There's an energy that's making them

to howl and growl too much. So, you take them gently into the wash area and just make a *wudu*. Just like how water brings down fire, they also can acquire a fire because of the subtlety of their nature. So, they wear the *ta'weez* like we wear the *ta'weez* (prayer for protection). They yell and scream uncontrollably. Then it's your responsibility to discipline them and control that wildness, and the use of water is highly advised. So, you water it and put out the fire of someone getting too aggressive and too much screaming and yelling, *inshaAllah*.

## What Are the Angelic Realities of Food?

The food has an immense reality. That everything we are doing is unlocking the power within the food and water. That every *tajalli* (manifestation) that coming for *insan* (human being), and the shaykhs and all the associations, they put all the *tajallis* of whatever they are doing upon the water and the food. Because the hearts of men are not capable of absorbing that reality, where we pray, we

keep water and food. And in our homes where we make *zikr* (Divine remembrance), we keep water and food.

They understood that every association, every *zikr*, every *salah* (prayer), every action that you are doing, its dress is most powerful upon water and food. That the *malaika* (angels) inside the water and the food, they  are the ones saying *ameen* at the level of angelic purity. So soon as we make our *salah*, we make our *zikr* (Divine remembrance), we make our *du'as* (supplications). When we are making the *du'a*, the angels, and the angels in the water, the tea, the food, we have an entire store place of food. Every angel upon them is saying *"Ameen, ameen, ameen,"* not at our level, but at an angelic level. What reality that carries is unimaginable.

On top of that, whatever *du'a* the shaykh is pushing through – again, light upon light, light upon light, light upon light of realities. Then from the understanding of Sayyidina Muhammad ﷺ, that every bite of a generous person's food, 300 angels enter into that *insan* (human being) to begin to make a *shifa* and healing for them. And on top of that, if one of those generous people are from Abdul Qadir, that they are *Qadiri* people of *Laylatul Qadr* (Night of Power), everything they do is multiplied by 30,000. Because Allah ﷻ says, 'We grant them, *Salaamun Hiya matlail Fajr.*'

سَلَامٌ هِيَ حَتَّىٰ مَطْلَعِ الْفَجْرِ ﴿٥﴾

*97:5 – "Salamun, hiya hatta matla'il Fajr." (Surat Al-Qadr)*

*"Peace it is until the emergence of dawn." (The Power, 97:5)*

They're granted 30,000. 1,000 months in every day, which is by 30 – 30 days times 1,000 months. Every day of theirs, Allah ☬ is blessing them 30,000 times more than anyone else. So, one of those *Qadiri* (people from the Ocean of Power) people making *du'a* (supplication), their food is blessed 30,000 times more. Their water is dressed 30,000 times more, their *salah* 30,000 times more *barakah* (blessings). Their *zikr*, 30,000 times more *barakah*. On top of that – because it keeps going – then Sayyidina Muhammad ﷺ sweetens the deal, says, 'Oh, if Allah ☬ giving that, then let me tell you what Allah ☬ gave me to give to that servant.'

If they do one hour of *tafakkur* (contemplation) that is accepted, and they become *Ahle Tafakkur* (People of Contemplation), and the people of that reality, every hour of theirs is like somebody else's seventy years of worship. One hour with them is as if you find somebody for seventy years has to worship, if you spend just one hour with them.

تَفَكُّرْ سَاعَةٍ خَيْرٌ مِنْ عِبَادَةِ سَبْعِينْ سَنَة

*"Tafakkur sa'atin khairun min 'Ibadati sab'een sanatan."*

*"One hour of contemplation is more valuable than seventy years of worship." (Prophet Muhammad (pbuh))*

One hour times seventy years, we said was like 1,500 years – one day with them. Because these *Ahle Tafakkur* (People of Contemplation), they're continuous live *tafakkur*. When they have been granted the station of *tafakkur*, their connection is live all the time. They're streaming all the time. They shut off for people, but their heart is alive and awake, and they're streaming twenty-four hours a day. So, it means their day is equivalent to 1,500 years of worship. If you spent one day with them, it's as if you spent 1,500 years with somebody else.  So, knowing one of them has a tremendous amount of light and blessings and dressing.

So then imagine the angels in their food, the angels in their water, how much Allah ﷻ sending. That's why some men, their *amal* (actions) are like mountains. Not because they're jogging, you know, 50 hours a day. Because Allah ﷻ is dressing and dressing and dressing and dressing. And that's Allah's ﷻ *Ni'mat* and blessing upon their soul. It's not something that is coming from *zakah* (charity), it's from Allah's ﷻ *Ni'mat* (blessing). Allah ﷻ inspire them to be from these people of *tafakkur* (contemplation).

Allah ﷻ inspired them to reach to that reality. And as a result, they are like abundant fountains of Allah's ﷻ Grace and *Rahmah* (Mercy) upon the Earth. And by means of them, everything is kept green. By means of that, everything is revived. By means of that, they are *muhyil qulub* (reviver of hearts). Any heart that comes dead around them, through them, through their signal, Allah ﷻ will revive it and bring it back to life.

If Sayyidina Khidr ﷺ used his power upon a dead fish, imagine through the *shajarah* (spiritual lineage) of the Naqshbandi Silsila, what he is sending into the hearts of these shaykhs. What Allah ﷻ cares for a fish to come back to life? Allah ﷻ cares for the heart of *insan* (human being). That bring their heart back to life.

قَالَ أَرَأَيْتَ إِذْ أَوَيْنَا إِلَى الصَّخْرَةِ فَإِنِّي نَسِيتُ الْحُوتَ وَمَا أَنسَانِيهُ إِلَّا الشَّيْطَانُ أَنْ أَذْكُرَهُ ۚ وَاتَّخَذَ سَبِيلَهُ فِي الْبَحْرِ عَجَبًا ﴿٦٣﴾

*18:63 – "Qala araayta idh awayna ilas sakhrati fa-innee naseetu alhoota wa ma ansaneehu illash shaytanu an adhkurahu, wat takhadha sabeela hu fee al bahri 'ajaba." (Surat Al-Kahf)*

*"He said, 'Did you see when we retired to the rock? Indeed, I forgot [there] the fish. And none made me forget it except Satan – that I should mention it. And it took its course into the sea amazingly.'"*
*(The Cave, 18:63)*

So, we said before they destroyed, *mahyidh dhunub* (destroyer of sins).

From just the *meem ha*, Sayyidina Muhammad ﷺ, they crush all of the rust and the badness that is around that *insan* (human being). That same light that comes and burns away everything, returns it as new. *SubhanAllah*, Allah ﷻ now has that technology for lasers for *insan* to see. So, they bring this really old and rusty, dirty piece of metal, and they have a new laser. And they bring the laser, and they're just hitting the metal and it's going 'kshh' [Shaykh makes burning noise], looks like it's burning it. And with a laser light, they take away all the rust and this device becomes as if brand new. The laser light is at such a frequency that it's burning through all of the rust and returns that piece of metal as if it's brand new, and they show you brand new. And they use this in industrial cleaning now with this laser light.

This for Allah ﷻ to show *insan* (human being), 'What you people think you can make it and you don't think Allah has it?' Allah ﷻ has servants through their eyes. They merely look more powerful than that laser light and it burns away everything. They have laser lights now where they can detect a sickness within your body cell. They inject a dye that attaches to  that sickness, for example, and makes that sickness to have a blue colour. Then they make a laser that goes through your skin and only targets the blue colour. And from outside, they shine a light. It goes in and begins to attack everything that's blue. If they diagnose the problem, attach a colour to the problem, and then have a receiving light that identifies only it wants to burn blue. It goes through your skin, no problem. It goes through your blood, no problem. It finds that infected cell that's blue, and starts to burn it, burn it, burn it and clean.

 All these technologies, Allah ﷻ is showing, 'Toshiba made it, you don't think Allah's Heavens has it? Of course.' These are the eyes of the believer, their eyes and their souls. Their light merely moves where Allah ﷻ wants it to move. It can clean, it can cleanse, it can heal, it can everything. But we have to build our self for that reality and to dress ourselves from that reality, *inshaAllah*.

## How Do Devils Still Influence Us if They're Imprisoned in Ramadan?

*A'uzu Billahi Minash Shaitanir Rajeem Bismillahir Rahmanir Raheem.* Your devils are chained in Ramadan, not other people's devils because the nation has been more attacked during Ramadan. Because unbelievers heard of Ramadan then said, 'That's the time to fight these people, because they'll be weak from being hungry.' So, it's not devils are chained, but your devil will be chained by your fasting. And anytime you fast, Prophet ﷺ taught that, '*Shaitan* (satan) runs through your blood.'

عَنْ أَنَسٍ قَالَ، قَالَ رَسُولُ اللَّهِ ﷺ: إِنَّ الشَّيْطَانَ يَجْرِي مِنْ الْإِنْسَانِ مَجْرَى الدَّمِ ."
[اَلْمَصْدَرْ: صَحِيحْ مُسْلِمْ ٢١٧٤ ]

*'An Anasin Qala Rasulallahi* ﷺ, *"Innash Shaitana yajri minal Insani majra addami." [Sahih Muslim 2174]*

*Narrated by 'An Anas (ra) that the Messenger of Allah (pbuh) said, "Satan circulates/flows through the human being as blood circulates/flow in the body." [Authentic by Muslim 2174]*

It means a satanic energy is related to what you eat and drink and how

you breathe. And he comes into your system; we said *shaitan* is inside people. All the *wudu* (ablution) that you're making outside is for the outside *shaitan*. The stronger one is the inside *shaitan*. And as soon as you enter into fasting and restrict your food and drink, that one inside becomes weakened by your *siyam* (fast). That's why fasting is so hard. Because that *shaitan* inside is pushing you to break your fast. He needs energy. 'Break your fast so that I can attack you again, I need energy.' As soon as you restrict the food, he becomes weaker. You restrict the drinking, he becomes weaker.

That's why we said, 'The first ten days is *rahmah* (mercy).' The first ten days wasn't *maghfirah* (forgiveness). Allah ﷻ gave us a clue that, 'It's the

*rahmah* that I send down a light that chains your *nafs* (ego), so that allows you to enter into the Ramadan, and into the fast.' If Allah ﷻ had not granted a *rahmah* in the ten days, everyone's *nafs* would have destroyed them from fasting.

عَنْ سَلْمَانَ اَلْفَارِسِيْ رَضِيْ اللهُ عَنْهُ، أَنَّ رَسُوْلُ اللهِ ﷺ قال: " شَهْرُ رَمَضَانَ أَوَّلُهُ رَحْمَةٌ ، وَأَوْسَطُهُ مَغْفِرَةٌ ، وَآخِرُهُ عِتْقٌ مِنَ النَّارِ."
[المصدر: الإِمَامُ اَلْأَلْبَانِي (مِشْكَاةُ اَلْمَصَابِيْح) ، كتاب ٧، حديث ٩]

*'An Salman al Farsi (ra), an Rasulullahi ﷺ qala, "Shahru Ramadana awwalahu rahmatun, wa awsatuhu maghfiratun, wa akhiruhu 'itqun minan naar."*
*[Al Imam al Albani, Meshkatal Masabih - 1965, Book 7, Hadith 9]*

*Narrated by Salman al Farsi (ra), that the Messenger of Allah ﷺ said, "The first (ten days) of the month of Ramadan is mercy, the middle (ten days) is forgiveness, and the last (ten days) is salvation/freedom from the fire."*
*[Al Imam al Albani, Meshkatal Masabih - 1965, Book 7, Hadith 9]*

That's why every other nation, they were denied that *rahmah*, and they did not keep the fast. They have Lent, where they leave Coca-Cola for a day, this was the fast thirty days. So, then they say Lent, they were supposed to fast thirty days, but then they say okay, 'Just abstain from something you like.' Somebody says, 'I like chocolate,' 'Then don't eat chocolate for a day.' So, it means their devils are so strong, that they can't stop for one day to do.

This is a *rahmah* from Allah ﷻ. It's not easy for two billion people to be fasting on this Earth. It's an *isharat* and a sign. The *rahmah* of Allah ﷻ on this nation because it's the *rahmah* of Sayyidina Muhammad ﷺ.

And that Allah's ﷻ chosen messenger, to show that, 'My Chosen Messenger, his people will keep the fast because I'm chaining their bad character, bad desire, so that they can enter it in.' Once ten days, they have entered in it, that *shaitan* becomes so weakened that they  continue through with *maghfirah*, Allah ﷻ begin to burn.

*Sifat* (attribute) of this month is under 81. *Dhul Fadl* (The Possessor of Grace) is the name of Sayyidina Muhammad ﷺ, the source of every

goodness. And Allah's ﷻ name is *Al-Muntaqim* (The Avenger). That, if not for Allah ﷻ to send and say, 'I'm going to avenge my creation from what *shaitan* has done to them,' because *Al-Muntaqim* comes and begin to beat and put fire onto the *shaitan* and they're running. So, their fasting is burning devils, burning *shaitans* (satans), *inshaAllah*.

311

## Do Solar and Lunar Eclipses Affect Us Spiritually?

That best to know that Prophet ﷺ had concerns during the eclipse. And that they would enter into the *salah* (prayer) and stay in *sujood*

(prostration) while the eclipse is taking place. And there is an importance with the sun, the moon, and the Earth. And everything that happens is a sign and an *isharat* (sign). And generally, these are warning signs of difficulties that come to Earth and that are heading onto Earth. And we know that we are in difficult times already.

Best not to look at those because of the energy that comes and whatever difficulty is being. And the guidance of that difficulty or sign of that

difficulty that coming onto Earth, don't go out staring at it. It may have a negative effect upon *insan* (mankind) and an unpleasant energy for those who are sensitive and subtle towards energy. Best to avoid those situations of looking at that and to pray that, '*Ya Rabbi* if anything is of a difficulty coming, that grant us a *najat* and a salvation through it, a protection through every type of difficulty.'

# Understanding Energy and Experiences During Meditation

## What Realities Does Practicing Meditation Open?

The meditation and *tafakkur* (contemplation) has basic concepts and principles. Be strong in your understanding of *wudu* (ablution); be strong in the practices of keeping your energy to be safe and secure, washing, cleaning, keeping oneself clean, wearing these *ta'weez* (prayer for protection), and having the understanding of energy. Anytime you're dealing with energy, the more you build yourself up the more there's going to be negative, and you're going to feel the negative. What may have been heedless before of negative energy all around you, as soon as you practice, you become what's called *lateef*, subtle. You start to feel what's uncomfortable. It has always been there; you just didn't feel it because we were in a state of heedlessness.

When Allah ﷻ wants you to wake up from heedlessness, 'Hey there's things crawling on you.' So, it's not insanity, it's just that you become more subtle. As soon as you become subtle you feel the energies that are not correct, not right. And that's why only through energy practices people understood they cannot do it themselves. Allah ﷻ didn't want us to be by ourselves.

That's what *shaitan* (satan) wants. He takes a herd of people and break them into groups; divide and conquer. And make everybody just to be divided and by themselves and then he conquers them and attacks them because his might has been here for all of this creation of *Bani Adam*.

What Allah ﷻ wants for us is to keep our fellowship. Keep the fellowship of the people of reality and to keep it at all times. The understanding of the *madad* (support) is to call upon that, '*Ya Rabbi*, I want to be with you I want to be with *Nabiyeen, Siddiqeen, Shuhadai was Saliheen.*'

وَمَن يُطِعِ اللَّهَ وَالرَّسُولَ فَأُوْلَـئِكَ مَعَ الَّذِينَ أَنْعَمَ اللَّهُ عَلَيْهِم مِّنَ النَّبِيِّينَ وَالصِّدِّيقِينَ وَالشُّهَدَاء وَالصَّالِحِينَ وَحَسُنَ أُولَـئِكَ رَفِيقًا ﴿٦٩﴾

*4:69 – "Wa man yuti' Allaha war Rasula faolayeka ma'al ladheena an'ama Allahu 'alayhim minan Nabiyeena, was Siddiqeena, wash Shuhadai, was Saliheena wa hasuna olayeka rafeeqan."*
*(Surat An-Nisa)*

*"And whoever obeys Allah and the Messenger (pbuh) are in the company of those on whom Allah has bestowed His Favours/Blessings - of the prophets, the sincere Truthful, the witnesses to the truth (who testify), and the Righteous, and excellent are those as companions."*
*(The Women, 4:69)*

Keep me in their presence and guide me into understanding how to always be in their presence, asking for the *madad* and support and energy and energy beings. '*Ya Rabbi*, these people whom, and these creations that you've given them a light and a blessing, surround me by that light and blessing.' So, then the practice of the *madad*, practice of *wudu*, practices of energy – all of these are important.

How to keep a balance in life of doing good, struggling, living amongst people, struggle with whatever work we have, whatever things we have to do, and at the same time practicing to reach our reality. The more the struggle, the bigger the reward. We don't run off into the bushes to hide for Allah ﷻ. That we live amongst people, communities, and work. And in that work and family and children, we struggle, struggle to keep our connection. There lies the immense reward. One whom can struggle, keep with their family and community and obligations, and at the same time build their spiritual practices. This means they work hard by day and they

pray all night. They do their practices at night if that's when it's more peaceful and quiet. They do their meditations; they do all their *zikrs* (Divine remembrance) and *awrads* (daily practices) throughout the day and at night. So, all of these keep us to be balanced and reaching towards Allah ﷻ Satisfaction, *inshaAllah*.

## Are There Physical Effects on the Body When Meditating?

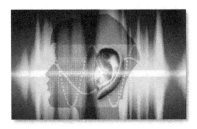

When Allah ﷻ want to open the senses, there are going to be many physical effects. They are going to feel different energies entering into their ears. They are going to feel different subtleties upon their hands and upon their feet because you become *lateef*, you become more subtle. When you focus on these senses and you focus on these body parts, it means that it becomes more sensitive to the energy and to the vibration. When Allah ﷻ wants to open a sensitivity, it means your focus is on your ears and you are trying to live a life of, *"Sam'ina wa ata'na."*

سَمِعْنَا وَأَطَعْنَا غُفْرَانَكَ رَبَّنَا وَاِلَيْكَ الْمَصِيْرُ ﴿٢٨٥﴾

*2:285 – "Sam'ina wa ata'na, ghufranaka Rabbana wa ilaykal masir."*
*(Surat Al-Baqarah)*

*"We hear, and we obey: (We seek) Thy forgiveness, our Lord, and to Thee is the end of all journeys." (The Cow, 2:285)*

You become very sensitive to hearing. You hear things. You feel vibrations. You have a depth in understanding of sound, and *salawats* (praises upon Prophet Muhammad ﷺ), and all these realities. The more you are focusing on your hearing, the more sensitive you become and more attuned to it. And also, with sound – loud sounds and agitations and vibrations, everything. So, yes, of course. Anything that you focus in will

become much more sensitive under the different characteristics of subtlety from *sifat al Latif*.

## Why Do Our Ears Heat Up During Meditation?

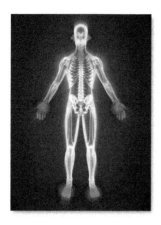

*InshaAllah*, make sure that you always have the *ta'weez* (prayer for protection) on because this is now a battle in energy. So, make sure that you started the meditation with *wudu* (ablution), that you have your *ta'weez* on, that you make your connection and your *madad* (support). And the rest, leave to Allah ﷻ. Energies are going to come and you're going to get heated, either in your neck, your hands, your feet, your ears.

There's going to be an exchange of energy. An energy that you're trying to bring is a positive energy and there's going to be all the negative energy that people have upon themselves. So, one's got to go. The positive energy is going to come, and the negative energy is not going to try to release very easily. So, there is going to be an exchange of energy and heated energies and cold energies.

Just make sure yourself is all washed and clean and you have your *ta'weez* (prayer for protection) and you're doing your practices. And it goes along with everything else that we're taught. It is that when you enter into the energy world and this energy training, you have to be hypersensitive to everything. Don't smoke, don't drink. It goes without even saying, don't do crazy things. Because once you open the door to energy and you engage in behaviour that is not to

the benefit of your spiritual being, you're now in a dangerous area.

Because then *shaitan* (satan) can come big time and attack and make your life really upside down.

Somebody grabbed a *ta'weez* and bought a *ta'weez* and then decided he would go every night to a nightclub. Of course, he's going to have

tremendous problems. Because now you're bringing in positive energy, positive beings and taking them into the satanic realm and like making them fight each other. You start seeing the dishes flying in and out and things going on all over the place. So, you try to say, 'Okay, I'm going to leave the bad to the best of my ability and I want to improve myself towards the good.' *InshaAllah.*

## What is the Significance of Hearing Sounds During Meditation?

It's good because everything is about becoming more subtle. That Allah ﷻ describes, *'They have ears, but they don't hear, they have eyes, but they don't see.'*

وَلَقَدْ ذَرَأْنَا لِجَهَنَّمَ كَثِيرًا مِّنَ الْجِنِّ وَالْإِنسِ ۖ لَهُمْ قُلُوبٌ لَّا يَفْقَهُونَ بِهَا وَلَهُمْ أَعْيُنٌ لَّا يُبْصِرُونَ بِهَا وَلَهُمْ آذَانٌ لَّا يَسْمَعُونَ بِهَا ۚ أُولَٰئِكَ كَالْأَنْعَامِ بَلْ هُمْ أَضَلُّ ۚ أُولَٰئِكَ هُمُ الْغَافِلُونَ ﴿١٧٩﴾

*7:179 – "Wa laqad zara'naa li jahannama kaseeran minal jinni wal insi lahum quloobul laa yafqahoona bihaa wa lahum a'yunul laa yubisiroona bihaa wa lahum aazaanul laa yasma'oona bihaa; ulaaa'ika kal an'aami bal hum adall; ulaaa'ika humul ghaafiloon."*
*(Surat Al-Ar'af)*

*"Many are the Jinns and men we have made for Hell: They have hearts wherewith they understand not, eyes wherewith they see not, and ears wherewith they hear not. They are like cattle – nay more misguided: for they are heedless (of warning)." (The Heights, 7:179)*

What we're trying to open is the second sense of everything. Every sense has two doors. I have eyes; as soon as I close them, my spiritual eye will

open. If I live my life only on my physical eyes, I have to see everything; I have to see it to believe, never my spiritual eye opens. My spiritual eye opens when I take a life of saying, 'I don't trust with my eyes because I saw so much deceit with my eyes, I'm not going to ruin my

life by my eyesight, so I'll close my eyes.' Soon as I close my eyes I say, '*Ya Rabbi*, it's like I'm in my grave; I don't want to see from these eyes.' Make my *zikr* (Divine remembrance), make my *zikr*. Then Allah ﷻ begin to make the sensitivity of your spiritual eye to open.

Same thing then when I clean my ears. 'I don't want to hear the bad. I don't want to hear the unnecessary things. I want to walk away from every type of unnecessary talk.' We don't sit and confront and argue people. Not the *dunya* (material world). D*unya* is like, 'Where are you going, you're like chicken, you're walking away from everything.' Yes of

course, every type of difficulty, my job is to walk away. That's why Prophet ﷺ would get up and walk away. We don't sit and begin to argue with *shaitan* (satan). Because you're now no longer dealing with a person, you're

dealing with their devil that's now in their presence. We walk away from every type of argument, no confrontation. Just, 'Thank you very much, peace be upon you, I'm out.' Soon as you guard your ears and listen to *salawats* (praises upon Prophet Muhammad ﷺ), listen to *salawats*, and you're playing the *salawats* and closing your eyes, your ears and your spiritual hearing becomes more sensitive, *inshaAllah*.

## What Does Hearing a Whistle Sound Mean When Meditating?

Anything can mean anything, but do you focus on it? No. So that's why you are trying to keep your focus. So imagine that you are on a bus to the presence of Sayyidina Muhammad ﷺ, and on this bus you keep looking at the view and the scenery instead of doing the *salawats* (praises upon Prophet Muhammad ﷺ), the practices that you are preparing yourself now to enter into the presence of that reality. So, the whole process of distraction is to distract the servant from their target. So, those horizons and visions on the side, and left, and front, they are not as significant as negating one's self.

That, '*Ya Rabbi*, I don't need to see anything; I'm nothing, I'm nothing. I close my eyes and I want to be in *Madinatul Munawwara*. Let me to reach to oceans of power.' Now you see this coming and that could be a distraction. You can see a vision of this coming and these are all distractions. That, tell and negate yourself to be nothing. 'I'm nothing, I'm nothing, and I'm not here for the visions, *ya Rabbi*. I want to reach towards this ocean

of power. I want to be in the presence of Sayyidina Muhammad ﷺ and I want to do my *salawats* and feel the energy of my *salawats*.'

Because if you allow the imaginary world of visualizing, and those whom have a very strong imagination, can all of a sudden lose themselves in an imaginal world. 'You know I saw the fairies coming, I saw these things are floating. I saw all these stars were shooting.' And then instead of your focus and your *zikr* (Divine remembrance) where you are trying to achieve and reach your destination, you become distracted. And that's why Naqshbandiya veils the servant until they reach their destination. The destination is not the Heavenly Kingdom, but the destination is into the inner core of their bad character.

Naqshbandiya, the minute they join and partake in the Naqshbandiya way, Shaykh Abdullah al-Faiz Daghestani's ق promise is that, 'I will lift that servant immediately to my *maqam* (station). What Allah ﷻ dressed me from, I will dress that servant.' And their journey is not into the heavens, but into their bad character. And until they go deep into their bad character, resolve their bad characteristics, take away all their bad desires, then that vision will become clearer and clearer because you already achieved those stations within the heavens. So, it is moving to the heavens, but the most powerful way is to move inside yourself.

So, you rid the veils of your humanity which are the thickest veils of bad character. So, as you're burning through them and the shaykh is describing this interaction with the shaykh is so to burn your bad characteristics, most of which you didn't know existed within you. Because once you start to deal with the shaykh you start to debate and argue, and you didn't like this advice. You thought that this advice was something else and, 'But my mum advised this, and my dad

advised this, and my brother advised that.' And all of those who bring out those characteristics of the most difficult characteristics, and these are *hijab al bashariya*, the veils of humanity and the thick, bad characteristics that have to be drilled through, *inshaAllah*.

## What is the Significance of Hearing a Calibration Tone During Meditation?

One, in the *tafakkur* (contemplation), we ask that you always play

*salawats* (praises upon Prophet Muhammad ﷺ). If you're playing the *salawats*, playing Holy Qur'an and meditating, I think it would be very difficult to hear anything, and any type of whisper that's coming into the ear. This sense of speech is not something you physically hear through the ear. That's something

else maybe trying to whisper to you, to talk to you. If you're doing it with the *salawats* and playing the *salawats*, you're not actually hearing that. You're trying to block out anything from physical hearing.

This reality is about shutting down the physicality and opening your second level of hearing, which is the hearing from your soul. As soon as

you open the hearing from your soul, it's your lower conscience. The reality of your soul that's in the body that begins to communicate with your higher conscience. The reality of your soul that's always in the heavens, always in Allah's ﷻ protection and kept away from you. Your soul will begin to talk to you and give you your inspirations. Your inspirations, not *wahy* (revelation), 'They call what inspiration?' *Ilham*. That your soul will give you your

inspirations and the soul is continuously trying to give out the inspirations, but mankind is busy.

They're running, running, running, running – never stopping to hear. So, it means that the real spiritual hearing is when they shut, and they can hear through their soul. That they hear the guidance of their shaykh pushing their soul to speak to them. And the soul is speaking to you about yourself, 'You should be praying. You should make *istighfar* (seeking forgiveness). You should be doing like this. You should be doing…' Anything that the soul speaks about is based on being hard to yourself.

If you ever hear a voice speaking to you about, 'You are correct and the shaykh was wrong,' that's *shaitan* (satan). If you hear a voice talking to you about giving yourself credit and that you're a good person, it's *shaitan*. Because the two, what they want is like you have to understand the flavour. The ego wants to always find something correct about the body because he's the one doing all the damage, 'So no, no, no. We're right, we're great, you're a perfect guy. You're a perfect person, everything is perfect.' And it always wants to validate the self and say bad about everybody else. The soul, when it inspires you, it tells you, 'You are wrong, you did wrong. You did bad. So, how can I be mad? That's horrible. I can't do like that.'

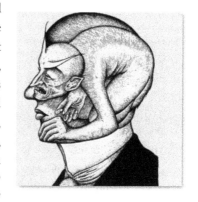

That's from the soul because it wants to crush you.

Anything that happens to you, the soul comes and tells you, 'Allah ﷻ sent that to you. Take it with your understanding and your faith. There's nothing for you to say back.' So, the soul is continuously helping us to be nothing. So, then when Sayyidina Ibrahim عليه السلام was going to take Sayyidina Ismail عليه السلام, the soul comes out and gives a guarantee for Sayyidina Ibrahim عليه السلام 'Don't worry, you'll find me to be patient.'

فَلَمَّا بَلَغَ مَعَهُ السَّعْيَ قَالَ يَا بُنَيَّ إِنِّي أَرَىٰ فِي الْمَنَامِ أَنِّي أَذْبَحُكَ فَانظُرْ مَاذَا تَرَىٰ ۚ قَالَ يَا أَبَتِ افْعَلْ مَا تُؤْمَرُ ۖ سَتَجِدُنِي إِن شَاءَ اللَّـهُ مِنَ الصَّابِرِينَ ﴿١٠٢﴾

*37:102 – "Falamma balagha ma'ahus sa'ya qala ya bunayya inni ara fee almanami annee adhbahuka fanzhur ma dha tara, Qala ya abati if'al ma tu maru, satajidunee inshaAllahu minas Sabireen."*
*(Surat As-Saffat)*

*"And when he reached with him [the age of] exertion, he said, "O my son, indeed I have seen in a dream that I [must] sacrifice you, so see what you think. He said, 'O my father, do as you are commanded. You will find me, if Allah wills, one of the Patient/steadfast.'"*
*(Those Who Set the Ranks, 37:102)*

This means the reality and the *haqqaiq* of the soul is that it wants to come and give us the guidance of Allah ﷻ. The higher path, the higher way. Don't shake off this difficult order that coming. Allah ﷻ wants something. And that's why we said that in this reality of Sayyidina Ibrahim عليه السلام, Sayyidina Ismail عليه السلام represents *Maqamul Ihsan* (Station of Moral Excellence).

Allah ﷻ will make a reality of your soul to come out to assist you on your guidance. That these coordinance, this is what the soul wants. Don't  listen to what your *nafs* (ego) is saying to answer back. You may get a heavy test in life. You say, 'I want to now use my ability to come against a shaykh, come against a *wali* (saint), come against anyone.' So, then they teach you, if you don't have that training now then stay quiet, stay quiet. So that that reality can become a reality within the heart. So, real hearing is through the subconscious where you hear the consciousness and it begins to dress you, bless you.

Different types of hearing and sounds are based on your training. If you're training in *tafakkur* and contemplation, they may begin to open up an alert system. An alert system is that when you've been trained in meditation and *tafakkur*, the connection with the shaykh is understood. You have an alarm system like ADT. Do they have ADT in Canada? House alarm. It means Allah ﷻ will wire you with an alarm system on all of your body's openings, everywhere.

And as soon as a being with incorrect intention enters your proximity, you hear a tremendous buzzing like all your energy is 'zzz' and very painful to ignore. A warning is coming that something is trying to enter into your field of protection. And that will be a different level of training for a student who's reached an understanding. They have a protection system that Allah ﷻ put because the vibration of their energy is being elevated. As a result of their perfected vibration, 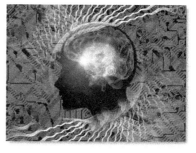 anything of a lower and dirty frequency agitates that field of energy. 'Zzz,' coming in something dirty.

So, we said before that it's like getting a battery, the nine-volt battery and test it on your tongue. It gives you like, 'ooh,' that hurt. That feeling is when an energy is trying to come around your body that's not at the cleanliness of your level. A dirty energy trying to hit a clean energy causes a shock in the energy and the vibration. Then later on, that will be training and energy; how to defend the self, how to push all the negativities away – that's with the *madad* (support).

That's why then the first level of *tafakkur* and meditation is just to contemplate, to begin to understand myself, how to breathe. Then to introduce my shaykh into the meditation. That, 'I want to be with my shaykh, my heart to be connected with my shaykh, to feel the love and the presence that keep your *nazar* (gaze) upon me always. I don't want to be in this world alone. I don't want to be left to my *nafs* (ego) for the blink of an eye.'

Prophet ﷺ asked Allah ﷻ is, 'Don't leave me to myself, my *nafs*, for even a blink.'

اللَّهُمَّ لَا تَكِلْنِي إِلَى نَفْسِي طَرْفَةَ عَيْنٍ وَلَا أَقَلَّ مِنْ ذَلِكَ

*"Allahumma laa takilnee ila nafsee tarfat `aynin wa laa aqala min dhalika."*

*"O Allah! Don't leave me to my ego for the blink of an eye or less."*
*(Prophet Muhammad (pbuh))*

How to avoid that is then to master the *muraqabah* (spiritual connection) and *tafakkur*. That, 'I'm always in the presence of the *shuyukh*. They're looking at me, watching me, I'm feeling their presence. Their *nazar* comes and begin to push away any type of negativity, any type of badness. They become like the light for the fly killer. You know, when you put that light on every type of bad fly that comes to you, 'zzz' and then falls. 'Zzz,' falls because their light is guarding and all over you. When their light over you, anything that comes into your field, 'zzz' and goes down, *inshaAllah*. The more stronger, stronger that light and love is, the stronger and stronger the field of energy and protection becomes.

## Is It Our Voice or the Shaykh's Voice We Hear?

No, the real hearing is that you hear yourself. That when you sit, you're in a continuous state. Your being that's inside you, the being that wants to communicate with you and then the being that is in the highest association. This means it wants to send you your coordinance from Allah ﷻ, but you have to be at a state at which you can silence every sound to hear what you have to say to yourself. What is the guidance that my

Lord has sent upon my soul for me to understand? That's why the *tafakkur* (contemplation) is so powerful.

Most people live their life with never slowing down. So, then they just listen to whatever they are doing in the speed of their emotion. As soon as you sit to contemplate, and then through their practices and through their training on how to shut off all the different sounds, they begin to try to hear their voice. And the shaykh will push their voice onto them. Later at different levels, when they have an extreme love for their

guide, they have the flavour and the mannerisms of how their guide talks to them. And they can hear that dialogue with the shaykh. That's at a much higher level, *inshaAllah*.

## How Can We Differentiate Inspirations From Whispers?

Definitely, the whisper never ends. That's the station that the whispering is always whispering. So, there is no protection against that. We seek refuge in Allah 'ﷻ and make the *salawats* on Sayyidina Muhammad ﷺ to

bring that light and that protection. The whispering will be there. Then they train you on what to listen for. This means that in all of this training for inspiration, follow the inspirations that have to do with worshipness. That I should pray more. I should make my *salawats*. I should sit down and begin to read

my Qur'an, read *Dalail ul Khairat* (book of praisings on Prophet ﷺ). All these things that are in reference to worshipness, those can be inspirations.

Any inspiration in which to deal with a person, we would believe it to be not good and *nafsani* (egocentric), where *shaitan* (satan) is talking to you to talk to a person. The only person I'm supposed to be worried about is myself. So, the only inspiration is on how to be hard on myself in my worshipness. Anything that's coming of a whispering of this person, 'Tell this one they're doing something wrong. Tell this one this, like tell this,' that's from *shaitan*. And that gets you in trouble and that's the big downfall of most spiritual people. They think they should advise everybody, but yet

they don't follow the advice themselves. And then they enter into an ocean of hypocrisy which is a very dangerous ocean for Allah 🕌 to punish the servant.

Because you're calling people to that which you don't do. So, to avoid that then, 'I only call people to goodness and I only worry about myself and being hard upon myself and my practices. Everyone else, *alhamdulillah*, they're free to do as they like.' Unless you're under the orders of the shaykh that, 'Please tell this person this, or give this rule for this.'

## How Do We Protect Ourselves From Whispers of Satan?

In the time of meditation, that's why we meditate with sound. It means

anytime we're going to isolate ourselves and sit and make our *tafakkur* (contemplation) it's with the power of sound. So, when we're listening to the *salawat*, it actually is to block the *waswas* (whispering) of *shaitan* (satan). That when we try to sit and contemplate, last thing we want to do is contemplate in silence because that's when *shaitan* is going to come. He has an active audience and begin to teach to the servant and gossip and complain to the servant.

And the other time is you're going to be attacked is in the wash facilities. As soon as you enter in, he begins to give a *khutbah* and lesson and teaching; take no teaching within the facilities. Anything you think is an inspiration is not an inspiration, it's the *waswas* of *shaitan*. And then the *salawats*, that throughout the day making *istighfar* (seeking forgiveness) it begins to block that *waswas*. That's why all these prescriptions are already in advance of what your questions are. It means that when you make your *istighfar* all day long, you're blocking this *waswas*. It's the time that we become idle is then the time in which he whispers into the ear to get the attention of the servant. When we're making *salawat* on Sayyidina Muhammad ﷺ, again it counters any type of *waswas* coming into the ear, *inshaAllah*.

## During Meditation is it Our Consciousness or Our Ego Speaking?

When we said before that the conscious being from the soul and the ego being the *nafs* (ego); anytime the *nafs* talks, it's a defence of the self. 'This happened because of this, this happened.' The *nafs* is always trying to defend. The soul is happy with all sorts of difficulty. So, the soul never defends something wrong that was done to you. The soul is happy with it. It says, 'You deserved it and that you should be crushed for Allah's ﷻ sake.' The *nafs* says, 'No, no, no, I have to take retribution.'

The *nafs* is always in a state of defending the body and the soul is very content in crushing the body. And inspiration of the *nafs* is to defend the body. So, 'Let me be inspired to go tell him he's wrong.' This is from *nafs*. The soul's inspiration is, 'I should pray about fifty *rakahs* (cycle of prayer) as a *tawbah* (repentance).' And those are the hardest to follow. The soul's inspiration is for worshipness. When

you feel that you are being inspired by your soul and say what is the inspiration of the soul? It is for worshipness. 'I should do now 20,000 *salawats* (praises upon Prophet Muhammad ﷺ) and I shouldn't move until that's finished. I should do 10,000 *istighfar* (seeking forgiveness). I should pray 20 *rakahs* in my *salah* (prayer).' Those inspirations come and people brush that away really quick and say, 'Oh, I don't feel like it.'

But the *nafsani* (egocentric) one is all based on the self, glorify the self, and vindicate the self. And that's why we said western words is based on completely egoistic understandings which we would never use those

words from Sufi training. 'Self-realization.' That's like saying 'ego-realization.' Self-help, ego-help. You don't want help from your ego and you don't want the ego to help you in your realization. So, this play of words is very dangerous. So, our way is based on how to destroy the ego and how to bring the power to the soul and they both want different things.

## How Do We Know We're Hearing the Heart and Not the Ego?

Yes, for sure know that you're hearing your *nafs* (ego) and *shaitan* (satan). The general rule in *tafakkur* (contemplation) and trying to listen is that it's always to tell myself that, 'My *shaitan* is going to say everything.' So, anything related to *'ibadah* and worship is from the soul. Anything in relationship to anything other than that is from the *nafs*. So, for example when you sit and meditate, if your soul tells you, 'Sit here another ten hours. Read half the Qur'an. Pray 200 *rakahs* (cycles of prayer),' that's the one you're going to ignore. You say, 'Oh no, I'm not going to listen to that.'

But if all of a sudden, your *nafs* (ego) tells you, 'You know what, you should call up your friend and they did something wrong.' That completely is the *nafs*. So, it means that the soul is never in inspiration to do with anyone other than the self. But when you're inspired by your soul to pray more, to give more, to do more, to do everything that's hard upon the self, it's *ruhani* (spiritual). If it's about doing something to someone else, clarifying to someone else,  something that makes you to feel better by going out and bothering somebody else, it's all *nafsani* (egocentric).

## Why is There So Much Disturbance When Trying to Meditate?

Because *shaitan* (satan) is not happy with you meditating. That if a person reaches to be a *rijal* (people of maturity) and Allah 🕮 grant them sincerity; they're the equivalent of 1,000 men on this Earth – men, women doesn't matter. It means a state of maturity. *Shaitan* is not interested in having a field of people of who are the power of a thousand  people. So, he's very interested in destroying any type of spiritual growth.

As soon as you take a path, the *shaitan* that you had before will be fired and a new more advanced *shaitan* will be sent. So, every level that you're

 improving, the *shaitan* is also being sent and changed to attack you in a different way, a more expertise version of that is coming. So, it means he's not leaving the process. He's more trained in the understanding. That's why *awliyaullah* (saints) understand what he's trying to do to their servants. And that's why again, following their guidance and following their *nazar* (gaze). Their spiritual vision understands and as a result of them taking their path with their shaykh, they know what these *shaitans* are trying. They know their system of how they're playing. *InshaAllah.*

## What Are the Signs That Spiritual Hearing and Sight are Opening?

*InshaAllah,* that you are actually following the shaykh. That these ears don't open without *itiba'*, without following. We are the people of *"sam'ina wa ata'na."*

سَمِعْنَا وَأَطَعْنَا غُفْرَانَكَ رَبَّنَا وَإِلَيْكَ الْمَصِيْرُ ﴿٢٨٥﴾

*2:285 – "Sam'ina wa ata'na, ghufranaka Rabbana wa ilaykal masir."* *(Surat Al-Baqarah)*

*"...We hear, and we obey: (We seek) Thy forgiveness, our Lord, and to Thee is the end of all journeys." (The Cow, 2:285)*

Anyone who has spiritual openings, but they don't listen to the instructions, then those are again *nafsani* (egocentric). Those are from

the ego, from *shaitan* (satan) and *jinns* (unseen beings) playing with people. This way of following their teaching, following their orders. Even if you're at a distance and you heard the *suhbah*, you heard the talks, then you go back and fight with everybody, you do whatever you want. You can't say that, 'Now I'm hearing the shaykh.' The hearing of the shaykh or hearing of inspiration is when Allah ﷻ is pleased with the servant and they came against, and they come against their desires. And they begin to listen to their inspiration.

Inspiration of the soul is always a difficulty against the body, not the inspiration of the *nafs* (ego). That, 'Go and tell this person this. Go correct this. Go say like this to somebody.' But when you hear from your soul, it means, 'Go pray twenty *rakahs* (cycles of prayer) right now. Right now, go read your *Dalail ul Khairat* (book of praises upon Prophet ﷺ). Go give whatever is in your pocket to that person over there.'

Everything that's hard upon the soul, upon the *nafs,* coming from the soul. That level, then they begin to hear. And they'll hear the inspirations that are coming into their heart of what Allah ﷻ wants from them, to them. Then they begin to get heated up and they feel heat coming upon them and slowly, slowly the *khashf.* That Allah ﷻ begin to open different visions within their heart of inspiration and visions, *inshaAllah.*

## What Does it Mean if We Start Seeing Insects and Creatures?

It's just spiritual vision; there are many of these creatures and energies

everywhere. Our world – imagine all the bugs and creatures in our physical eyes – the spiritual world of the *jinn* (unseen beings) is ten times more than that. Ten times the amount of spiders, ten times the amount of ants, ten times the amount of snakes, ten times the amount of personalities and beings.

If spiritual vision opens for certain people, they may sense certain energies and certain beings around. Don't focus on that; just focus on your *tafakkur,* your contemplation. Think of the presence of Sayyidina Muhammad ﷺ and how to reach that reality, how to do your *salawats* (praises upon Prophet Muhammad ﷺ) at *Rauza e Sharif* (holy burial chamber), and keep yourself in the presence of *Rauza e Sharif,* in the presence of Sayyidina Muhammad ﷺ.

## What is Khashf and How Does it Affect Our Body and Mind?

Again there's – this is a place of interpretation. When this authorized connection and authorized practices are coming, then what these *awliyaullah* (saints), what Allah ﷻ sending by order of Allah ﷻ to Prophet ﷺ and then to these guides is going to be a *khashf* that is authorized and is enough to give the servant hope. They get hope that what they're learning is true. Their way is real and it's like little glimpses, glimpses for them to reach towards that reality. *Haal* (spiritual state) – same thing. They give a *haal*, like a taste. They feel an energy, they feel an excitement, it's like Allah's ﷻ gift and a draw that, 'Come, keep coming. Keep coming.'

Not one to be lost in it where it's too strong and it's overwhelming and the person can no longer function. And then the difficulty of other types of things that people may think is a *khashf* and it could be from other sources where they start to hallucinate or feel different experiences. That's why they teach a very systematic approach. That you come, you abide by the *shari'ah* (Divine Law). That, 'Oh! You people don't follow *shari'ah*,' and all these ridiculous things. If anyone's heard the teachings, they're teaching from the *'azimah* of *shari'ah*. That your understanding of *shari'ah* is *La ilaha illAllah Muhammadun Rasulallah* ﷺ, very basic.

لَا إِلَهَ إِلاَّ اللهُ مُحَمَّدًا رَسُولُ الله

*"La ilaha illallahu Muhammadun Rasulallah."*

*"There is no deity but Allah, Prophet Muhammad is the messenger of Allah."*

336

They're going even to the *haqqaiq* (realities) of what is this *La ilaha illAllah* and the reality of *Muhammadun Rasulallah* ﷺ. So, no doubt

they're following *shari'ah*. So, then the student has to be at the same – that they're following the Islamic laws, guidelines, they're following the practices, they're keeping the limits of the *shari'ah*. That they're not doing bizarre and inappropriate actions. When you follow the discipline and the way of Sayyidina Muhammad ﷺ and asking, 'Would Prophet ﷺ be doing this right now and would he be sending what you're feeling and how you're feeling?' If all of that is, 'Yes, 100%. This is all clean and right,' and when it's done right, yes, the feelings are coming.

But there are those who have other issues in their mind and in the different practices and they start to go all over the place, and they start to hallucinate and visualize inappropriate things and all sorts of places the mind can go. This has nothing to do with the mind and a weakened mind. This has to do with the heart and that heart is very difficult to open. It's not something that comes easy. That's why the shaykhs know when someone's lying. This is like a high-level security training.

When Allah ﷻ want to open the heart, He looks to the person, says, 'This is a clean, sincere person.' That one, you know their heart when they're seeing is clean and true. Someone comes to you with no background in Islamic understanding, no purity in their practices and doing bizarre things. No, this is not *tariqah* (spiritual path). That's either playing with *jinn* (unseen beings), hallucinations, mental disabilities, all spectrum of things can be happening.

This is very specific, very clean, purified people who have been authorized and Allah ﷻ sent them through TSA training. You know, like security check training, step by step security, step by step security, that these people are good, clean, struggling in their way. Then we begin to open for them that realm. But just straight off the streets saying, 'I see this, I see that.' No, no, that could be *jinn*, that could be your imagination, that could be lack of medication, that could be many things. That's why in that environment it's disciplined, and it comes in the doses that the shaykhs can control and not too much of anything, *inshaAllah*.

## Should We Keep Notes of What We See During Meditation?

You keep a journal of important understandings or if the shaykh is inspiring your heart to understand something. But don't worry about the world of seeing because that can become very *nafsani* (egocentric). You know, you just keep an

understanding for yourself. And even Imam Ali ؑ that, 'I annihilated in my annihilation.' It means that in every *tafakkur*, in contemplating, they'll train higher that annihilate and negate everything. Because if you're sitting there and say, 'I'm meditating and now they're bringing a sword for me. They bring a *jubba* (robe) for me, they brought a turban for me. I'm going here, I'm going there.' You're now letting your *nafs* (ego) to take over the meditation and the contemplation.

Just always telling ourselves, 'I'm nothing, I'm nothing. I'm not worthy of any of these things. *Ya Rabbi,* let me just to keep the company of my

shaykh. By keeping his *nazar* (gaze) upon me, let me just to enter an ocean of energy and light. All I want, *ya Rabbi,* is energy and light. Send me into energy and light.' Until you can reach a place in which you feel energy and light incoming from every direction and dressing your soul. Everything else to be negated, 'I'm nothing, I'm nothing. I don't need that, *ya Rabbi,* thank you very much, I don't want it.' Because you don't want to be rude in case it really was something and it's a gift.

## Is it Normal to Feel Our Body Moving During Meditation?

The movement of the body or the sensation of movement is because the soul is moving. And actually, this Earth is moving at a tremendous speed, we just don't sense it. Once you enter into the spiritual realm, you begin to sense many things. You'll be meditating and you feel like your body is collapsing and dying. Because as you're pulling your energy out and learn how to separate yourself from your physicality, the body enter like a state of death and just sort of collapsing upon itself. So, then many different understandings begin to open as the person begins to meditate and contemplate.

The main thing is that don't focus on these issues. Don't focus on all of

these minor issues. Try to reach your goal. Your goal is that you want to enter into an ocean of power. That, '*Ya Rabbi,* dress me from Your oceans of power, dress me from the oceans of power, that I'm nothing. I'm nothing and that I want to be with my shaykh.' So, one step is to learn the *tafakkur* and the contemplation – how to visualize the presence of the shaykh, how to keep that presence and then do your *zikr* (Divine remembrance) and your *awrads* (daily practices). Not so much about all the different sensations that we're feeling; just move through them, pay no attention to them.

Whatever they show you in the spiritual world, pay no attention to it. That, 'Even within my annihilation, I was annihilated.' Many times, they begin to meditate, and the spiritual realm begins to open, and you see somebody coming with a spiritual gift for you. Even in that meditation, you just say, 'Thank you very much,' and pay no attention to it.

Whatever's coming to you, keep annihilating yourself that you're nothing, you're nothing, you're nothing. Otherwise, the *nafs* (ego) will begin to enter into that meditation and then it's all about thinking, 'I'm something. I got gifts, I got this, I got that.' And that's what has to be

negated. That if you got a gift then you think it's coming from the spiritual realm. That, 'Oh, we're giving you a gift. We're giving you a light; we're giving you this.' Just say, '*Alhamdulillah, ya Rabbi, shukr* (gratitude), I'm nothing. Let me to enter into Your oceans of light, *ya Rabbi. Ana abdukal 'ajeez,* I'm nothing, I'm nothing, *ya Rabbi.*' And keep negating the self, *inshaAllah.*

## What Does Thumping Between the Eyebrows Signify During Meditation?

You're going to feel in *tafakkur* (contemplation) – again, don't focus on anything. Don't worry about anything coming to you. We used to train and have to go into the *maqam* and do our meditation every day. And

when we would enter into the meditation, start making *tafakkur,* and it literally felt like something slapped me, 'cha' [Shaykh makes slap sound]. And then we would run out later on saying, 'I'm doing my *tafakkur.* Something hit me.' Said, 'What do you care if someone hit

you? That's not your job. Your job was to keep your heart connected through good and bad. Don't focus on the bad because the bad now just won and took your attention off of your *tafakkur.*'

So, it means then they begin to train you under duress and stress. That's at a different level but just an entry level of understanding is as soon as

you meditate, you're going to become sensitive. Then you're going to understand there's an entire creation that you were unaware of. You become *lateef* and you become of a subtle nature. So, when you sit and meditate and breathe and you feel, or you see, or you hear, ignore everything.

Keep your *tafakkur*, keep your *madad* (support). Have your faith that if you're making your *madad* and asking for the shaykhs, there's nothing that's going to bother you. I mean nothing going to really harm you, but everything is coming to bother you, to distract you, to stop you from the meditation. Don't worry about what you see. Don't worry about what begin to touch you. They would begin to touch and then face would swell up from their energies, like a bee sting. And you just keep focusing, keep focusing. Something begins to bite you, keep focusing.

You should have a strong connection and the *madad*. You understand once you make your *madad* that, 'Come and dress me, dress me.' The energy of the *madad* should come in and begin to push every negativity away so that you come to the realization of how weak

we are. And that when this *madad* and energy comes, it begins to push every type of negativity away. So, don't focus on what you see and what you hear and what you can, because if it frightens you, it's to stop you.

So, Shaykh Abdullah al-Faiz Dagestani ق, immense *maqam*. So, there's

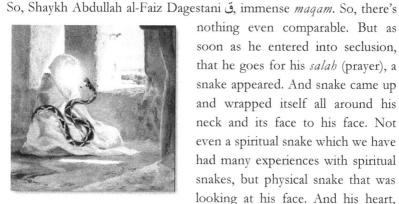

nothing even comparable. But as soon as he entered into seclusion, that he goes for his *salah* (prayer), a snake appeared. And snake came up and wrapped itself all around his neck and its face to his face. Not even a spiritual snake which we have had many experiences with spiritual snakes, but physical snake that was looking at his face. And his heart, because it's connected, that if you focus on this snake, it will for sure bite you. You'll probably die in this seclusion.

So, he was taught, 'Don't focus on that snake. Focus on your *salah*.' He said that he prayed – every time he would go for *sujood* (prostration), the snake moved out of the way and he would make his *sujood*, come back up, make his prayer. So, he doesn't know how long he prayed like that with the snake as his companion around his neck. Why? To make sure

your focus is on what? Your focus not to be distracted upon anything. You're not here for the treasures and you're not scared of the fears and somebody, 'Woo,' trying to scare you out of your *tafakkur*. *InshaAllah*.

## Why Do We Feel a Breeze During Meditation?

Each has its reality, so we don't want to say yes or no. The breeze, when you know the environment is closed off, most definitely *awliyaullah* (saints) will be present, spiritual beings will be present. You may smell a good fragrance of rose and amber and sandalwood, known fragrances for holy souls of angels, *mu'min jinn* (believing unseen beings), *awliyaullah*. Those are all beatific. And those are to encourage the servant to continue. These are the *khashf* (spiritual vision) and *haal* (spiritual state).

That when the servant is struggling with themselves, lowering bad desires and trying to improve themselves, Allah ﷻ gives reward. The *khashf* is that when they sit, Allah ﷻ may give a glimpse of something beatific. Somebody emailed, 'Oh, I was feeling beatific things. It went away. Have I done something wrong?' You know best if you did something wrong, but in reality, even if you don't do anything wrong, Allah ﷻ will close the tap. It's not meant to worship when everything is beautiful. Allah ﷻ sends and closes and wants to see that, 'When I close, do you struggle harder? Or do you only respond when everything is great?'

And they give the examples. When you come home and your kids, they only kiss you if you give them five dollars, 'Hi baba.' 'Here, you get five dollars.' 'Hi baba.' 'Here's five dollars.' And if the day you come, you don't give the five dollars, 'Oh, what do I care he came home today?' Allah ﷻ doesn't want that relationship where He is only encouraging only that He gives you a tip and you do good.

That reward came as a gift from Allah ﷻ, say, '*Ya Rabbi, shukr, shukr, shukr* (gratitude), that you made me to have more *yaqeen* (certainty).' And when things are not coming, you worship even harder to take yourself to the next level in which Allah ﷻ will be pleased with you. And then Allah ﷻ again can send his reward.

The *haal* (spiritual state) – same, the feeling. You enter the *zikr*, you enter the association, you feel what's transpiring and fight through the badness and bad character. Maybe a very, very holy night and *shaitan* (satan) wants to destroy it, and to make you to be angry and angered so that you don't receive the *tajallis* (manifestation). But the *rijal* (people of maturity), they understood that those are the nights where they have to fiercely fight to keep their connection and not worry about a reward.

The reward comes from Allah ﷻ. It can come through the back end or can come through the association. You may not feel it in the association. When you go home, you feel whatever Allah ﷻ wants you to feel or sends you something beatific. But we don't struggle and strive for those realities. We struggle to make Allah ﷻ happy. *"Ilahi anta Maqsood wa Ridha ka Matloob."* Our *zikr*, this whole way. *"Ilahi anta maqsudi wa radhaaka matloob."* 'I beg your forgiveness and seek your satisfaction with me, *ya Rabbi*.'

إِلَهِى اَنْتَ مَقْصُوْدِيْ وَرِضَاكَ مَطْلُوْبِيْ

*"Ilahi anta maqsudi wa radhaaka matloob."*

*"My God, You are my aim, and Your Satisfaction is what I seek."*

And same for Prophet ﷺ, that we're begging for Prophet's ﷺ forgiveness, and that we seek his satisfaction. That, 'I'm not here to feel this or see that. It would be nice if you felt some pity for me so that I

could feel it, but it's okay if you don't want to.' And then you don't seek it, don't seek it. That which you put in your heart, when you know your communication is very strong with them, if you put something in your heart, you're guaranteeing yourself to have that closed. You just gave them a big test. It's like going into your class in math and saying, 'I don't know multiplication. I don't know plus and minus,' and then sit down on your table. What did you just tell the teacher? He doesn't know multiplication, plus and minus? What do you think is going to be on your test? Multiplication, plus and minus.

You just gave yourself a very hard test. So, that's why our way was based on silence and spiritual silence. That, 'Oh, I want to see. I want to see that. I want to see that. I want to see that'; you're guaranteeing it's not going to come. Because now they say, 'Let's test him in *sabr* (patience), because he's asking for it, keep it away.' So, they don't ask anything they say, 'Don't

expect anything, you'll be happy with everything.' Take all expectation out of the heart. '*Ya Rabbi*, I'm not expecting anything. I'm a *zalim* and an oppressor to myself, and I do my worshipness as good worshipness.'

...لَّا إِلَـٰهَ إِلَّا أَنتَ سُبْحَانَكَ إِنِّي كُنتُ مِنَ الظَّالِمِينَ ﴿٨٧﴾

*21:87 – "...La ilaha illa anta Subhanaka, innee kuntu minazh zhalimeen." (Surat Al-Anbiya)*

*"...There is no god/diety except You; Glory to you: Indeed I have been of the wrongdoers/Oppressor to Myself!" (The Prophets, 21:87)*

If Allah ﷻ wants to send, then *alhamdulillah*. But if I keep saying this, 'Oh I want to see it, I want to see it, I want to see it,' you'll be like this a hundred years. Because as much as you are saying the *zikr*, 'I want to see it,' as much as it's going farther and farther and farther away. So, you're putting your tests out there. That's why they say don't say things, 'Oh, I can't stand when this happens.' As soon as you say it, write it, or even speak it from your heart, know that now it's the next test on your exam.

That's why we stay quiet. And when we talk to people say, 'Oh, don't say that. That's going to come really hard.' 'I can't stand when it's like this. I get so hungry.' And then next day, what happens? And that is exactly the condition Allah ﷻ will put the person in. That's why in this way the microphone is live. They are listening, they are observing because you are trying to get that live connection. It's going both ways. So, when we have an interview, we say, 'I'm going to get the interview that's going to be on television,' but many people forget that the mic was live. The camera cut off, but they are still talking. And all of a sudden, it's called the 'hot mic' where they put on television all these crazy things the person was saying. Same with spirituality, even more so.

The mic is live with Prophet ﷺ, with *awliyaullah* (saints), with angels, with the heavens. Everything you don't say you don't like, it will be on your next test. Everything that you're asking that you want to have, you want to have, it will be on the test and be farther away from the servant. The true servanthood is one whom wants nothing, desires nothing, put into their hearts nothing, nothing,
nothing, 'And *ya Rabbi*, I'll be happy with whatever you choose for me.' Then Allah ﷻ can surprise you with a gift.

Now take that back to your home and you have a certain gift you want to give to your kids. And your kid comes and says, 'Oh, I need this new super huge computer,' but you were hoping to bring just a box of candy to make them happy. Now between you and them there is a big problem because whatever I give, they just set the standard so high they would never be happy. So better not to give it. And why did you set a standard in that relationship like that?

So, it happens all the time in our daily lives. Why do it with Allah ﷻ? So,

if the child comes and says, 'I want nothing baba, I'm happy. I love you. I want nothing, I want nothing.' Anything you bring to them they are happy. And then you got happy that they're happy, so you continuously do it. That's the concept of not asking and not wanting anything. Everything you ask for, it makes you to have a distance with Allah ﷻ.

## What Does it Mean to Have Pain in the Heart During Meditation?

That's an energy. Any type of energy that's coming is going to find a conflict because of the good and the bad. The positive, any type of energy that comes, if it's of a positive nature and any type of negative

energy comes, there could become a conflict of something that has to be cleansed out of the body or something that's around in the environment. It could be through the home, through the

children, through anything that's around. So, that energy has to be cleansed and just continue with that, with your *salawats* (praises upon Prophet Muhammad ﷺ) and your energy. And then you have to contact the shaykh if it's continuing. If the energy is too strong and too negative, then the *zikrs* will be weakened and lowered down so that not to have that.

## If the Heart Heats Up, How Do We Nourish It?

Keep doing the meditation. As soon as your heart begins to heat up, you're breathing, you're feeling the energy of all these goodnesses, the *zikr* (Divine remembrance) that's good. You feel your heart, feel the energy, feel your heart, feel the energy and then you begin to feel your hands heating up and the back of your neck to heat up. Your hands, when they become hot, it's a good symbol that your heart is actually active. So, warm and heated hands

means they have a warm heart and heated. It's an activated heart.

Those are the hands also for healing. That when they touch something and make *du'a* (supplication), that Allah ﷻ through that energy and that

*qudra* (power), they can begin to heal. But they don't want to do any healing now because they haven't trained in that. Anything you touch to heal will be transferred over to you. So, it has to be very careful on how you heal. If there's a negative charge that's causing a sickness for a person and you're a positive hand, positive person – as soon as you come and touch, that negativity will come into you.

So, that's why they don't touch on people and they heal by stick or by some sort of separation between them and that energy. And that they don't take it onto their person. And the *zikrs* and trainings that they have is that any energy that does come becomes processed. And as a result, they can give out more light by that processing of

taking in the negativity becomes like a fuel for their energy. And as a result, they give out light as a result of what's coming in. But that has to be trained and to be understood at that level.

## What Can We Do if We Smell Bad Fragrances During Meditation?

*InshaAllah*, the whole way is based on hypersensitivity. So, that anytime you're going to practice your spiritual practices, every sense has a duality. There is hearing, that, 'I can hear shaykh.' No, but can you really hear? It means then you're going to train yourself on how to shut this hearing off, listen to *salawats* (praises upon Prophet Muhammad ﷺ) and begin to meditate. The *salawats* will pull you in the direction that you're supposed to be going in the meditation. This means they have a secret for everything. If you meditate without the sound, we don't know where your soul is trying to go because the soul, it knows exactly how to go back to Sayyidina Muhammad ﷺ. Right? Like a ship it knows exactly how to go in the direction Allah ﷻ wants it to go.

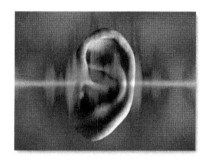

So that's why they come and they teach that when you're going to meditate, first thing you do is don't meditate in silence and leave this [Shaykh indicates ears] like an open microphone. There's a hot mic; you're having a conversation with someone and they tell you, 'Shaykh your mic was on the whole time.' Good God, I don't know what I was saying because it was a private conversation. Don't leave this mic on [Shaykh points to ear] and said, 'I am going to sit in quiet, I'm going to sit by myself. Oh, you're never by yourself; *shaitan* (satan) is right there. *Shaitan* is just going to be talking in your microphone all day long and you think like it's *futuhaats* (openings of the heart) and knowledges and all sorts of wisdoms coming. But it could be him whispering, whispering, whispering and then subtle throw in, 'You know what this person did to you?' Whisper, whisper, whisper. 'You know what this person did.' So, then they (shaykhs) recommend no, no, turn this system to *salawats*.

351

As soon as you're listening to *salawat* on Prophet ﷺ, your soul is like being mesmerized. It's feeling now an energy. You're meditating trying to get your energy away, and now release the energy of my soul. If you can relax yourself and meditate and contemplate, ask for the *nazar* (gaze) of these *awliya* (saints), ask for the presence of these guided souls to be present

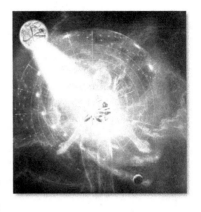

with you that, 'I don't want to meditate alone my Lord.' "*Wa kono ma'as sadiqeen.*"

يَا أَيُّهَا الَّذِينَ آمَنُوا اتَّقُوا اللهَ وَكُونُوا مَعَ الصَّادِقِينَ ﴿١١٩﴾

*9:119 – "Ya ayyuhal ladheena amanoo ittaqollaha wa kono ma'as sadiqeen." (Surat At-Tawbah)*

*"O you who have believed, have consciousness of Allah and be with those who are truthful/Pious/sincere (in words and deed)."*
*(The Repentance, 9:119)*

'You promised that to keep the company of pious people, I want to keep their spiritual company. So, I'm keeping and asking for my *madad* (support) and my shaykh is there present with me, I don't want to be alone.' And I begin to listen. As I'm listening to these *salawats*, I'm trying to relax myself and let my hearing to really hear.

If it begins to really hear the *salawat* and the praising, you may begin to start to cry because your soul is now at a level of feeling. It's not only hearing anymore; it's feeling as if these angels and these recitations are reciting directly in the presence of Sayyidina Muhammad ﷺ. Then your soul will 'whoosh,' fly. Fly into the presence of Sayyidina Muhammad ﷺ like the – 'whoosh.' As soon as you call the *salawats* the soul is moving, and you just let your body to release it and get out of the way and your soul moves into the presence of Sayyidina Muhammad ﷺ.

Smell is of an angelic reality. As soon as you meditate and contemplate and bring your ears into submission, bring your eyes into submission, sit, and close your eyes. Say, 'I don't want to close my eyes because too many things your eyes have been seeing.' So again, you discipline yourself to close the eyes and meditate, contemplate. Then you begin to open up the faculty of the breath. As you begin to smell and meditate and breathe the *zikr* *"Hu"* and you try to close off your mouth, that not to breathe from the mouth but to breathe from the nose. It's like making a

fireplace, you're going to now learn how to bring the fire within your heart to ignite it. If you bring too much oxygen, you're not going to ignite the fire.

So, if you breathe with the mouth it's a different type of energy. You're going to learn how to lock your tongue to the roof of your mouth and seal your mouth. And as you're making your *zikrs* with your breath, you're saying *'Hu'* in your heart and pushing with your breath  out exhaling and all the energy coming out [Shaykh breathes out through his nose]. And then meditating, breathing in all the energy that you bring in with your breath. Your *salawats* are playing, you're asking for these Divine Lights that you're in the presence of the shaykh and you're breathing, breathing. As you begin to breathe and practice the breath, the sensitivity of smell should begin.

 So, bad smell, good smell. Bad smell, bad things. Good smell, good things. Easiest way to understand. Bad energy has a very bad smell. That *awliya* (saints) they can see people, they can see souls, they can see the dead and they can smell them. And they have really bad, bad, bad fragrance. That's why they need the area to be continuously put with *bakhoor* (incense) and fragrances to compensate for the bad smell that people have put upon themselves by bad actions. So, it means then every negative action brings about a bad energy. That bad energy has a bad smell.

Every beatific action has a beatific fragrance. So, it means then they do *zikr*, they do their *salawats*, they do their *namaz* (prayer); they do the all the positive things and it brings about tremendous fragrances. And beatific fragrances and brings about beatific souls and energies all around them. Those, you may begin to smell musk and amber and all these beatific sandalwood. That these are the souls of the *jinns* (unseen beings), the angels, *awliya* that all around, releasing these fragrances.

And then again, the negative ones that are around, they smell like waste, the smell like urine, they smell like many different things because these are the negative beings and dirty beings that come around. So, you have to clean your environment, beautify the environment, put fragrances and *bakhoors* and do your *zikr*, your meditation, your *salah* (prayer) all in those areas. Play *salawats* in the house continuously to push out any type of negative energy. The truth and the falsehood, they don't occupy the same space.

وَ قُلْ جَآءَالْحَقُّ وَزَهَقَ الْبَاطِلُ، إِنَّ الْبَاطِلَ كَانَ زَهُوقًا ﴿٨١﴾

*17:81 – "Wa qul jaa alhaqqu wa zahaqal baatil, innal batila kana zahoqa." (Surat Al-Isra)*

*"And say, Truth has come, and falsehood has perished. Indeed falsehood, [by its nature], is ever perishing/ bound to perish."*
*(The Night Journey, 17:81)*

Any time you find that there's a negative energy, negative smell, you play *Dalail ul Khairat* (book of praising on Prophet ﷺ) in the house, put your *bakhoor*, put your fragrances, *inshaAllah*.

## Is Smoking Bad Spiritually and How Do We Quit Addictions?

*InshaAllah*, again if we go into the meditation, those things will be resolved. Somebody sent us a show to be an *imam* (religious leader) on their show and let's ask *fiqh* (Islamic jurisprudence) questions. That's not our specialty. To give you an answer based on the *fiqh* and say that, 'This is *haram* (forbidden), this is *halal* (permissible), this *haram*.' But the wisdom of *awliyaullah* (saints), that we hope to be under their feet and under their *barakah* (blessings), is to give us the *hikmah* and the wisdom of something so that it makes sense in your deep heart. That it's not a debate of *halal* and *haram* and, 'If this is *halal*, and this is *haram*, and this is not mentioned.'

But your most important power is your breath. All your spirituality, and the forty golden shaykhs, the forty golden chain masters said that, 'This

*tariqah* (spiritual path) is built in the breath.' If the whole reality of this *tariqah* is based on you mastering the breath, unlocking the power of the breath, and that breath coming into the lungs, nourishing the lungs, nourishing the heart, powering the blood and powering all of your organs. Then your answer is, 'Can you contaminate that breath?' Everything else will be destroyed. That then you understand what's *halal* and what's *haram*. If your objective is to destroy your breath, destroy your lungs, destroy your heart, destroy your blood, then you have become overcome by *shaitan* (satan).

Same thing with cannabis. Anyone tell you that because of pain and sickness and difficulty you have to smoke, it's a certificate to destroy your heart. To kill your lungs, destroy your heart, destroy your blood and take away your spirituality. 'Why don't you take oil? It doesn't require you to burn your lungs in the process.'

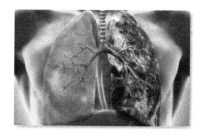

And we said that when they brought the cold smoke, the e-cigarette, they

try to fool the children saying, 'This is just vaping, it's like a fog. You take it in.' No, actually that cold fume went deeper into your lungs and killed in you in ways that the hot smoke couldn't do. So *shaitan* is attacking *insan* (mankind). He wants to take out your breathing, wants to take out your lungs, wants to take out your heart so that you don't reach your finish line.

If you should reach this reality of *tazkiyah* and reach the kingdom of Allah ﷻ in which Allah ﷻ, *"Qalb al mu'min baitullah."* That your heart become the house of Allah ﷻ, you'll have the power of 1,000 men, whether you're a man or a woman. You think *shaitan* wants that? No.

قَلْبَ الْمُؤْمِنْ بَيْتُ الرَّبْ

*"Qalb al mu'min baytur rabb."*

*"The heart of the believer is the House of the Lord."* (Hadith Qudsi)

To relieve the addiction, the addiction is to ask to stop, make an intention to stop. Recite Suratul Fatiha seven times on the water, up to forty times onto water and drink that water. Making the *madad* (support) the energy, all the spiritual practices come in line. That learn how to do the *madad*, recite on the water forty Suratul Fatiha. And then drink that jug of water, recite that Fatiha on that water, and then drink from that water. And every time the water goes down for the

next day, keep replenishing the water and adding upon it seven Suratul Fatiha upon that. And Allah 🌟 should push away that badness that entered into your body to make that addiction for smoking.

Drug and alcohol addiction – there are places to go for that so that you have a support group and that's a bit more complicated based on your

location and who you are hanging out with, and all the different things that are around you in your life. That requires for you to go to a group and to find an AA (Alcoholics Anonymous) meeting, and to be

a part of a community of people who want to clean themselves and sober up, *inshaAllah*. But for cigarette smoking then to recite the Fatiha and make your *madad* and your connection with the shaykhs, *inshaAllah*.'

## What is the Significance of Happiness and Sadness During Meditation?

The weepiness is generally related to the soul. When the proximity of a holy energy begins to enter near the soul, there's a tremendous amount of weeping because of the proximity of that Divinely presence through that soul. If the soul of Prophet ﷺ comes, immediately all crushing and crying and crying because of the soul's reality in the immense understanding of how it knows it's

done everything wrong. It's not like the *nafs* (ego) to be proud. The soul knows that we came onto the Earth. We didn't achieve what we promised to achieve to Allah ﷻ.

The soul knows that, 'I miss you. I'm yearning for you. I've been far from you; I'm stuck on this abode.' And begin to cry, and cry, and cry

like a reunion with something very beloved. So, it means there's a very holy soul entering into that presence and the *tajalli* (manifestation) becomes very sort of heavy upon the soul and the crying and crying. Then the euphoric dress is by its nature is euphoric. You feel the energy,

you feel happy, you feel good. The energies are coming into the heart, filling the heart. So, both *jalali wal jamali*. You have to mix. There has to be a Might and Majesty to make everything to crush and to cry. And then Allah ﷻ send the *jamali* like a rain to make the soul to be happy and the heart to be sort of joyful, *inshaAllah*. Mixing, they come in mixes, *inshaAllah*.

## Should We Have Spiritual Openings in Every Meditation Session?

No, again the striving for the carrot and a stick. The concept of the carrot and a stick is that you put the treasure that somebody wants on a stick in front of them so that you create a forward movement. If Allah ﷻ was to bestow everything based on our actions, we would do nothing. We would actually just sit there and meditate, and all-day long illusions and delusions would begin.

What Allah ﷻ grants is a *khashf* (spiritual vision) and *haal* (spiritual state). So, these two realities are you may be doing your *tafakkur*, your contemplation; you may be in *salah* (prayer), you may be in *zikr* (Divine remembrance) – 'woohphh' – Allah ﷻ open a trailer like a show from a

movie. 'Wow!' And then it goes away and then you keep trying to do practices to catch it again, catch it again. Wrong! It's not that you chase those things but continue your sincere actions that made Allah ﷻ happy with you to grant you that. Not that you try to chase now let me try to see another trailer. *Ya Rabbi,* let me get another. No, no, because Allah's ﷻ not on-demand where you make a request and Allah ﷻ says, 'Okay, I'm listening to you, My servant.' *Astaghfirullah!* It's we are the servant of Allah ﷻ so trace back to what were you doing consistently that made Allah ﷻ so happy?

Some say, 'Oh, so many things have stopped for me.' Yes, because you stopped. You stopped all your practices. You stopped your meditation. You stopped all the things that you were doing. You thought that you reached to a place so high and that's now okay, nothing else is coming now. So, then the *tariqah* (spiritual path) comes and says

to be annihilated and effaced, that I'm not searching for those, *Ya Rabbi*, and I go back to my sincere practices. And, lo and behold, Allah ﷻ will surprise and send His *khashf* (spiritual vision). And He doesn't want you to chase it and don't ask for it because then the relationship becomes something that's not proper. So, like we said before, you come home, you kiss your loved one and your children and it's a sign of love. But if they line up and say, 'Give me five bucks, give me five bucks' and you have to pay everybody to get a greeting, it's a different relationship.

So, Allah ﷻ doesn't want the servant asking for these things. Say you do what you had to do out of sincerity. I will give from my gift the way I want to give it and same for the *haal* (spiritual state). They do their *zikr* (Divine remembrance), they do their practices And Allah ﷻ may send them into a *haal* in which they feel energies, they feel emotions, they feel all sorts of experiences and they're not to chase it. So, Imam Ali ؑ said, 'I annihilated even my annihilation.' This means I reached to a point in which I continuously annihilated myself. I'm not worthy, *ya Rabbi*, I'm not chasing that.

Don't chase like, 'Oh, they came to me. They gave me a sword, they gave me a *jubba* (robe), they gave me a crown,' because then your *nafs* (ego) is entering into that and you're now making those images to come. That

I'm sitting there, they're giving me this, they're giving me that, it's all delusion because you should have annihilated. If an opening of your heart is opening and they're bringing things. Say, '*Alhamdulillah*, I'm not that servant. I'm not worthy of that. I'm nothing. I'm no one, I'm no one, I'm no one.' and that's what they want to hear.

Otherwise the state of delusion enters, and they begin to, 'Oh my gosh! I got this, I got this!' And the first they want to do when they come to shaykh, 'Do you know I had a dream? I sat on a chair like this, they came and they gave you a *jubba*, they gave me an *'arsh* (throne), they gave me a sword, they gave me a crown.' So, then okay, you take my job. I'll leave. It's not our way. It's to come and say I'm nothing, I'm nothing. Even you saw the seven heavens with your own eyeballs open, I'm nothing, I see nothing, I don't know anything. I don't know anything because that's keeping our cup empty. And my cup is empty, Allah ﷻ fills it  with immense joys and pleasures from this universe, from unseen universes and creation. So, the concept of keeping the cup empty – nothing. I'm nothing, I'm nothing and annihilate even in my ocean of annihilation, *inshaAllah*.

## If We've Never Had Spiritual Experiences Are We Doing Something Wrong?

No, it doesn't mean that anyone's doing something wrong, but everyone is going to advance at the speed Allah ﷻ wants them to advance. So, it's a motivation. Sometimes when you hear these types of questions that there are students that are experiencing things, there are students whom Allah ﷻ is opening for them. It's just a motivation in a course and in classes that I should study harder. I should try harder. I should do my practices with more *himmah* (zeal) and make it to be more real.

So, when I have a time to do my *salah*, I close off the doors, I make everything to be purified, I put my candle there, I put my water there for

blessings and then I begin to make my *namaz* (prayer). And at the end of my *namaz*, I connect my heart, I play some *salawats*, the prayer is already over. I'm playing some *salawats* and asking, 'Ya Rabbi, please I made this *salaam* coming into Your presence, dress me from these lights and just let me to breathe from Your energies and from Your *Ni'mat* (Blessing).' And they practice it with all sincerity and all their practices. No doubt Allah ﷻ will give. And that's why Allah ﷻ says, 'Ask and you receive.'

﴿وَقَالَ رَبُّكُمُ ادْعُونِي أَسْتَجِبْ لَكُمْ ۚ ... ﴿٦٠﴾

*40:60 – "Wa qaala Rabbukum ud 'ooni astajib lakum;..."*
*(Surat Al-Ghafir)*

*"And your Lord says, "Call upon Me, I Will Respond/Answer to your (prayer)..." (The Forgiver, 40:60)*

But if they're not doing it with that type of firmness and they just periodically come and go, come and go, then you know as much as you put into it is what you get out of it. Put little in, you probably get very little out.

# Chapter 5

## Tafakkur (Contemplation) and Muhasabah (Self-examination)

# Understanding Tafakkur and Muhasabah

### What is the Recommended Amount of Time to Contemplate For?

For a beginner, *inshaAllah,* it's a few minutes. That don't make something so heavy that you just don't want to continue it. To do something light and consistent is better than to do something heavy and keep dropping it. That it has to be a spiritual dress in which is not so heavy, you want to dump it and never do it again. You try to do everything light and consistent. So, that consistency is what Allah ﷻ is looking for and as soon as you're consistent in that amount of four, five minutes after every *salah* (prayer) connecting your heart.

The whole of *salah* is the realities of *tafakkur* (contemplation) because the *salah* is a means in which to reach to the Holy Ka'bah, that you're doing all of what Islam had prescribed to you in the *salah.* You have to do your *shahadah* (testimony of faith), you have to do your washing, you have to do your *zakah* (charity) because you're stopping everything. Mawlana Shaykh's ق teaching you, you're stopping from working so that's a *zakah*. You're giving charity as soon as you stop and take a half hour of *salah*. You could be working and making money; that's considered a *zakah* at that time. And you are fasting because you can't eat during your *salah* and it's a pilgrimage to Allah's ﷻ Ka'bah because you have to face the direction of the Ka'bah. So, you have all of Islam in that one *salah*. So, the *tafakkur* and its reality is all the *salah*.

So, it means then this is a principle of our belief. The entire foundation of the belief and how to connect your heart. How to be nothing, how to make your *salah* and connecting your heart that, 'I'm nothing, I'm nothing, *ya Rabbi*, let me to be at the holy Ka'bah. Let me to be praying at that Ka'bah. That I'm nothing and let me be with the *Nabiyeen, Siddiqeen, Shuhada, wa Saliheen* and You said these are the best of company.'

وَمَن يُطِعِ اللهَ وَالرَّسُولَ فَأُوْلَئِكَ مَعَ الَّذِينَ أَنْعَمَ اللهُ عَلَيْهِم مِّنَ النَّبِيِّينَ وَالصِّدِّيقِينَ وَالشُّهَدَاء وَالصَّالِحِينَ وَحَسُنَ أُولَئِكَ رَفِيقًا ﴿٦٩﴾

*4:69 – "Wa man yuti' Allaha war Rasula faolayeka ma'al ladheena an'ama Allahu 'alayhim minan Nabiyeena, was Siddiqeena, wash Shuhadai, was Saliheena wa hasuna olayeka rafeeqan."*
*(Surat An-Nisa)*

*"And whoever obeys Allah and the Messenger (pbuh) are in the company of those on whom Allah has bestowed His Favours/ Blessings - of the prophets, the sincere Truthful, the witnesses to the truth (who testify), and the Righteous, and excellent are those as companions."*
*(The Women, 4:69)*

You even make *tafakkur* on the words of what you're saying in your *salah*. *"Assalamu Alaika ayyuhan Nabi."* Did you see Prophet ﷺ? You're making a *salah* in your *attahiyat* (sitting on knees during prayer), *"Assalamu Alaika ayyuhan Nabi."* So, it means Prophet's ﷺ head, the back of his head, is not facing you because Allah ﷻ wouldn't give you words to recite that would be *bey adab* (disrespectful). It has to be the best of *adab* (manners). So, then Allah's ﷻ saying, 'How come you recite but you don't even understand what you're saying?' So, you're saying in *attahiyat*, *"Assalamu 'alayka ayyuhan Nabi ﷺ."* So, Prophet ﷺ must be always looking at his nation in their *salah*. Always.

التَّحِيَّاتُ لِلَّهِ وَالصَّلَوَاتُ وَالطَّيِّبَاتُ . السَّلاَمُ عَلَيْكَ أَيُّهَا النَّبِيُّ وَرَحْمَةُ اللَّهِ وَبَرَكَاتُهُ، السَّلاَمُ عَلَيْنَا وَعَلَى عِبَادِ اللَّهِ الصَّالِحِينَ، أَشْهَدُ أَنْ لاَ إِلَهَ إِلاَّ اللَّهُ وَأَشْهَدُ أَنَّ مُحَمَّدًا عَبْدُهُ وَرَسُولُهُ .

*"Attahiyatu Lillahi wa salawatu wat tayyibatu. Assalamu 'alayka ayyuhan Nabiyu ﷺ, wa rahmatullahi wa barakatuhu. Assalamu 'alayna wa 'alaa 'ibadulllahis saliheen. Ashhadu an a ilaha illallahu wa ashhadu anna Muhammadan 'abduhu wa Rasuluhu."*

*"All the best compliments and the prayers/praising and the pure/good things are for Allah. Peace and Blessings be upon you, O Prophet (pbuh)! Peace be on us and on the righteous servants of Allah. I testify that there is no deity but Allah, and I testify that Prophet Muhammad (pbuh) is the servant and Messenger of Allah."*

Now if you don't see Prophet ﷺ, this is your problem. But to know Prophet ﷺ sees you and that Allah ﷻ is making you to give your greetings in present tense, not past tense, not *"Assalamu Alaikum."* *Assalamu 'alayka Ya Sayyidi, Ya Rasulallah* ﷺ and *Assalamu alaikum 'ibadulllahis*

*Saliheen,"* because some may be present, and many may not be present at that level. But even Allah ﷻ wants you to know that *'Ibadullahis Saliheen* are also facing you. When do they stop facing you?

If Allah ﷻ has no time and has asked you to pray five times a day to cover your whole *yawm*, your whole day. When is it a time in which Prophet ﷺ is not facing you? Your soul is always in the presence of Sayyidina Muhammad ﷺ. It's always facing Prophet ﷺ and *'Ibadulllahis saliheen* are always facing you. Now you don't see it. So, this is not something people make up. It's in the words of our most basic *usool* (principles), is the *salah* and Prophet ﷺ says, 'If you don't make *salah*, you're outside of your belief.'

عَنْ جَابِرٍ أَنَّ النَّبِيَّ ﷺ قَالَ: " إِنَّ بَيْنَ الرَّجُلِ وَبَيْنَ الشِّرْكِ وَالْكُفْرِ، تَرْكَ اَلصَّلَاةِ ." [اَلْمَصْدَرْ: صَحِيحْ ْ مُسْلِم٨٢]

*'An Jabirin anna AnNabi* ﷺ *qala, "Inna baynar rajuli wa baynash shirki wal kufri, tarka asSalah." [Sahih Muslim 82]*

*Narrated by Jabir (ra) that the Prophet (pbuh) said, "Verily, between a man and polytheism and disbelief is abandoning the daily obligatory prayer." [Sahih Muslim 82]*

So, it's the foundation of our entire being. We're praying but we're not really thinking about what we say when we pray. So, one is that, 'Oh my gosh, *ya Rabbi*, I'm facing Prophet ﷺ and I don't see it and I don't feel

it.' And *'Ibadullahis Saliheen*, that all of these pious souls, they're staring at me. Why Allah عز وجل wants Prophet ﷺ to be staring at your soul in your *namaz* (prayer)? And why *'Ibadullahis Saliheen* and all the pious souls? So, that the *nazar* (gaze) of Prophet ﷺ to be on

his nation. That they're going to pray, and their prayer counts as nothing without you watching them. Because he is the great intercessor. That when our souls are praying, the *nazar* of Prophet ﷺ must be watching that *salah*. And that's why Prophet ﷺ said 'If my nation's *'amal* is presented to me, if it's good, I say *alhamdulillah*. If it's bad I ask, '*Ya Rabbi, astaghfirullah*!'" He asks for forgiveness.

قَالَ رَسُولُ اللهِ صَلَّى اللهُ عَلَيْهِ وَسَلَّمَ : حَيَاتِي خَيْرٌ لَكُمْ ، تُحَدِّثُونَ وَيُحَدَّثُ لَكُمْ ، فَإِذَا أَنَا مُتُّ كَانَتْ وَفَاتِي خَيْرًا لَكُمْ ،تُعْرَضُ عَلَيَّ أَعْمَالُكُمْ ، فَإِنْ رَأَيْتُ خَيْرًا حَمِدْتُ اللَّهَ، وَإِنْ رَأَيْتُ غَيْرَ ذَلِكَ اسْتَغْفَرْتُ اللهَ لَكُمْ

*Qala Rasulullahi ﷺ, "Hayatee khayrun lakum tuhadithona wa
yuhdatha lakum, fa idha anaa mutta kaana wafati khayran lakum.
Tu'radu `alayya `amalukum, fa in ra`itu khayran hamidtu Allah, wa in
ra`aytu ghayra dhalik astaghfartullaha lakum."*

*The Messenger of Allah said, "My life is good for you, as you will relate
from me and it will be related to you, and when I die my passing will be
better for you. I observe the deeds of my ummah/Nation. If I find good
[in it] I thank/praise Allah, and if I see bad, I ask forgiveness for
them/on their behalf." (Prophet Muhammad (pbuh))*

So, then Prophet 🕮 is responsible. The *nazar* is responsible upon their *salah* to clean and to wash it and to present it to Allah 🕮 pure and purified. It's like a *pardeh* (veil) between creation and entering into the Divinely Presence. We don't understand that until we understood meditation, *tafakkur*, contemplation – whatever it is that we want to call it in which you stop and contemplate. 'What are these words that I'm saying? What is it that I'm trying to achieve? What's happening in the reality of my being?' *InshaAllah.*

## How Can We Improve Our Contemplation?

Then meditate – sit and meditate. Meditation is not easy as western people because you're a believer. And Allah 🕮 knows that as a believer, *shaitan* (satan) is after you. Now if you're not a believer and you have all sorts of markings all over your place and you have dreadlocks, of course meditation is wonderful for you because *shaitan* already has you. He's not going to bother you. He's going to say, 'You go sit by this tree and the bears will be nice with you.' Because you're already  his *mureed* (devoted disciple). He has no interest in bothering his students. He makes them hallucinate. They think that they're seeing everything beautiful and the angels are coming and the fairies are coming. No, no, no, they're all demons disguised as angels.

But when you believe in Allah 'و and you believe in the heavens and you take a way of the Prophetic reality, that the prophets of oneness. Of course, now you're an enemy to *shaitan*. And *shaitan* going to make every obstacle possible so that you don't reach your contemplation and you don't have *tafakkur* (contemplation) and you don't have *tazakkur*. That you don't remember what Allah 'و bestowed upon you. That's why it's hard.

So, then every time I sit to contemplate. As soon as the *zikr* (Divine remembrance) begins, the *zikr* is the perfect time for contemplation

because of the energies of the shaykh. The energy comes to hit the ego and to give you a sense or time of serenity. In that time, you make your *madad* (support), your contemplation, that connect your heart. And then every night, you make a little of your contemplation but more important, 'What did I do wrong? What did I say wrong? What did I do wrong? What was my interaction with the fellow students or the shaykh?'

That one is rare because not that many people have an interaction with the shaykh because of its danger. And it's very dangerous. Because they said that when you go for *hajj* (pilgrimage), if you start to commit sins in the Haramain, it's a million times more sin then if you sinned at home. That was the concept. So, that's why Allah 'و doesn't let that many in their presence because the sins of those who come close is multiplied. So, that they have to have good character and restrain themselves from their bad character. But all of this is to reach that perfection and to reach what Allah 'و wants.

Now everyone's motivated because they're in lockdown. Then by Ramadan, it'll be everybody fasting because there's not that much food. Rajab, the whole world went into seclusion. Imagine Ramadan. And

those who have training they say, '*Alhamdulillah*, we'll eat a little bit. We'll lose some weight, not a problem.' Others are like, 'What you talking about, McDonalds is closed? Burn it down, burn it down.' [Laughter]. And they're not going to be very happy with anybody saying, 'No.'

## What is the Difference Between Zikr and Fikr?

They go hand in hand. It's not something you start and then don't do the other one. The way of the *tariqah* (spiritual path), that's why the *tariqahs* all do *zikr* and they all do *fikr*. This means that the *zikr* is an energy, "*Bi dhikrillahi tatma'innul Qulob.*"

$$\text{الَّذِينَ آمَنُوا وَتَطْمَئِنُّ قُلُوبُهُم بِذِكْرِ اللَّهِ ۗ أَلَا بِذِكْرِ اللَّهِ تَطْمَئِنُّ الْقُلُوبُ ﴿٢٨﴾}$$

*13:28 – "Alladheena amano wa tatma'innu Qulobu hum bidhikrillahi, ala bi dhikrillahi tatma'innul Qulob." (Surat Ar-Ra'd)*

*"Those who believe, and whose hearts find satisfaction in the remembrance of Allah. For without doubt in the remembrance of Allah do hearts find satisfaction." (The Thunder, 13:28)*

That we come to the *zikr* (Divine remembrance) to be washed and to be cleaned and to take away. You know, everything if you follow our teachings – let's reduce everything to an energy. So, the importance of understanding the energy and how to build the good energy. So, we come with a negative energy in our lives to the associations and Allah 'ﷻ sends us for guidance. So,

when we have a negative energy, our responsibility is to go somewhere that we can clean that energy.

The *zikrs* are a washing machine. As soon as you enter into the *zikr*, the energy that is coming into the *zikr* is washing because the angels are

circumambulating. All the holy souls that are present, the *zikr* is washing, washing, washing all of the badness and bad character away. And then the student also has a responsibility to participate. It's not just you sit and do the *zikr*, but the homework is to

do the thinking and contemplation. That if I am coming in as a sinner and coming in with bad character, at some point I want to step in this circle without that bad character. So, *tafakkur* (contemplation) and *tazakkur* (remembrance).

The *tafakkur* is to take a life in which Allah 'ﷻ says basically, 'Stop and smell the roses.' That you're moving through this life too fast. You're not getting a sense of what Allah 'ﷻ wants for us. So, we're coming then, we're being washed. We're being cleaned. And then *tafakkur*. *Tafakkur* is, 'I stop and slow down. 'O my Lord, what is it that you want from me? What is my bad character? What am I doing wrong every night?'

That's why we said the isolation now can draw people to be very mad, insane mad, or they can become very beatific. Beatific because they sit and realize and begin to cry, 'I wasted my life. I wasted my time and I could have done beatific things with what Allah ﷻ gave me of my wealth, of my possession, of my time. I could

have done my *zikr*. I could have built *masjids*. I could have done many things. But I was so engaged in myself and my self-desires, everything was lost.' And they may change towards goodness. And there are those who go in and they realize that they're just angry. They don't want to be caged. They want to be out partying. They want to be out doing every type of sinful and forbidden thing. And they regret very much that they're being locked up and then they become angrier and angrier.

That's *tafakkur*, to stop and to get a sense. *Tazakkur* is at a much higher

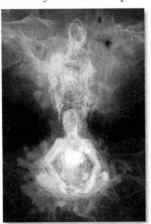

level in which you remember. Once you stopped and took a life of *tafakkur*, its contemplation, contemplate; contemplate is now a God-consciousness and a self-conscious. That your soul in Divine Presence will begin to communicate with you, tell you what you should have been doing. And *tazakkur* is now 'remember.' Remember what Allah ﷻ taught us. Remember the knowledges Allah ﷻ gave us. Remember everything that Allah ﷻ, *"Allamal Qur'an. Khalaqal Insaan."*

عَلَّمَ الْقُرْآنَ ﴿٢﴾ خَلَقَ الْإِنسَانَ ﴿٣﴾

*55:2-3 – "Allamal Qur'an (2). Khalaqal Insaan (3)."*
*(Surat Ar Rahman)*

*"It is He Who has taught the Qur'an. (2) He has created Mankind. (3)"*
*(The Beneficent, 55: 2-3)*

In this *Allamal Qur'an*, what Allah ﷻ taught? The soul will begin to ask us, 'What Allah ﷻ taught us of reality? How come you're not remembering?' And *tazakkur* is then to now reach to a level in which you stopped, you contemplated, and now your soul will begin to teach you to remember the ocean of reality that Allah ﷻ has taught you. And that's why when we think from energy and the world of light, everything we do has been given to our soul. And the soul's dress and nobility and honour, it's all these gifts that are being dressed upon the soul. It's the soul that doesn't trust the body.

The soul does not trust our physical body and doesn't want to give us any of the gifts. It thinks always, 'If I give you, you're going to ruin it.' So, there are actually two beings. There is the soul of somebody that is reaching their purification and there's the physicality of *insan* (mankind). If they purify and clean their physicality, Allah ﷻ will give a command from, *"Atiullaha wa atiur Rasula wa Ulil amre minkum."*

...أَطِيعُوا اللَّهَ وَأَطِيعُوا الرَّسُولَ وَأُولِي الْأَمْرِ مِنكُمْ... ﴿٥٩﴾

*4:59 – "...Atiullaha wa atiur Rasula wa Ulil amre minkum..."*
*(Surat An-Nisa)*

*"...Obey Allah, Obey the Messenger, and those in authority among you..." (The Women, 4:59)*

That now your soul can begin to teach you, and begins to now give you the *haal*, the feelings, *khashf*, the visions and the knowledges. But that's

until your body reaches a trustworthy state. That's why people don't want to reach that state. Say, 'No, no, no, Shaykh, just you got to open it. You got to open it.' Even the family members. 'Just open it, open it.' It doesn't work that way. Your soul doesn't trust you, more or less the shaykh to trust you. Your soul is, 'No way.' And every time a test comes and you explode, you get angry, you exhibit these characteristics, the soul is saying, 'No, no, no, no. See? See? This is why.'

Because if the soul was to give you realities and you're not in control of

your body, can you imagine what type of harm that would do onto this Earth? That's a *fir'aun* (pharaoh). Your body would go out and be like a wizard and a magician and doing every kind of crazy deceitful thing all from *haqqaiqs* (realities). So, the soul is much tougher than the TSA, CIA, Mossad, everything. It's going to evaluate your physicality, watch all of the tests that are coming from Allah 󠀠, that your physicality has to be trustworthy, clean, correct, and that your characteristics have to be under control. Then the soul begins to send its *futuhaats*, its understandings and contemplations, *inshaAllah*.

## Will We Know and Understand Our Seven Names During Contemplation?

Understanding the seven names – it's more important that, 'Who knows himself will know his Lord.'

مَنْ عَرَفَ نَفْسَهُ فَقَدْ عَرَفَ رَبَّهُ

*"Man 'arafa nafsahu faqad 'arafa Rabbahu."*

*"Who knows himself, knows his Lord."* (Prophet Muhammad (pbuh))

That this process of knowing oneself is the journey. So when I look to myself, and the depth of that Holy *Hadith*, 'Who knows his *nafs* (ego), will know his *Rab* (Lord),' of what Sayyidina Muhammad ﷺ was describing is that you don't have to die to find your Lord. You don't have to physically die to find your Lord and that which governs the entire universe. Your journey starts by looking inward and not outward. And the most difficult journey is the journey inward.

So, we just described now in the meditation and we just described it in the light that, that was it. Do you understand how to build your light? Do you understand how to nourish your light? Do you understand that what are the lords that are governing you now that are trying to destroy that light? Right? Drinking, smoking, anger; those whom are governed by anger – it's disbelief. Every time they let anger and rage overtake them, it's like a tornado on that light trying to extinguish it. Because in one instant you can harm somebody, harm yourself and do something that takes

complete light and faith away. The candle will be blown and that person perishes not in an eternal state.

First was to know all the lords that govern me and my character. That I go through all of those and reach towards sincerity and *mukhles* in which I've been granted from Allah 🕮 to be a sincere servant. And in my sincerity Allah 🕮 begin to open to myself who I am. And what's the name of this name, of my *dunya* (material world) name. What it means? What's its reality? And I have seven names in seven paradises. And what are those names? And what is the support of that name upon myself? And how that name is to support me on my journey in *dunya*, and in my journey into the realities of  the heavens? So very deep; that is a very deep reality. We have to conquer all of the badness and the trash.

## Is the Soul the Oppressor Within Us or is it the Ego?

 Your soul is never a *zalim* (oppressor). Your *ruh* (soul) is never a *zalim*. So, let's just keep it in English before you try to understand Arabic. And there's a secret behind the Arabic. The English is very easy. It's your *nafs*, your ego. The ego has to be brought down and can never be killed. The *nafs* (ego) cannot be killed. The *nafs* will be something that rides you or becomes your *buraq* (noble mystical horse) in which you're riding your *nafs* and will shoot you into the heavens. Because the *nafs* is under your

control and you have flipped the situation. But the *nafs*, if you don't control it, will be partner with *shaitan* (satan) and there's the *sharik* (partner). The *shaitan* never partners with the soul, the soul has nothing to do. The soul is *haq* (truth) and *shaitan* is false and the truth never come together.

$$وَ قُلْ جَآءَالْحَقُّ وَزَهَقَ الْبَطِلُ، إِنَّ الْبَطِلَ كَانَ زَهُوقًا ﴿٨١﴾$$

*17:81 – "Wa qul jaa alhaqqu wa zahaqal baatil, innal batila kana zahoqa." (Surat Al-Isra)*

*"And say, Truth has come, and falsehood has perished. Indeed falsehood, [by its nature], is ever perishing/ bound to perish."*
*(The Night Journey, 17:81)*

So, the only *sharik* that somebody can make is through their *nafs*. Their *nafs* becomes a partner with *shaitan* against Allah ﷻ. But the soul is always pure. It's a pure light from Allah's ﷻ Divinely Presence. The *nafs* will partner to destroy the soul. So, then you have to bring the *nafs* down. So, every time and all year-round, the *nafs* is riding you.

Ramadan is the only time that you can see how you ride the *nafs* because you tell your *nafs*, 'Look, no matter what you say, I'm a Muslim. I'm going to do my fasting or we're going to die.' If the *nafs* believes that yes, you're going to do Ramadan, he wakes you up at 3:30 am. Because he's like, 'We're not doing the hunger. I'm not going to starve. Get up, eat now, big buffet.' Now, you're riding the *nafs* because it's helping you to do your worshipness. So, that's the sign that Allah ﷻ wants to show you, 'No, this can be done.'

381

If you push and you push and you push enough in your life, your *zikrs* (Divine remembrance), your love, your *muhabbat* (love), the *nazar* (gaze) of Prophet ﷺ – it will push it so far down that the *nafs* will begin to be ridden and realize that you seem to be the boss; now let me help you. I will give you – instead of fighting – I will give you a *himmah*. I will give you a push and a zeal to do your worshipness, to do what you have to do to make Allah ﷻ to be pleased. But not for a blink of an eye, Prophet ﷺ described, to leave yourself to the badness. Always know that it's there and you're continuously doing all your practices to bring that beast down, *inshaAllah*.

اللَّهُمَّ لَا تَكِلْنِي إِلَى نَفْسِي طَرْفَةَ عَيْنٍ وَلَا أَقَلَّ مِنْ ذَلِكَ

*"Allahumma laa takilnee ila nafsee tarfat `aynin wa laa aqala min dhalika."*

*"O Allah! Don't leave me to my ego for the blink of an eye or less."*
*(Prophet Muhammad (pbuh))*

## How Can We Make Ourselves Believe That We Are Nothing?

You have to keep believing, *inshaAllah*. That if we keep repeating to myself that, 'I'm ignorant, *ya Rabbi*. I'm ignorant and then I watch the teachings because the teachings have an energy; there's a light.' Attending the *majlis* (association) of the *zikr* (Divine remembrance), by coming online and listening to the *zikr*. There's an energy that they're sending onto the soul that energizes the soul and begins to push down the *nafs* (ego) and the bad character of

the *nafs*. As long as I'm taking a path in which, *"La ilaha illa anta Subhanaka, innee kuntu minazh zhalimeen."*

لَّا إِلَٰهَ إِلَّا أَنتَ سُبْحَانَكَ إِنِّي كُنتُ مِنَ الظَّالِمِينَ ﴿٨٧﴾

*21:87 – "...La ilaha illa anta Subhanaka, innee kuntu minazh zhalimeen." (Surat Al-Anbiya)*

*"...There is no god/diety except You; Glory to you: Indeed I have been of the wrongdoers/Oppressor to Myself!" (The Prophets, 21:87)*

And keep repeating *ayatul kareem* (the generous verse of Holy Qur'an) and keep repeating to ourselves that, 'I'm nothing, I'm nothing, *ya Rabbi.* That, *'Ana abdukal 'ajeez, wa dayeef, zhalim wa jahl,* and that have mercy upon me forgive me, forgive me.' And then taking an accounting of every night. Every night that when you sit and contemplate, 'My Lord, I'm asking please inspire my heart. What did I do wrong? What did I say wrong and whom did I hurt with my tongue?' And Allah ﷻ never forgive those whom break the heart of people. This means it's a big *gunah*, it's a big sin. So when we identify, then at least we know that we're asking forgiveness. 'Ya Rabbi*, forgive me. I may have talked harshly. I may have acted inappropriately. Please forgive me, *ya Rabbi*, please forgive me.' And then making the *istighfar* (seeking forgiveness) in the day, and in the afternoon making the *salawats* on Sayyidina Muhammad ﷺ, *inshaAllah.*

## How Can We Understand the Concept of Nothingness in Our Daily Activities?

Again, the sensitivity of our subjects in lieu of all the people who have completely no understanding of *tariqah* (spiritual path), that to have a self-worth. Because a lot of these words that we use in English psychology and in English teachings may have a negative understanding and that's not at all what the *tariqah* is about. And one reality is that, how can we expect people to love us when we don't love ourselves? So, this is supreme.

Now, to love myself is to appreciate what Allah ﷻ has given to me as a gift of everything. Everything that Allah ﷻ has given to me is a gift. In which I love it and I respect it and I reach a level in which I stopped from pride of it. Not to be proud of what Allah ﷻ has given as a gift, but to respect. And that's why our *zikr* every day is *"Alhamdulillah wa shukran lillah"* 100 times at *Salatul Fajr*. *"Alhamdulillah wa shukran lillah," Salatul Shukr.* Why, because *hamd*, everything is praising Allah ﷻ and I should, and I too must join in that praising.

سَبَّحَ لِلَّهِ مَا فِي السَّمَاوَاتِ وَمَا فِي الْأَرْضِ ۖ وَهُوَ الْعَزِيزُ الْحَكِيمُ ﴿١﴾

*57:1 – "Sabbaha lillahi ma fis Samawati wa ma fil ardi, wa Huwal Azizul Hakeem." (Surat Al-Hadid)*

*"Whatever is in the heavens and whatever is on the earth exalts/Praises Allah, and He is the Exalted in Might, the Wise." (The Iron, 57:1)*

And *shukr* (gratitude) for what Allah ﷻ has given to me, not what I wanted but, what Allah ﷻ has given. To be thankful for what Allah ﷻ has  given, and the *tariqah* comes to teach that reality. That before you make all these requirements, then become upset because you didn't get those requirements or those things that you had asked for from Allah ﷻ. You never stopped to thank Him for what He did give of health, of wealth, of possessions, of mind and *aqel* (intellect), and just a common sense. Some people have no sense. Whatever health Allah ﷻ gave you, there are people who have less of that. So, at every condition and in every state, we are being gifted by our Lord these realities.

So then *tariqah* comes to teach, 'Don't you love yourself. Don't you love that what God has given to you. Respect yourself. You want respect from other people but yet you don't respect yourself.' Now within that secret of respecting yourself comes the secrets of these *awliyaullah* (saints). For if you truly respect yourself, you would listen to their guidance. Because their guidance will expose your character defects and magnify what God has given to you.

## How Can We Stop Obsessing About Certain Issues in Our Life?

It's not what you're running after this *dunya* (material world) for. Some people are so obsessed with a target and it becomes a box for them. They want a specific issue and why this specific issue is not opening for them. They become depressed and sad and every type of characteristic. And the danger is your mind has boxed you

into a place and has actually locked you. And the purpose of guidance is that if you talk to a guide and one whom is guided, they may inspire you to look out literally out of the box. So, someone may say, 'How come I'm not on this project, working on this project, doing this project, doing this.' But then all of a sudden, the shaykh may say, 'There are ten other projects you could be doing. Why are you boxed onto this one issue?'

That's the danger of our life, that our mind and *shaitan* (satan) has the ability to come and lock onto something. And then create a panic, a sadness, a disappointment with our Lord, disappointment in everything. And the *tariqah* is to come and teach, 'Be happy with yourself, proud of yourself in the sense that what God has given to you, you have a responsibility. How am I to serve You to the best of my character. How am I to have the best of example and therefore magnify everything that Allah ﷻ has given to us.' So, the *tariqah* comes to teach these and how to have this good characteristic and how to respect yourself. And stop at the line of becoming ignorant and proud of who you are.

## How Should We Deal With People Who Always Test Us?

I give you an example that an animal characteristic, that when we look around at ourself and then begin to observe other people. The shaykh's personal life has gone through many abuses, many, many difficulties that you would never know it, unless you're very close. Abused by other shaykhs, by people in their lives, by many things. But because of their training, you never see it on their face, on their lips, or on their typing and their hands. They live their life, because everything is like beads that they sew together like a *tasbih* (prayer beads). If they're teaching you *muraqabah* (spiritual connection) and meditation, and all their meditation is about being at the presence of Sayyidina Muhammad ﷺ. Whether you arrived or you didn't arrive – you fake it until you make it! That, 'I'm at *Rauza e Sharif* (holy burial chamber), if my heart opened and I can see Sayyidina Muhammad ﷺ, *alhamdulillah*. And if I can't, it

makes no difference, I still placed myself at *Rauza e Sharif*.' If your life is governed by this rule, then you are at *Rauza e Sharif* and a shaykh has offended you, a Muslim has offended you, a non-Muslim has offended you. Something has gone wrong. Do you think in the presence of Prophet ﷺ – who is the judge, he's the law maker, the law giver that what Allah ﷻ has given to Prophet ﷺ – how would the reaction be? If you stated the case and Prophet ﷺ is listening, what would he have said? 'Oh, destroy him. Go after him. Ridicule and insult him.'

All these things that people with bad character do; it shows who they really are. That they had no training, they never went through *tazkiyah* (purification), and they have no sense of being in the presence of Sayyidina Muhammad ﷺ. So, then their knowledge became a source of arrogance and pride for them. They think they copied and pasted and learned something, and the sickness of pride entered. Had they taken and completed their path of *tazkiyah* and *tariqah*, they would have understood that, 'I'm always in the presence of Sayyidina Muhammad ﷺ.' And Prophet ﷺ would have said, 'Watch out. As you are my family, he is my family. Just stay quiet for the love of me.' And they stay quiet. And he says, 'If you want your reward by bringing my family

down, I'm not happy with you for that. If you stay quiet, I will give you my reward, I will dress you, I will bless you.' And the whole path was only for that anyways.

So maybe that was the secret of the problem that was sent to you. Without that problem, you didn't have that account with Sayyidina Muhammad ﷺ. With that problem, you now have that account with Prophet ﷺ. That, 'Stay quiet for my sake, have good character for my sake. If you want from them your solution, go get it. But in your badness of character, you may become distant from me.' So, because of their training, they would never risk anything like that. So, then they're ordered, 'Stay quiet.' So, when you see them not at those associations, not sitting with those people, not in the groups of those shaykhs, it's because they've been ordered by Sayyidina Muhammad ﷺ, 'Stay away. Stay quiet and I will raise you, I will dress you.' That's it. We are not a people who enter into conflict and argument and, 'Let's debate this.'

Then they give an example that look to the internet, when they describe how people will have characteristics. And you know what the characteristic of a rat is? It's dirty, it's filthy. And you know why it's filthy? Because it sends its poo-poo everywhere. How does the guy find the rat? When they come and say, 'You have mice and you have rats in your home,' why is it bad, why is it dangerous? It's because the rat is poo-pooing on everything. He's putting his droppings on every closet, in every cabinet, on every spoon, on every plate. And that's how they're tracking him. They say, 'Oh look at all these droppings everywhere.' You follow the tracks of the waste to find the creature. And along the way, the waste was causing all the sickness and the problems.

So then now look at the characteristics of people online, they are rats. They go from page to page throwing droppings. Making bad comments, throwing bad comments. What is that? It's not from teaching, it's not from Sayyidina Muhammad ﷺ; it's just their excrements, their waste. Just the garbage of *shaitan* is coming through their fingers, they throw it on page to page to page. So, you follow the page, and you're following a rat. That's just going page to page making satanic comments, against *Ahlul Bayt* (holy family of Prophet ﷺ), against *awliyaullah*, against the descendants of Sayyidina Muhammad ﷺ.

Imagine one whom may have an *uloom* and a knowledge, he represents a piece of the heart of Sayyidina Muhammad ﷺ. And that's why *tazkiyah*, and *taqwa* (consciousness), and *tariqah* comes to teach us. Is that any knowledge or  anything to be built, any power in your prayer to be built, anything that you're seeking out of this relationship with Allah ﷻ, if its foundation is not the beatific character and all of these mannerisms that they teach, of what benefit is it for? Become *hafiz* (one who memorized Qur'an) and you become like a rat making bad comments every time? You memorize *hadith* and become like a rat making bad comments? So, what is the benefit of that knowledge? That's *tariqah*.

## How Do We Know We Achieved a Level of Being Nothing?

Oh, you'll feel that you are cooked. When everything is in difficulty, every type of crushing, every type of crushing-ness, you'll understand when life is crushing you, and sadness is surrounding you, and every type of difficulty is all around. You feel yourself – it's been crushed. You'll know it when you get there. And the more you're crushed and the more these types of difficulties come in life, the stronger your connection is if you're practicing. Because your practicing works best with the sad and broken-hearted. So that when they build that connection through difficulty, then when everything becomes good and the days are sunny, their connection is also strong and made.

But to make the connection with everything great, it doesn't work that way. Tell somebody to sit down and meditate, 'Oh, I can't. I have to go to the beach, I have to go here, I have to go there, I'm doing all these

things.' Then Allah ﷻ put everybody, said, 'Beach is even closed. Pandemic is coming, you're all going to die, you're all going to die'. 'What you mean?' Say, 'You're all going to die.' Body pictures everywhere. Say, 'All these people are going to die, I got to go to the room and meditate now.' Because that room became like a *qabr*

(grave) for you. You think, 'I am really going to die so I better make sure I'm good with Allah ﷻ and my room becomes like my grave and I start making my *zikr.*'

Then we understood through difficulty, there is an understanding of why Allah 🕮 sends that difficulty. When it makes us to cry, makes the heart to become soft and this then draws us towards that reality, *inshaAllah*.

So that when days are good we've made that connection, we're thankful to Allah 🕮, that, '*Ya Rabbi*, I don't need another beating, I got it, I understand, and I'm going to submit to the best of my ability. I don't need to see more of the difficult days,' and then the believer begins. But there are some people who only function through crisis. Every time something is good, they forget, and they go. Their practices are gone, you don't see them, nothing. They're crisis actors.

As soon as things become horrible again, 'Oh Shaykh, I'm here again, everything's falling apart.' So, we try to not be of those, we try to be that, '*Ya Rabbi*, when difficulty comes, I learned and in good days I believe more and do more, *ya Rabbi*.' And *inshaAllah*, they become more *istiqam* and firm in what they believe, *inshaAllah*.

## How Do We View Ourselves as Nothing in the Presence of Prophet Muhammad 🕮?

Yes, what was the answer that we gave yesterday, 'Every day is a new *tajalli* (manifestation).' This was somebody asking that, 'They want to see themselves at *Rauza e Sharif* (holy burial chamber).' So, the concept

of negating yourself is to continuously tell yourself and your *nafs* (ego) that, 'You're nothing, you're nothing, you're nothing, you're nothing.' But to see yourself always at *Rauza e Sharif*, so that I am always at *Rauza e Sharif*, but I'm telling my *nafs*, 'I'm nothing.' So, nobody can see themselves as nothing, unless they've trained themselves to be nothing; then they would feel themselves disappearing. That's a different level of training. When you close your eyes and see yourself as nothing, you'll probably see a silhouette of yourself to show you that you can't really believe that you're nothing.

Later, when you ask to be in the *hudur* (presence) of the shaykh is that, 'I am asking to be in the presence of my shaykh and that I'm just a dust in his *jubba* (robe).' And see if you can keep the image of the shaykh and that you're non-existent there – very difficult. People can't see that, then they only see themselves. That's your *nafs* telling you that it's not disappearing, 'I am right here, you can dream all you want but I'm right here!' So then that gives the sign you need a lot more scrubbing, a lot more scrubbing. So, one, is the understanding, 'I am nothing.' And then the most important is to place myself always at *Rauza e Sharif* that, 'I am nothing, I'm no one; I don't think I deserve anything, but I'm here at *Rauza e Sharif* to be under the *nazar* (gaze) of Sayyidina Muhammad ﷺ and to reach to just be a carpet under the holy feet of Sayyidina Muhammad ﷺ.'

# Building Good Character Through Tafakkur and Muhasabah

## How Do We Stop Bad Habits?

*Alhamdulillah,* that keeps the shaykh in business. If people didn't have sins, who would need a shaykh? It's like saying if the world was cured of all sicknesses there would be no need for a doctor. So, it means that the

fellowship that Allah ﷻ is creating, He knows what sins the servants are doing. As a result, He wants to build the relationship that, 'This character you have, go to this one to teach you to stop from that.' Because this one's

training was to deal with that so it's a relationship, what they call a symbiotic relationship; it's a relationship that needs each other. The shaykh needs students that sin and sinful people need a shaykh.

And that's why we said the *tariqahs* (spiritual path), *zikr* (Divine remembrance) is a washing machine. It's not the circle of *saliheen* (righteous), although everyone wants to think they're the circle of *saliheen.* The reality is that everybody, if left to their own, would do bad things. So, Allah ﷻ gathers them and says, 'At least cleanse and purify yourself,' because He loves you. That He is guiding you to clean now before the cleaning of the grave which is 70,000 times more difficult. Wash now, clean now, take away the sins now, build the character now.

That's why we say it's a *ni'mat* (blessing). Mawlana Shaykh ق describes it's a *ni'mat* from Allah ﷻ. Because when Allah ﷻ doesn't give that *ni'mat* there is a difficulty coming in the grave. Those whom He granted them

a special gift, 'Sit with the circle of paradise they're going to wash and clean all of this badness now.' So no, the shaykh is in need of the students. And whatever badness they're doing, they're doing. And that's you know whatever's been written upon that student. But to change the bad character then is the goal. How to change and how to discipline, and how to teach the student to discipline themselves from the bad characteristics, *inshaAllah*. But nobody's perfect.

## What Can We Do When We Have Flashbacks of Our Sinful Past During Contemplation?

You cry. You make *istighfar* (seeking forgiveness) and they say that *awliya* (saints), they forgive but they never forget. That when Allah ﷻ

want to open their consciousness, that the state of heedlessness stops from them. So, regular people, they forget. Every day, they do something wrong, they forget it. Next day, they repeat it right away. They forgot what they did wrong. They forgot that they

made *tawbah* (repentance). They forgot all the things, and as a result of that, *shaitan* (satan) keeps tripping them every day. 'Ah! I wasn't going to do that again.' They do it again, they do it again. So, they're continuously forgetting.

When Allah ﷻ begins to open higher states of their consciousness, higher states of sincerity, He begins to teach them, 'Don't forget.' You know, forgive. That ask your forgiveness, don't do that again. Make your *tawbah*, but don't forget how *shaitan* tricked you into falling into that again.' And they have a character in which they forgive everything and they forget nothing. They know everything that has been done, but they forgive. And their character is a consistent *istighfar, istighfar*, asking for forgiveness.

But in our characters, it's to wake from a state of heedlessness in which every moment we're forgetting what we promised, what we were not  going to do. And then *shaitan* make us to do it again the next day. And that's why then the *zikr* (Divine remembrance). So far for us, that's coming in these last days, is throughout the day making *istighfar*, "*Astaghfirullahal 'Azim, wa atubu ilayh. Astaghfirullahal 'Azim, wa atubu ilayh*" all the way till midday.

أَسْتَغْفِرُ الله الْعَظِيْمِ وَأَتُوْبُ إِلَيْه

"*Astaghfirullahal 'Azim, wa atubu ilayh.*"

*I ask for forgiveness of Allah the Magnificent, and I turn to Him in repentance.'*

"*Astaghfirullahal 'Azim*," because *sifat al-'Azim* will wash everything away and Allah's ﷻ *'Azimah* (Magnificence) – nothing is of a big nature. Everything will be diminished into nothingness. And when we ask for *istighfar*, Allah's ﷻ reply, *inshaAllah*, "*Bismillahir Rahmanir Raheem.*"

بِسْمِ اللهِ الرَّحْمَنِ الرَّحِيْمِ

*"Bismillahir Rahmanir Raheem."*

*"In the Name of Allah, the Most Beneficent, the Most Merciful."*

We're asking for forgiveness and Allah's ﷻ, *"Bismillahir Rahmanir Raheem,"* to wash it. And then after midday, *salawats* (praises upon Prophet Muhammad ﷺ). So, the *istighfar* is a shower, washing ourselves. After midday, *salawat* on Sayyidina Muhammad ﷺ all the way till nighttime while you watch TV, play with your children. *"Allahumma salli 'ala Sayyidina Muhammad wa 'ala aali Sayyidina Muhammad."* to make the tongue and the heart to be sweet with the fragrance and the love of Sayyidina Muhammad ﷺ, *inshaAllah*.

اللَّهُمَّ صَلِّ عَلَى سَيِّدِنَا مُحَمَّدٍ، وَعَلَى آلِ سَيِّدِنَا مُحَمَّدٍ وَ سَلِّمْ.

*"Allahumma salli 'ala Sayyidina Muhammadin wa 'ala aali Sayyidina Muhammadin wa Sallim."*

*"O Allah! Send Peace and blessings upon our master Prophet Muhammad and upon the Family of our master Prophet Muhammad (pbuh)"*

## How Do We Counter Whispers, Negative Thoughts, and Fears During Contemplation?

Yes, that's the whole process. It's that *shaitan* (satan) is gaining access to the ear and to the heart and that he's trying to overtake the faith of the believer. So, those faculties are the ones that you're going to focus on when you're doing the *tafakkur* (contemplation). When you're doing the *tafakkur*, it's such a tremendous power, *shaitan* doesn't allow it.

That as soon as you want to make your connection that, 'I want to connect my heart, *ya Rabbi*. Keep me with You, keep me with Prophet ﷺ. Keep me with these *ulul amr* (saints), that dress your light upon me, dress your *nazar* (gaze) upon me.' Then they begin to teach you all the different things that you're supposed to do. How to keep your *wudu* (ablution), how to make your *salawats* (praises upon Prophet Muhammad ﷺ), how to keep the house with all these *ta'weezes* of Qur'an and all these beautiful calligraphies so that to fortify and sanctify yourselves.

As you build your energy, the more powerful your energy becomes, the

more it pushes away these devils and these bad energies; pushes them to stay further away by the strength of the energy that you're building within the heart. So, it's important to build that energy and to begin to push these things away. But not for a blink of any eye, Prophet ﷺ said, 'Don't leave me to my *nafs* (ego) for a blink of any eye.'

اللَّهُمَّ لَا تَكِلْنِي إِلَى نَفْسِي طَرْفَةَ عَيْنٍ وَلَا أَقَلَّ مِنْ ذَلِكَ

*"Allahumma laa takilnee ila nafsee tarfat 'aynin wa laa aqala min dhalika."*

*"O Allah! Don't leave me to my ego for the blink of an eye or less."* (Prophet Muhammad (pbuh))

So, don't think for a moment that *shaitan's* not waiting to attack. That 'Oh, he's gone away.' Never – he's waiting for a mistake.

## What is the Best Way to Do Muhasabah?

Every night, people, places, and things that you don't like, take a writing of 'why?' *Muhasabah* is to take an accounting of one's self, like an inventory. You say, 'Oh, what are all the people, places, and things that I don't like?' But the importance of this inventory is, 'What is my role in not liking them.' This means the blame is always on myself.

'I don't like this person because they have this car,' but what is my role in that is that? 'I'm jealous that his car is nicer than my car.' And that's the sickness Allah 'ﷻ wants you to identify.

Other people's accounting is they put the blame on everyone except themselves. Especially western understanding is they raise the *nafs* (ego), 'self, *nafs* awareness.' What are all these realities of self-glorification? 'Be happy with yourself.' The self is the *nafs*.

Our way is to defeat the *nafs*, and that the *nafs* is to blame for everything wrong. So, once I identify, 'Why I don't like this person?' Be really truthful; why I don't like him? 'Because his car, he has a nice car; I'm jealous of the car he has.' When I put myself to be guilty, I'll find the character defects. Those defects are what Allah 'ﷻ wants us to find. If you're finding the defect is jealousy, enmity, anger – all of these then are the root of the sickness.

The majority now is anger. And anger we said is like a fire, it's like a pilot light. Everyone's heart has a little light, and Allah ﷻ wants to know if this light, are you going to strike it for Divine love, or are you going to make it to be a source of explosion within your being? So, then every bad quality comes like a little gas. It drops on the light, and then Allah ﷻ wants to see, 'Jealousy – did

you explode and turn on fire?' So, the pilot light is already there. Allah ﷻ is going to test it before He ﷻ makes you to be from *ahbab* and lovers. Enmity, it lights up. Now the most dangerous one is anger. You know the light is there. Just a little bit of gas of anger comes in. Instead of controlling and containing it, it explodes like an explosion. And this is the difficulty that everyone's facing now in their *muhasabah* – how to control their anger.

And the biggest defence against anger is *wudu* (ablution), is to keep 24 hours a day, to the best of our ability, our state of *wudu*. Is to wash, pray two cycles of *wudu*, and don't leave the *wudu*, as if you're going to be attacked and killed if you're out of *wudu*. You don't leave *wudu*. You don't go to work, and you know, just do whatever your business is and

keep your *wudu*; you keep your *wudu* at all times. *Shaitan* (satan) is watching to see you leave *wudu*, and your shield of protection drop, and full on attack into the being, which now that attack can lead to severe sickness in this time of difficulty.

## How Can We Remove Bad Character Identified During Muhasabah?

The removal of the character is the working on the opposite of that character. This means once you identify, you can email and ask a specific question that, 'Shaykh, I have a lot of anger and I identified my anger.' Then they teach you how to make the *zikr* (Divine Remembrance), the *salawats* on Prophet ﷺ, the *istighfar* (seeking forgiveness), how to make *zikr* of *"Ya Halim"* to calm yourself and most important is put an outside reminder for an inner sickness.

So, it means wrap something around your arm and say, '*Ya Rabbi,* I am going to work on this character of *ghadab* and anger for 40 days at least. And every time I'm about to get angry, I'll see this red or this yellow or this sign of something that reminds me I'm working on my anger. As soon as I'm about to open my mouth and give a reply or get angry, then they teach you – go wash.

So, there's a whole remedy for the characteristic, the majority of which 99% of people are now suffering from anger. As soon as the testing comes, they're 'hit' with a test from Allah ﷻ. Most people are so toxic like petroleum. Their blood is like gasoline. It doesn't take much to spark them. Their entire complexion changes and they are lit up. They are on fire and you can't even calm them down, they're so hot and heated. So, that as soon as you

get angry, there has to be a training, 'I'm going to go wash.' It's not the time to talk. It's not the time to argue. You entered into a state where *shaitan* (satan) has ignited you.

You are now in isolation. There's no need to talk to anyone in your satanic state. And most people say, 'No, no, I have to resolve it right now.' No, because in your satanic state, the shaykh has no permission, the person has no permission to be around someone in a satanic state. That's why Prophet ﷺ walked away. He says, 'Because now *shaitan* will be present. Because of your arguing, *shaitan* will come, and me and *shaitan*, we don't occupy the same space.'

عَنْ أَبِي هُرَيْرَةَ رَضِيَ اللَّهُ عَنْهُ: "أَنَّ رَجُلًا شَتَمَ أَبَا بَكْرٍ وَالنَّبِيُّ ﷺ جَالِسٌ، فَجَعَلَ النَّبِيُّ ﷺ يَعْجَبُ وَيَتَبَسَّمُ. فَلَمَّا أَكْثَرَ رَدَّ عَلَيْهِ بَعْضَ قَوْلِهِ. فَغَضِبَ النَّبِيُّ ﷺ وَقَامَ. فَلَحِقَهُ أَبُو بَكْرٍ، فَقَالَ: يَا رَسُولَ اللهِ كَانَ يَشْتُمُنِي وَأَنْتَ جَالِسٌ. فَلَمَّا رَدَدْتُ عَلَيْهِ بَعْضَ قَوْلِهِ، غَضِبْتَ وَقُمْتَ.
قَالَ ﷺ: "إِنَّهُ كَانَ مَعَكَ مَلَكٌ يَرُدُّ عَنْكَ. فَلَمَّا رَدَدْتَ عَلَيْهِ بَعْضَ قَوْلِهِ، وَقَعَ الشَّيْطَانُ، فَلَمْ أَكُنْ لِأَقْعُدَ مَعَ الشَّيْطَانِ." [المَصْدَر: مُسْنَد الإِمَام أَحْمَدْ: ٩٦٢٤]

*'An Abi Hurairah (ra), "Anna rajulan shatama Aba Bakrin (as) wan Nabiyu ﷺ jalisun, faja'ala AnNabiyu ﷺ ya'jabu wa yatabassamu. Falamma akthara radda 'alayhi ba'da qawlihi. Faghadaba AnNabiyu wa qama. Falaheqahu Abu Bakrin, faqala: "Ya Rasulallahi kana yashtumuni wa anta jaalis. Falama radadtu 'alayhi ba'da qawlihi, ghadebta wa qumta.*

*Qala: "Innahu kana ma'aka malakun yaroddo 'anka. Falamma radadta 'alayhi ba'da qawlihi, waqa'ash shaitanu, falam akun li aq'oda ma'ash shaitan."*

*Narrated Abu Hurairah (ra) that, "Once, a man was verbally abusing Abu Bakr (as) while the Prophet (pbuh) was sitting, watching curiously with a smile. After taking much abuse quietly, Abu Bakr (as) responded to a few of his comments. At this, the Prophet (pbuh) exhibited his disapproval, got up and left.*

*Abu Bakr (as) caught up with the Prophet (pbuh) and said, "O Messenger of Allah, he was abusing me and you remained quiet. When I responded to him, you disapproved and left!"*

*The Messenger of Allah (pbuh) responded, "There was an angel with you responding to him. When you responded to him, Shaitan took his place. [Source: Musnad Al Imam Ahmad: 9624]*

So, it means that's not the time to have a discussion when you're angry and when you're on fire. It's a time for you to go wash, to calm yourself. First battle your *shaitan* before you try to resolve outside issues with people, places, and things. *InshaAllah.*

## Is There a Recitation to Jumpstart Our Humility?

Be careful for what you pray for. Because humility, it's not self-humility where you bring somebody a cup of water and, 'Oh, how are you, I bring you.' This is where Allah ﷻ is going to send you through a washing machine of humiliation. Where people will humiliate you; people at work will humiliate you, family members will humiliate you. And you'll have to resist fighting and saying and saying. So, the path of humiliation is very difficult. Try to approach that with patience and slow.

There is no fast relief to realities. This is not a drive-thru where we try to double up on everything and get everywhere quick. It is a life-long process. So, by doing the *zikr* (Divine remembrance), by doing the meditation, by doing the *tafakkur* (contemplation), you're building up the tools you need that when someone insults you, you don't reply. You just smile and understand that this is now a test for you. Or you interact with the shaykh and the shaykh will begin to poke at you. So that to say, 'You're wrong on this, wrong on that, and you're quick to make a reply, quick to say I want to do this or that.' All of these characteristics, they have to be brought down. So, path of humility is going to take time, it's not something that's easy and there is nowhere to reach in a hurry. This is a life-long process, *inshaAllah*.

## How Do You Fix Jealousy?

When you take the *muhasabah* (accounting) and you start to write all of these issues in our lives. And then to understand the sickness is the first step in it. That when you confront your sickness and say that, 'I have

jealousy issues,' at least then you'll get your *zikr* (Divine remembrance), your *istighfar* (seeking forgiveness), your *salawats*. And keep asking Prophet ﷺ that, 'I know that I'm a jealous person. Take

this off of my eyes. Take this *nazar* (gaze) off my eyes. Let my eyes to be content with what life Allah ﷻ has given to me.' And then they begin the *"Alhamdulillah wa Shukrulillah, Alhamdulillah wa Shukrulillah."*

اَلْحَمَّدُلِلَّهْ وَ اَلْشُّكُرُ لِلَّهْ

*"Alhamdulillah wa shukrulillah."*

*"Praise belongs to Allah and all thanks to Allah."*

Because when the eye is too hungry, it's not content with what Allah ﷻ has given to you. And then it makes us to be in a difficult situation with Allah ﷻ. So, the first level is to identify. And most people will go through their whole life thinking they have no character defects. So, when you point out all the problems and say, 'What's the root of that problem?' It must be *hasad* and jealousy. I can't stand why this person has this and I don't have it.

403

Then we identified it. This is a huge step that, *'Ya Rabbi*, I have *hasad*.

I have *hasad*. *Ya Sayyidi, Ya Rasulul Kareem* (The Most Generous Prophet), keep your *nazar* upon me. *Ya awliyaullah* (saints), keep your *nazar* upon me and take this from my heart. Take this from my eyes. Take this sickness from my eyes and from my heart.' Then every *salawat* and *istighfar* that we're doing is now directed towards the sickness that we know we have. And then

"*Alhamdulillah wa Shukranlillah,*" that *ya Rabbi*, I'm happy with what You have given me. I'm *radhi* with what You have, "*Bi qismatika radhiyan wa bi iz-zatika sajdan.*" *Ya Rabbi*, I'm happy. *Du'a Kumayl*, it's from *Du'a Kumayl*. "*Bi qismatika radhiyan wa bi iz-zatika sajdan.*"

وَتَجْعَلَنِي بِقَسَمِكَ رَاضِياً قَانِعاً، وَفِي جَمِيعِ الأَحْوَالِ مُتَوَاضِعاً

"*Wa taj-'alani bi-qasamika radhiyan qani'n wa fi jamii'l-ah-wali mutawadhi'aa.*"

"*And to make me satisfied and content with Your (appointment/ Distribution), and to make me humble in every state.*"

That I am *radhi*, I am happy with what You have written for me and I'm making my *sujood* (prostration) into Your *Izzah* and Your Might. I can't change my condition.

أَتُسَلِّطُ ٱلنَّارَ عَلَىٰ وُجُوهٍ خَرَّتْ لِعَظَمَتِكَ سَاجِدَةً

"*Atusal-litun-nara 'ala wujuhin khar-rat li-'azhamatika sajidah.*"

"*Whether You wilt give the Fire dominion over faces fallen down prostrate before Your Tremendousness.*"

Only you can change, *ya Rabbi*. If You see that I need more than, it's only up to You. That I am *radhiyan, rida* (satisfaction) with what You have given to me. And Allah's ﷻ happy with the servant who's happy with Allah ﷻ.

## Who is Iblis?

Iblis was a *jinn* (unseen being) and his worshipness was so strong and that was always the example that *tariqah* (spiritual path) comes and teaches. That some people, they have a lot of *himmah* (zeal) in which they do whatever they want to do. And they do it and they do it and they do it. They say for 70,000 years, he worshipped Allah ﷻ in which he made a *sujood* (prostration) everywhere. There's nowhere from Earth into the heavens that he did not make his *sujood* and his worshipness for Allah ﷻ.

But because his worshipness was based at his own time and his own pace and the way he wanted, he didn't know that his actions were filled with arrogance. And Allah ﷻ allowed him to continue until he reached the station of heavens in which the angels would come to his associations of teachings. And when he would give a *bayan* (discourse), they were listening. And that's where *awliyaullah* (saints) come to teach us is not only the *bayan* that come to you, say, 'Oh, it's very interesting talk he had,' but the guy's yelling and screaming and every other word he's spitting form his mouth. He's exhibiting characteristics that are not with the love and the *muhabbat* of Sayyidina Muhammad ﷺ.

The one talking must always assume that Sayyidina Muhammad ﷺ is straight in front of you, looking at you while you're giving *bayan*. You cannot yell. You cannot scream. You cannot become insulting. You cannot do anything that would make the presence of Sayyidina Muhammad ﷺ to leave that *bayan*. And that's what they call their *madad* and their support. Because all their shaykhs come with a Muhammadan light. So, when the shaykh is coming, he's coming with a Muhammadan light, as if Prophet ﷺ is in front of them in a Muhammadan dress.

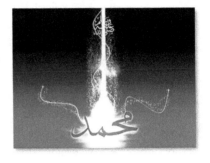

So, it means that then *shaitan* (satan) was exhibiting characteristics and the angels were being dressed by it. And that's why Allah ﷻ wanted to show when He said, 'The *khalifa* (deputy), bow down,' to show their *taslim* (submission) and this was a *sujood al-ihtiram* (prostration of respect) and the angels went into *sujood*, except *shaitan*. He didn't.

وَإِذْ قُلْنَا لِلْمَلَائِكَةِ اسْجُدُوا لِآدَمَ فَسَجَدُوا إِلَّا إِبْلِيسَ أَبَى وَاسْتَكْبَرَ وَكَانَ مِنَ الْكَافِرِينَ ﴿٣٤﴾

*2:34 – "Wa idh qulna lilmalayikati osjudo li Adama fasajado illa ibleesa aba wastakbara wa kana minal kafireen." (Surat Al-Baqarah)*

*"And [mention] when We said to the angels, 'Bow Down/make prostration to Adam'; so they prostrated, except for Iblis. He refused and was arrogant and became of the disbelievers/who reject faith."*
*(The Cow, 2:34)*

Then the angels, they came back up to look and they saw, 'Oh!' They're scared that he's not making *sujood* to Allah ﷻ and they went down again. That's why we make the two *sujood*. They made one, came up, and they saw he's still not bowing. They were scared and went back into *sujood*. And when they got up and finished, then the ones whom had been his students, they took it to ask a question. Say, 'Why the *khalifa*?' And that's what Allah ﷻ wanted to bring as an example. Those angels that Allah ﷻ allowed them to even speak so that to be as an example.

وَإِذْ قَالَ رَبُّكَ لِلْمَلَائِكَةِ إِنِّي جَاعِلٌ فِي الأَرْضِ خَلِيفَةً قَالُواْ أَتَجْعَلُ فِيهَا مَن يُفْسِدُ فِيهَا وَيَسْفِكُ الدِّمَاء وَنَحْنُ نُسَبِّحُ بِحَمْدِكَ وَنُقَدِّسُ لَكَ قَالَ إِنِّي أَعْلَمُ مَا لاَ تَعْلَمُونَ ﴿٣٠﴾

*2:30 – "Wa idh qala rabbuka lil Malayikati innee ja'ilun fil ardi khaleefatan, qaloo ataj'alu feeha man yufsidu feeha wa yasfikud dima a wa nahnu nusabbihu bihamdika wa nuqaddisu laka, Qala innee a'lamu ma la ta'lamon." (Surat Al-Baqarah)*

*"And [mention, O Muhammad], when your Lord said to the angels, "Indeed, I will make upon the earth a Deputy/Representative." They [angels] said, "Will You place upon it one who causes corruption/mischief therein and shed blood, while we praise and glorify You?" Allah said, "Indeed, I know that which you do not know." (The Cow, 2:30)*

## What is the Story of the Fallen Angels, Harut and Marut?

Harut and Marut were two other angels. There are stories of angels falling. When Allah ﷻ want to test them for whatever reason, Allah ﷻ

does whatever Allah ﷻ wants to do. You don't say, 'No, it can't be done.' When the two angels – when Allah ﷻ was describing later in creation – that look how difficult their life is on this Earth, how much they have challenges from *shaitan* coming after them. There were angels thinking, 'That's not so hard. Why don't they just stay pure like us?' And then Allah ﷻ told to Harut and Marut, 'If you think that's easy, then we'll make you to go down. And I'll give you *Ismullah al-Azam* in which you go, and you become human at that time. Live amongst them. But if you should commit a sin, immediately you will stay in that realm and you'll no longer be allowed to repeat that name to come into the heavens.'

They thought they were on a very easy mission, 'We're going to go there and it's going to be great and we're going to show how you should be as an angel in this realm.' The minute they came in, they went to a *maikhana* where they were drinking in a tavern. And they said, 'Wow, these humans have it great,' and they started to drink. And as soon as they're drinking, they saw a very beautiful woman. And they said, 'Wow, these human women are something else,' because now they're in a human form. They use that name to come in human form. So, they went and approached the beautiful woman. She was waving say, 'Come, come.' So, they went and approach.

Said, 'Do you want to be with me?' And (angels) said, 'Okay.' (Woman) said, 'But I have you to do one thing for me.' (Angels) say, 'What?' Say, 'Kill my husband.' And (angels) said, 'Hmm?' (Woman), 'Kill my husband.' (Angels) said, 'Okay.'

And they went and they killed the husband. And they're cut. And then they cried and repented, 'We don't what happened to us, *ya Rabbi*. We came, we drank from their drinks that we don't have in heaven, and we lost our mind, and we went after a woman. We've never seen a woman before. We wanted her. We said we'll do whatever you want, and she asked us kill this man. We killed him and now we don't know how to go back.' Say, 'Go back? For all of eternity, you're on this Earth.'

This Harut wa Marut were thrown into the well of Babel and they're held upside down inside that well till today. Where all the magicians, they make their *ziyarah* (pilgrimage) to that well and they ask from those angels, the magic of deceit. So, the knowledges of this magic are real because it's coming from these angels. And they give a warning that, 'Before we tell you this, know that you will be eternally punished.' Because Allah ﷻ describes in Qur'an, they give a disclaimer that we are angels of the heavens and that Allah ﷻ will punish you. And they will take that knowledges regardless of the threat of punishment. And the majority of the angelic knowledges they take is how to break families. So, the satanic empire is very big on how to break relationships and break families.

وَاتَّبَعُوا مَا تَتْلُو الشَّيَاطِينُ عَلَى مُلْكِ سُلَيْمَانَ ۖ وَمَا كَفَرَ سُلَيْمَانُ وَلَٰكِنَّ الشَّيَاطِينَ كَفَرُوا يُعَلِّمُونَ النَّاسَ السِّحْرَ وَمَا أُنزِلَ عَلَى الْمَلَكَيْنِ بِبَابِلَ هَارُوتَ وَمَارُوتَ ۚ وَمَا يُعَلِّمَانِ مِنْ أَحَدٍ حَتَّىٰ يَقُولَا إِنَّمَا نَحْنُ فِتْنَةٌ فَلَا تَكْفُرْ ۖ فَيَتَعَلَّمُونَ مِنْهُمَا مَا يُفَرِّقُونَ بِهِ بَيْنَ الْمَرْءِ وَزَوْجِهِ ۚ وَمَا هُم بِضَارِّينَ بِهِ مِنْ أَحَدٍ إِلَّا بِإِذْنِ اللَّـهِ ۚ وَيَتَعَلَّمُونَ مَا يَضُرُّهُمْ وَلَا يَنفَعُهُمْ ۚ وَلَقَدْ عَلِمُوا لَمَنِ اشْتَرَاهُ مَا لَهُ فِي الْآخِرَةِ مِنْ خَلَاقٍ ۚ وَلَبِئْسَ مَا شَرَوْا بِهِ أَنفُسَهُمْ ۚ لَوْ كَانُوا يَعْلَمُونَ ﴿١٠٢﴾

*2:102 – "Wattaba'oo maa tatlush Shayaateenu 'alaa mulki
Sulaimaana, wa maa kafara Sulaimaanu wa laakinnash Shayatteena
kafaroo, yu'al limoonan naasas sihra wa maaa unzila 'alal malakayni bi
Baabila Haaroota wa Maaroot; wa maa yu'allimaani min ahadin hattaa
yaqoolaa, innamaa nahnu fitnatun falaa takfur; fayata'al lamoona
minhumaa maa yufarriqoona bihee baynal maryi wa zawjih; wa maa hum
bidaarreena bihee min ahadin illaa bi iznillah; wa yata'allamoona maa
yadhurruhum wa laa yanfa'uhum; wa laqad 'alimoo lamanish taraahu
maa lahu fil Aakhirati min khalaaq; wa labi'sa maa sharaw biheee
anfusahum; law kaanoo ya'lamoon." (Surat Al-Baqarah)*

*"And they followed [instead] what the devils had recited during the reign
of Solomon. It was not Solomon who disbelieved, but the devils
disbelieved, teaching people magic and that which was revealed/came down
to the two angels Harut and Marut, at Babylon. But the two angels do
not teach anyone unless they say, "We are a trial, so do not disbelieve [by
practicing magic]." And [yet] they learn from them that by which they
cause separation between a man and his wife. But they do not harm
anyone through it except by permission of Allah. And the people learn
what harms them and does not benefit them. But they certainly knew that
whoever purchased the magic would not have any share (in the happiness)
in the Hereafter. And wretched is that for which they sold themselves, if
they only knew." (The Cow, 2:102)*

### Are There Any Practices to Control Sudden Feelings of Anger?

The *zikrs* of *Ya Haleem*, keeping of *wudu* (ablution), keeping the *salawats* (praises upon Prophet Muhammad ﷺ), all of the practices, the *muraqabah* (spiritual connection), the meditation. Then we have a form letter just on asking about energy because the base and foundation of these practices is a strong adherence to what we understood of energy. So, we don't always have to repeat the same thing.

You have to make *wudu*, you have to make *Salatul Wudu* (Prayer of Ablution), you have to do your *zikr*, you have to do your *salawats*, you have to do the *muraqabah*. You have to understand the basics of how to keep your energy practices. If you're not doing any of that nothing is going to make any sense. So, when you keep the foundation strong that, 'I'm doing all of these, I'm doing all my *salawats*, I keep my *wudu*, I keep my energy practices. I'm meditating and asking how to connect to you.

Then I'm praying *Salatun Najat* (prayer of salvation), that take away my *ghadab* and my anger, *ya Rabbi*. I have an anger that I can't control.' Then *Salatun Najat* – you open the app, go to *Fajr* and go to *Salatun Najat;* click on it and say, 'Ya Rabbi

I'm going to specifically pray every night *Tahajjud* (late night prayer), *Salatun Najat* to take away my *ghadab*,' And in that *sujood* (prostration), is a long *sujood* say, 'Ya Rabbi I'm asking for forgiveness.' *"Tawbatan 'abdin zalimin li nafsihi, la yamliku li nafsihi mawtan wa la hayatan wa la nushura."*

تَوْبَةَ عَبْدٍ ظَالِمٍ لِنَفْسِهِ لاَ يَمْلِكُ لِنَفْسِهِ مَوْتًا وَ لاَ حَيَاةً وَلاَ نُشُورًا

*"Tawbatan 'abdin zalimin li nafsihi, la yamliku li nafsihi mawtan wa la hayatan wa la nushura."*

*"The repentance of a servant who has oppressed himself, who neither has power over his death, nor his life, nor his resurrection."*

We have a whole *du'a* (supplication) there – *Sultan at Tawbah, Sultan al Istighfar,* that asking in that *sujood* and that *sajda* (prostration) that, 'Ya Rabbi, I am asking please grant me a forgiveness; grant me the ability of this anger to be taken and take away my bad characteristics, *inshaAllah.*'

## How Can We Control Our Anger?

Again, the power of water and all the tools come together. That one, we took a path of silence. So, if you or we know that we have anger, put

lollipops in your pocket because it's just a matter of time before Allah's going to test it. As soon as you feel, 'Hmm, I got to say something' and you're about to say something, take your lollipop out, put it into your mouth. If you feel that you're becoming overwhelmed by the energy of anger, then again, go make

a *wudu* (ablution). Wash, pray your two cycles of *namaz, Salatul Wudu* (Prayer of Ablution), and ask that Allah seal your energy. Come out, *"Qulna ya Naaru, kuni Bardan wa Salaman 'ala Ibrahim."* 'Ya Rabbi, make the fire to be cool and peaceful.'

قُلْنَا يَا نَارُ كُونِي بَرْدًا وَسَلَامًا عَلَىٰ إِبْرَاهِيمَ ﴿٦٩﴾

*21:69 – "Qulna ya Naaru, kuni Bardan wa Salaman 'ala Ibrahim."* *(Surat Al-Anbiya)*

*"We said, O fire, be cool and Peaceful upon Abraham."* *(The Prophets, 21:69)*

And that the power of water and the understanding of how to put water on ourselves when the anger of *shaitan* (satan) is overwhelming us. And after your *namaz*, again, back with your lollipop in your mouth to control the mouth. The more that you make a conscious effort to control it and not say, 'Oh it came out again.' Yes, of course it's going to come out. Once it comes out, it's already finished, that test was lost. To keep it from coming is the importance and how to have the lollipop, how to recognize 'I'm not feeling well. I'm going to go wash.'

How to avoid certain confrontations when you know it's going to be confrontational and the person just wants to resolve the issue. It's not  so much, you know, trying to resolve the issue. You have to fear more your Lord. That, 'I don't know about your issue or resolving it, but I'm worried about my grave. And every time I'm going to deal with you, it's going to be combative. It doesn't resolve anything, and it makes Allah ﷻ angered.' So, people think that you have a tendency to run away. No, it's not run away. It's actually Prophet's ﷺ way. If something is incorrect and it's going to be satanic, Prophet ﷺ walks away.

If somebody's characteristics exhibit anger, they can't stay in the presence of *shaitan* because now *shaitan* is coming through that person's anger. They're not going to sit and start to talk and debate and discuss a situation because they know that they're not dealing with that person, they're dealing with a *shaitan*. So, you have to walk away from the *shaitan*. You just  walk away, and we'll resolve it another time when *shaitan* gives up and he walks away from you. But people insist that they want to resolve the issue. They want to talk. And say, 'No, no, that's not important. This is more about my place and my grave. If I keep failing this test, then Allah's ﷻ anger begin to dress upon the servant.'

## How Can We Control Our Bad Desires With All the Media Around?

We talked on that before many times that all these practices, all these *zikrs* (Divine remembrance), all these *salawats* (praises upon Prophet Muhammad ﷺ) are a fire against the *nafs* (ego). And why *zakah* (charity) and why giving is a cleansing? Because it has a deep reality in following

the *tariqah* (spiritual path), following the advice of the shaykh is give. That every time you give, you're taking away a sickness that's been put upon you through your *rizq* (sustenance). So why Allah ﷻ

asks for *zakah*? Because what you make has a burden in it. Who you made it from, what you did to make that? You're the number one credit card sales guy that all these people have credit cards that they don't need. There are burdens in everything. Everything that someone does is accountable for something to Allah ﷻ. So, He ﷻ knows that whatever we're going to do in life is making burdens.

So, the concept of *zakah* was what – is to clean it. It's like an infection that *insan* (mankind) can't see upon themselves. When the infections are

festering, and festering, and festering, they only see the bad characteristics. But what *awliyaullah* (saints) are supposed to see, the scabs. They see that all these difficulties that *shaitan* (satan) is putting upon the body of all these sicknesses

and all these things that are making the desire upon the person. So, every time they give, it's as if they went to the doctor and he cut the abscess. Right? Because if you have a big abscess you just say, 'I have a lot of pain

I can't move my leg.' But what the doctor sees, he sees an infection so if he cuts the abscess means he cuts all of the bacteria to come out. Only then can healing begin.

So then there's a tremendous reality in being of service. Your *zakah* can be your time, can be your ability, can be whatever Allah ﷻ has given to you. You put into that way to heal yourself, to participate. Anytime you do something wrong, punish yourself. That if you're continuously watching something you're not supposed to be watching, then say, 'Every time I watch it, I'm going to give fifty dollars to *Mawlid* (celebration of the birthday of Prophet ﷺ).' It makes something against your *nafs*. Before, Shaykhs punished themselves, but we don't want to talk like that because then people can, you know, inflict difficulty.

But there has to be a consequence in yourself otherwise it's a continuous line that you pass. So, say that, 'Every time I do something wrong that I didn't want to do, I'm going to pay a fine.' So that fine is not only something on your ego that, 'Oh  gosh we're going to empty our accounts like that.' But at the same time, it's an immense *barakah* (blessing) because you're giving in the way of Allah ﷻ. So, there's all sorts of ways that you can handle that. Anyone who wants to pray, drink a lot of water before you sleep so all night long you have to wash and make *wudu* (ablution). So then there's all systems in which to implement to achieve what we have to achieve.

## How Do We Stay Positive in Times of Uncertainty?

*InshaAllah*, not to be a party-pooper, things are not changing for good. Everything has a phase, and this *dunya* is in a death phase. And anything that is in a phase of dying, one reality is dying and a new is always opening. Our concept of death is not something understood by most people. Even a human when they die, they're actually being born. One phase is like going but that's not the end; something much more beatific is coming.

Same, we have given talks on the seed. You plant a seed, for the seed it's thinking, 'Why are you putting me in the ground? I'm going to die.' Because Allah ﷻ has a plan that a much more beautiful flower, tree that bears fruits and other flowers is going to be coming out. And the seed has to perish for the tree to appear and the flower and the rose to appear. So, everything has a phase. This *dunya* is in that phase, it's going down. And by guidance of Sayyidina Muhammad ﷺ, has warned us of all the difficulties, all the catastrophes, all the turmoils, all of the things that would be visiting upon this Earth. And *subhanAllah* with this, the events that have happened in the last three to four months, nobody could have imagined that without a single shot fired, one unseen has shut down all the doors of this *dunya* (material world).

You know they worship, when they say 'GOD,' and that they worship

God, it's not our Allah ﷻ. When they say 'GOD,' it stands for 'Gold, Oil, and Drugs. Gold, Oil, Drugs, GOD.' Gold, the source of all wealth. They took the gold and gave you worthless paper; if

416

you have you can blow your nose with it. It's not based on anything. Oil, was the spice, was the fuel for every factory and everything. How Allah ﷻ brought that oil now down to nothing, it's not a dollar a barrel. Because there's not a ship moving, not a factory turning on. Who wants all this oil? So, they're pumping it into the desert and throwing it into the sand. He brought that their entire desire and brought it all and crushed it down. And you're wondering if this is coming back? It's been dealt a death blow, 'Pow!'

And then drugs, those are the things they worship. Why? Because they send out the sickness to give you a remedy. They make people sick to make them, 'Oh, here's your remedy.' The biggest industries are the drugs and pharmaceuticals. This is what they worship when they say *dunya* and *mulk* (earthly realm) and 'In GOD, we trust.' No, it's gold, oil and drugs they trust. It's not in Allah ﷻ, and it's not in the Prophet of Sayyidina Muhammad ﷺ, but it's in, 'P-R-O-F-I-T.' *Shaitan* is playing. So, this *dunya* is in a difficult phase. As a result, make your connection.

Keep the way of *zikr*, keep the way of love, keep the way of *tazkiyah* and *tafakkur*. Because it's a way in which to contemplate and take an  account. Before Allah ﷻ sends something to decimate and destroy something, why don't you just take an account of yourself? '*Ya Rabbi*, let me clean myself before you send this calamity upon my hand. Let me make my *istighfar* (seeking forgiveness), let me make my *salawat* (praising), let me try to attend the *zikrs*, in which I will try to clean with Your blessings and Your *barakah* before You have to scrub me in a way that's not pleasant.'

So, we pray that Allah ﷻ inspire us to this way of *tazkiyah* which means cleaning. And this way of *tafakkur* and contemplation in which I can see that we're not going to be faultless, but we are going to have many faults.

But to be from the people who ask for Allah's ﷻ forgiveness, not that *shaitan* fool us and say, 'Oh you're so good you don't ever ask, you don't need to ever ask or God's forgiveness.' But our *wazifa* (spiritual practice) and our *awrad* (daily practices) is to

continuously ask everyday a thousand, 10,000, 20,000 times *istighfar*. *"Astaghfirullahal 'Azim Ya Rabbi, wa atubu ilayh."*

أَسْتَغْفِرُ الله الْعَظِيمِ وَأَتُوبُ إِلَيْهِ

*"Astaghfirullahal 'Azim, wa atubu ilayh."*

*"I ask forgiveness from Allah Almighty, and I turn to Him in repentance."*

Through Your *Sifat al-'Azim* (Attribute of the Magnificent), Your Might and Majesty, that nothing can compare to it; I'm begging your forgiveness. *InshaAllah.*

## What is the Best Way to Deal With Difficulties Knowing They Are Pre-ordained?

The best *adab* (manner) to deal with difficulties is telling ourselves that it's already been written. And that, '*Ya Rabbi*, did I make the right choices, and did I have the correct character?' And that because the person, if he's from or she's from *ahle tafakkur*, they're contemplating everything. Every time a test comes, they contemplate. 'Was this a result of bad character or was this a result of Allah ﷻ wanting to raise a *darajah* (spiritual rank)?' You know, you make a turn and you enter into a wrong neighbourhood, you're going to have a lot of difficulty. So, am I making the wrong choice and that difficulty coming?'

Then I still have to increase my *salawats*, increase my practices, control my anger, my bad characteristics, make and improve my *muraqabah* (meditation) so that my communication is coming correct. If I'm doing everything that I perceive to be good because everyone takes an account of themselves. That's why every night is a *muhasabah* (accounting). If a difficulty came and, 'Oh Shaykh, everything is good,' but you don't say about how you just fought last week, horrific fight. You yell and  scream at all sorts of things. Of course, then difficulty came your way. And we say, 'No, in my true and sincere understanding of myself, I pray that Allah ﷻ be happy with me. I tried my best. I did my *zikrs*. My occasional up and down, *inshaAllah*, no problem. But this then is just a test Allah ﷻ is sending for me to have *sabr* (patience). And in my *sabr* training was that I expected nothing and I was happy with everything.'

As soon as you expect people to call you at a specific time, people to do  for you a specific chore, a specific gift, a specific anything, that specificity is what *shaitan* (satan) is going to play. You expect that I was going to do this and I thought something would open from Allah ﷻ. I'm going to do this and something is going to open from this person. Take all, all of what we expect out of life. If we can destroy those expectations, we would be so happy with whatever comes. 'I don't expect a gift. I don't expect anything. Oh, *mashAllah* look something happened.' But as soon as you expect – we said before the kids would expect a gift and you would come with like, a book, they're going to beat you up. 'What's this? Baba, what happened? It wasn't supposed to be like that.'

And Allah ﷻ is saying, 'Do you see that character? How can I give you anything when you're expecting something maybe completely ridiculous to what I want to give you. And had I have given it to you, it would have caused you great harm.' Because don't ask that which will harm you.

يَا أَيُّهَا الَّذِينَ آمَنُوا لَا تَسْأَلُوا عَنْ أَشْيَاءَ إِن تُبْدَ لَكُمْ تَسُؤْكُمْ ... ﴿١٠١﴾

*5:101 – "Yaaa aiyuhal lazeena aamanoo laa tas'aloo 'an ashyaaa'a in tubda lakum tasu'kum…" (Surat Al-Maidah)*

*"O you who have believed, do not ask about things which, if they are shown to you, will distress you. …" (The Table Spread, 5:101)*

And most people asking excessively, too much that which would harm them, especially money. Most people, if they're granted money, it would definitely harm them. They would find  themselves not doing any *zikr* (Divine remembrance), any practices, and everything forbidden. So, then it means our life is about understanding not asking for anything, being happy with everything, living a life of *sabr* (patience) and Allah ﷻ knows best. And if we did do bad things and things Allah ﷻ not pleased with – harming other people, yelling and screaming, fighting, shouting – all of these, they have consequences.

And that's why then *istighfar* (seeking forgiveness). And that's why people who make *istighfar*, they make excessive amounts of *istighfar*. It's different than making *salawats* (praises upon Prophet Muhammad ﷺ). *Istighfar* is that you are asking Allah's ﷻ forgiveness. If a hammer is headed towards somebody, you have to make *istighfar*. It's a different *tajalli*, different reality. Because every time you make *istighfar*, you are asking, '*Ya Rabbi, Astaghfirullahul 'Azim* (I ask for forgiveness, O Magnificent). *Azimat al 'Azim*, by your *sifat al-'Azim*, I'm begging your forgiveness.' And the reply from Allah ﷻ, *inshaAllah*, "*Bismillahir Rahmanir Raheem*." That He dressed the servant with the secret of *Bismillahir Rahmanir Raheem*. That's a different dress upon the soul.

And when you're making *istighfar* for ourselves, then make *istighfar* for our children because they are not making *istighfar*. And you don't know what they do behind the closed doors or what they say with friends and what they do. So, we make *istighfar* for them especially if they are growing older. You don't even see your kids and what they're doing. So, you make *istighfar* for them and then how *awliya* were trained is

that they make so much *istighfar* that it's even for their community. '*Ya Rabbi*, forgive them for they know not what they do.' Sayyidina Isa عليه السلام kept asking. Allah ﷻ said 'I'm going to punish them. They made *sharik* (partner) and they called you Allah ﷻ. Did you say that to them?' How angry Allah ﷻ was. 'Did you tell them to say that?'

وَإِذْ قَالَ اللَّهُ يَا عِيسَى ابْنَ مَرْيَمَ أَأَنتَ قُلْتَ لِلنَّاسِ اتَّخِذُونِي وَأُمِّيَ إِلَـٰهَيْنِ مِن دُونِ اللَّهِ ۖ قَالَ سُبْحَانَكَ مَا يَكُونُ لِي أَنْ أَقُولَ مَا لَيْسَ لِي بِحَقٍّ ۚ إِن كُنتُ قُلْتُهُ فَقَدْ عَلِمْتَهُ ۚ تَعْلَمُ مَا فِي نَفْسِي وَلَا أَعْلَمُ مَا فِي نَفْسِكَ ۚ إِنَّكَ أَنتَ عَلَّامُ الْغُيُوبِ ﴿١١٦﴾

*5:116 – "Wa iz qaalal laahu yaa 'Eesa ibna Maryama a-anta qulta linnaasit takhizoonee wa ummiya ilaahayni min doonillaahi; Qaala Subhaanaka maa yakkoonu lee an aqoola maa laisa lee bihaqq; in kuntu qultuhu faqad 'alimtah; ta'lamu maa fee nafsee wa laa a'alamu maa fee nafsik; innaka Anta 'Allaamul Ghuyoob." (Surat Al-Maidah)*

*"And [beware the Day] when Allah will say, 'O Jesus, Son of Mary, did you say to the people, 'Take me and my mother as deities besides Allah?' He will say, 'Glory to You! Never could I say what I had no right (to say). If I had said it, You would have known it. You know what is within my myself, and I do not know what is in Yours. Indeed, it is You who is Knower of what's hidden.'" (The Table Spread, 5:116)*

'Ya Rabbi, astaghfirullah, you know when I was amongst them what I was saying. And now that I'm not with them, ya Rabbi, forgive them. They are Your creation. You want to destroy them, destroy. But they are Your creation, ya Rabbi, tawbah (repentance).'

إِن تُعَذِّبْهُمْ فَإِنَّهُمْ عِبَادُكَ ۖ وَإِن تَغْفِرْ لَهُمْ فَإِنَّكَ أَنتَ الْعَزِيزُ الْحَكِيمُ ﴿١١٨﴾

*5:118 – "In tu'azzibhum fa innahum 'ibaaduka, wa in taghfir lahum fa innaka Antal 'Azzizul Hakeem." (Surat Al-Maidah)*

*"If You should punish them – indeed they are Your servants; but if You forgive them - indeed it is You who is the Exalted in Might, the Wise." (The Table Spread, 5:118)*

So even Sayyidina Isa ﷺ was making *istighfar* for his nation. Prophet ﷺ making *istighfar* for their nation. And then this Muhammadan *haqqaiq* (reality) is teaching us, 'Make *istighfar*. Ask people's forgiveness. You have to ask for forgiveness for Allah ﷻ to grant that forgiveness.' And those whom are heedless – the biggest trick from *shaitan* is to inspire you not to make *tawbah*. 'Oh, you're so good, you're so great. Why you have to make *tawbah*?' Because he put a lock on it because that has its own *tajalli* (manifestation) and its own reality. When you ask for forgiveness, Allah ﷻ says, 'Ask me and I forgive you.' And for all our loved ones and all our community, and that's the cleaning, cleaning, cleaning.

$$\text{وَقَالَ رَبُّكُمُ ادْعُونِي أَسْتَجِبْ لَكُمْ ... ﴿٦٠﴾}$$

*40:60 – "Wa qaala Rabbukum ud 'ooni astajib lakum;..."*
*(Surat Al-Ghafir)*

*"And your Lord says, "Call upon Me, I Will Respond/Answer to your (prayer)..." (The Forgiver, 40:60)*

So, you don't put on your beatific dress when you're *najes* (unclean), right? You say, 'I have a beautiful suit.' You have *junub* and *najes* and say that, 'I'm going to go put that suit on.' No, so what do you do first? You shower, you clean. The shower was the *istighfar*, washing, washing, washing. Then you beautify yourself with *salawatun Nabi* ﷺ. That, I feel  ashamed to even ask Prophet ﷺ, I haven't made my *istighfar* yet. How am I going to bring the *ruhaniyat* (spirituality) of Prophet ﷺ when these sins are upon me, the sins of my children and loved ones are upon me, the sins of my community upon me?

I'm going to go with this dirtiness into the presence of Sayyidina Muhammad ﷺ, and throw that dirtiness upon Prophet's ﷺ reality? Or we sit and busy ourselves washing, cleaning, washing, cleaning, 'Ya Rabbi, I can't do no more, forgive me, *tawbatan 'abdin zalimin.'*

تَوْبَةَ عَبْدٍ ظَالِمٍ لِنَفْسِهِ لاَ يَمْلِكُ لِنَفْسِهِ مَوْتًا وَ لاَ حَيَاةً وَلاَ نُشُورًا

*"Tawbatan 'abdin zalimin li nafsihi, la yamliku li nafsihi mawtan wa la hayatan wa la nushura."*

*"The repentance of a servant who has oppressed himself, who neither has power over his death, nor his life, nor his resurrection."*

And that's why in the app in the Fajr, it's all the big *Sultan e Tawbah* (King of Repentance), the king *salawats*, and the king *istighfar* is why? To wash, everything clean and now I'm presentable to make my *salawats* on Sayyidina Muhammad ﷺ. With that *ihtiram* and that respect, *inshaAllah*, that light to dress our souls, bless our souls, so that the *ruhaniyat* of Prophet ﷺ stick to us, dress us, and bless us.

## How Do We Keep Our Faith Strong in the Last Days?

When we're trying to teach people to meditate and contemplate just so

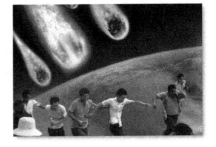

that we can get an understanding of the drop of the depth of that reality. So that we appreciate what guidance is and that we appreciate the ability to try to excel and improve ourselves. But in last days, because of the extent of testing and the immensity of difficulties upon the Earth, many people will be hit by a test and run away, run away. So, you'll begin to see many people leave and you begin to see many people, new people come.

Because as we begin to approach that reality, closer and closer, these are the difficulties of testing. One will be tested and will begin to lose completely their faith and leave. And we pray that Allah ﷻ save us from

that door. Others will be tested and completely gain their faith. And that's why the *hadith* of Prophet ﷺ, 'In last days, one will go to sleep with belief and wake up with disbelief.' He went to sleep as a believer, woke up as an unbeliever. What happened in that nighttime? 'And one who will sleep as a disbeliever wakes as a believer.'

عَنْ أَبِي هُرَيْرَةَ رَضِيَ اللهُ عَنْهُ، أَنَّ رَسُولَ اللهِ ﷺ قَالَ " بَادِرُوا بِالْأَعْمَالِ. فِتَنًا كَقِطَعِ اللَّيْلِ الْمُظْلِمِ. يُصْبِحُ الرَّجُلُ مُؤْمِنًا وَيُمْسِي كَافِرًا، وَيُمْسِي مُؤْمِنًا يُصْبِحُ كَافِرًا. يَبِيعُ أَحَدُهُمْ دِينَهُ بِعَرَضٍ مِنَ الدُّنْيَا. "
[ الْمَصْدَرْ: جَامِعُ اَلتِّرْمِذِي ٢١٩٥، كِتَابْ: ٣٣، حَدِيثْ: ٣٨ ]

*'An Abi Hurairah (ra), anna Rasulullahi ﷺ qala, "Baadiro bil a'maali fitanan kaqeta'yil laylil muzlimi yusbehur rajulu muminan wa yumsi kefiran, wa yumsi muminan yusbehu kafiran. Yabi'yu ahaduhum deenahu be'aradhin minad dunya."*
*[Jami' at-Tirmidhi 2190, Kitab 33, Hadith 38]*

*Abu Hurairah (ra) narrated that the Messenger of Allah (pbuh) said, "Rush to do good deeds. A fitnah will occur that is like a portion of the dark night. Morning will come upon a man as a believer, who will be a disbeliever in the evening, and evening will come upon a believer, who will be a disbeliever in the morning. One of them will sell his religion for goods of the world." [Jami' at-Tirmidhi 2190, Kitab 33, Hadith 38]*

*InshaAllah,* just keep us awake. Something's wrong in the sleep process, that's the scary part. But *alhamdulillah,* Allah ﷻ dress us, bless us and teach us more and more the understanding of light and the reality of light. And what's happening in the grave, *Hayat al Barzakh* (the Abode of the grave). They asked the other night, but which is an ocean of understanding on the realities of what's happening with this world of light. Why do we need to make this connection now? So, that this light and this perfection can be done in a wakeful state.

The separation of body and soul is not an easy process and if people are waiting for having that separation in the grave, that's what they call the

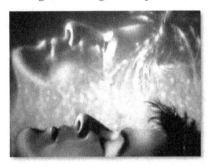

torment of the grave because the two friends are not separating. But if all your life, you took a path of being crushed and being tested and being tested and being tested, of course your body and soul have separated. As a result of that separation, you feel the emanations of the *zikr.* You feel the *barakah* and the blissfulness of the *zikr* (Divine remembrance) and becomes like a paradise garden for you, *inshaAllah.*

## How Can We Keep Balance in Life?

That it's very important to keep balance. I think we started tonight by saying that. The way is not based on hearing these things and say, 'Now I'm going to go run into a jungle.' And that would be easy and the principles that Mawlana Shah Naqshband ق left for us, *Khalwah dar Anjuman*. So, they're not happy with anyone who tries 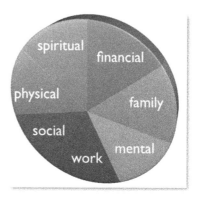 to retreat. You know we don't want to get phone calls from family members, wives, and parents that, 'Oh! Where is my husband, he's nowhere to be found? He doesn't want to go to work anymore. He wants to sit in a closet and just do his *zikr*.' That's cheating; that's not Naqshbandi.

Naqshbandi wants your *dunya* to be very busy, very complicated life, children, family; everything all around you and confusion but you have to find your solitude. You have to find your peace within your heart. If you're isolating, you're doing it wrong. If you're trying to avoid everyone, you're doing it wrong! You're trying to cheat and that's not what they want. Cheating – anybody can do that. Go sit in a bush and then hide yourself from all of creation. But to be in the crowd and to be amongst people and train yourself on how to lock out and go into your heart. People talk, but you're not there. That you're keeping your connection with the shaykh, you're keeping your connection with your *zikr*, with your *salawat* (praises upon Prophet Muhammad ﷺ). That brings the reward of Allah ﷻ and that's what Allah ﷻ wanted from Naqshbandi *awliya* (saints), that they're amongst people. They're not hidden in the mountains of Pakistan, that was a different group.

These *awliya*, they're under the order to be amongst people everywhere and the *tajalli* (manifestation) that they receive is very strong because of that. If you hide, they give you ten watts, because you're hiding, you're not benefiting anyone. You get your ten watts of power. But if you go into the city where you're a *shifa* and a healing, you are a *barakah* and a blessing for everywhere you go, they give you 10 million watts because the wattage has to be a lot more for

the amount of people that are all around. So, it means the more difficult, the more reward. When you try to make something simple, that's not what Mawlana Shah Naqshband ق wanted for us. So, it means that we keep amongst people. We work hard. We do everything that we can and we do our *zikr* and our contemplation. We struggle to keep the connection and to attend the *zikr*, *inshaAllah*.

## How Do We Balance Our Worldly and Spiritual Life?

Well, it just got a lot simpler because Allah's ﷻ making you stay home. That's why we said, *'Ya musabbibal asbab* (O Originator of causes!).' Nobody was believing. You know that the viewership goes up, the belief goes up, the practices all go up because Allah ﷻ started a marketing campaign. It's very difficult to get people to believe and do their practices when McDonald's is open and the blue beautiful skies. But as soon as *'azaab* (infliction) starts to fly and come down, this one bug from the heavens entered this atmosphere and then what happened? *"Zahoqa."*

وَ قُلْ جَاءَالْحَقُّ وَزَهَقَ الْبَطِلُ، إِنَّ الْبَطِلَ كَانَ زَهُوقًا ﴿٨١﴾

*17:81 – "Wa qul jaa alhaqqu wa zahaqal baatil, innal batila kana zahoqa." (Surat Al-Isra)*

*"And say, Truth has come, and falsehood has perished. Indeed falsehood, [by its nature], is ever perishing/bound to perish."*
*(The Night Journey, 17:81)*

Every falsehood now is 'kssh, kssh,' shaking from one unseen. From one

unseen has begun to collapse every falsehood. The stock markets are collapsing. How? Who, who saw what? Businesses are collapsing. Every type of industry collapsing. Mighty nations with trillions of dollars of warfare and machinery, it goes down. How? Who's doing that? The only One who can bring it with not a single drop of warfare.

It's just a bug that nobody could see that entered into this *dunya* (material world). So, it means everybody is now motivated. Sit at home. You have no work to do. Start doing your *awrads* (daily practices), start doing your prayers. And think that every type of difficulty is coming to you and are you reciting? Are you believing? Are you good with Allah ﷻ? And try to push away any type of negativity from yourself, from your home and from your family, *inshaAllah*.

Do the *madad* and it play inside your home. If you think these viruses are going to be moving into the home and attacking into the home, play within the home the *zikr* (Divine remembrance). Watch the teachings. It's all on YouTube. Do the live *zikr* within the home. Make the home a *masjid* and the *masjid* to be filled with spiritual beings. This was always the *tariqah* (spiritual path) teaching. If you make your home a *masjid*, adorn it. Make it to be perfected, make it to be beautiful. *Awliyaullah* (saints) will send other spiritual beings to pray there. Then it becomes like a *maqam* because the people who love that shaykh, they are coming by and passing by and praying there.

The *jinn* (unseen beings) are praying there, *malaika* (angels) are praying there; *Budala, Nujaba, Nuqab, Awtad wal Akhyar* are all praying there when they're passing in that region because you made it to be beatific for them. You made it to be fragranced for them. No doubt, can you imagine if you pass a *maqam* and you don't pray there? No! They rather pray there versus somewhere that doesn't have that belief. So, when they make that belief, Allah 🕮 send. That house becomes like a *maqam* for them and many spiritual beings will be there.

## What is the Realm of Barzakh and the Realm of Malakut?

That requires a whole show, *inshaAllah*. *Alhamdulillah*, the teaching is all about *malakut*, the world of light, and to reach towards that world of

light in this life. How to be dressed from the world of light and how to take the understanding from *malakut* and not the *mulk* (earthly realm). Not the physical realm for every understanding but the realm of light and what's the importance of the world of light. One

understanding is it's timeless, there is no time; light has no time – it's constant. So then anything from the world of light is timeless. So that then has a huge understanding for us.

The *barzakh* (purgatory) and what happens within the grave is our whole preparation of *tariqah* (spiritual path). That, what do you want to do with your light? Do you want to build it now or you want to build it in the grave? Where then becomes the separation of *mulk* and *malakut*. Because as soon as you enter the grave, your physicality – ashes to ashes, dust to dust – your physicality is going to go away. And your spirituality, your soul has to

separate. That process of separating can be very painful for people.

Or if you took a path in which all your life you practiced that separation. You were able to separate from your physicality, by your meditation, contemplation and by asking Allah ﷻ you're able to move your spirituality out of your physicality, so then why would the grave be difficult for you if you achieved that in physicality? But if you're locked and you never practiced that, can you imagine then the difficulty of trying to separate these two realities. And that's what becomes the difficulty of *barzakh*. And everything has to be in the grave, the service has to be in the grave and

many different realities they taught from the world of light, *inshaAllah*.

## Can We Speak on Political Matters Through Social Media?

Right now is a dangerous time. This social media is not designed for you

to spread a message of politics and injustice because then you're saying you're trying to change it to 'A time of justice.' When Allah ﷻ has already told through Sayyidina Muhammad ﷺ, 'In the last days there would be injustice everywhere.' And Sayyidina Mahdi ؏ wouldn't appear until the Earth was filled with injustice.

عَنْ أَبِي سَعِيدٍ اَلْخُدْرِيِّ رَضِيَ اللَّهُ عَنْهُ : قَالَ رَسُولُ اللَّهِ صَلَّى اللَّهُ عَلَيْهِ وَآلِهِ وَسَلَّمَ :
" لَا تَقُومُ السَّاعَةُ حَتَّى تَمْلَأَ اَلْأَرْضَ ظُلْمًا وَجَوْرًا وَعُدْوَانًا. ثُمَّ يَخْرُجُ مِنْ أَهْلِ بَيْتِي
مِنْ يَمْلَؤُهَا قِسْطًا وَعَدْلًا كَمَا مُلِئَتْ ظُلْمًا وَعُدْوَانًا.
[ اَلْمَصْدَرْ: اَلْأَلْبَانِي (سلسلة الأحاديث الصحيحة) ٧١١ ]

*'An Abi Sa'yid Al Khudriyi (ra), qala Rasulullahi (Sallallahu 'Alayhi wa Aalihi wa Sallam), "La taqoomos sa'atu hatta tamla al arda zhulman wa jawran wa 'odwanan.*

*Thumma yakhrojo min Ahli Bayti min yamlaoo haa qistan wa 'adlan kama mule'at zhulman wa 'odwanaa."*
*[Almasdar: Al Albani (Sisilatal Ahadithi As Sahihah) 711]*

*Narrated Abi Sa'yid Al Khudriyi (ra), that the Holy Prophet (peace and blessings be upon him and his holy family) said, "The Hour will not be established until this world will be filled with oppression, and injustice and enmity. Then a person will reappear from my progeny who will fill it with equality and justice as it would be filled with injustice and tyranny."*
*[Source: Al Albani (Chain of Authentic Hadith) 711]*

Injustice (is) 'Just Us' – you are not included in their 'Just Us' group. It means in social media is to bring out your name, who you are and what do you think. For those 'Just Us' people they begin to come after you.

That 'Hey, he's not just with us. He's exposing himself.' So those who know this is a destined time, Allah ﷻ has already destined this time. And these events are coming and we are going to see Sayyidina Mahdi ﷺ. So why do you want to go out and say anything. You thought you were going to change it? Or you'll just let people know you're aware of it? Well, we are aware of it too. Don't have to say anything. But more important, build your connection with Sayyidina Muhammad ﷺ and let Prophet ﷺ teach us about the injustice of ourselves! That when Allah ﷻ said, 'Verily they are an oppressor to themselves.

إِنَّ اللَّـهَ لَا يَظْلِمُ النَّاسَ شَيْئًا وَلَـٰكِنَّ النَّاسَ أَنفُسَهُمْ يَظْلِمُونَ ﴿٤٤﴾

*10:44 – "Innal laaha laa yazlimun naasa shai'anw wa laakin nannaasa anfusahum yazlimoon" (Surat Yunus)*

*"Indeed, Allah does not wrong the people at all, but it is the people who are oppressor to themselves/their soul." (Jonah, 10:44)*

Why are you worried they suffocated this poor man on the street when every day we suffocate our soul and suffocate ourselves from the reality that Allah 'ﷻ wanted from us. We talked about that when the soul is called the she-camel. *Naqatullah*, the analogy of *Naqatullah* is that the soul is Allah's 'ﷻ Divinely lights and reality that He sent upon the human being. It's not from an ocean that we feel; Allah 'ﷻ made that to be *Al Hayyul Qayyum* (The Ever-Living and Self-Sustaining).

وَإِلَىٰ ثَمُودَ أَخَاهُمْ صَالِحًا ۗ قَالَ يَا قَوْمِ اعْبُدُوا اللَّهَ مَا لَكُم مِّنْ إِلَٰهٍ غَيْرُهُ ۖ قَدْ جَاءَتْكُم بَيِّنَةٌ مِّن رَّبِّكُمْ ۖ هَٰذِهِ نَاقَةُ اللَّهِ لَكُمْ آيَةً ۖ فَذَرُوهَا تَأْكُلْ فِي أَرْضِ اللَّهِ ۖ وَلَا تَمَسُّوهَا بِسُوءٍ فَيَأْخُذَكُمْ عَذَابٌ أَلِيمٌ ﴿٧٣﴾

*7:73 – "Wa ila thamooda akhahum Salihan. Qala: ya qawmi 'abudo Allaha malakum min ilahin ghayruhu. Qad ja atkum bayyinatunn mir Rabbikum, Hadhihi Naqatullahi lakum ayatan. Fadharoha takul fee ardi Allahi, wa la tamassoha biso in, faya khudhakum 'adhabun aleem." (Surah Al A'raf)*

*"And to the Thamud [We sent] their own brother Salih. He said, "O my people, worship Allah; you have no deity other than Him. There has come to you clear evidence from your Lord. This is the she-camel of Allah is a sign for you. So leave her to eat within Allah's earth/land, and do not touch her with harm, or you shall be seized with a painful punishment." (The Heights, 7:73)*

Allah ﷻ said, 'I sent it upon and you don't let her to drink from My realities; it means you don't give her *zikrullah* (remembrance of Allah), you don't give her your *tafakkur* (contemplation), you don't give her from your lights and realities of the heavens.' Allah ﷻ is going to say, 'You put your foot on her neck, and

that you hamstrung her and punished her.' And that's why Allah ﷻ makes reference that, 'They are oppressors to themselves.'

It means it's a warning, 'You're responsible for what I gave you.' It is not your life to live and destroy. It's not your life to tattoo your body and mark up your being. It's nothing of yours. Everything was a trust for us. The body is a trust that I have to keep it clean, conditioned, in proper order, and it goes back to the dirt. That Allah ﷻ gave my soul, I had to nourish it and teach it of its Lord, feed it from these oceans of Divine reality.

And those who wish to harm themselves, and think maybe they can check out from the world, they will be in a perpetual difficulty. We said before if you jump, every moment, Allah ﷻ will give you the pain and the anguish of what you felt. You'll feel the entire jump, you smash into

the ground, and Allah ﷻ will instantly bring you back. And you'll keep perpetually doing that action that was displeasing. With all of its pain, at 150% of your senses, because now you're numb to who your real senses are. Nobody escapes what Allah ﷻ wants. And *shaitan* (satan) just wants to punish you more and says, 'Go do something.' And those whom have a spiritual vision they'll go somewhere, especially these bridges where everybody jumps. And they see these people jumping all the time, all the time. Because of what they did, they put a glitch into a program.

As a result, Allah ﷻ looped it. They didn't get to the next scene, Allah ﷻ just put a loop in their program and now they are always jumping. And they get their form back, they go there, they jump, and they feel all the pain, all the misery of what they are doing. So, it's horrific. If you thought you know your day was bad, imagine living that day for all of eternity. So, it's not an option for anyone. And anyone who doesn't know.

And at the same time, we don't burn our bodies, and put them in the grave! 'Oh, I just want to burn myself because I don't want my family to pay for it.' Let them pay! Who cares? 'Put all your inheritance, you first

bury myself, if you have no money left, I don't care.' Because people say, 'No, I don't want to spend any money, let them burn me.' No, no, as soon as the fire begins, you'll feel everything five hundred percent. Because now your *nafs* (ego) is out of the way, your soul is in full attention. Soon as you begin the burning process, that person will feel every bit of that fire. And again *shaitan* came and played with them, to fool them – how much he hates *insan* (mankind) that, 'If I couldn't get you and destroy you on this Earth, on your departing I will make sure that you're tormented and tortured through that difficulty.'

So, it means that we pray Allah ﷻ guide us continuously in this way of *muhabbat* (love). And whom Allah ﷻ guides to guidance is not something small. That, 'Okay I see, not see, maybe I go see shaykh.' No, the actual reality of these shaykhs is beyond imagination for the living people. They are the ones who continuously make your case in Divinely Presence. They are the lawyers who represent you

continuously in the presence of Sayyidina Muhammad ﷺ. And their most powerful action is on your last breath.

Those who die without a *wakeel* (representative), *shaitan* will be present right there with them tormenting them on their last breath, giving them the anguish of thirst in which they are dying from thirst. And *shaitan* will come to them and say, 'I will give you something to drink that takes away this pain of thirst, I want you to denounce Sayyidina Muhammad ﷺ,' and take away their faith. And many have stories that on the death bed the death person would start to say horrific things. Things that were not in their Islamic belief because *shaitan* had come to them.

So, it means a *wakeel*, its most powerful time is in the time of death. When they appear by the permission of Allah ﷻ and Sayyidina Muhammad ﷺ, and they begin to do what Allah ﷻ has destined for them to do.

That, 'Not to talk, don't say anything.' That they are representing that person in Divinely Presence. We pray that Allah ﷻ keep us under their *nazar* (gaze), *awliyaullah* (saints) *fis samayi wa fil ard* (in the heavens and on earth), *inshaAllah*.

**Should We Stop Working During Covid-19?**

Everybody's advised to do what they have to do according to their *rizq*, their sustenance, what is required of them. If they feel they can work and they have to work, then go to work. If you feel you have the ability to not work and stay home, then not work and stay home.

**Do the Events of Covid-19 Relate to Any of the Realities of Lataif al Qalb?**

Yes, the war. That the station of the knowledge is all opening. That the knowledge and the sin of mankind, that both are opening. That for the *qalb* (heart) to open was under the authority of Sayyidina Adam ﷺ, that to understand that you've sinned, '*Ya Hamid bi Haqqi Muhammad.*' The *du'a* (supplication) of Sayyidina Adam ﷺ was not accepted until he praised the praise upon Sayyidina Muhammad ﷺ.

Qalb (Heart)
Adam (as)
Angel Jibreel/Gabriel
Hz. Uthman

At that time Allah ﷻ gave permission, 'Now make your *du'a*.' "*Ya Hamidu bi Haqqi Muhammad* ﷺ, *Ya 'Aliyu be Haqqi 'Ali* ﷺ, *Ya Khaliqu bi Haqqi Fatimatuz Zahra* ﷺ, *Ya Rahmanu bi Haqqi Hassan* ﷺ, *Ya Raheemu bi Haqqi Hussain* ﷺ.*"

بِسْمِ اللهِ الرَّحْمَنِ الرَّحِيمِ

يَا حَمِيدُ بِحَقِّ مُحَمَّدٍ ﷺ، يَا عَلِيُّ بِحَقِّ عَلِي (عَلَيْهِ السَّلَامْ)، يَا خَالِقُ بِحَقِّ فَاطِمَةُ الزَّهْرَاءِ (عَلَيْهِ السَّلَامْ)، يَا رَحْمَنُ بِحَقِّ حَسَنْ (عَلَيْهِ السَّلَامْ) ، يَا رَحِيمُ بِحَقِّ حُسَّيْنِ (عَلَيْهِ السَّلَامْ)

*"Bismillahir Rahmanir Raheem*

*Ya Hamidu bi Haqqi Muhammad* ﷺ, *Ya 'Aliyu be Haqqi 'Ali (as),*
*Ya Khaliqu bi Haqqi Fatimatuz Zahra (as), Ya Rahmanu bi Haqqi*
*Hassan (as), Ya Raheemu bi Haqqi Hussain (as)."*

"In the name of Allah, the Most
Compassionate, the Most Merciful

O' the Praiseworthy for the sake
of Prophet Muhammad (pbuh), O'
the Most High for the sake of
Imam 'Ali (as), O' the Creator
for the sake of Fatima Zahra (as),
O the Most Compassionate for the
sake of Imam Hassan (as), O' the
Most Merciful for the sake of
Imam Hussain (as)."

And Allah ﷻ say, 'Where you learned these?' Said, 'I was taught them in
paradises.' Said, 'Had you asked anything by these names, I will grant it
to you.' So, it means this is the station of the *qalb* to understand that key
and that light, and that reality of Sayyidina Adam ﷺ. That Allah's ﷻ
kingdom, the *qalb*, is the house of Allah ﷻ. It's the kingdom of Allah ﷻ.
It's not a *lataif* (subtle energy points). The *lataif* is just words they're
using because Allah's ﷻ saying, 'I'm not in heaven, not on Earth but I'm
in the heart of my believer.'

مَا وَسِعَنِيْ لَا سَمَائِيْ ولا اَرْضِيْ وَلَكِنْ وَسِعَنِيْ قَلْبِ عَبْدِيْ الْمُؤْمِنْ

"Maa wasi'anee laa Samayee, wa la ardee, laakin wasi'anee qalbi
'Abdee al Mu'min."

"Neither My Heavens nor My Earth can contain Me, but the heart of my
Believing Servant."
(Hadith Qudsi conveyed by Prophet Muhammad (pbuh))

So, what you're actually opening is the kingdom of Allah ﷻ. The kingdom of Allah ﷻ is on the heart of the believer. And Allah's ﷻ kingdom is coming down. As it is on heaven so shall it be on Earth. So, then that *lataif al qalb* begins to open. This difficulty and this hardship is now the test of Sayyidina Nuh عليه السلام, which is the *sir* (secret). That we all have to be tested with our faith.

This means the difficulty comes and we talked from that of Sayyidina Nuh عليه السلام. And that was the analogy, that every test we did and how much *shaitan* (satan) came against us for trying to build our soul. And now Allah ﷻ make everybody flooded in difficulty. Everybody is in a difficulty and their only salvation is through the realization of Islam. They accept it, they don't accept it. They're learning how to wash. They are learning how to make their *wudu* (ablution). They're learning how to cover. They're learning how to stay home. Don't fornicate, don't dance, don't do all of these things that bring about social mixing and bad actions and bad character.

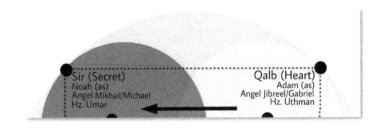

So, it is the *qalb* and the *sir* opening onto Earth. Why? Because the *sirr e sir* (secret of the secret) is going to be dressing. The kingdom of light is coming, right? How can the kingdom of light come if you didn't pass the first two? That the knowledges and the understanding of the Muhammadan reality is the first door into that heart and the Kingdom of Allah ﷻ. Then the fight and the struggle against oneself and that everything has to be brought down and now you enter into – actually, the *akhfa* (most hidden) is before because the black is the centre where everything is annihilated before the kingdom of light arrives.

## How Can We Prepare for the Coming of Sayyidina Mahdi ☝?

Good character. That's what we said in previous talks that Sayyidina Mahdi ☝ is coming to bring *muhabbat* and love. Every type of bad character is going to be taken away from this Earth. Every type of bad character that Allah ☝ is not pleased with will be taken through all of Allah's ☝ Divine anger that's now dressing the Earth. That anger is directed towards every type of badness and that will perish. And that is false and all falsehood perishes.

وَ قُلْ جَاءَالْحَقُّ وَزَهَقَ الْبَطِلُ، إِنَّ الْبَطِلَ كَانَ زَهُوقًا ﴿٨١﴾

*17:81 – "Wa qul jaa alhaqqu wa zahaqal baatil, innal batila kana zahoqa." (Surat Al-Isra)*

*"And say, Truth has come, and falsehood has perished. Indeed falsehood, [by its nature], is ever perishing/bound to perish."*
*(The Night Journey, 17:81)*

Those whom represent Sayyidina Mahdi ☝, their mission was to spread good character because that would be the attraction of hearts. When you teach people to have good character, good understanding, don't enter into arguments. Don't break the heart of someone for it should anger Allah ☝. Have a *muhabbat* and love, love for Allah ☝, love for Sayyidina Muhammad ﷺ, a fellowship, a brotherhood and sisterhood in which you come together. And there's no gossiping, backbiting, but learning how to have the prophetic character within our lives.

All of that was for the training of Sayyidina Mahdi ؏. That they would be people of *muhabbat* and love, and Allah's ﷻ *ni'mat* would dress them and bless them. And only the blessed can be in the reality and enter into that reality. Not the angry people, they'll burn. Not the greedy people, not the arrogant people – these are all the characteristics that leave the Earth. We pray that Allah ﷻ increase our *muhabbat* and love and good character, *inshaAllah*.

## How Do We Know Our State of Account With Allah ﷻ?

How much do you love Allah ﷻ? And how much do you love Prophet ﷺ? As much as you love them, and you love with good character and good actions. Again, we've talked on other times with some people you meet and they say, 'Yeah, I love God.' Then why are you so mean and rotten? So, how can somebody claim to love the Divine but have a rotten heart, with rotten actions, harsh words? So, it's a whole package.

When I know that I'm trying my best to be good, to be polite at times, to correct myself when I'm being aggressive, and I have an immense love, I have an immense love for Allah ﷻ a love for Prophet ﷺ and trying my best to be sincere. Then you must know that this love that's in your heart is a gift from Allah ﷻ. You didn't get it. You didn't get it by you going outside and ploughing the garden. Allah ﷻ gave you a *ni'mat* (blessing) and a gift. That is the result of this good character.

So, when we have good character, and we have this love and this compassion, it's Allah ﷻ saying, 'This is My gift to you.' That's when we talked before – when a sincere person cries, Allah ﷻ is in the tear. Allah ﷻ is in every emotion of His beloved servant. He's the cause for them to have emotion. He is the cause for them to be happy and to be sad. And if they love, the greatest gift is this love; not lust, but love. When

they have a true compassion and a love for the Divine, then this is an immense gift from Allah ﷻ. That's why we said, 'Reduce everything to energy.' If somebody doesn't have love, doesn't have good energy but they say they're making their *salah* (prayer), it's of no value. You wasted your life. What's the purpose of your praying and you're rotten? Who are you praying for? Allah ﷻ didn't need your prayers. You needed your prayers!

So, these people were focusing on just *'amal, 'amal, 'amal* (actions). But they never talk, 'Is your heart good or is it rotten?' If your heart is dead, then it's a dead man praying. Do the dead prayers count? No, it's *najes* too, it's dirty. Because dead is not something that goes and prays. So, it means the heart has to be alive and the sun has to be alive. When they're alive with good and loving heart, everything they do is blessed and dear to Allah ﷻ, *inshaAllah*. And Allah's ﷻ gift is love.

# Resources

## Daily Awrad (Practice)

## Bayah
## (Pledge of Allegiance to
## The Naqshbandi Way)

AWRAD

# Daily Awrad (Practice)
# of Naqshbandi Tariqah

**1. 3X Shahada** (Testimony of Faith)
Raise right hand's index finger and recite.

أَشْهَدُ أَنْ لَا إِلَهَ إِلاَّ الله وَأَشْهَدُ أَنَّ مُحَمَّدًا عَبْدُهُ وَرَسُولُهُ

*Ashhadu an la ilaha illallah, wa ashhadu anna Muhammadan 'abduhu wa Rasulu.*

*I bear witness that there is no god but Allah and Muhammad ﷺ is His servant and Messenger.*

**2. 70X Astaghfirullah**

أَسْتَغْفِرُ الله

*I seek Forgiveness from Allah.*

**3. Surat al Fatiha** (1ˢᵗ Chapter of Holy Qur'an)
(With intention of being dressed with the manifestations and blessings that were sent down with this surah when it was revealed in Makkah)

بِسْمِ اللَّهِ الرَّحْمَنِ الرَّحِيمِ ﴿١﴾ الْحَمْدُ لِلَّهِ رَبِّ الْعَالَمِينَ ﴿٢﴾ الرَّحْمَنِ الرَّحِيمِ ﴿٣﴾ مَالِكِ يَوْمِ الدِّينِ ﴿٤﴾ إِيَّاكَ نَعْبُدُ وَإِيَّاكَ نَسْتَعِينُ ﴿٥﴾ اهْدِنَا الصِّرَاطَ الْمُسْتَقِيمَ ﴿٦﴾ صِرَاطَ الَّذِينَ أَنْعَمْتَ عَلَيْهِمْ غَيْرِ الْمَغْضُوبِ عَلَيْهِمْ وَلَا الضَّالِّينَ ﴿٧﴾

447

*Bismillahir Rahmanir Raheem. Alhamdulillahi rabbil 'alameen. Ar Rahmanir Raheem. Maliki yawmid deen. Iyyaka na'budu wa iyyaka nasta'een. Ihdinas siratal mustaqeem. Siratal lazeena an'amta 'alayhim, ghayril maghdoobi 'alayhim walad dalleen. (Surat al Fatiha)*

*In the name of Allah, the Most Compassionate, the Most Merciful. (1) Praise be to Allah, Lord of the worlds. (2) The Most Gracious, Most Merciful. (3) The Sovereign King of the Day of Judgement. (4) It is You we worship and You we ask for help. (5) Guide us to the Straight path. (6) The path of those on whom you have bestowed your favor/blessing, not of those who have evoked (Your) anger or of those who go astray. (7) (The Opener)*

## 4. **Amana ar Rasul** (Holy Qur'an, Surat al Baqarah, 2:285-286)

آمَنَ الرَّسُولُ بِمَا أُنزِلَ إِلَيْهِ مِن رَّبِّهِ وَالْمُؤْمِنُونَ ۚ كُلٌّ آمَنَ بِاللَّهِ وَمَلَائِكَتِهِ وَكُتُبِهِ وَرُسُلِهِ لَا نُفَرِّقُ بَيْنَ أَحَدٍ مِّن رُّسُلِهِ ۚ وَقَالُوا سَمِعْنَا وَأَطَعْنَا ۖ غُفْرَانَكَ رَبَّنَا وَإِلَيْكَ الْمَصِيرُ ﴿٢٨٥﴾ لَا يُكَلِّفُ اللَّهُ نَفْسًا إِلَّا وُسْعَهَا ۚ لَهَا مَا كَسَبَتْ وَعَلَيْهَا مَا اكْتَسَبَتْ ۗ رَبَّنَا لَا تُؤَاخِذْنَا إِن نَّسِينَا أَوْ أَخْطَأْنَا ۚ رَبَّنَا وَلَا تَحْمِلْ عَلَيْنَا إِصْرًا كَمَا حَمَلْتَهُ عَلَى الَّذِينَ مِن قَبْلِنَا ۚ رَبَّنَا وَلَا تُحَمِّلْنَا مَا لَا طَاقَةَ لَنَا بِهِ ۖ وَاعْفُ عَنَّا وَاغْفِرْ لَنَا وَارْحَمْنَا ۚ أَنتَ مَوْلَانَا فَانصُرْنَا عَلَى الْقَوْمِ الْكَافِرِينَ ﴿٢٨٦﴾

*Amanar Rasulu bima unzila ilayhi min rabbihi wal muminona, kullun amana billahi, wa malaikatihi, wa kutubihi, wa rusulihi, la nufarriqu bayna ahadin mir rusulihi, wa qalu sami'na wa a'tana ghufranaka Rabbana wa ilayka almaseer. La yukallifullahu nafsan illa wus'aha, laha ma kasabat wa alayha maktasabat, Rabbana la tuakhidhna in naseena aw akhtana, Rabbana wa la tahmil alayna isran kama hamaltahu alal ladheena min qablina, Rabbana wa la tuhammilna ma la taqata lana bihi, wa'afu anna, waghfir lana, warhamna, anta mawlana fansurna alal qawmil kafireen. (Surat al Baqarah, 2:285-286)*

*The Messenger has believed in what was revealed to him from his Lord, and [so have] the believers. All of them have believed in Allah and His angels and His books and His messengers, [saying], "We make no* distinction between any of His messengers." And they say, "We hear and we obey. [We seek] Your forgiveness, our Lord, and to You is the [final] destination." (2:285) Allah Doesn't place a burden on a soul/body greater than it can bear. It gets every reward that it has earned, and it suffers for every ill/evil that it has earns. (Pray:) "Our Lord! Do not punish us if we forget or fall into error; our Lord! and Lay not on us a burden Like that which you laid on those before us; Our Lord! and Lay not on us a burden greater than we have strength to bear. And pardon us, and forgive all our sins, and have mercy on us. You are our master and Protector; Give us victory over those who stand against faith [the unbelievers within]." (The Cow, 2:285-286)

## 5. 7X Surat ash Sharh (94th Chapter of Holy Qur'an)

بِسْمِ اللَّهِ الرَّحْمَنِ الرَّحِيمِ
أَلَمْ نَشْرَحْ لَكَ صَدْرَكَ ﴿١﴾ وَوَضَعْنَا عَنكَ وِزْرَكَ ﴿٢﴾ الَّذِي أَنقَضَ ظَهْرَكَ ﴿٣﴾
وَرَفَعْنَا لَكَ ذِكْرَكَ ﴿٤﴾ فَإِنَّ مَعَ الْعُسْرِ يُسْرًا ﴿٥﴾ إِنَّ مَعَ الْعُسْرِ يُسْرًا ﴿٦﴾ فَإِذَا
فَرَغْتَ فَانصَبْ ﴿٧﴾ وَإِلَى رَبِّكَ فَارْغَب ﴿٨﴾

*Bismillahir Rahmanir Raheem*
*Alam nashrah laka sadrak. Wa wada'na 'anka wizrak. Alladhee anqada zhahrak. Wa rafa'na laka zikrak. Fa inna ma'al 'usri yusran, Inna ma'al 'usri yusra. Fa idha faraghta fainsab. Wa ila rabbika farghab. (Surat ash Sharh)*

Did We not expand for you, [O Muhammad ﷺ], your Chest? (1) And We removed from you your burden. (2) Which had weighed upon your back. (3) And We raised high your Zikr (remembrance). (4) For indeed, with every difficulty, there is relief. (5) Indeed, with every hardship is ease. (6) So when you are free and have finished [your duties], then stand up [for worship]. (7) And to your Lord turn all your attention/invocation/longing. (8) (The Relief)

449

## 6. 11X Surat al Ikhlas (112<sup>th</sup> Chapter of Holy Qur'an)

بِسْمِ اللَّهِ الرَّحْمَٰنِ الرَّحِيمِ

قُلْ هُوَ اللَّهُ أَحَدٌ ﴿١﴾ اللَّهُ الصَّمَدُ ﴿٢﴾ لَمْ يَلِدْ وَلَمْ يُولَدْ ﴿٣﴾ وَلَمْ يَكُن لَّهُ كُفُوًا أَحَدٌ ﴿٤﴾

*Bismillahir Rahmanir Raheem*
*Qul Huwa Allahu Ahad. (1) Allahus Samad. (2) Lam yalid wa lam
yolad. (3) Wa lam yakul lahu, kufuwan Ahad. (4) (Surat al Ikhlas)*

*Say, "He is Allah, [who is] One. (1) Allah, the Eternal
Absolute/Refuge.(2) He neither begets nor is born. Nor there is none like
unto Him." (3) (The Sincerity)*

## 7. Surat al Falaq (113<sup>th</sup> Chapter of Holy Qur'an)

بِسْمِ اللَّهِ الرَّحْمَٰنِ الرَّحِيمِ

قُلْ أَعُوذُ بِرَبِّ الْفَلَقِ ﴿١﴾ مِن شَرِّ مَا خَلَقَ ﴿٢﴾ وَمِن شَرِّ غَاسِقٍ إِذَا وَقَبَ ﴿٣﴾
وَمِن شَرِّ النَّفَّاثَاتِ فِي الْعُقَدِ ﴿٤﴾ وَمِن شَرِّ حَاسِدٍ إِذَا حَسَدَ ﴿٥﴾

*Bismillahir Rahmanir Raheem*
*Qul auzu bi Rabbil falaq. Min sharri ma khalaq. Wa min sharri
ghasiqin iza waqab. Wa min sharrin naffathati fil 'uqad. Wa min sharri
hasidin iza hasad. (Surat al Falaq)*

*Say, "I seek refuge int he Lord of the daybreak/dawn. (1) From the evil
of whatever He has created. (2) And from the evil of darkness when it
overspreads. (3) And from the evil of the blowers in knots (destructive
witchcraft) (4) And from the evil of envier when he envies. (5)"
(The Day Break)*

## 8. Surat an Nas (114<sup>th</sup> Chapter of Holy Qur'an)

بِسْمِ اللَّهِ الرَّحْمَٰنِ الرَّحِيمِ

قُلْ أَعُوذُ بِرَبِّ النَّاسِ ﴿١﴾ مَلِكِ النَّاسِ ﴿٢﴾ إِلَٰهِ النَّاسِ ﴿٣﴾ مِن شَرِّ الْوَسْوَاسِ
الْخَنَّاسِ ﴿٤﴾ الَّذِي يُوَسْوِسُ فِي صُدُورِ النَّاسِ ﴿٥﴾ مِنَ الْجِنَّةِ وَالنَّاسِ ﴿٦﴾

*Bismillahir Rahmanir Raheem*
*Qul a'uzu bi rabbin naas. Malikin naas. Ilahin naas. Min sharril*
*waswasil khannas. Al lazee yuwas wisu fee sudorin naas. Minal jinnati*
*wan naas. (Surat an Nas)*

*Say, "I seek refuge in the Lord of Mankind. (1) The Sovereign King of*
*Mankind. (2) The god of Mankind. (3) From the evil of the whisperer*
*(devil), (4) Who whispers (evil) into the hearts of mankind. (4) from*
*among the jinn and mankind. (6)" (The Mankind)*

## 9. 9X La ilaha illAllah

لَا إِلَهَ إِلَّا اللهُ

*There is no God but Allah.*

## 10. 1X La ilaha illAllah, Muhammadun Rasulallah

لَا إِلَهَ إِلَّا اللهُ مُحَمَّدُ رَّسُولُ اللهِ

*There is no God but Allah, Muhammad ﷺ is the messenger of Allah.*

## 11. 10X Salawat

اَللَّهُمَّ صَلِّ عَلَى سَيِّدِنَا مُحَمَّدٍ، وَعَلَى آلِ سَيِّدِنَا مُحَمَّدٍ وَ سَلِّمْ

*Allahumma salli 'ala Sayyidina Muhammadin wa 'ala ali Sayyidina*
*Muhammadin wa sallim.*

*O Allah! Send Peace and blessings upon Muhammad ﷺ and upon the*
*Family of Muhammad ﷺ (Peace and Blessings be Upon him).*

## 12. Ihda (Dedication) and Surat al Fatiha

(With intention of being dressed with the *tajalli* (manifestations) that
come down to *Madinatul Munawwara* (the illuminated City of Prophet
Muhammad ﷺ).

إِهْدَاءٌ:

## IHDA (Dedication)

اَللَّهُمَّ بَلِّغْ ثَوَابَ مَا قَرَأْنَاهُ وَنُوْرَ مَا تَلَوْنَاهُ هَدِيَّةً وَّاصِلَةً مِّنَّا اِلَى رُوْحِ نَبِيِّنَا سَيِّدِنَا مُحَمَّدٍ (صَلَّى اللهُ عَلَيْهِ وَسَلَّمَ) وَإِلَى أَرْوَاحِ إِخْوَانِهِ مِنَ الْأَنْبِيَاءِ وَالْمُرْسَلِين وَخُدَمَاءِ شَرَائِعِهِمْ، وَإِلَى أَرْوَاحِ الْأَئِمَّةِ لْأَرْبَعَةِ، وَإِلَى أَرْوَاحِ مَشَائِخِنَا فِي الطَّرِيْقَةِ النَّقْشْبَنْدِيَةِ الْعَالِيَّةِ، خَاصَةً اِلَى رُوْحِ اِمَامِ الطَّرِيْقَةِ وَ غَوْثِ الْخَلِيْقَةِ خَوَاجَهْ بَهَاءُالدِّيْنِ اَلنَّقْشْبَنْد مُحَمَّدٌالْأُوَيْسِي الْبُخَارِيْ، وَاِلَى سُلْطَانُ الْأَوْلِيَاءِ الشَّيْخْ عَبْدِاللهِ الْفَائِزْ اَلدَّاغِسْتَانِيْ، وَاِلَى سُلْطَانُ الْأَوْلِيَاءِ مَوْلَانَا الشَّيْخ مُحَمَّدْ نَاظِمْ الْحَقَّانِي ، وَمَوْلَانَا الشَّيْخْ مُحَمَّدْ عَادِلْ الرَّبَّانِيْ، وَمَوْلَانَا الشَّيْخ مُحَمَّدْ هِشَامْ اَلْقَبَانِي، وَمَوْلَانَا الشَّيْخ اَدْنَانْ اَلْقَبَانِي. صَاحِبِ الزَّمَانْ سَيِّدِنَا مُحَمَّدْ الْمَهْدِي(عَلَيْهِ السَّلَامْ)، رُوْحُ الله سَيِّدِنَا عِيْسَى(عَلَيْهِ السَّلَامْ) و سَيْفُ الله سَيِّدِنَا عَلِيْ (عَلَيْهِ السَّلَامْ)، وَ اِلَى سَائِرِسَادَاتِنَا وَالصِّدِّيْقِيْنَ. الْفَاتِحَةُ.

*Allahumma balligh tawaba ma qaraanahu wa nura ma talawnahu, hadiyyatan wasilatan minna ila ruhi Nabiyina Sayyidina Muhammadin (SallAllahu 'alayhi Wa sallam), wa ila arwahi ikhwanihi minal Anbiyai wal mursalyin, wa khudamaai sharay'ihim, wa ila arwahil a'imatil arba'ah, wa ila arwahi mashayikhina fit tariqatin Naqshbandiyatil 'aaliyah, khasatan ila ruhi Imamit tariqat wa ghawthil khaliqati Khwaja Bahauddin anNaqshband Muhammadal Uwaisil Bukhari, wa ila sultanul Awliya Mawlana Shaykh Abdullah al Faayiz adDaghestani, wa ila sultanul Awliya Mawlana Shaykh Muhammad Nazim al Haqqani, wa Mawlana Shaykh Muhammad Adil ar Rabbani, wa Mawlana Shaykh Muhammad Hisham al Qabbani, wa Mawlana Shaykh Adnan al Qabbani. Sahibul Zaman Sayyidina Muhammadul Mahdi ('alayhis salaam), wa Ruhullah Sayyidina 'Isa ('alayhis salaam), wa Sayfullah Sayyidina 'Ali ('alayhis salaam), wa ila sayiri sadatina wa Siddiqin. Al Fatiha.*

*O God! Grant that the merit of what we have read, and the light of what we have recited, are (considered) and offering and gift from us to the soul of our Prophet our Master Muhammad (pbuh), and to the souls of his brothers; all Prophets and messengers, and to our honoured Shaykhs of Naqshbandi Order, especially the leader of the Way and arch-intercessor of the created world; Khwaja Bahauddin Muhammadul Uwaisil Bukhari, and to our Master Sultanul Awliya (King of saints) Shaykh Abdullah al Fa'iz adDaghestani, and Sultanul Awliya (King of saints) Mawlana Shaykh Muhammad Nazim al Haqqani, and Mawlana Shaykh Muhammad Adil ar Rabbani, and Mawlana Shaykh Muhammad Hisham Qabbani, and Mawlana Shaykh Adnan Qabbani, and to all our masters, and those who are Truthful.*

*(Recite First Chapter of Holy Qur'an Al Fatiha (The Opening)).*

*(This presents the reward of the preceding recitations to the Prophet ﷺ and to the Shaykhs of Naqshbandi Order).*

# Part Two of the Daily Awrad

Sit on the knees, meditate and try to keep the connection *(rabita)* to your Shaykh, from your Shaykh to the Prophet ﷺ and from the Prophet ﷺ to the Divine Presence, reciting:

**13. 3X – "Allahu Allahu Allahu Haqq"**     اللهُ اللهُ اللهُ حَقْ

*Allah, the Absolute Truth.*

**14. 1500X** (Minimum)

Zikr of the Glorious Name 'Allah, Allah'     اللهُ اللهُ

(You can increase it to 2500 or 5000 times by tongue and then by heart)

1. **Beginners (Mubtadi)** – **1500X** by tongue,
           **1500X** by heart (silently)
2. **Prepared (Musta'id)** – **2500X** by tongue,
           **2500X** by heart (silently)
3. **People of Determination (Ahlil 'Azm)** –
           **5000X** by tongue and
           **5000X** by heart (silently)

**15. 100X (Minimum) Salawats/Durood**

Praising upon Prophet Muhammad ﷺ

**300X** on Mondays, Thursdays and Fridays

(You can increase it to 500X daily and 1000X on Mon, Thurs and Fri)

اَللّٰهُمَّ صَلِّ عَلَى سَيِّدِنَا مُحَمَّدٍ، وَعَلَى آلِ سَيِّدِنَا مُحَمَّد

*Allahumma salli 'ala Sayyidina Muhammadin wa 'ala aali Sayyidina Muhammad ﷺ.*

*O Allah! Send Peace and blessings upon Muhammad ﷺ and upon the Family of Muhammad ﷺ (Peace and Blessings be Upon him).*

1.  **Beginners (Mubtadi)** – **100X** Salawat/Durood daily,
    **300X** on Mon, Thurs, and Fri
2.  **Prepared (Musta'id)** – **300X** Salawat/Durood daily,
    **500X** on Mon, Thurs, and Fri
3.  **People of Determination (Ahlil 'Azm)** –
    **1000X** Salawat/Durood daily,
    **2000X** on Mon, Thurs, and Fri

## 16. 1 Juz (Section) of Holy Qur'an OR 100X Surat al Ikhlas

(if one is not able to read 1 Juz of Qur'an)

## 17. One Chapter of Dalail al-Khairat OR 100X Salawat/Durood

(if one is not able to read one chapter of Dalail al Khairat)

<h1 dir="rtl">اَلْبَيْعَةُ فِي الطَّرِيقَةُ النَّقْشَبَنْدِيَّة</h1>

# Al Bay'atu Fit Tariqatun Naqshbandiya
# Pledge of Allegiance to The Naqshbandi Way

1. Put Your Right Hand Up
2. Recite the following Du'a (supplications) with the intention of giving Bay'ah (Pledge Allegiance) to the Naqshbandi Way.

اَعُوْذُ بِاللهِ مِنَ الشَّيْطَانِ الرَّجِيْمِ

بِسْمِ اللهِ الرَّحْمَنِ الرَّحِيْمْ

إِنَّ الَّذِينَ يُبَايِعُونَكَ إِنَّمَا يُبَايِعُونَ اللهَ يَدُ اللهِ فَوْقَ أَيْدِيهِمْ فَمَن نَّكَثَ فَإِنَّمَا يَنكُثُ عَلَىٰ نَفْسِهِ وَمَنْ أَوْفَىٰ بِمَا عَاهَدَ عَلَيْهُ اللهَ فَسَيُؤْتِيهِ أَجْرًا عَظِيمًا (٤٨:١٠)

رَضِيْتُ بِاللهِ رَبًّا، وَبِالْإِسْلَامِ دِيْنًا، وَبِسَيِّدِنَا مُحَمَّدٍ صَلَّى اللهُ عَلَيْهِ وَسَلَّمَ رَسُوْلاً وَنَبِيّاً، وَبِالْقُرْآنِ كِتَابًا، وَاللهُ عَلَىٰ مَا نَقُوْلُ وَكِيْلٌ. وَالْحَمْدُ لِلَّهِ رَبِّ الْعَالَمِينَ.

وَقَبِلْنَا بِسَيِّدِنَا سُلْطَانُ الْأَوْلِيَاءُ مَوْلَانَا اَلشَّيْخُ مُحَمَّدْ نَاظِمْ اَلْحَقَّانِيْ شَيْخُنَا وَ مُرْشِدِنَا، وَمَوْلَانَا اَلشَّيْخُ مُحَمَّدْ عَادِلْ اَلرَّبَّانِيْ شَيْخُنَا وَ مُرْشِدِنَا. وَبِبَرَكَةِ مَوْلَانَا اَلشَّيْخُ مُحَمَّدْ هِشَامْ اَلْقَبَّانِيْ، وَمَوْلَانَا اَلشَّيْخُ عَدْنَانْ اَلْقَبَّانِيْ. وَاللهُ عَلَىٰ مَا نَقُوْلُ وَكِيْلْ.

اللهُ، اللهُ، اللهُ، حَقّْ

اللهُ، اللهُ، اللهُ، حَقّْ

اللهُ، اللهُ، اللهُ، حَقّْ

*A'uzu Billahi Minash Shaitanir Rajeem*
*Bismillahir Rahmanir Raheem*

*Innal lazeena yubayi'oonaka innama yubayi'oon Allaha, yadullahi fawqa aydihim, Faman nakatha fa innama yankuthu 'ala nafsihi, wa man awfa bimaa 'aahada 'alayhu Allaha fasa yuteehi ajran 'azima.*
*(Surat al Fath, 48:10)*

*Radheetu billahi Rabban, wa bil Islami dinan, wa bi Sayyidina Muhammadin sallallahu 'alayhi wa sallam, Rasulan wa Nabiyan, wa bil Qur'ani kitaban. 'Wallahu 'ala ma naqulu Wakil.' 'Walhamdulillahi Rabbil 'alamin.'*

*Wa qabilna bi Sayyidina Sultanul Awliya Mawlana Shaykh Muhammad Nazim Al Haqqani, Shaykhuna wa Murshidena, wa Mawlana Shaykh Muhammad Adil ar Rabbani, Shaykhuna wa Murshidena. Wa be barakati Mawlana Shaykh Muhammad Hisham Qabbani, wa Mawlana Shaykh 'Adnan Qabbani.*
*'Wallahu 'ala ma naqulu Wakil.' (Surat al Qasas, 28:28)*

*Allahu, Allahu, Allahu, Haqq*
*Allahu, Allahu, Allahu, Haqq*
*Allahu, Allahu, Allahu, Haqq*

*Indeed, those who give Bay'ah (pledge allegiance) to you [O' Muhammad ﷺ] – they are actually giving Bay'ah (pledge allegiance) to Allah. The hand of Allah is over their hands. So he who breaks his oath/pledge only breaks it to the detriment/harm of his own soul. And he whoever fulfills their (bay'ah/covenant) that which he has promised Allah (AJ) – He will Grant him a mighty reward. (The Victory, 48:10)*

*We accept and are pleased with Allah (AJ) as our Lord, and with Islam as our religion, and with our Master Prophet Muhammad (pbuh) as our Messenger and Prophet, and with the holy Qu'ran as our book. And Allah (AJ) is witness over what we say. And All praises are due to Allah, the Lord of the worlds. And we accept our Master the King of Saints Mawlana Shaykh Muhammad Nazim Al Haqqani as our master and our spiritual guide and Mawlana Shaykh Muhammad Adil ar Rabbani as our master and our spiritual guide, and by the blessings of Mawlana Shaykh Muhammad Hisham Qabbani, and Mawlana Shaykh Adnan Qabbani. "And Allah (AJ) is witness over what we say." (Surat al Qasas, 28:28)*

*Allah is, Allah is, Allah is the Absolute Truth.*

DUAS

إِهْدَاء - إِلَى شَرَفِ النَّبِيِّ ﷺ

## IHDA – Ila Sharafin Nabi ﷺ
### Dedicated to Prophet Muhammad (pbuh)

إِلَى شَرَفِ النَّبِيِّ ﷺ وَالَى آلِهِ وَصَحْبِهِ الْكِرَامِ، وَإِلَى أَرْوَاحِ إِخْوَانِهِ مِنَ الأَنْبِيَاءِ وَالْمُرْسَلِين، وَخُدَمَاءِ شَرَائِعِهِمْ، وَإِلَى أَرْوَاحِ الأَئِمَّةِ لِأَرْبَعَةِ. وَإِلَى أَرْوَاحِ مَشَائِخِنَا فِي الطَّرِيقَةِ النَّقْشْبَنْدِيةِ الْعَالِيَةِ، خَاصَّةً إِلَى رُوحِ إِمَامِ الطَّرِيقَةِ وَ غَوْثِ الْخَلِيقَةِ خَوَاجَهْ بَهَاءُالدِّينِ النَّقْشْبَنْد مُحَمَّدُالأُوَيْسِي الْبُخَارِيْ، وَالَى سُلْطَانُ الأَوْلِيَاءِ مَوْلَانَا الشَّيْخ عَبْدِاللهِ الْفَائِزْ الدَّاغِسْتَانِيْ، وَالَى سُلْطَانُ الأَوْلِيَاءِ مَوْلَانَا الشَّيْخ مُحَمَّد نَاظِمْ الْحَقَّانِي، وَمَوْلَانَا الشَّيْخ مُحَمَّد عَادِلْ الرَّبَّانِيْ، وَمَوْلَانَا الشَّيْخ مُحَمَّد هِيشَامْ الْقَبَّانِي، وَمَوْلَانَا الشَّيْخ اَدْنَانْ الْقَبَّانِي، وَ صَاحِبِ الزَّمَانْ سَيِّدِنَا مُحَمَّدُ الْمِهْدِي(عَلَيْهِ السَّلَامْ)، وَ رُوحُ الله سَيِّدِنَا عِيْسَى (عَلَيْهِ السَّلَامْ) ، وَ سَيْفُ الله سَيِّدِنَا عَلِيْ (عَلَيْهِ السَّلَامْ) وَ إِلَى سَائِرِسَادَاتِنَا وَالصِّدِّيقِيْنَ . الْفَاتِحَةُ.

*Ila sharifin Nabi (SallAllahu 'alayhi wa Sallam) wa ila aalihi wa sahbihil kiram, wa ila arwahi ikhwanihi minal Anbiyai wal mursalin, wa khudamayi sharay'ihim, wa ila arwahil a'imatil arba'ah. Wa ila arwahi mashayikhina fit tariqatin Naqshbandiyatil 'aaliyah, khasatan ila ruhi Imamit tariqati wa ghawthil khaliqati Khwaja Bahauddin Naqshband, Muhammad al Uwaisil Bukhari, wa ila sultanul Awliya Mawlana Shaykh Abdullah al Faayiz ad Daghestani, wa ila sultanul Awliya Mawlana Shaykh Muhammad Nazim Adil al Haqqani, wa Mawlana Shaykh Muhammad Adil ar Rabbani, wa Mawlana Shaykh Muhammad Hisham al Qabbani, wa Mawlana Shaykh Adnan al Qabbani, wa Sahibul Zaman Sayyidina Muhammadul Mahdi ('alayhis salaam), wa Ruhullah Sayyidina 'Isa ('alayhis salaam), wa Sayfullah Sayyidina 'Ali ('alayhis salaam), wa ila sayiri sadatina wa Siddiqin. Al Fatiha.*

*Honour be to the Prophet Muhammad ﷺ, and his family, and his distinguished Companions, and to the souls of his brothers; all the Prophets and messengers. And to our honoured Shaykhs of Naqshbandi Order, especially the leader of the Way and arch-intercessor of the created world; Khwaja Bahauddin Muhammadul Uwaisil Bukhari, and to our Master Sultanul Awliya (King of saints) Shaykh Abdullah al Fa'iz adDaghestani, and Sultanul Awliya (King of saints) Mawlana Shaykh Muhammad Nazim al Haqqani, and Mawlana Shaykh Muhammad Adil ar Rabbani, and Mawlana Shaykh Muhammad Hisham Qabbani, and Mawlana Shaykh Adnan Qabbani, and to all our masters and those who are Truthful.*

*(Recite First Chapter of Holy Qur'an, Al Fatiha (the Opening)).*

*(This presents the reward of the preceding recitations to Prophet Muhammad (pbuh) and to the spiritual guides of the distinguished Naqshbandi Spiritual Order).*

# nsan al Kamil
## The Universal Perfect Being
ﷺ

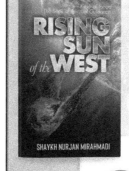

*Featuring over 1,000 full-colour images including custom teaching diagrams!*

## nsan al Kamil
### The Universal Perfect Being

*Kitab al Irshad*

*The Book of Spiritual Guidance*

SHAYKH NURJAN MIRAHMADI

## OUT THE BOOK

der to be known, the Divine created a sublime
re for all of creation - the glorious light and soul
Insan al Kamil, Prophet Muhammad ﷺ.
niverses, including every particle in existence, came
anifestation through this all-encompassing ocean of
tion. This book is a source of inspiration, reminding
ader how Prophet's ﷺ essence is truly within each
empowering us with his light, and constantly
ing our souls to be brought into the Divinely Presence.

## ABOUT THE BOOK

An essential spiritual guidebook filled with
invaluable knowledge of the elements within
our cosmos. The journey examines the Divine's
most powerful sun of all universes,
Prophet Muhammad ﷺ, and progresses to an
insightful overview of the stars, represented by the
Holy Companions and the full moons, the spiritual guides,
who reflect the sun and exemplify the best in character.

## E-STAR REVIEWS

e these teachings as they bring home for me truths
eard on many different settings, religion, self help
ology. Universal truths coupled with concrete
ces and rational behind them. It's not just nice
o think and talk about a path to actual get to the
God willing, that the seeker is trying to get to."

one is a must for those interested in awakening the
nd receiving much needed inspiration during these
lt times."

## FIVE-STAR REVIEWS

*"A unique look at spiritual guidance through the
understanding of our universe. It provides the
reader a perfect blend of ancient knowledge with
today's science. A perfect companion for those
seeking truth and realities hidden within us."*

*"The immense power for the soul that lies within the
book unbelievable. It uplifts the souls, and makes
one feel connected at a deeper understanding.
The examples and analogies are so relevant."*

Available at
## amazon

## ORDER YOUR
## COPY TODAY!

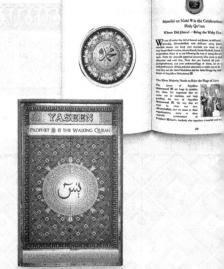

# In PURSUIT *Angelic* POWER
A Path Towards Divine Healing Energy

# The Healing Power
# of Sufi Meditation

The Healing Power
of Sufi Meditation

Foreword by Shaykh Muhammad Nazim Adil al-Haqqani
Introduction by Shaykh Muhammad Hisham Kabbani

by as-Sayyid Nurjan Mirahmadi and Dr. Hedieh Mirahmadi
Naqshbandi Haqqani Sufi Order of America

## OUT THE BOOK

heavenly beings, our souls are eternally in suit of healing energy through Divine and elic Power. By understanding the origins nergy through light and sound, the seeker ns to attune to the guides of heavenly wledge and discovers essential techniques cquire and increase positive energy within beings.

## E-STAR REVIEWS   By Amazon Reviewers
⭐⭐⭐⭐⭐

s invigorating book broadens and promotes a wledge of the affinity and interactions between els and Humans."

*nust have in every home,*
*Pursuit of Angelic Power" serves to mankind an duction and insight to our illuminating friends."*

## ABOUT THE BOOK

For those who have reached a level of understanding of the illusory nature of the world around us and seek to discern the reality that lies behind it, Sufi meditation (muraqabah) is the doorway through which we can pass from this realm of delusion into the realm of realities. Through meditation the seeker has a means to return to his or her perfected original self.

## FIVE-STAR REVIEWS   By Amazon Reviewers
⭐⭐⭐⭐⭐

*This is a one-of-a-kind book by an actual authorized teacher of Sufi meditation. Not only it details the methods of meditation, but it also gives the practical advice regarding everything a seeker needs in order to pursue such a journey, first of which is to have a guide!"*

*"The book is rare gem in English language, providing the much needed instructions of Sufi meditation in a clear way. It contains some extra-ordinary illustrations, which is a huge plus for a beginner.*

Available at
amazon

## ORDER YOUR COPY TODAY!

# LEVELS OF THE HEART
## LATAIF AL QALB

# SECRET REALITIES
## OF HAJJ

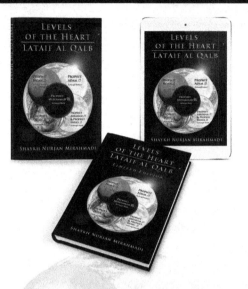

## ABOUT THE BOOK

There are subtle energies and realities that are dressing the heart – these are the Levels of the Heart (Lataif al Qalb). Shaykh Nurjan has composed an exceptional work on the map of the heart, intertwining the teachings of its spiritual attributes and how they affect every aspect of a seeker's path.

## ABOUT THE BOOK

Secret Realities of Hajj features invaluable teachings and spiritual insight into the Islam holy pilgrimage of Hajj. From the historical references of holy prophets to the remarkab scientific explanations of the circumambulation, this book provides a deep understanding of this important pillar of faith

## FIVE-STAR REVIEWS
BY AMAZON REVIEWERS ★★★★★

"I've learned more about Islam in 6 months than in 20 years reading Shaykh Nurjan's books, reading the articles on his app and watching his YouTube channel videos. His teachings transcend the worldly divisions we've created and helps unveil our deeper spiritual and universal realities within."

"To finally have all this information in one book is simply incredible. It is an ocean of spiritual knowledge."

## FIVE-STAR REVIEWS
By Amazon Revie ★★★★★

"Amazing! A rare jewel filled with illuminating knowledge. Highly recommended for non-Muslir and Muslims equally, as the secrets referred to are, in reality, secrets related to creation itself, and the inner reality of the human heart."

"A must-read for people interested in the spirititu dimensions and secrets of the Hajj. The author intimate knowledge of the topic from a long linea of Sufi Masters. Pick up and enjoy, I did."

Available at
amazon

ORDER YOUR
COPY TODAY!

# CHECK US OUT ON SOCIAL MEDIA

Shaykh Nurjan
Mirahmadi

The Muhammadan Way

shaykhnurjanmirahmadi

Shaykh Nurjan
Mirahmadi

The Muhammadan Way

WhatsApp

# SMC MERCHANDISE

**SUFI SUNNAH APPAREL**
NO FEAR COLLECTION

**ACCESSORIES**
UNIQUE ITEMS WITH
ORIGINAL CALLIGRAPHIC
DESIGN

**SUFI ESSENTIALS**
TAWEEZ / PRAYER BEADS
STICKERS AND MORE

**BAKHOOR AND PERFUMES**
BLESSED SUFI SCENTS
FEATURING
PREMIERE ARABIAN BRANDS

**WELLNESS TEAS**
CUSTOM-BLENDS WITH
HEALING PROPERTIES

**LIMITED EDITION PRODUCTS!**

VIEW THE FULL SELECTION OF ITEMS AT

## SMCMERCH.COM

GIVE
THE
PERFECT
GIFT!

*...pired from Traditional*
*Islamic Armor and*
*...ection with Qu'ran Ayat,*
*...Allah and Ism Rasul ﷺ*

SHOP
ONLINE
TODAY!

# THE MUHAMMADAN WAY

*"Give charity without delay, f
it stands in the way of calamity
- Prophet Muhammad*

# nurmuhammad.com/donate

## General Donations

You may donate to many different projects.

You can add a dedication or
prayer (du'a) requests you have.

## Sadaqah

Please add a note on which Sadaqah the
payment is for and prayer (du'a) requests.

Sadaqah Nafilah
Sadaqah Wajibah

## Zakat

Please add a note on which type of Zakat
payment is being made.

Use the online calculator for current values.

The collected funds will be paid to specific
recipients of the Muslim community in
accordance to zakat principles.

## Help Those in Need

Fatima Zahra Helping Hand volunteers
prepare and distribute meals on a monthly basis.

Clothing and other basic necessities are
collected or purchased and distributed to the less
fortunate including the Orphan Donations Program
in Pakistan.

## Mawlid

Donations go towards Mawlid Events such as
the Annual Grand Milad un Nabi ﷺ.

These are special programs to commemorate
the life and times of our
Holy Prophet Muhammad ﷺ.

*"Give charity without delay, for it stands in the way of calamity."*
*- Prophet Muhammad ﷺ*

# Support is the Way of Love - Donate Today!

## Qurban / Zabiha

Payment for any program requiring Qurban offerings including Udhiyyah for Eid ul Adha sacrifice.

## Khums / Hadiya

Khums = one-fifth
Hadiya = gift

Please add specific note whether payment is for khums or hadiya.

Please also add any prayer (du'a) requests you have.

## Canada
### Sufi Meditation Center Society

CRA no. 856872817 RR0001

*Also for donations from United Kingdom, Australia, New Zealand & Other Commonwealth Nations

## United States
### Mystic Meditation

Zelle Direct Deposit - No fees
donation@mysticmeditation.org

EIN No. 84-2681459
*Also for International donations but will not get non-US tax receipt.*

## Pakistan

For

Fatima Zahra Helping Hand in Pakistan
&
Orphan Donations Program in Pakistan

CPSIA information can be obtained
at www.ICGtesting.com
Printed in the USA
JSHW011109100523
41520JS00002B/4

9 781989 602037